Venture Capital Fund Management

A Comprehensive Approach to Investment Practices &
the Entire Operations of a VC Firm

Lin Hong Wong

D1522414

Mat #40686911

BOOK & ARTICLE IDEA SUBMISSIONS

If you are a C-Level executive, senior lawyer, or venture capitalist interested in submitting a book or article idea to the Aspatore editorial board for review, please email AspatoreAuthors@thomson.com. Aspatore is especially looking for highly specific ideas that would have a direct financial impact on behalf of a reader. Completed publications can range from 2 to 2,000 pages. Include your book/article idea, biography, and any additional pertinent information.

ISBN 1-59622-359-6
Library of Congress Control Number: 2005936981

For corrections, updates, comments or any other inquiries please email AspatoreEditorial@thomson.com.

First Printing, 2005
10 9 8 7 6 5 4 3 2 1

Aspatore Books is the largest and most exclusive publisher of C-Level executives (CEO, CFO, CTO, CMO, Partner) from the world's most respected companies and law firms. Aspatore annually publishes a select group of C-Level executives from the Global 1,000, top 250 law firms (Partners and Chairs), and other leading companies of all sizes. C-Level Business Intelligence™, as conceptualized and developed by Aspatore Books, provides professionals of all levels with proven business intelligence from industry insiders—direct and unfiltered insight from those who know it best—as opposed to third-party accounts offered by unknown authors and analysts. Aspatore Books is committed to publishing an innovative line of business and legal books, those which lay forth principles and offer insights that when employed, can have a direct financial impact on the reader's business objectives, whatever they may be. In essence, Aspatore publishes critical tools—need-to-read as opposed to nice-to-read books—for all business professionals.

Table of Contents

Foreword 7
    Chapter 1: Introduction 11

Part I: VC Financing & Organization
    Chapter 2: VC Financing 25
    Chapter 3: VC Organization 45

Part II: Raising Funds
    Chapter 4: Raising Funds 65
    Chapter 5: Limited Partnership Agreement 89

Part III: Finding & Screening Deals
    Chapter 6: Deal Sourcing 107
        Appendix 6A: Non-Disclosure Agreement 119
        Appendix 6B: Deal Log 121
    Chapter 7: Deal Screening 125
        Appendix 7A: Deal Alert 139

Part IV: Conducting Due Diligence
    Chapter 8: Due Diligence Basics 143
    Chapter 9: Due Diligence of Management 157
    Chapter 10: Due Diligence of Marketing & the Market 169
    Chapter 11: Due Diligence of Manufacturing 185
    Chapter 12: Due Diligence of Financial & Legal Aspects 203

Part V: Making the Deal
    Chapter 13: Valuation 219
        Appendix 13A: The Venture Capital Method 254
        Appendix 13B: A Spreadsheet Model for the Venture Capital
        Method 264
    Chapter 14: Investment Securities 267
    Chapter 15: Deal Structuring 301
    Chapter 16: Term Sheet 323
        Appendix 16A: Term Sheet 343

Part VI: Closing the Deal
 Chapter 17: Deal Negotiation 359
 Chapter 18: Conditions Precedent 371
 Chapter 19: Investment Documentation 383

Part VII: Nurturing & Harvesting the Investment
 Chapter 20: Monitoring & Adding Value 401
  Appendix 20A: Quarterly Monitoring Report 413
 Chapter 21: Realizing & Recovering Value 415

Part VIII: Achieving Quality Performance
 Chapter 22: Fund Performance 431
  Appendix 22A: Valuation Report 449
 Chapter 23: Qualities of a VC Firm 451
  Appendix 23A: GP's Letter to Shareholders 461

List of Abbreviations 467
Index 469
About the Author 491

Foreword

The venture capital industry is globalizing. Funds are being raised internationally and invested globally. Venture capital is now a recognized asset class for fund managers. More and more venture capital firms have established multinational operations. The leading venture capital firms are becoming renowned household names.

Venture capital fund management firms have matured. Their investment policies, procedures, and systems have been refined over decades of experience, and are becoming formalized and structured. Venture capital fund management and investment is fast becoming a professional practice, like an accounting or legal practice.

More and more universities and financial training institutions worldwide conduct venture capital courses, or have private equity and venture capital electives in their business administration, entrepreneurship, or finance courses, at undergraduate or post-graduate levels, such as those in Harvard, Wharton, and Stanford, and many in Europe, Japan, Australia, and elsewhere.

The purpose of this book is to contribute to the advancement of professionalism in venture capital fund management and investment practices and to add to the growing educational literature and training materials on the practice.

There are many books teaching entrepreneurs how to raise funds from venture capital firms. There are also many that tell interesting war stories and experiences of venture capitalists. There are fewer books on the venture capital investment practice, aimed at venture capital investment professionals and students who wish to join the venture capital industry. However, such practitioner-targeted books usually focus only on isolated aspects of the venture capital investment practice, such as due diligence, deal structuring, or valuation. With the emergence of venture capital investment as a professional practice, there is urgent need for a comprehensive and integrated book on the practice, for practitioners and would-be practitioners.

This book therefore aims to provide a comprehensive and complete treatment of the entire professional practice of a venture capital firm. It describes how venture capital firms raise funds; search for and screen investment opportunities; conduct due diligence on management, marketing, manufacturing, financial, and legal aspects of the businesses under evaluation; how they value, structure, negotiate, and legally document the deals; how they monitor, add value to, and realize value from their investments, to finally achieve superior financial returns from the investments.

A professional practice encompasses the expertise, concepts, principles, theories, methodologies, unique terminologies, systems, and standards of the profession. All these are elucidated in this book. In addition, this book suggests best practices, systems, report formats, internal documentation, and database structures that a venture capital firm should adopt to become a world-class organization. Furthermore, issues affecting a venture capital firm, such as corporate governance, public disclosure, corporate structure, corporate qualities and performance measures, tax, legal, and staffing, are also discussed.

This book may be used as a reference handbook for practitioners in the venture capital industry. It is also suitable for professionals in the private equity industry, as the concepts and practices are very similar. The practices described in this book are those of U.S. firms, and are therefore relevant to all venture capital and private equity firms worldwide. U.S. practices have become de facto standards due to the dominance of the U.S. industry and the spreading of U.S. firms into Europe and Asia.

Many venture capital professionals learn on the job. It is hoped that this book will help to fill in knowledge gaps and raise standards in the profession, by providing a comprehensive reference on important aspects of the practice. In particular, the systematic approach to due diligence described in this book, an original methodology conceived by the author, could be a useful practical aid to practitioners in this difficult but critical process.

This book may also be used as a textbook for undergraduate and post-graduate students attending courses or electives in private equity and venture capital investment. It could also be used as a complete self-study book for those who wish to pursue a career in the private equity and venture capital industry.

Professionals such as lawyers, accountants, bankers, consultants, and investment advisers, as well as business angels and entrepreneurs, will find this book useful to learn more about the internal processes and mentality of venture capitalists, to assist them in their work and relationships with venture capitalists.

Finally, casual readers who may be fascinated by the occasional publicity of venture capitalists making astronomical financial returns, can find out more about how venture capitalists work, so that perhaps they can learn how to apply some of the techniques in their own investments.

Little or no financial knowledge is required of readers, with the sole exception of the concept of internal rate of return, which is readily referenced in a basic book on accounting or finance, or from the Internet. A comprehensive index provides pointers to explanations, given within the text, of financial or venture capital industry terms used.

L H Wong

1

Introduction

The history of investing parallels the history of commerce. Trading, the purchase of goods for resale at a profit, is a form of short-term investing. When royalties, wealthy families and groups, cooperated to explore, capture, mine, grow, build, or produce essentials or valuables of one kind or another, they were making longer-term investments with the objective of gaining wealth.

Investment opportunities exploded with the industrial revolution, as innumerable businesses unceasingly sprouted and expanded to directly or indirectly serve the insatiable appetite of the growing populace. The wealthy initially invested through their own efforts or with the help of family members. As the task of seeking, evaluating, and managing investments grew more complicated, professional staff were hired in the 1930s in the U.S. This marked the beginning of professional private investment management. The coining of the term "venture capital" to refer to such investments is attributed to Jean Witter, president of the Investment Bankers Association of America, who first used this term in a speech at a convention in 1939.[1]

The first venture capital firm in the world is acknowledged to be American Research and Development (ARD), USA, which was formed in June 1946

---

[1] See Chapter 1 of William Bygrave and Jeffry Timmons, *Venture Capital at the Crossroads*, Boston: Harvard Business School Press, 1992, for an account of the history of the Venture Capital industry in USA, and Chapter 2 of Rick Lake and Ronald Lake (eds.), *Private Equity and Venture Capital*, London: Euromoney Books, 2000 for an overview of U.K. venture capital.

by Ralph Flanders, president of the Federal Reserve Bank of Boston, Karl Compton, president of MIT, and General Georges Doriot, professor of the Harvard Business School, together with other professors and business leaders. ARD raised US$3.5 million of initial capital, and although the overall investment results were not spectacular, it made a very successful investment in Digital Equipment Corp, which was set up by four MIT students.

The first venture capital limited partnerships were formed in the U.S. in the late 1950s and the 1960s. The industry languished after the stock market downturn in 1969 and it was only between 1978 and 1981 that the big spurt in growth arose, fueled by new legislations allowing pension funds to invest in venture funds, and by a reduction in the capital gains tax. Venture capital fund investors poured more than $550 million into the industry in 1978, a tenfold increase compared to the levels in prior years, although this pales in comparison to present-day figures where a single venture fund can amount to one billion.

Another industry spurt was experienced in the mid-1980s, after stories spread of venture capital firms getting back more than twenty times their investments in technology companies such as Apple Computer and Lotus Development. Public interest in venture capital was again ignited during the dot-com boom years in the late 1990s when Internet and Internet-related companies were listed at exceptionally high valuations, giving many venture investors more than fifty times, and some more than 1,000 times, returns.

The venture capital industry has now spread globally. The U.K.'s venture capital industry, the second largest after that of the U.S., traces its roots to the Second World War. The rest of Europe is about the same size as that of the U.K. The venture capital industries in Japan and Australia started in the 1970s and other parts of Asia in the 1980s. Many U.S. and European venture capital firms raise funds and invest globally.

In this chapter, we shall have an overview of venture capital investing, starting with a definition of venture capital, a look at the role of venture capital in economic and entrepreneurial development, and an examination of the characteristics of venture capital investments. We shall discuss the venture capital investment process, and in so doing, get an overview of the contents of this book.

Definition of Venture Capital

Venture Capital (VC) may be defined as capital for equity investment in higher risk start-up and early stage private companies, with the objective of achieving above-average medium term investment return. The return is mainly through capital gain from the appreciation in value of the shareholding in the company over a number of years.

There are different definitions of VC. In most countries, VC would be limited to smaller investments in more risky enterprises, particularly start-ups and young technology companies. In some countries, VC is considered to be a subset of private equity, a generic term for all equity investments in private companies (as against public listed companies). In some other countries, VC is considered to be separate and distinct from private equity. In this case, private equity takes on a narrower meaning, covering only larger investments in less risky and more mature private companies, buyouts and special situations.

In rare instances, VC is considered as a superset, including higher risk, smaller investments and all private equity type investments. This would be an error and sometimes occurs in Asia, where many so-called VC firms also invest in mature family-owned companies and management buyouts, due to a lack of start-up or early stage high-technology companies. They should more rightly be called private equity investment firms. To add to the confusion, some European countries consider VC to include buyouts, whereas in the U.S. venture capital and buyouts are separate and distinct classes.

In this book we shall use VC to mean the higher risk, earlier stage investments. Earlier stage companies may be defined as those that are about two years or more away from IPO, although most VC investments would be targeted at those that are at the younger end of the spectrum. Late stage, mezzanine stage, and buyouts would be excluded from this definition, although we may include such investments for the purpose of comparative discussion. The VC investment concepts and processes described in this book could largely be applied to all private equity investments.

Role of VC

The role of VC firms in a local economy is multi-faceted:

o They encourage entrepreneurship and support the development of entrepreneurs and entrepreneurial businesses.

o They support start-ups which in turn contribute to the revitalization of mature industries and often the development of new industries.

o They support start-ups which exploit and commercialize local technology, innovations, and discoveries.

o They assess business risks and help channel scarce economic resources to businesses that are more likely to grow and succeed.

o They often help local businesses expand their operating and marketing territories, including overseas.

o They often help small, medium, and family businesses to corporatize and modernize.

o They often help companies to forge synergies and strategic alliances.

o They bridge the gap between entrepreneurs and large sources of funds, such as pension funds, and provide the expertise to do this effectively and successfully.

o They help to leverage the expertise of experienced CEOs and senior executives to help young companies, and also tap retired and semi-retired executives to continue to lend their expertise.

Many governments have recognized the vital role played by VC firms in industrial ecosystems, and offer incentives to develop the local VC industry, as well as offer VC funding directly to entrepreneurs or indirectly by investing in VC funds.

VC as a Funding Source

Besides meeting their own returns objectives, VC firms have to satisfy the needs and expectations of entrepreneurs in order to successfully close the desired investment deals. To the entrepreneur, VC could be an attractive source of funding compared to other alternatives:

- Wealthy individuals: The amount of funding is usually limited and the investors are usually passive.
- Business angels and incubators: Although the business angels or incubators provide assistance or infrastructure support, funding is limited. These investors would be more suited to entrepreneurs who are at the stage of conceptualizing the business.
- Corporations: They can provide strong management and infrastructure support, but would usually require majority ownership or management control, and perhaps strategic benefits such as an exclusive technical license or marketing rights.
- Financial institutions: Financing is usually in the form of debt requiring collateral or personal guarantees, and the company has to generate income to service the debt.
- Government: Funding is limited and the company has to meet developmental criteria.

The VC firm looks purely for attractive financial return, has no hidden agenda or strategic intent, does not require ownership or management control, and adds value to the investment by providing management support and business linkages. The VC also shares in the business risk by investing in equity instead of debt, although it usually enjoys certain preferential rights. Some entrepreneurs may find the price of VC financing to be high, but they have to recognize the lack of attractive alternatives, the risks incurred by the VC firm, and the value add that it provides.

Characteristics of VC Investments

The typical characteristics of VC investments are as follows:

- The investments are in private companies that have strong management and high growth potential.
- The investment objective is to achieve high financial returns, not for strategic reasons or for management control.
- The investments are in equity and hence there is risk sharing with the founders of the companies, although there are protective and negative covenants imposed on the companies.

o   The VC firm evaluates the investment opportunities, negotiates the investment terms, and monitors and adds value to the investments.

o   The VC firm holds the investments for up to seven or eight years and exits through trade sales or post-IPO sales of its shareholdings.

The VC firm would typically aim to achieve a return of more than ten times its original investment in seven years or earlier. This means an internal rate of return (IRR) of 39 percent or better. How can the VC firm hope to achieve such a high return?

The VC firm works very hard to minimize the risks inherent in the investments and to maximize the returns. It does this through various rigorous ways and means that constitute the entire venture capital investment process, including pre-investment and post-investment processes. We shall call this entire process the "VC Process." The core of this book is on the VC Process and its constituent sub-processes, as well as the concepts and techniques that support the Process.

The VC Process

The VC Process is all about minimizing investment risks and maximizing investment returns. The key areas within the VC Process are:

o   Searching extensively for quality deals

o   Selecting the best deals through stringent evaluation and exhaustive due diligence investigation

o   Negotiating low valuations and tight investment terms

o   Staging investments into several rounds based on achievements of milestones

o   Adding value to the investee companies

o   Monitoring and helping to manage the performance of investee companies

o   Seeking high exit valuations proactively

o   Salvaging as much value as possible from failed investments

These and other processes, which shall be discussed in this book, combined with the efforts of the founders and managements of the companies, perhaps together with some luck, work towards reducing investment risks and achieving high returns.

Despite all the efforts, it is inevitable that some of the investments will not perform well, due to the high business risks and uncertainties of management performance, markets, and competition. It is typical that out of ten VC investments, three or four may fail with total or near total loss, another four or five may result in mere recovery of capital or provide three or four times return on amounts invested. The aim is that one or two will give ten or twenty times return. The VC firm's objective is to achieve an overall return for the portfolio of investments that is better than two and a half times the total invested, or a portfolio IRR of better than 20 percent, for the ten year period over which the investments are made and divested. This is to satisfy the expectations of investors in the funds raised by the VC firm.

In going through the VC Process, the VC firm raises many questions and investigates many areas to help it decide on the investment. These are some of the key questions:

- How valuable is the company now?
- How low is our entry valuation?
- How big can the company be?
- How high will be our exit valuation?
- What are the internal factors affecting the success of the company?
- How positive or negative are these internal factors?
- How will they change with time?
- What are the external factors affecting the success of the company?
- How positive or negative are these external factors?
- How will they change with time?
- What investment terms can we impose to protect our investment?
- What investment terms can we impose to enhance our investment return?
- How and what value can we add to the company?
- How can we divest with the best possible return?

The answers will of course be different for each company. Often the answers will be vague and variable, depending on the source, and even conflicting. How does the VC firm assess and consolidate all the information gathered to arrive at useful decisions?

After the investment is made, the hard work does not stop. Most of the preceding questions will continue to be asked. Due to the uncertainties and risks faced, and the many inevitable stumbles encountered as the company progresses, the VC firm has to keep a close watch and assist whenever and however possible. Here again, there will seldom be clear answers, and many problems and issues faced by the company will affect its value and hence the VC firm's investment return.

Ultimately, business sense and business judgment must rule. However the VC firm may call upon analytical tools, management principles, expert advice, and other resources to help. All these will be more effectively and successfully applied if the VC firm itself puts in place a rigorous, thorough, and disciplined VC Process that incorporates the best practices that prevail in the industry. It is my hope that this book can contribute towards the understanding and implementation of best practices in the VC Process.

This book is laid out in eight parts, mostly following the flow of the VC Process. In Part I of this book, we follow from our introductory chapter with Chapter 2: VC Financing, which describes how a VC-backed venture typically goes through several rounds of VC financing before aiming for a public listing. VC firms have inculcated such a basic and common practice to minimize risks and maximize returns, as will be explained in the chapter. Chapter 3: VC Organization describes how a VC firm organizes its management company and the funds that it manages, and what qualities the firm seeks in its investment staff.

Before a VC firm can make investments, it has to raise funds from investors who are called Limited Partners. In Part II, we have two chapters describing the VC fund-raising process and the important Limited Partnership Agreement, which captures the understanding reached between the VC firm and the Limited Partners on the management of the fund.

Part III kicks off the VC Process. Figure 1.1 shows an outline of the VC Process. Chapter 6: Deal Sourcing describes the first step, which is to look for investment opportunities or investment deals. Effective and extensive deal sourcing results in continuous inflow of quality deals. Without the availability of good seeds to start with, the harvest will never be plentiful. Thus deal sourcing is an important part of the VC Process.

FIGURE 1.1   THE VC PROCESS

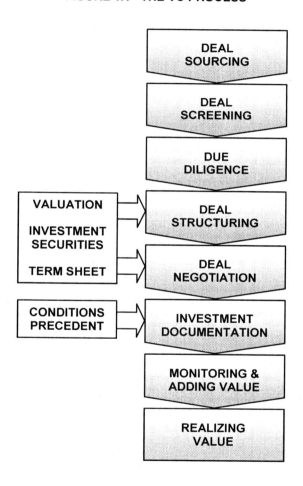

The selection process is of course also important. Because the VC firm receives a large number of deal proposals, it has to screen out deals that would clearly be rejected, so no further time or effort is wasted on following them up. Chapter 7: Deal Screening describes this process and the common screening criteria used.

When a deal passes through the screening process, it would then be subject to a very extensive and intensive investigation process by the VC firm, called due diligence. Along the way, the deal may be dropped because of one or more significant negative aspects uncovered during the due diligence. Part IV describes the due diligence process, starting with Chapter 8: Due Diligence Basics, which describes the basic principles of the work involved. Experience has shown that the work can often deteriorate to haphazard, inefficient investigation resulting in low productivity, time wasted, and non-meaningful information gathered. Therefore I propose herein a systematic approach and provide a working framework for the conduct of due diligence. The chapter also gives some suggestions on how to arrive at overall conclusions after completion of due diligence.

Chapters 9 to 12 are devoted to the important areas of due diligence investigation: the management, the market and marketing strategies, the manufacturing operations, as well as financial and legal aspects. Using the same prescribed systematic approach and frameworks that are tailored to the area under investigation, we point out factors and issues that can contribute to the success or failure of the business, and these need to be validated and assessed for degree of seriousness in the due diligence.

In parallel with the due diligence investigation, the VC firm works towards concluding the deal successfully. Part V deals with different aspects of making the deal. Valuation of the company is often a thorny issue in deal negotiations and is an important determinant of the VC firm's return. Valuation as a subject is treated in many books, so Chapter 13: Valuation will mostly focus on concepts and methods that are related to venture deals, and only briefly cover other methods.

Chapter 14: Investment Securities describes the types of securities used by VC firms to make their equity investments, and the rights that may be attached to those securities. Chapter 15: Deal Structuring looks at how VC deals may be structured. The investment securities used, the rights attached, and the deal structure are important as they may affect the risks faced and the returns achieved by the VC firm. Wise choices and decisions on these factors can provide protection against downside risks and stretch upside potentials of the deal. Chapter 16: Term Sheet wraps up this part of the book by going through an important document, the term sheet, which captures all the key terms and conditions of the deal, for signature by the entrepreneur.

Part VI is on closing the deal. Chapter 17: Deal Negotiation describes the factors that affect the generosity or severity of the deal terms. The VC firm has to understand these factors well if it wants to negotiate successfully to close the deal. A skillful negotiation is important as ground given or taken affects the risks and returns, and lays the foundation for a win-win partnership with the entrepreneur. Chapter 18: Conditions Precedent describes the preparatory steps that need to be taken by the VC firm, the entrepreneur, and the company for the closing of the deal. Chapter 19: Investment Documentation reviews the important clauses in the investment and shareholder agreements. These are important, as deals have been broken because of sticky issues in the clauses.

With the conclusion of the deal and the disbursement of funds, work begins with the nurturing of the investment, which is described in Part VII. In Chapter 20: Monitoring & Adding Value, we discuss the reasons for close monitoring: to watch for early warning signs, to add value to the company, to ensure corporate governance, to enforce investment terms if necessary, and to explore divestment opportunities. Such efforts are necessary to manage and enhance the health of the investment and to be able to quickly grasp opportunities to realize good returns. In Chapter 21: Realizing and Recovering Value, we discuss the common methods that VC firms employ to divest from their investments, look at scenarios of an investment going bad, and what may be done by the VC firm to recover some value back.

It can be clearly seen that every step of the VC Process involves managing risks and enhancing value of investments. Such continuous and strenuous effort is necessary to achieve the high returns demanded by investors of the funds.

We end the book with Part VIII, on how performance of VC funds are measured and what are the qualities of a VC firm that are expected by investors, entrepreneurs, and the firm's own staff.

Notes on Terminology

All currencies are in US$

VC is the short form for Venture Capital or Venture Capitalist as dictated by the context. If referring specifically to the firm, VC firm will be used, but in many instances, VC may be applicable to either the venture capitalist (individual) or the venture capital firm.

Other short forms:

GP means either the individual general partner, or the general partnership firm
IPO means initial public offering
IRR means internal rate of return
LP means limited partner
LLC means limited liability company
LLP means limited liability partnership
M&A means mergers and acquisitions

The terms: GP, Fund Manager, Management Company are used interchangeably, although GP is more appropriate for partnerships

The terms: LPs and Fund Investors are used interchangeably, although LPs are more appropriate for partnerships

The terms: LLP and Fund Company are used interchangeably, as the only difference is the form of incorporation

A complete list of abbreviations is given on page 467.

PART I

VC FINANCING & ORGANIZATION

Chapter 1: INTRODUCTION answered the following questions: What is Venture Capital? What is its role in the economy and in the financing of companies? What characterizes venture investments? We also introduced the entire Venture Capital investment process, which we call The VC Process.

We now continue with Part I of this book where we answer the questions: How does a VC firm typically finance a company? How is a VC firm set up and staffed?

We start with Chapter 2: VC FINANCING which describes the financing rounds typical of VC investments and how this funding process helps the VC firm to achieve superior returns.

In Chapter 3: VC ORGANIZATION we describe how VC firms are set up and the qualities of the staff that they look for.

2

VC Financing

A VC firm manages several investment funds, and each fund invests into a portfolio of companies. In this chapter we shall explore how the economics work out when a VC invests and attempts to generate superior returns. How is the successful VC able to generate such superior returns?

Since VCs invest in high-risk and young companies, it is only common sense that the VC should *diversify* risks by investing into several companies. The expectation is that while several of the investments may be lost through business failure, there will be others that provide such spectacular gains that they will not only cover the losses, but will also result in a high investment gain for the whole portfolio. It is this *skew* that impacts the economics of a fund's portfolio.

It also makes sense that the VC should *minimize* its risks by not investing a large amount in a very young company with little or no track record. However, investing insufficient funds could stifle the company's growth. The solution is to identify critical stages in the company's growth, marked by significant milestones, and to invest sufficiently at each stage to enable the company to reach the next milestone, provided the progress has been satisfactory and the prospects remained good. This is called *staging* the investment, and the VC rounds of financing are simply called 1st Round, 2nd Round, 3rd Round, etc., or Series A, Series B, Series C, etc. The latter nomenclature follows the naming of the investment securities for the financing round. Some VCs invest in a round earlier than the 1st Round, which is called the Seed Round. It is this staging of investments that affects the investment returns of the VC.

In this chapter, we shall see how VCs typically finance a company by staging the investments through several rounds and how the skew effect works in a portfolio of companies. Let us first examine the different stages of development that a company will typically go through from its birth to maturity. This is because the staging of investments follows the progress of the company through its stages of corporate development.

Stages of Corporate Development

Figure 2.1 describes one of the ways of classifying the stages of corporate development and the respective characteristics of each stage. These stages are helpful in characterizing the development or progress of a company in its growth cycle. The development varies in speed and sometimes may retrograde. The dividing line between stages may not be clear and stages may overlap. Subsequent to these stages the company may move on to a mature stage, a decline stage or a restructuring stage, but we shall focus on the growth stages, which are the targets for VCs.

FIGURE 2.1 STAGES OF CORPORATE DEVELOPMENT

STAGE	CHARACTERISTICS
INITIAL CONCEPT	The founder (or founders) develops ideas for a new business venture, probably working during spare time.
PROOF OF CONCEPT	The original founders bring in a few others to help develop prototypes to prove that the ideas work. Some of the founders may work full time. A company is formed and a business plan is written (through many revisions).
PRODUCT DEVELOPMENT	An initial development team of founders and hired engineers is formed. Patent filings may start. Market research is conducted to determine product features. The alpha version of the product is completed and tested. Staff strength may be ten to fifteen.

MARKET LAUNCH	Beta versions of the product are tested at selected potential customer sites. Market feedback is used to modify the product. Marketing personnel are hired. Marketing strategies are developed. The business plan is updated. Staff strength may be about thirty. The senior management team is almost complete.
MARKET DEVELOPMENT	Revenues are generated. Hiring speeds up. Staff strength increases to fifty or more. New product extensions and offerings are developed. New market niches are penetrated. The company is still unprofitable.
EXPANSION	The company is profitable. Aggressive plans are developed to expand geographically and through acquisitions. Plans for IPO are initiated.

There are many ways to characterize and name the development stages, and sometimes the same name may have different definitions in different systems. Figure 2.2 attempts to clarify and to show three commonly used nomenclature systems. Note that the demarcations of the stages are only roughly equivalent from one system to the next.

FIGURE 2.2 NAMING OF STAGES OF CORPORATE DEVELOPMENT

Initial Concept	Seed	Early Stage
Proof of Concept	Start-up	
Product Development	Development	
Market Launch	Revenue	Expansion
Market Development		
Expansion	Profitable	Later Stage or Mezzanine

Rounds of Financing

Figure 2.3 illustrates the typical rounds of financing associated with the various stages of corporate development. Note that some rounds may be skipped, and a financing round need not be closed at the very beginning of a stage. Some companies may take more rounds of financing than shown in the figure, arising from the need for more than one round for a particular stage of development. Of course, some companies may fail along the way, may be bought out, or choose not to IPO.

FIGURE 2.3   TYPICAL ROUNDS OF FINANCING

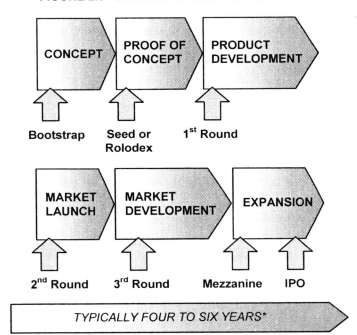

(*Not considering the dot-com era, when this period was more typically 2 to 3 years, and in some cases as fast as a year, with fewer rounds of financing.)

Successful companies typically take four to six years from start-up to IPO. This is not considering the dot-com era, in the late 1990s and 2000, when companies took two to three years, and some even as short as a year. This is now rare, as companies are reverting to the need for a profitable track record before IPO.

It is typical for each round to last six months to two years, since VCs want to see achievement of significant milestones within a year or eighteen months from funding. Companies therefore need to raise enough funds to last for a year to two years, but may end up burning money faster, which could be either good or bad. The company may be accelerating its plans due to better than expected progress or prospects, or it may have lost control of costs or incurred unplanned major expenditures. In some cases, companies may have to stretch the *burn rate*, if they face difficulties and fail to achieve the milestones sufficiently well or in time.

Timing for raising funds may also be affected by the VC market. During a VC market boom, funds are chasing after companies, enabling them to raise funds earlier or raise more funds than planned. If the VC market is dry, or if the company's industry sector has fallen out of fashion, money has to be stretched, and the next round may only be raised perhaps more than twenty-four months after the previous round.

There is usually an increase in the valuation of the company, called a *step-up* in valuation, from one round to the next due to the progress made. If no progress is made, or if overall market valuations have deteriorated significantly, the company may face a drop in valuation (compared to the previous round) and this round is called a *down round*. Step-up in valuation is frequently 1.5 to 2.5 times, but there is a wide variation due to the many factors that affect a company's valuation, which we shall discuss in a later chapter.

Investors of one financing round may or may not participate in future rounds depending on their own perception of the company's future prospects, any limitations they may have on the maximum amount that may be invested in any one company or industry, or whether they have any funds left over from their existing active funds. Referring back to Figure 2.3, let us now examine each financing round in greater detail.

Bootstrap

The funding is from the founders' own pockets. The name is derived from "pulling oneself up by one's bootstraps." This is typically at the initial concept stage, where the company is not yet formed, and the founders are working part time, usually without any salary. The objective is to investigate the feasibility of the business ideas or technology, or to determine the existence of market potential. The milestone here would be reached when a strong level of confidence is attained on the feasibility and market opportunity.

Seed or Rolodex Round

The funding is usually from the founders and their friends, relatives, and possibly business angels also. Hence the name "Rolodex," which implies flipping through the rolodex to search for personal contacts. The name Seed implies the germination of ideas. This is typically the proof of concept stage when prototypes are to be developed to test technical or business concepts or very preliminary market surveys are conducted. A company would likely be formed to enable issue of shares to investors. A preliminary business plan may be drawn up with rough numbers. A core team would be gathered together although some may still be working behind the scenes. The milestone here would be reached when there is adequate evidence that the concepts work.

A Rolodex round consisting of founders, friends, and relatives may amount to $500,000, with each individual investing $10,000 to $100,000, and shares would likely be issued at par. Seed funding may sometimes also come from VCs that focus on seed deals or VCs that allocate a portion of their funds to early stage investments. Seed funding would typically amount to one million, with valuation around $3 million post-money.[2]

1ˢᵗ Round or Series A Round

The funding would be principally from VCs. The shares issued would be Series A Preferred Shares, hence the name Series A Round, or simply A Round. This is typically the product design and development stage. Filings of patents may be commenced for intellectual property that is being developed. The company would also be building a management team. In this round about $4 million would be raised and the company would be valued at about $10 million post-money. The milestone here is the completion of the alpha (first) version of the product.

---

[2] Post-money valuation is the valuation of the company after an investment is made into the company. For elaboration see page 221 of Chapter 13.

2nd Round or Series B Round

The funding would likely be all from VCs in view of the relatively larger amounts raised. The company would be launching the product, hence requiring larger amounts of funding to build marketing and market support teams, and to launch marketing promotions. The management team should be in place at this stage. The company would be raising about $10 million with a valuation of about $25 million post-money. The milestone here would be successful conclusion of beta site tests (testing the beta or second version of the product at potential customer sites), and receiving strong market interest, or even some initial orders.

3rd Round or Series C Round

Funding would be from VCs and perhaps from mezzanine funds as well, with the expectation that the company could IPO in a year or two. At this stage, the company would be generating revenue, although it may not be profitable yet. The funds would be deployed to penetrate markets and to expand product range. Probably about $20 million would be raised and the company would be valued at $80 million post-money. The milestone here would be the building of a strong customer base and establishing a market position.

Mezzanine Round

If the company has been growing well, this round may be skipped and the company may instead prepare for IPO. On the other hand, the company may be confident that further fast growth is within reach and may want to build a longer profit track record before IPO, so that a much higher IPO valuation can be attained. It may also mean that the IPO market sentiment may have turned down, delaying the IPO plans. The company would then raise a mezzanine round, with the amount of funds to be raised being enough to bridge the delay. The milestone here would be the filing of an IPO.

Other Rounds

If the company did not progress well, there could be more intervening rounds. One or two of the rounds could be down rounds and may involve restructuring or a management buyout. On the other hand, a new round may be raised for unplanned opportunities such as mergers, acquisitions, joint ventures, or overseas expansions.

IPO

This is the ultimate round of concern to the VC as it provides the opportunity for the VC to divest its shares. Funding would be from the public offering and from public and institutional investors.

Figure 2.4 summarizes the characteristics of the financing rounds. Amounts raised and valuations are only indicative, as there is wide variation depending on the company's business and prevailing financial market conditions.

FIGURE 2.4   TYPICAL CHARACTERISTICS OF FINANCING ROUNDS

FINANCING ROUND	AMOUNT RAISED	TYPICAL VALUATIONS*	INVESTORS
Bootstrap	Nil	Nil	Founder(s)
Seed or Rolodex	$1 million	$3 million	Founders, friends, relatives, angels, VC seed funds
1st Round	$4 million	$10 million	VCs, angels
2nd Round	$10 million	$25 million	VCs
3rd or Mezzanine	$20 million	$80 million	VCs, mezzanine funds
IPO	$50 million	$300 million	Public

(*Not considering the dot-com era, when valuations were much higher. Since the dot-com crash, valuations have fallen back to those prevalent in the mid-nineties as shown here, which are representative of technology companies. The valuations are post-money values.)

Examples of Financing Rounds

Let us now look at examples of financing rounds for three successful companies, Ideal Inc, LessIdeal Inc, and Ideal.com. These examples show how the shareholdings of the VC as well as the founders increase in value as the company grows. Eventually, when the company has its IPO, the VC can dispose its shares to realize gains. For simplicity, we shall only look at what happens to a single investment of one million by the VC.

In the case of Ideal Inc in Figure 2.5, the column titled "Seed" shows that the company raised one million from the VC. In this seed round, Ideal had a *pre-money* valuation (valuation before the investment) of $2 million. After the one million investment, the *post-money* valuation (valuation after the investment) was $3 million. The VC's 33 percent share in the company was then obviously worth the one million that it had just invested.

FIGURE 2.5   ROUNDS OF FINANCING OF IDEAL INC

($ million)

Financing Round	Seed	1st	2nd	3rd	IPO
Pre-money Valuation	2	6	15	60	250
Amount Raised	1	4	10	20	50
Post-money Valuation	3	10	25	80	300
% Share Offered	33%	40%	40%	25%	17%
Founders' Share	67%	40%	24%	18%	15%
Founders' Share Value	2	4	6	14	45
VC's Share	33%	20%	12%	9%	8%
VC's Value	1	2	3	7	23

In the subsequent 1st Round of financing, Ideal was valued at $6 million pre-money. It raised $4 million from other investors and the VC did not participate. The VC's shareholding was hence diluted from 33 percent to 20 percent. This amount of dilution arises from the following calculation. Since 40 percent new shares were offered in the 1st Round, the VC's shareholding was diluted to 60 percent of 33 percent (0.6×0.33) or 20 percent. However, this shareholding of 20 percent is worth $2 million, as it is 20 percent of the whole company's valuation of $10 million.

It can be seen that despite having a smaller and smaller percentage share of the pie, the VC's share was in fact increasing in value, since the whole pie had been growing in size. On IPO, the VC's shares were valued at $23 million. By making a very high risk investment into a company at its early beginning stage, the VC made a healthy return of twenty-three times its investment, in this example.

The founders paid nominal amounts for their shares, perhaps $100,000 in total. Their shares were worth $45 million at IPO. It is such substantial gains that motivate founders to work their guts out to grow the company successfully.

Figure 2.6 shows a less successful example. LessIdeal Inc had to go through a Rolodex Round, raising money from friends and family, as the technology required extensive validation before seed VCs could be convinced to invest. Progress was slower than Ideal Inc, and hence the step-ups in valuation were smaller. After the 3rd round of financing, the company decided to seek a *trade sale* instead of going IPO, as it concluded that a large corporation in the same business would see strategic value in acquiring its enabling technology, whereas the public may not appreciate or even understand the technology.

FIGURE 2.6   ROUNDS OF FINANCING OF LESSIDEAL INC

($ million)

Financing Round	Rolodex	Seed	1st	2nd	3rd	Acquired
Pre-money Valuation	0.5	2	5	12	30	40
Amount Raised	0.2	1	2	4	8	-
Post-money Valuation	0.7	3	7	16	38	40
% Share Offered	29%	33%	29%	25%	21%	-
Founders' Share	71%	48%	34%	26%	20%	20%
Founders' Share Value	0.5	1.4	2.4	4.1	7.7	8.1
VC's Share		33%	24%	18%	14%	14%
VC's Value		1.0	1.7	2.9	5.4	5.6

The VC and the founders did not gain that much from this effort. However the 5.6 times return is still respectable, given the high percentage of failures in early stage investments.

Finally, Figure 2.7 shows an example of a successful Internet company. Not only did the founders and the VC make astronomical gains, it was achieved in a shorter period, resulting in very high IRRs.

A notable example of very successful Internet companies is Netscape which had its 1st round in September 1994, raising $6.4 million at a valuation of $20.8 million. In less than one year, it raised $140 million at its IPO in August 1995, with a valuation of over one billion. An investor putting in one million in the 1st round would have reaped $48 million on the IPO, not counting any run up in value post-IPO. Another example is eBay. Its 1st round financing was in June 1997, raising $3 million at $30 million valuation. Its IPO was in September 1998, raising $63 million at a valuation of $740 million. An investment of one million in the 1st round would have returned $25 million after just one year.

FIGURE 2.7   ROUNDS OF FINANCING OF IDEAL.COM

($ million)

Financing Round	Seed	1st	2nd	IPO
Pre-money Valuation	20	60	180	500
Amount Raised	5	10	20	60
Post-money Valuation	25	70	200	560
% Share Offered	20%	14%	10%	11%
Founders' Share	80%	69%	62%	55%
Founders' Share Value	20	48	123	309
VC's Share	4.0%	3.4%	3.1%	2.8%
VC's Value	1.0	2.4	6.2	15.4

It should be reiterated that following the dot-com crash in early 2001, valuations of dot-com companies have progressively declined to more down-to-earth levels, reminiscent of mid-1990s levels. The examples given are reflective of real situations, but there can be wide variations

from company to company, industry to industry, geographical region
to region, as well as from time to time arising from varying market
factors.

Staging of Investments

Let us now look at the effect of staging investments. In the case of Ideal
Inc in Figure 2.5, the VC invested one million in the seed round. Ideal
decided to raise $4 million in its first round at a pre-money valuation of $6
million, a step-up of two times the post-money valuation of $3 million after
the seed round. Ideal had received strong validation for its technology and
its initial market surveys had shown huge potential demand for its proposed
products. The company wanted to raise sufficient funds that would allow it
to rapidly develop and deploy the products. Under these circumstances, the
VC would have willingly followed on to invest in the first round. Figure 2.8
shows the position after the VC took up the whole allocation of $4 million
in the 1st round.

FIGURE 2.8   STAGING OF INVESTMENTS IN IDEAL INC

($ million)

Financing Round	Seed	1st	2nd	3rd	IPO
Pre-money Valuation	2	6	15	60	250
Amount Raised	1	4	10	20	50
Post-money Valuation	3	10	25	80	300
% Share Offered	33%	40%	40%	25%	17%
Founders' Share	67%	40%	24%	18%	15%
Founders' Share Value	2	4	6	14	45
VC's Share	33%	20%	12%	9%	8%
VC's Value	1	2	3	7	23
VC's Follow-on Share		40%	24%	18%	15%
VC's Follow-on Value		4	6	15	45
VC's Total Share	33%	60%	36%	27%	23%
VC's Total Value	1	6	9	22	68

We see that the VC's shares, from a total investment of $5 million, would be worth $68 million on IPO, a substantial gain in absolute terms and therefore in terms of return multiple.

It is interesting to note that the initial investment of one million had a return of twenty-three times, while the follow-on investment of $4 million had a return of about eleven times. This is rightly so, as the later investor normally faces lower risks than the earlier investor, and hence should receive lower returns, although this is not always necessarily the case. In fact, assuming that it took a year between each round, the IRR for the initial investment was 118 percent, while the IRR for the follow-on investment was 124 percent. In terms of IRR, the returns for both stages were similarly high, which validates the wisdom of the follow-on investment.

What if the VC had invested all the $5 million at once in the seed round? The shares would theoretically be worth $5 \times 23 = $115 million on IPO. But would the VC have been willing to take the big risk of losing all the $5 million, should the company fail? By placing a small initial bet on the company, the VC had the chance to monitor its progress, and placed the big bet when the company proved itself. If the company had floundered, the VC would have stopped investing or invested less in the follow-on rounds.

In the first place, the founders would not have accepted such a big investment at the seed stage. Figure 2.9 shows what happens to the founders' shareholding, if this were the case. For comparability, this alternative financing would skip the 1st Round shown in Figure 2.5, since the $5 million raised would last long enough. The total amount of funds raised would be $85 million in both cases.

Instead of having 15 percent share worth $45 million, the founders would now have 11 percent share worth $32 million, the result of the heavy dilution in the seed round. Neither would the VC wish to severely dilute the founders, and reduce their incentive to work hard. Ideal Inc may then not fully realize its potential for a $300 million IPO.

The multiple rounds of financing reduce risks for the VC and reduce dilution effects on the founders' shareholdings. Staging of investments through several financing rounds, usually matching achievement of milestones, has become a well accepted VC practice.

FIGURE 2.9   ALTERNATIVE FINANCING OF IDEAL INC

($ million)

Financing Round	Seed	1st	2nd	IPO
Pre-money Valuation	2	15	60	250
Amount Raised	5	10	20	50
Post-money Valuation	7	25	80	300
% Share Offered	71%	40%	25%	17%
Founders' Share	29%	17%	13%	11%
Founders' Share Value	2	4	10	32
Seed VC's Share	71%	43%	32%	27%
Seed VC's Value	5	11	26	80

Skew Effect

The term *skew* is from the statistical study of distributions of variable values. We are familiar with *normal* distribution, which is the bell-shaped curve, where the values are distributed symmetrically around the mean value and tailing off equally on both ends. A skewed distribution is an asymmetrical or lop-sided distribution, either having more values on the lower end or on the higher end, as shown in Figure 2.10. In our case, the desired objective is to have our investments skewed positively, towards higher returns, which means having more investments providing higher returns.

How does the VC firm achieve positive skew for its portfolio of investments? The secret is in the staging of investments. This practice not only helps to reduce investment risks, it also helps to improve investment returns as it allows the VC to selectively invest more funds into the more successful companies. This obviously means that the less successful and certainly the failing investee companies would receive little or no follow-on funding, unless the VC is convinced that there is a good chance of recovery.

Investment gains are enlarged through the addition of funds into successful companies, while investment losses are minimized through the stoppage of funding into failing companies. This leads to the skewing of the investment returns towards the positive end.

FIGURE 2.10   DISTRIBUTIONS OF INVESTMENT RETURNS

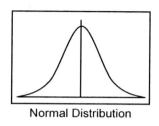

Normal Distribution

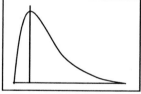

Skewed Distribution:
More investments with
lower returns

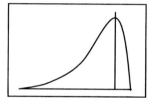

Skewed Distribution:
More investments with
higher returns

This is like playing blackjack in a casino where you are allowed to increase your bet if you wish, after seeing the cards that have been dealt to you. Obviously if you have a strong hand you will increase your bet, although it is not guaranteed that you will win, since the dealer's hand is not exposed yet. If you have a weak hand, you will not add on to your bet. By varying the size of your bet according to the strength of your hand, you are skewing the payoff in your favor.

Let us see how the staging of investments skews a portfolio in the VC's favor. A VC's portfolio typically has this profile: about 40 percent of the companies would be losers, 30 percent would have mediocre performance (they are called *living dead*), 20 percent would give two to five times return, around 8 percent would give five to ten times return, and about 2 percent would be star performers, giving more than ten times return. However, let us use a simplified example—the portfolio of a $50 million six-year fund. Figure 2.11 shows what would have been the portfolio performance if the VC had merely placed equal bets of $10 million on each investment. Negative numbers are investment disbursements, and positive numbers are receipts of divestment proceeds.

FIGURE 2.11   PORTFOLIO A

($ million)

Year	1	2	3	4	5	6	Return Multiple
Inv#1	-10	0	10				1.0
Inv#2	-10	0	0	20			2.0
Inv#3		-10	0	0	0	0	0.0
Inv#4		-10	0	0	100		10.0
Inv#5			-10	0	0	5	0.5
Cash Out	-20	-20	-10				-50
Cash In			10	20	100	5	135

Investment #1 returned $10 million, resulting in a return multiple of 1.0. Investment #2 did better with a return multiple of 2.0. Investment #3 was a loser. Investment #4 was a star, returning ten times the investment, while Investment #5 returned half. Total proceeds amounted to $135 million and the portfolio IRR, calculated from the cash flow, was 40 percent.

The skew effect is already in play in Portfolio A. If Investment #4 gave a return of $15 million instead of $100 million, the total portfolio proceeds would have been $50 million and the portfolio IRR would have been 0 percent. The substantial return from Investment #4 has skewed the portfolio return positively.

Figure 2.12 is more representative of how a VC would invest. This VC initially invested $5 million into each company. If the company performed well, follow-on investments were made. Of course, the VC could make wrong calls, as exemplified by Investment #5, which turned sour after doing well initially. Well, even VCs make mistakes!

FIGURE 2.12 PORTFOLIO B

($ million)

Year	1	2	3	4	5	6	Return Multiple
Inv#1	-5	0	5				1.0
Inv#2	-5	-5	0	20			2.0
Inv#3		-5	0	0	0	0	0.0
Inv#4		-5	-10	-5	200		10.0
Inv#5			-5	-5	0	5	0.5
Cash Out	-10	-15	-15	-10			-50
Cash In			5	20	200	5	230

Portfolio B shows how the staging of investments further skews the portfolio performance positively. After the respective initial investments, Investments #2, 4 and 5 were found to be doing well, and hence follow-on investments were made. Investments #1 and 3 did not do well and no more money was put in. Investment #4 was found to be doing extremely well and hence larger and more follow-on investments were made. All these actions contributed towards skewing the returns more positively. The total divestment proceeds amounted to $230 million and the portfolio IRR was 79 percent, about double the performance of Portfolio A.

The skew effect from staging of investments is a major contributing factor to improving returns from a VC's portfolio of investments. However it should be noted that this is not the only factor. VCs work to improve returns in many other ways, such as sourcing and selecting quality deals, conducting intensive due diligence, thoroughly evaluating them, adding value, closely monitoring the investments, and finding the best exits. Investments that are failing are also worked on to try to turn them around and to recover as much as possible from them. These are important parts of the VC Process that help to improve returns and will be discussed in other chapters.

Capitalization Table

So far we have been looking at simplified tables of shareholdings through a company's rounds of financing. Such tables are called *capitalization tables*. To complete the picture, we now look at a more representative capitalization table, shown in three parts for clarity, in Figures 2.13A, B, and C.

FIGURE 2.13A   IDEAL INC CAPITALIZATION TABLE NUMBER OF SHARES HELD AFTER EACH ROUND

('000)

	Boot-strap	Seed Round	ESOS Reserve	A Round	B Round	ESOS Adjust	C Round	IPO
Founders	2,000	2,000	2,000	2,000	2,000	2,000	2,000	2,000
ESOS			750	750	750	2,400	2,400	2,400
Angels		1,000	1,000	1,000	1,000	1,000	1,000	1,000
A Series				2,500	2,500	2,500	2,500	2,500
B Series					4,167	4,167	4,167	4,167
C Series							4,000	4,000
Public								3,125
Total	2,000	3,000	3,750	6,250	10,417	12,067	16,067	19,192

FIGURE 2.13B   IDEAL INC CAPITALIZATION TABLE AMOUNTS INVESTED (*IN ITALICS*) AND VALUES OF SHARES HELD AFTER EACH ROUND

($'000)

	Boot-strap	Seed Round	A Round	B Round	C Round	IPO
Founders	*100*	2,000	3,200	4,800	10,000	32,000
ESOS			1,200	1,800	12,000	38,400
Angels		*1,000*	1,600	2,400	5,000	16,000
A Series			*4,000*	6,000	12,500	40,000
B Series				*10,000*	20,833	66,667
C Series					*20,000*	64,000
Public						*50,000*
Valuation	100	3,000	10,000	25,000	80,333	307,067
Price/share	$0.05	$1.00	$1.60	$2.40	$5.00	$16.00

FIGURE 2.13C   IDEAL INC CAPITALIZATION TABLE
PERCENTAGES HELD AFTER EACH ROUND

	Boot-strap	Seed Round	ESOS Reserve	A Round	B Round	ESOS Adjust	C Round	IPO
Founders	100%	67%	53%	32%	19%	17%	12%	10%
ESOS			20%	12%	7%	20%	15%	13%
Angels		33%	27%	16%	10%	8%	6%	5%
A Series				40%	24%	21%	16%	13%
B Series					40%	35%	26%	22%
C Series							25%	21%
Public								16%

The founders started Ideal Inc with $100,000 of their own money, issuing themselves 2,000,000 of common shares. About six months later they gathered together friends, relatives, and a couple of business angels to put in a total of one million, issuing to them 1,000,000 of common shares. A year later the founders successfully raised $4 million, mostly from two VCs, issuing Series A preferential shares at $1.60 each. These preferential shares were convertible into common shares on the basis of one common share for each preferential share, and held certain rights required by the VCs.

Prior to the first round, the VCs requested that the company establish an Employee Stock Option Scheme (ESOS), by reserving 750,000 new common shares. In this way, the Series A investors would not be diluted by the ESOS.

After the Series A round, Ideal had 6.25 million shares outstanding. The founders' shareholdings were worth $3.2 million. About eighteen months later, the company completed its product development successfully and raised $10 million in a Series B round to fund its market launch. The two VCs continued to support the company by investing the $10 million.

A year later, the company planned a major expansion that would require $20 million funding. A major VC was brought in and the two existing VCs continued to support, although with smaller amounts this time. The ESOS allocation was adjusted prior to this round, to bring the percentage back to 20 percent, to sustain the motivation of existing management staff, and to cater for new staff that would be hired for the expansion. In less than two years later, the company had its IPO, raising $50 million.

This example gives a fuller picture of how the various shareholders, the founders, angels, management staff, Series A investors, Series B investors, Series C investors, and the public (institutional investors and individuals) participated in the staged funding of the company as it developed.

Chapter Recap

In this chapter, we explored the following:

- o The different stages of corporate development
- o The rounds of financing raised by a growing company
- o The typical valuations and amounts raised in financing rounds
- o The staging of investments by VCs
- o The skew effect in a VC portfolio
- o The impact of staging and skew on investment return
- o The capitalization table

3

VC Organization

T here are many different organizations that carry out VC activities in one form or another, essentially investing into private companies with the objectives of achieving high returns, accessing new technologies or businesses, or promoting local economic development.

Large corporations may set up a VC division or subsidiary with the aim of having a window to emerging technologies, gaining opportunities for possible diversification, or supporting companies that might have synergy with its core business. Banks may also set up a VC arm, for investment return and for synergy with its investment banking activities, such as M&A and IPO services. The large corporations and banks would typically invest their own funds. At a later stage some of them may spin off the VC operations in order to raise third party funds and avoid conflicts of interest. Wealthy families may invest directly or employ professionals to manage their funds, for investment return. Individuals, such as retired CEOs and senior executives, called business angels, may invest for the return and the opportunity to contribute their expertise to the investee companies. Sometimes the angels may form a group or an investment club to extend their network and widen their range of expertise. Countries or states may set up investment companies to fund start-ups and early stage companies, to promote local economic development and entrepreneurship. Universities and research organizations may form incubators to exploit and commercialize their discoveries. All these are different forms of venture capital investing, by different organizations and individuals.

We shall focus on the mainstream VC organization, which is an independent firm usually set up by a group of individuals with some experience in VC investing, managing funds raised from third parties such as pension funds, insurance companies, university endowments, funds of funds, banks, large corporations, and wealthy families. The objective of the mainstream VC firm is to achieve high returns.

Since a venture fund has a limited life of usually ten years, and has to be wound up at the end of its life, separate companies are set up for each fund. In USA and those countries that have corporate laws that allow it, the fund company is set up as a Limited Liability Partnership. A Limited Partnership Agreement (LPA) is signed between the investors, known as Limited Partners (LPs) and the fund manager, known as the General Partner (GP). The LPA spells out the fund's objectives and policies and the partners' respective rights and obligations, and fees payable to the GP. We shall discuss the LPA in Chapter 5.

In those countries that do not allow limited liability for partnerships, it would be typical to set up two separate limited liability corporations, one as the management company and the other as the fund company. There would be a Management Agreement between the two companies, setting out the terms similar to the LPA.

In this chapter we shall discuss how the VC fund and management companies are typically structured, and the management fee structure consisting of an annual fee and a share of the profits, often paid by multiple funds. We end the chapter with a description of how VC management firms are organized and staffed.

Fund Company Structure

Limited Liability Partnership

A Limited Liability Partnership (LLP) is a partnership where the LPs, as the name implies, are not liable beyond the amount of capital contributed respectively. These are the investors in the fund. The GP, which is the investment manager, has unlimited liability, but it is usual that the partners limit their liability by organizing a separate entity such as a Limited Liability

Company (LLC), to hold their partnership interests in the LLP, as shown in Figure 3.1.

FIGURE 3.1   LIMITED LIABILITY PARTNERSHIP STRUCTURE

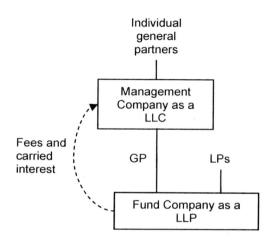

Relatively recent legislation in the U.S. allows the LLC to elect to be treated as a partnership for tax purposes, while still enjoying limited liability. As a partnership, the LLC is not taxed. It is a flow-through entity, like the LLP, with the LLC's ordinary income and capital gains flowing through to the individual owners of the LLC.

There may be variations in tax treatments from state to state, but generally, the LLC owners, like shareholders of a corporation, are not held personally liable for the LLC, unlike an LLP where the managing partners have unlimited liability. This is why the GP holds its interests in the LLP through an LLC. Since the LLC offers the tax advantage of a partnership and the limited liability of a corporation, in the future more VCs may just form a LLC as the fund company, instead of the traditional two-layer structure in Figure 3.1.

The total amount raised for the fund is called the total committed capital, which is drawn down progressively as the fund makes investments. The GP usually contributes one percent of the committed capital and is hence also a

LP in the fund. All the investors commit to their respective amounts and would face penalties if the commitment is not met when a capital drawdown is called.

VCs in the U.S. adopt the LLP structure because of the many advantages:

- o Limited liability: The LLP has limited liability, as mentioned in the preceding paragraphs. Unlimited liability occurs only in the event of fraud, negligence, or malpractice.

- o Tax advantage for LPs: A corporation faces two levels of tax—a corporate tax on income and a tax on dividends received by the shareholders. A LLP is not taxed, as its income is flowed through to the LPs pro rata to their respective committed capital, and each LP is taxed based on its income from all sources after deducting expenses. However many LPs such as employee pension funds enjoy tax exemption, and distributions received from the LLP would not be taxed provided certain conditions are met. The conditions include: the LLP must be purely an investment company and must not operate any business; the LLP cannot incur debt to finance its investments; the LP cannot be involved in the management of the LLP, but may provide internal investment advice and not to third parties.

- o Tax advantage for the GP: For its investment in the fund, the GP is treated like any other LP. If the limited liability company or other entity that holds the GP's interests is a pass-through entity, tax will only be paid on the respective distributions received by each partner in the GP. The GP's share of profits, or carried interest, retains its capital gains nature and is taxed in the hands of each partner. If there are profits earned from management fees in excess of the VC firm's expenses, these profits retain their ordinary income nature.

- o Ease of capital drawdown: Each drawdown of the committed capital only requires a simple notification to LPs within the prescribed notice period, unlike an increase in capital in an incorporated company which requires complex and lengthy processes. The process is further simplified because no shares are issued by the LLP.

○ Ease of returning capital and distributing capital gains: Unlike a corporation, distributing profits or capital gains does not require having net income or accumulated profits. Return of capital does not require court permission. The only requirement is that the LLP must have sufficient assets to meet liabilities.

○ Selective allocations of expenses and capital calls: Each LP has its own capital account, showing its capital contributed, distributions received and fund expenses deducted. A LP may have preferred terms over other LPs because it may be a sponsor and the first to invest, or it may have committed an exceptionally large amount. Thus this LP may enjoy a slightly lower management fee. The LLP structure allows non-pro rata deduction of management fees from each LP capital account. On rare occasions an LP may not participate in a particular investment because of conflicts of interest or other reasons allowed in the partnership agreement. The particular capital call will have to exclude this LP, and subsequent capital calls will be based on amounts not drawn down.

○ Non-pro rata distributions: In a corporation, dividends have to be distributed pro rata to the shareholding held. This is not required in an LLP. This facilitates distribution of carried interest to the GP which is not derived from any share of the committed capital. The carried interest is distinct from a one percent distribution received by the GP for its one percent investment in the fund. Sometimes a LP who is a sponsor of the fund may be entitled to part of the carried interest, and hence distributions to LPs may not be pro rata.

○ Distribution of marketable securities: It is common for VCs to distribute in specie instead of cash; that is the VC distributes the shares held in a listed investee company pro rata the value of the shares to the respective LPs. This may be because the VC holds a large percentage shareholding of the investee company, such that selling the shares in the stock market will cause the share price to plunge. For an LLP, distribution of marketable securities is treated as distribution of cash, based on the market value of the shares at the time of distribution.

o Confidentiality and flexibility of limited partnership agreement: The LPA is deemed to be private in nature and need not be filed publicly. Therefore the terms and conditions can be kept confidential. There are also few statutory limitations or regulations governing the LPA, allowing all parties flexibility in negotiating terms.

o Few corporate rules and regulations: There is no need for Annual General Meetings, although the VC normally holds an annual meeting to brief LPs and for the sake of investor relations. The process of forming and dissolving an LLP is simple—making it easy to have an LLP for each fund.

Perhaps the only disadvantage is the need to negotiate a new LPA every time a new fund is raised. We shall discuss the LPA in Chapter 5.

Corporation

In those countries that do not have legislation providing for formation of limited liability partnerships, it is common to form two separate incorporated companies; one is the operating Management Company and the other is the Fund Company, as shown in Figure 3.2. The two companies will enter into a management agreement, with terms and conditions similar to the LPA, approved by the fund investors. At the end of life of the fund, the Fund Company is wound up and a new one is formed for the new fund.

Unless the country of incorporation offers tax exemption as incentives to develop its VC industry, the two companies may be incorporated in a tax haven. The tax haven Management Company becomes a paper company, contracting out the management of the fund to an operating Management Company incorporated in the country where the VC operates. Income derived from fees and carried interest by the tax haven Management Company would be tax exempt, and it will fund the operating company on a cost plus basis, thus minimizing tax on the operating company.

FIGURE 3.2   FUND CORPORATION STRUCTURE

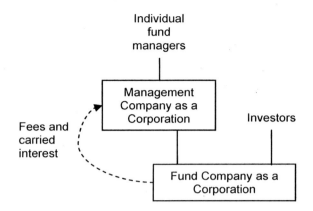

If the Fund Company is established in a tax haven, it may be readily operated like an LLP. If it is established in the country offering tax incentives and is an incorporated company, a structure has to be devised to allow easy return of capital and distribution of capital gains, also recognizing that the Management Company gets a share of profit from the Fund Company without a contributory shareholding.

The usual solution is to structure the Fund Company with high value redeemable preferred shares and very low value common shares. For example, a $100 million fund may consist of 1,000 units, each unit comprising 100 common shares at $1 per share, and 900 redeemable preferred shares (RPS) at $111 per share. Thus each unit costs $100,000. On full subscription, the investors will own 100,000 common shares and 900,000 RPS for the $100 million capital. The Management Company may invest one percent, or one million, thus subscribing for ten units. In addition, the Management Company would have paid in $25,000 for 25,000 common shares prior to sale of the fund units.

Return of capital to investors is facilitated by redemption of the 900 preferred shares at $111 per share. After full redemption, the Fund Company has 125,000 common shares, of which 25,000 shares are owned by the Management Company, which represents its 20 percent share as carried interest. The profits are distributed as dividends pro rata to the common shareholding. In this way, the Management Company receives its carried interest with just an injection of $25,000 into the Fund Company.

Multiple Funds

A VC fund takes about three to four years to be fully invested. Therefore, the VC firm raises a new fund every three or four years, provided circumstances such as market conditions allow, so that it can maintain continuity in investing. In its first year of operation, the VC manages its initial single fund. As new funds are raised, the VC firm will manage a staggered series of funds, as shown in Figure 3.3, which is simplified for illustrative purposes.

FIGURE 3.3   TIME PERIODS OF MULTIPLE FUNDS

Year	1	2	3	4	5	6	7	8	9	10	11	12	13	14...
Fund I														
Fund II														
Fund III														
Fund IV														
Fund V														

It can be seen that from Year 7 onwards, in a steady state situation, the GP will be managing three or four funds at a time, each with its portfolio of investee companies and each at a different stage of its life.

Sometimes the VC may raise two or more parallel funds at a time. Thus, for example, Fund III may be replaced by Funds IIIA, IIIB and IIIC, or whatever names they may be called, all starting at around the same time. This may be done to satisfy different groups of investors, who may require different fund structures for their own reasons, usually because of tax. This may also be done to tap different sources of funds. For example, an Asian VC may set up several country funds in parallel. Similarly a specialty fund may be set up in parallel with a general fund to meet the interests of different investors.

With a mix of earlier funds, current funds, and parallel funds, the VC must have clear policies on how a new investment or a follow-on investment is allocated to the different active funds, and all investors expect this from the VC so that there is no conflict of interests.

There are two investment policies that the VC must have. The first relates to a fund investing into the portfolio company of another fund. This is not allowed, except with the express approval of the VC's Advisory Committee. This is to prevent any attempt to rescue a failing company of a fund by using other funds, which may be a case of pouring good money after bad. If the follow-on investment is well justified by the strong potential for high returns, the VC has to convince the Advisory Committee of the newly participating fund. The valuation of the investee company for the follow-on round also has to be fair. Too high a valuation will disfavor the new fund, while too low a valuation will result in unfair dilution to the old fund.

The second policy relates to allocation of a new investment to parallel funds. Investors do not wish any one group to be favored by the VC with a disproportionate allocation in an extraordinarily good investment. The usual rule is to allocate the respective investment amounts in proportion to the total committed capital of each of the active funds. If a fund cannot participate because it is fully invested or prevented from doing so by its charter, the fund's allocation is reallocated to the other funds, also pro rata to their total committed capital. Thus the allocation is mechanistic and not a subjective exercise by the VC firm. The divestment of such parallel investments is also done on a pro rata basis.

Compensation Structure

The GP is paid a compensation for its fund management services consisting of an annual management fee and a share of the fund profits (called *carried interest*). When the GP sets up a fund, a compensation structure is proposed, and this is often subject to heavy negotiation with LPs.

Management Fee

The Management Fee has shown a slight decline over the years, and nowadays is usually 1.5 percent to 2.5 percent of the committed capital of the fund, payable quarterly or sometimes semi-annually, in advance. In rare cases, the fee could be lower than 1.5 percent or higher than 2.5 percent. The lower end may be applicable to larger funds, while the upper end is for smaller funds or those that specialize in early stage investments and hence require more intensive evaluation and monitoring work. In the early days of the VC industry in Asia, some GPs enjoyed as high a fee as 3.5 percent, but of late, fees have declined to be more in line with those of U.S. funds. A young VC may have to reduce the fees to the largest or earliest investors to be successful in raising its initial funds.

The management fee is meant to cover the cost of operations of the GP. About 60 to 70 percent of the fees go to salaries and bonuses for professional investment staff and support staff, while the remainder is for overhead expenses, particularly travel and entertainment.

When compared to management fees for mutual fund managers, which is typically 0.5 percent of assets managed, the fees for VCs appear to be high. This is because of the higher cost of making private equity investments, as against investing in public companies where corporate information is promptly and fully disclosed. Besides having to ferret out the private companies, carrying out intensive due diligence and evaluation, as well as close monitoring, the VC has to incur effort in adding value and seeking fruitful divestment opportunities, which are activities that are not required with public securities.

Nevertheless, the growth of VC funds into sizes that exceed a billion dollars has resulted in management fees ballooning to large amounts which more than cover the GP's expenses. This is compounded by the fact that VCs manage, and hence draw fees from, as many as three or four funds at any point in time, as shown in the previous section. Since each new fund is likely to be larger than prior funds, the fees get further magnified. In recent years, the more established VCs that were already managing several funds and had successfully raised new mega-funds have found that they were making significant profits from the fees alone. The LPs are therefore concerned that the GP would become not so driven to make successful investments in order to earn carried interest, thus adversely affecting investment performance and hence the LPs' returns.

LPs have indeed always been negotiating for lower fees and the trend continues in that direction. In Chapter 5 we shall discuss the ways in which management fees are structured to bring them closer to the GP's operating costs.

It should be noted that a 2.5 percent management fee for a $100 million fund with a charter life of ten years will mean a total fee paid by the fund amounting to $25 million, assuming that it is a fixed fee. This means that the fund theoretically has only $75 million to invest. However in practice, it is common for funds to invest about 80 to 90 percent of the committed capital for new and follow-on investments. In some cases, the GP may choose to invest 100 percent. Some of the proceeds from divestments will be used to pay management fees in the later years. By putting more money to work, the GP hopes to improve the performance of the fund.

Fees for Extended Fund Life

LPs may agree, at the request of the GP, to extend the life of a fund beyond ten years, by two or more years, to allow extra time to the VC to complete divestment of the remaining portfolio, instead of rushing and as a result realize lower returns. It is typical that management fees are reduced during the extended period, and may sometimes be completely waived, depending on what had been agreed previously and specified in the LPA. If not previously specified, it would be negotiated.

Carried Interest

Carried interest is usually 20 percent to the GP, with the remaining 80 percent of capital gains going to the LPs. This basis has been held steady over the years. During the dot-com boom years, some premier VCs were able to raise carried interest to 25 percent or even 30 percent, due to the strong oversubscription to their new funds. After the crash, the carried interest has returned to 20 percent for most of the new funds raised. A young VC may have to sacrifice a part of the carried interest to sponsors, which may be as high as 50 percent. This is frowned upon by other LPs, since they fear that the VC staff may not be sufficiently motivated.

The high carried interest is to align the interest of the VC with that of the LPs, which is to achieve as high returns as possible. Carried interest is usually based on the net capital gains for the portfolio, after deducting investment losses, management fees, and allowed expenses incurred by the fund. Usually the GP does not get its share of profits until after all the drawn down capital is returned to LPs. Thus the carried interest has to be sufficiently high to help retain staff, as it is not paid out until several years into the fund life.

During the VC industry boom years, more funds allow carried interest to be payable on a deal by deal basis, instead of only after returning all capital, to further incentivize and retain staff. In such cases, the funds need to have a mechanism whereby capital losses are reimbursed as soon as a profitable divestment is made. VCs have found creative ways to provide this mechanism. They will be discussed in Chapter 5.

Management Company Organization

The VC fund management company is typically organized functionally, with an investment division and support departments such as finance, investor relations, IT, and HR. For a small VC, all the support functions may be in one department, usually managed by the CFO. A management company organized as a partnership will designate its investment staff as in a professional services firm, with titles such as partner and associate. Again, like a partnership, each partner may have dedicated associates and analysts, or the partners may share a common pool of associates and analysts. Decisions on deals may be made by an Investment Committee consisting of the managing partner with two or all of the senior partners, on a majority or consensus basis. If organized as a corporation, the VC will have the usual corporate titles such as president, vice president, and investment manager.

Investment Division

Many VCs are organized with each partner or senior investment staff looking after several investments from cradle to grave. This provides continuity in the memory and understanding of the rationale behind the deal terms and issues faced by the company; continuity in rapport with entrepreneurs; as well as accountability for the outcome of the investment.

On the other hand, some VCs believe that different skill sets and temperaments are required for deal sourcing and deal making, as against investment monitoring and divestment. The former requires marketing and negotiation skills as well as a more outgoing personality for networking. Investment monitoring and divestment require more analytical skills, and corporate finance or investment banking experience would be useful. Because of this, some VCs break up the investment staff into two groups and hire according to the skills required. Deal evaluation would be carried out by both groups. The marketing group would carry out preliminary evaluation to screen off marginal deals. If the deal is straight forward, they may put up the investment proposal to the Investment Committee. The monitoring group, with their analytical skills, would evaluate more complicated deals. A deal team may be formed, with members from both groups. This promotes teamwork and provides continuity when responsibility of the deal moves from the marketing group to the monitoring group.

For a larger VC in Asia, it may be more economical and sensible to have marketing offices in several countries and the monitoring group centralized in the headquarters, instead of independent offices all over, or all centralized in one office. The presence of marketing offices provides the local knowledge and networking, which is important in view of the disparate cultures, languages, business practices, and laws in the Asian countries. Centralizing the monitoring and divestment group saves overhead and provides a common standard in evaluating deals and helps to detect cross-border M&A and exit opportunities.

While investment staff may have designated investment territories, many VCs adopt a matrix approach, with staff also designated with specializations according to industry sectors or types of businesses, to tap their specialized knowledge or interests.

Whether it is within a single office or among several offices, good communications and team spirit are important to facilitate tapping of each other's knowledge and assistance. VCs therefore hold weekly deal meetings within each office, and perhaps quarterly group meetings for staff from all offices to meet, discuss deals, exchange ideas, and socially interact. The staff may be rewarded by bonuses or shares of the carried interest partly based on the fund's overall performance and partly based on the investments made by each office, to promote team effort and spirit.

Finance Department

The finance department manages the VC's internal accounts and the LPs' capital accounts; ensures compliance with internal financial controls and procedures, including investment procedures; makes the necessary regulatory filings; helps investment staff with legal documentation and investment audit work; liaises with LPs on capital calls and distributions; and coordinates the submission of portfolio reports to LPs. The department also handles the necessary submission of applications and renewals of investment advisers' licenses for the company and the professionals. The CFO may also oversee the HR and IT functions.

Investment Staff

All the investment staff are called professional staff, while the rest are called support staff. In the U.S., a VC managing a $100 million fund would typically have three to five partners, or approximately $20 to 40 million per partner. In Asia, because of lower costs and smaller funds, it is typically $10 to 20 million per partner. The larger VCs in Asia would enjoy economies of scale and the ratio would be closer to that of U.S. VCs, around $20 to 30 million per partner. A larger VC in Asia would need several offices spread out in several countries, requiring a higher headcount than a U.S. VC.

The VC deals in the U.S. are generally larger in size than in Asia. While a U.S. VC would make investments averaging $5 to 10 million per deal, including follow-ons, the deals in Asia would average about $3 to 5 million. Thus each partner, whether in the U.S. or Asia, would do about four deals per fund, or on average a deal a year, since the investment period for a fund is about four years. During very active years in the VC industry, the investment rate may accelerate, and the fund may be fully invested in about two and a half to three years. Thus a partner may then do an average of one and a half to two deals a year.

At any time a partner should not be monitoring more than six investee companies, and ideally it should be four or five. A partner would be assisted by associates and analysts to help with due diligence, financial analysis, and research, and as back up in monitoring investments.

Staff Profiles

Without a doubt, the quality of investments depends heavily on the quality of the investment professionals. Evaluating and adding value to companies require skills, knowledge, and experience in a diverse range of areas, such as business strategies, operational experience, management practices, technology, industry structures, market trends, financial expertise, and some legal knowledge. Some VCs would prefer to hire engineers with MBAs; others may prefer accountants or consultants with MBAs. In any case, the VC firm should have a mix of all these expertise, so that help can be provided internally for simpler situations, and for interfacing with external consultants and experts, hired for more complex situations.

Besides character, qualifications, and experience, certain abilities are important in VC investment professionals:

o Judgment: People judgment and business judgment are probably the most important skills that a VC must be good at. While it is arguable that these skills are required in any job, the VC is called upon to judge a person's character and ability, and the correctness and prospects of business strategies, much more often than most other jobs. The success of investments is usually critically hinged upon such judgments.

o Investigative & interviewing skills: Very often, a VC is required to assess unfamiliar businesses, entrepreneurs, and managers. Due diligence investigation under pressure of limited time requires knowing where, how, and what to find out as well as the ability to ask the right questions in the right ways to arrive at the clearest answers possible. This also requires skills in listening and observing body language.

o Interpersonal skills: The VC must earn the trust and respect, and often the friendship, of the entrepreneurs and managers prior to and after the investment. In this way, the investee company will be prompt in keeping the VC abreast of developments and facilitate the help and value add that the VC firm can offer to the company.

o   Networking skills: The VC taps a network of networks, more so than most other professionals. There are networks of individuals and organizations to source deals, to carry out due diligence, for value adding, and for exit opportunities. These include entrepreneurs, industry leaders and executives, academic and research institutions, financial institutions, professional firms, regulatory bodies, etc. The VC must continually expand and update relevant and important networks.

Staff Incentivization

Besides salaries and bonuses, VC staff may have added incentives to align their interests with that of the company. Some VCs award a share of the carried interest to all professionals, while others limit it to senior investment staff. On the closing of a fund, and over a time frame of the initial three or four years of the fund, points are vested to staff in tranches, most likely according to seniority. At the time of distribution of carried interest, the staff's share is based on the percentage of points out of the total vested. Staff who join after the vesting period will not participate in the current fund, but in the next fund that would be raised. Support and investment staff who do not participate in the carried interest will be awarded relatively higher bonuses if the fund performs well.

The VC may set up an investment company to invest in parallel with the fund, providing an opportunity for staff to participate in the investment returns. Contribution to this investment company is voluntary. The company will invest in parallel, in all deals, in the proportion of its fund size to the committed capital of the main fund. The VC cannot cherry-pick which deals the staff investment company would invest in. This parallel investment company may be in addition to or in lieu of the GP's one percent committed capital in the main fund. The advantage of a separate staff investment company is that it would be easier to manage withdrawals due to resignations and transfers of shares between staff.

— *Chapter Recap* —

This chapter focuses on:

- ○ How a VC firm is organized into a Management Company with one or more Fund Companies
- ○ The structuring of a Fund Company as a limited liability partnership and as a corporation
- ○ The structuring of management fee and carried interest
- ○ How a Management Company is organized, in particular the investment division
- ○ The important qualities of investment staff and staff incentivization

PART II

RAISING FUNDS

Raising funds is crucial to the VC firm. Without funds to manage, invest, and earn fees, the VC firm cannot operate. How and from whom do VC firms raise money? How do they convince such investors to invest in their VC funds? What terms and conditions would the investors impose on the VC firm? What management fees would they pay to the VC? How will profits from investments be shared?

These questions are answered in Chapter 4: RAISING FUNDS and Chapter 5: LIMITED PARTNERSHIP AGREEMENT. The Limited Partnership Agreement is an important document that spells out the compensation terms to the VC firm and governs the conduct of the VC firm.

4

Raising Funds

A VC firm going out to raise a new fund is not very different from an entrepreneurial firm attempting to raise funds from VC firms. Potential investors of the new fund will evaluate the management team's track record, its investment strategies, and environmental factors such as the business climate, investment opportunities, and the economic growth trends of the territory in which the VC firm operates. The VC firm will have to capture all this information in an offering document or a private placement memorandum and will conduct road shows to make presentations to potential investors. In this chapter we shall discuss the mechanics of the fund-raising process, which consist of drawing up the offering document, identifying the target investors, understanding their investment criteria, and conducting the road show.

Just as a VC firm may receive on average as many as eight business plans per working day, an investment advisory firm managing a large pension fund may receive on average one or two placement memos per working day. If the VC firm is lucky enough to gain sufficient interest for an initial meeting, the road shows and interviews by the potential investors can be grueling, as these are sophisticated and experienced investors, used to dishing out high-pressure grilling. These initial meetings are often followed by due diligence questionnaires which may contain literally hundreds of questions, as well as several repeat visits, which may still end up in rejections.

An important decision by the VC firm is the timing of the fund-raising. The right timing can ensure a successful full subscription to the fund. A correct decision requires understanding of VC market conditions and market cycles, which we will discuss first, followed by the pros and cons of using a placement agent, who may provide useful advice on the fund-raising market. Then we shall dwell on the mechanics of the fund-raising process followed by some related issues.

VC Market Cycles

The VC market goes through short-term years of ups and downs in a cyclical manner while exhibiting overall long-term growth. In the boom years, new VC funds are successfully raised, and hence investment activity is robust. In the bust years, VC firms have difficulty raising new funds and investments by the VC firms slow down, so as to stretch out the remaining funds while awaiting an upturn in the industry. Why does the industry experience market cycles?[3]

During good times, with a growing economy and strong investor interest in IPOs, many VC firms are able to raise new funds, many of which are mega-funds with total commitments of a billion dollars or more. With so much new money, VC firms are pressurized to invest large amounts quickly, forcing an upward trend in company valuations. Many VC firms chase after certain industry sectors, especially emerging technologies, leading to a herd mentality which balloons valuations further. The euphoria infects the public markets as companies IPO at exceptionally high valuations. Soon realism sinks in, as company results reveal that they cannot support the market valuations, which then plummet. The IPO market dries up and VC firms find that their portfolio companies have to postpone their IPOs or IPO at low valuations. Since investments were made at high valuations, the VC funds start to show poor performance, LPs become disenchanted, and the VC market dries up. VC firms have to delay starting a new fund and concentrate instead on working on portfolio companies and are more selective in investments, and as a result private company valuations become

---

[3] See Chapter 6 of Paul Gompers and Josh Lerner, *The Money of Invention*, Boston: Harvard Business School Press, 2001, for a discussion on the boom and bust cycles of the Venture Capital industry.

more realistic. But memory does not last long. When capital markets revive, VC firms rush in to raise funds and the cycle repeats itself.

Such cycles are not unique to the VC industry. The semiconductor industry, for example, is very similar. As the economy shows signs of recovery from a recession, billions of dollars are sunk in to add wafer fabrication (fab) capacity. Such plants are designed for large production capacities to cater for market sizes that are anticipated several years later, since it is not economical and often not technically feasible to build a plant for the immediate future and incrementally add capacity year by year. Just like a VC firm with its newfound mega-capacity to invest, the semiconductor firm with its newly commissioned fab will scramble for market share to fill up as much of its overly large capacity as possible. However, many of these plants will find that demand is not as strong as anticipated, due to double or triple ordering arising from the supply shortages before the new fabs came on stream. As a result semiconductor prices plummet; the firms lose money and struggle until demand catches up with capacity again.

In the early years of the semiconductor industry, wafer fabrication plants were not so expensive. The wafers were smaller in diameter and fewer chips were squeezed into each wafer. Therefore the construction of new plants were spread out more evenly over the years, as each increment in capacity was relatively small and readily absorbed by the growing market. With tremendous advances in technology, it became feasible to have larger wafers and chips being more densely squeezed together. The capacity of each new plant became much larger. Due to the huge cost, companies spaced out such expansions and the timing by different companies tended to be delayed or accelerated to coincide with market turnarounds, which meant that they bunched together. Thus, on an industry basis, total capacity expansion was magnified exponentially by the larger plants and coincidence of timing, leading to larger swings in supply-demand cycles.

VC firms have found that economies of scale also work in their industry. Larger funds mean more fees and greater ability to hire better managers, have wider scope of investments, and to scale globally. Larger funds mean better reputation and ability to attract better deals. But larger funds also mean that proper timing of fund-raising is critical. Good timing for one VC firm is usually good timing for others as well, especially after a long dry period, such as from 2000 to 2003. The year 2004 saw the release of pent-up demand and the rush to raise funds. Thus we see a similar trend towards larger funds and coincidence of timing, which exacerbate the swings in the VC market cycles.

The world VC market behavior follows that of the U.S., since the U.S. VC industry is by far the largest and the U.S. pension and endowment funds are also the largest suppliers of funds to the VC industry worldwide. Therefore VC firms seeking funding inside and outside the U.S. have to be cognizant of the U.S. market cycles. This does not necessarily mean that the VC firm must time its fund-raising to coincide with others, since there will be much jostling and competition for funds. There are some firms that have successfully raised funds while all others were holding back. A strong team, with a good track record and a wise investment strategy, will be able to raise funds during off-peak years, or be able to stand out among the crowd during the peak seasons.

Besides affecting the timing of fund-raising, VC market conditions affect decisions on the size of funds raised, the investors to target, and the investment strategies to adopt. While these also depend on the VC team's capabilities and operating environment, they have to be fine tuned to suit the prevalent market preferences and meet the objectives of LPs.

Placement Agent

Placement agents who help VC firms raise funds may be investment banks, specialist or boutique firms, or single person consultant firms. VC firms are increasingly using placement agents because LPs are more and more sophisticated, and the competition for funding is getting to be fierce because of the increasing number of VC firms and the increasing size of funds raised. VC firms are becoming more global in terms of fund-raising as well as operations. Asian VC firms are raising funds in the U.S., while many U.S. VC firms are not forgetting to include Asia in their foray for funds.

The choice of placement agent is therefore not limited to fund-raising capability and track record in terms of network within a given territory, but is assessed on a global basis, in the case of VC firms intending to raise substantial funds. The tendency would then be to prefer the better known placement agents. However, the VC firm would have to be conscious of any conflict of interest, which may arise if the agent happens to be raising funds for a competing VC firm at about the same time. The VC firm would also have to ensure that adequate resources are dedicated to its effort throughout the exercise. Some VC firms therefore prefer to work with boutique firms that provide full attention and support.

The VC firm must remember to decide on a placement agent very early in the exercise, since a lot of the work, and hence the agent's value, go into the preparatory work. In the first place, the agent would advise on the market situation and timing for the fund-raising. The agent would help to work out the investment strategy and focus of the proposed fund and the fund-raising marketing pitch to prospective LPs. A great value of an agent is its knowledge of investment preferences of LPs. The VC firm should not waste time and effort in pitching to LPs who have little interest in the industry or geographical focus of the fund, or perhaps LPs who have exhausted their funds for the current fiscal year.

Knowledge of the LP's background, investment interest, and concerns, as well as investment experience, would be valuable in customizing the marketing pitch to evoke interest, and in preparing answers to anticipated questions. The agent's network and personal relationships with senior staff of LPs will also go a long way to opening doors, sounding out interest, and understanding concerns.

Another area of assistance by a placement agent is advice on local regulations and tax laws relevant to the VC industry. These have impact on the structure, investment policies, and administrative procedures of the fund. This would be of particular importance to a VC firm attempting to raise funds offshore. Some VC firms have found the need to structure parallel funds to serve the tax and regulatory needs of different groups of LPs.

A young VC firm will find that its fund-raising task may be made easier if it could first convince a reputable placement agent to sign up. This would in turn help to convince other prospective LPs. The placement agent brings along with it its reputation and credibility that are recognized by LPs. Many

LPs find it more comfortable to talk to a third party than directly to the VC firm, for feedback of opinions and concerns. Finally, a placement agent plays a useful supplementary role during road shows, by taking notes, observing the meeting dynamics and body language, and looking for improvements to the VC firm's presentation and answers to questions; which are tasks the VC partners may not always adequately perform, being engrossed in the interaction.

Fees charged by the placement agent typically range from 1 to 3 percent of the capital raised through its efforts, excluding funds raised directly by the VC firm itself or through other parties. Part of the fee may be in the form of a retainer and sometimes may include a share of the carried interest, especially for new or young VC firms.

A good way to find placement agents is through introductions by LPs, legal or accounting firms or banks, or perhaps even a friendly VC firm which has successfully raised funds using an agent. The VC firm would obviously have to carefully evaluate prospective agents and would be well advised to consult the opinion of one or two of the leading prospective LPs that it may be in touch with. This is because some LPs may have rather strong views on the placement agent's fees, which are paid from the fund, and some may have had an unhappy experience with the placement agent in question.

Limited Partners

Limited Partners (LPs) of VC funds include the following:

- o   State pension funds
- o   Corporate pension funds
- o   University endowment funds
- o   Fund-of-funds, limited partners of fund-of-funds
- o   Corporate venture operations
- o   Financial institutions such as banks, finance, and insurance companies
- o   Cash-rich companies
- o   Wealthy families including family funds and foundations
- o   Wealthy individuals including successful entrepreneurs

o Developmental organizations (state economic development organizations, industry-based organizations or industry associations, minority-based development organizations)
o Public market investors

Obviously, investors in the VC firm's prior funds will be of top priority in the fund-raising. These LPs already know the VC firm and will likely continue to invest, provided the past performance has been reasonable. The satisfaction and continuing support of existing LPs lend credibility to the VC firm in its fund-raising with new LPs. VC funds are now accepted as an asset class within the investment strategies and allocations of pension funds. Pension funds and endowment funds typically allocate 5 to 10 percent of their funds to higher risk investments such as VC funds.

Fund-of-funds, as the name implies, are funds that invest in other funds. Managers of fund-of-funds are known as *gatekeepers*. A corporate venture operation is a division of a corporation that invests in VC deals, usually with the main objective of seeking new business opportunities or acquiring new technologies. Such an operation may also invest in VC funds to enlarge it deal exposure.

Banks and other financial institutions may invest their own funds or funds organized from high net worth clients. Cash-rich companies and wealthy families also invest in VC funds. Their funds may be in-house managed or managed by investment consultants and advisers. Wealthy individuals may invest directly or through a group such as a group of business angels.

Country or state development organizations invest in VC funds to promote entrepreneurial development and investments in local companies. They would usually require a portion of the funds to be invested locally. Some state pension funds also have such a requirement to promote local job creation.

The VC fund investors listed above are not necessarily limited to those in the country or region in which the fund operates. Fund-raising is now pursued globally, especially for the larger funds. Asian, European, and American VC firms have successfully sought investors in each other's countries.

Some VC firms have successfully raised funds from public markets. Some of them have started new funds raised entirely from public subscription. Although at the time of the listing, the funds themselves have no performance to demonstrate—being new, the VC firms have depended on their track records of prior funds to convince public investors. However, such funds, in their initial years, have to face disgruntled investors who do not understand the nature of VC funds well. Such investors typically question why the fund is sitting on its horde of cash just recently raised, why it is not investing fast enough, and why it is not declaring dividends. It is typical for private equity investments that lemons drop before the plums mature. The initial bad investments leading to write-offs and write-downs further generate investors' displeasure.

Other VC firms have therefore found it more prudent to list a fund after establishing three or four years' investment track record. The portfolio could then be listed and funds would be raised for further investments. The existing investments would soon mature leading to divestments and declaration of dividends. It is typical that the profits from the divestments are distributed as dividends, while the investment capital is retained for reinvestment. Therefore the advantage of a listed fund is its evergreen nature, without needing a three- or four-year cycle of fund-raising. If the fund performs well, it would be easier to enlarge its capital base through a rights issue.

Another advantage of a listed fund is the liquidity that it offers to investors. A private VC fund locks up investors for ten to twelve years. Although there are secondary markets for VC fund holdings, these markets are still not well developed. Yet another advantage is that the listed fund does not have a limited life, and hence investments can be held longer. However the VC firm would have to balance between holding longer with the hope for higher gains, versus the risks, the need to declare dividends and the performance of the fund.

The advantage of liquidity for listed fund investors is somewhat reduced by a discount in the market value of the listed shares of the fund. Listed funds typically suffer a 15 to 30 percent discount from net asset value— sometimes as high as 50 percent. The rationale is that since the investments are in private companies, disposal will not be easy and will not realize the full value as assessed by the fund manager. The lack of public interest in and understanding of such funds also contribute to the discount in market value.

For the fund manager, the advantage of the evergreen nature of the listed fund is somewhat offset by the need to educate investors and to balance disclosures of investments and results. Being a listed company, the fund has to meet disclosure requirements, especially large new investments that are made, as well as the performance of the top largest investments held. As these are private companies, the fund has to be careful that confidentiality is not breeched and competitive information is not revealed in the disclosures. Such a fine balancing act is possible but can be difficult.

In the late 1990s there was a surge in interest in public listed VC funds. These were Internet-focused VC funds and they enjoyed the success of several quick IPOs of Internet related companies. Substantial amounts of money were raised from their public offerings and their share prices rose astronomically. A few years later, with the dot-com crash, their share prices crashed to as low as 5 percent of peak values, and listed VC funds fell out of favor. It remains to be seen whether they will re-emerge.

Fund Policies & Strategies

When raising a new fund, it is important for the VC firm to have well thought out and clearly stated fund focus, objectives, strategies, and policies. These would be highlighted in the offering document.

Fund Focus

A VC fund may be set up with a specific focus or as a general fund. Some funds may specialize by industry sector, such as information technology, nanotechnology, communications, media, energy, or healthcare; by investment territory, such as a country or region, or may be global; or by stage of company development such as seed companies, start-ups, mid stage, or later stage companies. The choice of focus may be dictated by the skill sets and interest of the general partners as well as the investment opportunities offered in the investment territory. Some VC firms may decide not to be too narrowly focused to diversify investment risks. As VC funds keep growing in size, the trend has been to move from country to regional and global funds. A larger VC firm may choose to have a global fund invested by large LPs and several parallel country funds to tap local fund sources.

Some funds may be set up by country or state organizations to foster local economic development and entrepreneurship. Such funds, without specific focus, were popular in Asia in the early years of the industry, because many countries offered good investment opportunities but with widely diversified economies and different levels of industry development, requiring a broad and opportunistic approach. However, LPs are nowadays demanding a more focused and strategic approach to differentiate a VC fund from the many me-too funds being set up.

Fund Size & Life

The VC firm's aim is to raise a larger fund each time. This would match its growth and increasing capacity to invest. Obviously the larger management fee and carried interest are strong incentives. Thus in the late 1990s, spurred by the dot-com boom, VC funds reached the billion dollars level. After the short-lived boom, some VC firms reduced the committed capital by as much as 30 percent or more, thus notionally returning funds to investors, as they realized that investment opportunities have become fewer and smaller. Nevertheless, the industry is showing an overall sustained trend of larger sized funds, ignoring the market swings caused by the VC boom and bust cycles.

The VC firm must determine the fund size not only based on the VC market sentiment, the investment climate, and the investment opportunities in its operating territories, but also based on the focus of the fund and the investment strategies. These must be consistent with each other. For example the size must be moderated if the focus is on early stage companies, since each investment will be relatively smaller.

The fund life is usually ten years, with provision to extend to twelve or sometimes thirteen years, subject to approval by LPs for each year of extension. The extension of the fund life is to allow completion of divestment of laggards in the portfolio. Usually the management fee would be reduced or waived during the extended period.

Investment Objective

The fund's investment objective is usually stated to be to achieve significant long-term capital appreciation through private equity or equity-related investments. This may be embellished with a description of the investment climate, growth potential, and opportunities in the target investment territories. Some offerings may indicate a target investment return.

Investment Strategies

In order to differentiate its fund and to stress the unique prospects offered, the VC firm will highlight the special investment strategies it will pursue, utilizing the expertise of its team and capitalizing on opportunities available in the investment territory, and quoting some examples that may achieve extraordinary returns. We shall discuss this further in the next section.

Investment Policies & Limits

The VC firm would perhaps stress a policy of creating a balanced and diversified portfolio, managing risks and optimizing returns. In this regard, it will specify a typical average investment size, and investment limits on amounts invested in a portfolio company, an industry sector, and in a country or region.

VC firms try to have fewer than forty companies in a portfolio as too many become unmanageable. Thus a $400 million fund would target an average investment size of $10 to 20 million. Typically a fund will not make a total investment, including follow-on investments, in a portfolio company amounting to 10 percent or 20 percent of total committed capital of the fund; in an industry sector amounting to perhaps 20 or 25 percent; and in a country or region amounting to 30 or 40 percent of total committed capital. Some funds will specify only a limit on a portfolio company.

The VC firm will also specify that it will not invest in listed securities and in other funds. These policies, as well as several others, are captured in the LPA, as described in Chapter 5 in the section on Covenants & Controls.

Monitoring & Divestment

Active monitoring and proactive divestment efforts are givens for VC investments. However, the VC firm may make specific statements to stress these, and highlighting how it will add value to the investments.

Distribution of Proceeds

The VC firm will state a policy on how proceeds from divestments will be distributed to LPs. This will include the VC firm's right to withhold a part of proceeds to meet payment of fees and approved expenses, and the right to distribute in specie if the VC firm wishes. The method of calculation and payment of carried interest to the VC firm will also be spelled out, as described in Chapters 3 and 5.

Valuation Policy

The VC firm will clearly state its policy on how the portfolio companies will be valued. This is described in Chapter 22.

Other Income

The VC firm may earn certain fees in the course of its work, and these are usually all accrued to the fund. These would be spelled out in the LPA. Some VC firms charge their investee companies an originating fee or investment banking fee for the effort in sourcing, evaluating, and structuring the investment. Some VC firms also charge their investees a management fee for the management support and value add provided to them. All these fees usually belong to the fund and not the VC firm. If the VC firm's representative sitting on the board of the investee is paid a fee and given stock options, the fee and options also go to the fund. Similarly loan interest and dividends, if any, are paid to the fund.

If the VC firm earns finder's fees for introducing deals to co-investors, the fees belong to the fund. Of course, if the VC firm has a one percent interest in the fund, it will receive its one percent share of the income.

Investment Expenses

Certain expenses incurred by the VC firm, as specified in the LPA, may be charged to the fund. These include costs incurred in organizing annual meetings for LPs, employing consultants for due diligence assistance and advice, or incurred for deals that were aborted. Some LPAs may spell out a formula to share costs between the fund and the VC firm. Since the fund bears such chargeable costs, carried interest will be net of such costs.

Expenses incurred in organizing the fund are usually not chargeable to the fund. Fund-raising fees paid to consultants, brokers or placement agents are usually borne by the VC firm. If such fees are chargeable to the fund, they would be subject to a cap. Professional fees, such as legal and audit fees, incurred for the investments are usually charged to the investee company.

Investor Criteria

When raising a new fund, it is also important for the VC firm to understand the criteria that LPs will use to evaluate and decide whether to invest in the fund. The following are factors that will be examined:

o   Quality of the Investment Team
o   Quality of Past Investments
o   Investment Strategies and Policies
o   Investment Climate and Opportunities

It is obvious that the foremost consideration is the quality of the VC firm. This is not limited to the senior general partners, but includes the whole investment team. It is also not limited to the people, but includes the partnership's investment process, controls, and documentation. We shall discuss these important qualities in Chapter 23.

Evaluation of the quality of past investments is also a good indicator of the quality of the team and the investment environment. A successful investment may have occurred as a result of coincidence or circumstances that may not be repeatable. The LP would have to evaluate the effort and contribution of the team towards the successful sourcing, evaluation, and post-investment management of the deal. Failed investments are also looked into to see whether the VC firm understood the causes and whether the lessons were learned.

The LP's analysis of prior funds can be very detailed. The VC firm would have to produce datasheets breaking down prior investments by categories such as industry sector, geographical location, stage of development, and deal source. Each category would have investment details such as amount invested, year invested, percentage ownership, realized value, year of exit, mode of exit, investment gains or loss, and IRR. Investments that are still held will have additional details of any write-downs or write-offs, as well as projections of year of exit, mode of exit, and exit values. Sometimes the LP would also want indications of whether the VC firm was the lead investor or syndicate member of a deal, or whether there were industry or other strategic partners in the deals. All these data will enable the LP to take the analysis further to look for strengths and weaknesses in the team and the investments.

The LPs will usually prefer focused investment strategies for the fund. During times of strong economic growth, an opportunistic and unfocused investment strategy could be acceptable. However in an economy where only certain sectors promise growth, the new fund has to encompass one or some of the sectors in order to deliver the high returns required. LPs also want to see the uniqueness and attractiveness of the strategies, to differentiate the VC firm from others.

If a VC firm does not give sufficient thought to its strategies, an experienced LP will quickly see through it. Firstly, the strategies have to be consistent with the skills and experience of the team members, or else it would be clear that there will be difficulties in execution. Secondly, the strategies, and even the size of the fund, have to be consistent with opportunities that are available in the fund's investment territory. Past successful strategies will have to be reviewed in the light of prevailing circumstances, as there is no guarantee that past strategies will continue to work. Thirdly, the LP will want to investigate prior investments to see whether they were consistent with the past stated strategies. If there were deviations, the VC firm should have clear reasons to justify them. Consistency in the actual execution of past strategies will provide confidence on the sincerity and determination of the VC firm to carry out the investment strategies of the new fund.

In evaluating the proposed investment territory of the new fund, the LP will consider a host of environmental factors, such as political stability, economic structure and growth, regulatory and tax structures, foreign exchange trends, capital markets, deal flow, entrepreneurial spirit, and investment climate. The LP will need to look at both short-term and longer-term trends, since the fund will be active for ten years or longer. The VC firm would have to provide data and may even have to commission essays from economists and consultants if the targeted LPs are not too familiar with the investment territory.

Besides the key factors described above, the LP will also take into account the proposed compensation structure for the general partners, how the carried interest is allocated to the senior staff, management staff continuity and succession issues, as well as portfolio valuation policies. Besides investment data, the LP may also ask for deal flow data, to get a feel of the richness and quality of deal opportunities in the investment territory.

Offering Document

Like the entrepreneur's business plan, the VC firm's offering document encapsulates relevant information on the background, experience, and capability of the VC firm and its senior partners individually, the details of the fund structure, investment strategies and policies, as well as fees and other compensation to be paid. An example structure of an offering document is given in Figure 4.1. This example is to show the types of information that would need to be provided and not so much the exact order or organization, which have wide variation.

The partnership information (or corporate brief in the case of a fund company that is set up as a corporation) is a listing of directors or advisors, corporate office address, auditors, lawyers, bankers, etc. This is followed by definitions of terms used; details of the invitation, such as the amount of committed capital being raised, life of the fund, minimum subscription, the capital commitment made by the VC firm, number of closings and date of the first closing; and procedures for making the subscriptions.

FIGURE 4.1   STRUCTURE OF OFFERING DOCUMENT

Offering Summary	Partnership Information
	Definitions
	Details of the Invitation
	Procedure for the Subscription
Organization Structure	Corporate Structure
	Fund Structure
	Partnership Agreement
Policies	Investment Objective
	Investment Strategies
	Investment Policies & Limits
	Monitoring & Divestment
	Distribution of Proceeds
	Valuation Policy
	Investment Expenses
Compensation	Management Fees
	Carried Interest
Management	Sponsors
	Board/Advisory Committee
	Management Team
	Track Record
Miscellaneous	Conflicts of Interest
	Risk Factors
	Taxation
Appendix	Financial Information
	Statutory Information
	(Articles of Incorporation, etc)

The section on Organization Structure describes the structure of the Management Company and the Fund Company. This may be followed by highlights of the Limited Partnership Agreement, or merely a reference to the document, which would be made available separately.

The next section has been described in the section on Fund Policies & Strategies in this chapter. Next is the Compensation Structure of management fees and carried interest, which are discussed in Chapters 3 and 5. The next section on Management would include short briefs on the fund sponsors, board members, and members of the Advisory Committee, if any, briefs on the principal members of the fund management team, and the track records of the management company and key members of the team.

In the Miscellaneous section, possible conflicts of interest situations (see Chapter 5), and the resolution processes are described. This is followed by a standard risk factors declaration. Taxation advice from a professional tax expert that is relevant to the target investors is also included. The Appendix may contain financial statements and relevant statutory information of the management company.

It must be remembered that the Offering Document is a marketing document, while the Limited Partnership Agreement is a legal document. The Offering Document should highlight only the salient features, and must convey an exciting message that this is unique, promising an opportunity for the LPs to achieve good returns, and substantiated by relevant information on track records, examples of investment scope, opportunities, and growth potentials. At the same time, the presentation should be honest, factual, and balanced by a description of the risks.

In some countries, if the number of investors is less than a specified number, say fifty or a hundred, the offering document may be in the form of an information memorandum instead of a prospectus. An information memorandum is less detailed, not lodged with the authorities as a legal document, and hence cheaper to produce than a prospectus.

Road Show

When a VC firm goes out to raise funds, it is not different from any company raising funds through a private placement or a public listing. The offering document will be prepared and the VC firm goes on a road show to promote itself to potential investors. A presentation will be prepared to highlight the important elements of the offering document and to anticipate key issues that LPs may be concerned with.

The following information is essential for inclusion into the presentation:

- o   Overview and unique features of fund
- o   Fund objectives and strategies
- o   Investment policies
- o   Track record
- o   Management team CVs
- o   Tax status
- o   Term sheet

Backup sheets may also be prepared for the following:

- o   Industry structure and potential in the investment territory
- o   Economic growth potential in the investment territory
- o   Deal sourcing, investment process, portfolio valuation policies
- o   Example deals, especially value add provided
- o   Lessons learnt from bad deals

The potential LPs would have received the prospectus or information memorandum ahead of time, and the road show is to provide the opportunity to discuss issues and to meet the key partners face to face.

The VC firm should tailor each presentation to suit the time available, and to address the interest and concerns of the particular LP. If these are not known, the VC firm or its placement agent should find out, prior to or at the start of the meeting. A side benefit of tailoring each presentation is that the VC firm escapes the boredom of too much repetition in making the presentation to LPs one after another, as the boredom will show through during the presentation.

A presentation in a flip-book is preferable to using a projector. There is no lost time in setting up the equipment or fumbling around. Also there is no need to darken the room, so that there is better eye contact and observation of body language. Notes should be taken of who were present and their respective areas of interest or concerns. These would be useful for the next visit or for follow-up information to be sent.

Some LPs may require several rounds of meetings and a lot of follow-up questions before deciding. Some of the more established LPs have developed a comprehensive due diligence questionnaire that contain hundreds of questions. For foreign VC firms, such as Asian VC firms raising funds in the U.S., the LPs may want to make due diligence trips to the domicile of the VC firm and the proposed investment territory.

A fund-raising round can take a year or longer. During VC industry boom periods, LPs would be rushing for a share of new funds raised by the premier VCs, so funds can be closed relatively fast. During the VC industry bust periods, there would be little interest from LPs, so many VC firms may have to delay fund-raising efforts, or may find that they can only raise funds that are smaller than desired, and the effort will take longer than anticipated.

Fund-Raising by New VCs

A newly established VC firm, like any start-up, will find it much more difficult to raise funds, due to a lack of track record. It is not only a lack of track record in investing, but also a lack of experience working together as a team. If LPs have other more established VC firms to invest in, the difficulty will be even greater. Let us look at an example of how this problem was addressed in the following brief case study.

Mini-Case: Transpac Capital Pte Ltd.

Transpac Capital Pte Ltd. (named Transtech Venture Management Pte Ltd. prior to 1990) was established in Singapore in 1986. It was the second VC firm formed in South-East Asia; the first was set up in 1983. The concept of venture capital fund management was hardly heard of in this part of the world in those days. Although several members of the initial team had some experience in a corporate venture capital operation and Transtech at that time was supported by Advent International of U.S. through a small equity ownership, Transtech itself had no track record.

It would have been impossible for Transtech to raise its initial funds, if it were not for its sponsor. The Development Bank of Singapore Ltd. (subsequently renamed DBS Bank Ltd.), one of the largest banks in South-East Asia, had a significant minority share in Transtech. The bank was a lead investor in Transtech's first funds and also introduced associate companies and corporate clients to the funds. As a shareholder, LP, and sponsor, DBS lent tremendous credibility to Transtech. In return, DBS had a share of Transtech's carried interest in the sponsored funds.

By 1993, Transpac had a demonstrable track record and successfully raised a US$75 million fund, mainly from LPs in the U.S.—one of the first Asian-based VC firms to raise a substantial fund in the U.S. A boutique placement agent was used for the fund-raising in the U.S. At the time, Transpac presented a unique opportunity for U.S. LPs to participate in the strong economic growth of the Asia-Pacific Basin. This was followed by a US$320 million fund, also invested mainly by U.S. LPs, which closed in January 1997, just before the Asian financial crisis in mid-1997.

The U.S. LPs in the 1977 fund were not happy to see a significant portion of the carried interest being cut away from the VC partners, especially when the bank's role as a sponsor had diminished over the years. Their fear was that the VC partners may not be rewarded or motivated as they deserved. The LPs also had the concern that the bank may influence the VC partners to favor its clients in the investment decisions, although in fact this was not the case. The bank subsequently agreed to reduce its share of the carried interest, and in fact later sold its shareholding to the VC partners.

The mini-case shows some of the ways the fund-raising difficulty was addressed by a new VC firm. In general, the problem can be addressed by one or more of the following ways[4]:

---

[4] The ways described are drawn from personal experience and from Chapter 5 of Paul Gompers and Josh Lerner, *The Money of Invention*, Boston: Harvard Business School Press, 2001.

o Have a sponsor, such as an investment bank as in the case above, or an industry association or private equity group. However, as exemplified by the case, the sponsor usually demands a share of carried interest, joint ownership of the fund management company and/or participation in the investment committee, which may give rise to problems or concerns from other LPs.

o Have a lead investor. In the above case, the lead investor was the sponsor as well and rightly so. By being the first to commit and contributing a significant, but not necessarily the largest portion of the committed capital, the lead investor opens the path for other LPs. In return the lead investor may receive special benefits, such as a reduction or complete waiver of the 20 percent carried interest to be paid to the VC firm. There may be additional benefits such as lower management fees and a share of the VC firm's carried interest. These benefits also create concerns from other LPs that the VC firm's motivation may be reduced, and may also trigger demands for similar treatment by the larger LPs.

o Fall back on the prior track records of the partners. Often a new VC firm will be started by one or more veteran VC partners who bring with them impressive track records.

o Seek investors who want strategic benefit. Countries such as Singapore, Malaysia, and Taiwan support the development of a domestic VC industry and would match government funds with private funds in certain ratios. Alternatively, an industry focused fund may attract corporate investors desiring exposure to related businesses and technologies.

o Seek individuals and wealthy families as investors, especially if they were friends or past business partners of the VC partners. In this case the fund is likely to be small.

o Have a very unique strategy or opportunity. Although easier said than done, such opportunities may arise, as in the mini-case above. Transpac Capital's 1993 fund, for example, provided a rare opportunity to U.S. LPs to invest in fast-growing private companies in Asia during the years of robust economic growth in the Asia-Pacific region.

o   Invest more than one percent of the fund. A larger contribution by the VC firm shows greater commitment, although some LPs may be concerned that this may result in the VC firm being overly cautious and unwilling to take risks, resulting in low investment returns.

Regulatory Requirements

The VC firm has to be aware of regulatory requirements affecting or imposed on certain LPs, so that appropriate measures may be taken to accommodate their investments into the new fund. Several important requirements are outlined here.

Accredited Investors

The LPs, whether institutions or individuals, must qualify as "accredited investors" or "qualified purchaser" or "sophisticated investors," as defined under the various securities investment acts of different countries. Usually they are defined to have specified minimum net worth or minimum annual income. This is to ensure that the investors are educated and understand the risks involved. For listed funds, the relevant authorities and stock exchanges have waived this requirement and allowed the public to invest to open up new investment alternatives for the man-in-the-street. Such listed funds are governed by the securities acts of the respective countries.

ERISA Requirements

In the U.S., if 25 percent or more of the fund is invested by employee benefit plans, the fund will be governed by the provisions of the Employee Retirement Income Security Act (ERISA) which are subject to onerous reporting requirements. Hence, the VC firm has to ensure that such pension fund investors do not commit in excess of 25 percent of the total committed capital, to avoid such onerous requirements.

Another ERISA requirement is that more than 50 percent of the fund must be in investments that carry management rights, such as a seat in the board. This is typically not a problem—as in any case it is common for the VC firm to insist on a board seat for monitoring and value adding purposes.

UBTI Requirements

The VC firm also has to be sensitive to LPs in the U.S. that may be concerned with Unrelated Business Taxable Income (UBTI). Investment gains distributed by the VC firm to the LPs are not taxable. However, if the partnership derives income not related to its VC investments, such income would be taxable. Some LPs may not mind paying the tax, as it is income after all, and provided the VC firm properly informs the LPs when making distributions. However LPs may put a cap on such income so that the VC firm's attention is not diluted by such efforts.

Chapter Recap

In this chapter we discussed the issues faced by a VC firm in its fund-raising effort:

- o The VC market cycles
- o The use of a placement agent
- o The types of limited partners
- o The fund policies and strategies
- o The criteria of limited partners
- o The structure of the offering document
- o The road show

We also highlighted the fund-raising issues faced by a new VC firm and how these may be addressed, and covered several regulatory requirements affecting LPs which the VC firm has to note.

5

Limited Partnership Agreement

The Limited Partnership Agreement (LPA) is an agreement between the Limited Partners (LPs) and the General Partner (GP), mainly covering the terms and conditions for the management of the VC fund, the investment policies, and the conduct of the General Partner during the management period.

While the other terms such as management fees and profit sharing arrangements are no less important, the terms dictating the conduct of the GP are important for corporate governance reasons. In a corporation, the board of directors makes major policy decisions, oversees the conduct of management, and can remove the CEO and other key managers. The directors themselves are elected in and may be voted out by shareholders. In a Limited Liability Partnership (LLP), there is no board of directors, and no Annual General Meeting for the LPs who are shareholders. The LPs cannot be involved in the GP's management decisions, as this would affect the tax status of the LPs.

A shareholder of a public listed company may sell the shares if he is unhappy with the performance of the management. A shareholder of a non-listed company may also do so, albeit with some difficulty and probably at a discount. A single discontented LP cannot simply stop making capital contributions when called within the committed capital amount. The LP stands to forfeit whatever amount that had been contributed so far. It would normally require a super-majority vote by LPs to freeze a fund. The LP may attempt to sell his holdings as there is a secondary market for partnership holdings, but it is a small market limited to mostly blue chip partnerships. In such partnerships, it is unlikely that an LP would sell for reasons of poor management or performance, but more likely due to its own financial reasons. Therefore, selling a holding in a less well-known partnership, and especially for performance reasons, would usually not be a viable option.

The LPA is therefore the mechanism by which LPs effect corporate governance controls on the GP while being careful not to be involved in management decisions. In the worst case, removal of the GP is difficult unless it is due to fraud or similar misconduct. Furthermore the LPs cannot amend the LPA, once signed, without the consent of the GP. A sufficient number of LPs could freeze the fund and not need to contribute any more capital, which means the GP cannot make any more new investments and would be limited to managing and divesting the existing portfolio.

Over the years, many safeguard mechanisms have been devised and incorporated into the LPA. In addition, it is usual for the partnership to form an Advisory Committee, consisting of representatives from the major LPs, to provide some degree of oversight, particularly with respect to conflict of interest situations, compliance requirements, and changes in investment policies.

In this chapter we shall examine the typical key terms and conditions in an LPA.

Organization of the LPA

For ease of discussion, we shall organize the limited partnership agreement into the sections shown in Figure 5.1. We shall discuss the key terms in each section. While the compensation terms are of pecuniary interest to the VC, the covenants, controls, and conflicts of interest provisions can sometimes be contentious. Recently, some Limited Partners have been required to publicly disclose the terms and performance of their investments in VC funds, which stirred some degree of controversy and discontent among GPs, and this will be discussed also.

FIGURE 5.1   ORGANIZATION OF THE LIMITED PARTNERSHIP AGREEMENT

PARTNERSHIP INFO	This section captures the corporate details of the partnership and the General Partner
CAPITAL COMMITMENTS	This section provides details of capital commitments, drawdowns, and distributions
COMPENSATION	The management fees, carried interest payments, and chargeable expenses are spelled out
COVENANTS & CONTROLS	These are corporate governance provisions
CONFLICTS OF INTEREST	Certain conflict of interest situations and resolutions are described
DISCLOSURE	Of increasing importance, these are restrictions on disclosure of confidential information by Limited Partners
TERMINATION	Provisions for the termination of the partnership

Partnership Information

This section provides corporate information such as the name of the partnership or fund company, incorporation details, the general partner, the fund management company, fund size, fund life, provisions for extension of the fund life, as well as fund investment objectives, and strategies. These have been covered in the previous chapter.

Capital Commitments

This section provides for initial and subsequent closings in the fund-raising process, the minimum capital commitment by LPs, the procedures for drawdowns from the committed capital, the period for such drawdowns, and the procedures for distribution of proceeds from divestments to the LPs.

Closings

It is typical to have an initial closing when 50 percent of the target fund size has been raised, so as to seal the commitments made by LPs so far, and to enable the GP to actively pursue investment opportunities. The initial closing will also help to swing the decision for those LPs who may be sitting on the fence. Subsequent closings would be to accommodate these uncertain LPs, or those who may need longer time for their internal approval process. LPs who participated in the initial closing may increase their commitment in subsequent closings. The period from the initial to final closing is typically a year or shorter. LPs who sign up in subsequent closings will pay their pro rata share of partnership expenses and management fees, as well as an interest payment charged from the date of the first closing.

Capital Calls

Minimum capital commitment by an LP is typically 1 or 2 percent of the fund size, although there is allowance for the GP to accept smaller commitments. The agreement will also spell out the procedure for the GP to make capital calls, such as the minimum amount and notice period, and penalties chargeable to LPs for late payments. The period for capital calls for new investments is usually five years, which would be the fund's investment period. The fund would not make new investments beyond the specified investment period. Capital calls after the five-year period would hence be for follow-on investments into companies in the fund's portfolio, investment commitments made by the fund prior to the end of the five-year period, and for payment of management fees and other allowed expenses. Of course the total drawn down must not exceed the total capital commitment. Any capital that remains not drawn down will be cancelled.

LPs are usually concerned about being given sufficient notice for capital calls. The notice period would be spelled out in the LPA. LPs also would not like to see excessive drawdowns resulting in idle cash sitting with the GP. The GP has to balance between the urgency of funding a deal and the possibility that it may be aborted, resulting in the drawdown not being utilized.

Distributions

Proceeds from divestments may be distributed back to LPs at any time at the discretion of the GP. It would not be to the interest of the GP to hold on to such proceeds as it would affect the performance of the fund, just as it would not be wise to make capital calls prematurely. Idle cash will adversely affect the IRR of the fund. The GP will only hold back and accumulate small amounts of proceeds before distributing, so that LPs are not inconvenienced by frequent receipts of small amounts. The GP will be allowed to distribute *in specie* (in kind) through the distribution of shares in the portfolio company. This will be covered in Chapter 21 on Realizing & Recovering Value.

Investor Rights

Usually the LPA will state that all LPs will receive most favored nation treatment—that is, all will be treated equally. However, it is accepted practice that one or some LPs may get special treatment as sponsors of the partnership. These may be LPs that help in fund-raising. For example if the LP is a gatekeeper, it may recommend its limited partners to invest directly into the fund as well. Such sponsors may pay lower management fees and may have a share of the carried interest from the GP. Such preferential treatment would be disclosed in the LPA or in appropriate side letters.

A common right that LPs ask from the GP is the opportunity to co-invest directly in the more attractive or larger deals. The GP would offer such opportunities to all those LPs that have indicated interest on a pro rata basis according to respective committed capital.

Compensation

As discussed in Chapter 3, the GP is compensated through a Management Fee and a share of the investment profits, called Carried Interest. Just as VCs have been very creative in structuring investment terms and incentive share options to motivate entrepreneurs, the LPs have, over the years, developed a variety of compensation schemes to motivate GPs and align their interests. LPs have also created structures for management fees to more closely match the costs of efforts made by the GP in seeking and making investments and in monitoring and adding value to investments. This brings the compensation structure more in line with the traditional VC industry principles that the management fees should cover operating costs and the carried interest should reward the GP for good investments.

Management Fee

Traditionally, the management fee has been a fixed percentage of the committed capital throughout the life of the fund. LPs have continuously pressed GPs to lower the management fees and have achieved this either through a simple reduction of the percentage, or through structuring the fee to incorporate progressive reductions. The basis on which the fee is calculated could also change as the fund progressed.

The aim is to structure the fees to more closely reflect the work done by the GP. One example is to structure a 2.5 percent fee into a fixed component of one percent and a variable component of 1.5 percent. The fixed fee of one percent is based on committed capital, which is meant to cover fixed operating costs of the GP through the life of the fund. The variable fee of 1.5 percent is based on the amount invested, at cost, on those deals that are active. Thus investment amounts that have been divested, written down, or written off would be excluded. This fee is therefore initially zero and increases as investments are made. It is decreased as divestments and write downs are made in the later years. The argument here is that the GP incurs greater effort in screening, evaluating, and monitoring deals as more investments are made. After the investment period, there is no need to source for and evaluate deals, and the amount of monitoring effort declines as divestments are made. This variable component is therefore sometimes called the monitoring fee. On the average the total fees would amount to about 1.7 percent of committed capital or 17 percent for a ten-year fund. This compares with 2.5 percent of committed capital or 25 percent total, if structured as a simple fixed percentage.

Another example is to simply vary the percentage by periods of the fund life. The fee could be 2.5 percent during the investment period, which is set to be the first five years. This could be reduced to 2 percent for the next five years, and one percent for any extended year. A variation would be to set the fee at 2.5 percent for the first five years, and then reduce it by 10 percent every year onwards. Yet another example is for the GP to work out annual budgets for approval by the Advisory Committee and the fees would reimburse budgeted costs.

Carried Interest

As discussed in Chapter 3, carried interest has largely remained constant over the years at 20 percent of net investment gains to the GP. Of late, LPs have shown some tolerance for a step-up in the carried interest, based on performance. Thus it is likely that in the future, during boom years, some funds may, for example, have the carried interest increased to 25 percent if the LPs achieve IRR exceeding 20 percent, or some other form of staggered increase for better performance.

Also, in line with the changing fortunes of the VC industry, many new funds are reverting to distributing carried interest to GPs only after all committed capital has been distributed back to LPs, instead of distributing on a deal by deal basis. In some cases, contributed (or drawn down) capital is the benchmark instead of committed capital for the commencement of payment of carried interest to the GP. This would be useful for high performance funds that recoup all contributed capital prior to fully drawing down the committed capital of the fund.

The clauses in the LPA relating to the carried interest specify the mechanisms for the calculation and distribution of carried interest to LPs and the GP. If carried interest is paid to the GP only after return of all committed capital, the clauses would be straightforward. If payment is on a deal by deal basis, the mechanism can be rather complex. The important rule is that any investment that incurs a loss of capital invested has to have its lost capital reimbursed as soon as possible.

A solution would be to have a priority system for distribution of proceeds from a divestment. The proceeds would consist of the capital invested or part thereof, and the capital gains, if any. The first priority would be to distribute the capital amount pro rata to the LPs. Then if there is capital gain, it would be used to reimburse any prior loss of capital. Any remaining capital gain would then be distributed in the ratio of 80:20 to LPs and the

GP. At the end of life of the fund an adjustment will be made if there had been any overpayment or underpayment of carried interest to the GP.

Another solution would be to pay only a portion of the entitled carried interest to the GP and the rest is kept in an escrow account, which would be used to reimburse capital losses. So long as there is a specified minimum sum in escrow, carried interest is payable to the GP. At the end of life, adjustment is made. This adjustment process is called a *claw back* of the carried interest. The objective is to keep sufficient funds in the escrow account to cover any potential claw back, yet not withholding an unduly excessive amount from the GP.

Claw back provisions are now common in LPAs. In many cases, the LPA would provide for an annual balancing of the escrow account to ensure that an appropriate amount is kept. Sometimes this is called a *loss carry forward* provision. This provision ensures that the GP is not paid its share of the carried interest until all losses in prior years have been recouped by the fund.

Some LPAs provide for a *hurdle rate*, which is the LP's preferred rate of return to be achieved by the fund before the GP gets its allocation of carried interest. The hurdle rate is typically 7 or 8 percent. Such a return rate appears ridiculously low when compared with the expected rate of return of at least 20 percent to be derived from the fund. However this provision acts in the same way as the claw back and loss carry forward provisions. It ensures that the GP is not allocated any carried interest if the fund has lost part of its committed capital or has been achieving a low rate of return. Once the hurdle rate is exceeded, the GP gets its full 20 percent allocation.

Some LPs object to paying carried interest on a deal by deal basis, as the VC may be tempted to delay recognition of investment losses.

Other Income & Expenses

The rules for recognition of other income and the chargeability of investment expenses are also included here. These are described in Chapter 4 in Fund Policies & Strategies.

Covenants & Controls

This is an important section to the LPs, and as a result, to the GP as well. Unlike a corporation, a partnership does not have a governing board. Many LPs cannot be involved in the management of the fund, as this will affect their tax status. Corporate governance over the GP is hence exercised through relevant clauses in the LPA, and to a smaller extent by the Advisory Committee, which mostly rules on conflict of interest issues.

The following are key corporate governance provisions in the LPA. The level of detail in which they are spelled out would depend on the LPs and the negotiation with the GP.

o   Appointment and services to be rendered: These specify the GP's duties, responsibilities, authority, and reports to be provided to LPs.

o   Fund size: The LPs want to ensure that the fund size is within the capability of the GP's team to manage and invest and is commensurate with the investment climate and opportunities within the focus of the fund. LPs do not want the GP to raise too large a fund to enjoy a big management fee, but ends up not finding enough deals or investing indiscriminately. On the other hand, a minimum fund size may be specified, below which the fund may not be closed. If the fund is undersubscribed significantly, the GP would not be able to successfully execute the stated investment strategies, hence the LPs would not want to proceed with the fund.

o   Investment decisions: LPs prefer an investment committee consisting of all the senior partners, so that there is shared responsibility and teamwork. The composition of the investment committee and investment approval procedure would be specified here.

o   Investment limits: These are specified in the LPA to ensure diversification of risks. An example may be that not more than 50 percent of the committed capital may be invested in a country or territory (for funds that invest in multiple countries or territories);

not more than 25 percent in any one industry sector; and not more than 10 percent (perhaps 20 percent for smaller funds) of committed capital in any one investee company. The LPA would have a clause allowing such limits to be waived by the Advisory Committee if justified on a case by case basis. Besides diversifying risks, such limits may be imposed to restrict investments to be within the fields of expertise or geographical knowledge of the GP. In such cases, limits would instead be imposed on investments made outside specified industry sectors or territories. In the same way, limits may also be imposed on stage of development of the investee company, especially if it is a stage-focused fund.

o   Investment period: This is usually set as the first four or five years of the fund. The fund is allowed to make only follow-on investments but no new investments beyond the investment period. This is because the investee companies need time to mature prior to the end of life of the fund.

o   Reinvestment of proceeds: This usually not allowed. The GP may be tempted to reinvest proceeds from divestments, whether the capital or profits or both, to hopefully increase the profits and hence the carried interest and the track record of the fund. In some cases the desire may be to increase the management fees, if it is wholly or partly based on the value of assets under management or amount invested. Some LPs may suspect that the GP may use such later investments, which are unlikely to have matured by the end of life of the fund, to extend the tenure of the fund. The key concern of the LPs is that the GP may be investing for the wrong reason. Nevertheless, the LPA may allow such reinvestments under certain restrictions. For example, the capital cost of the investment must be returned, and only profits from divestments can be reinvested; or reinvestment may be allowed only for a limited period, say within the investment period or a year or two after; or if the divestment is made within a short period after the investment, say within a twelve or eighteen month period.

o   Investment into other funds: This would be expressly disallowed, as it does not make sense for the LPs to pay management fees and carried interest to a VC firm that in turn pays fees and carried interest to another VC firm to make investments. If LPs were to invest in a fund of funds, they would pay a much lower management fee.

o Investment into public securities: This would again be expressly disallowed, as the GP would not have mutual fund management expertise, and cannot add value to the investments. Furthermore, LPs would pay lower fees to mutual fund managers. An exception would be made if the intent of the GP is to privatize, restructure, and redevelop the listed company.

o Debt and contingent liabilities: Usually the fund is not allowed to borrow funds to invest or incur contingent liabilities so that its financial exposure does not extend beyond the committed capital. In some cases debt may be allowed under certain restrictions, such as a limit based on committed capital or assets of the fund, and may also have a limited maturity to ensure that the commitment can be met within the life of the fund. If a fund provides a corporate guarantee for its investee's debt, the fund would have to set aside investment funds to meet the contingent liability. This would not be desired by the GP as the funds would be making little (if there is a guarantee fee) or no return. VCs therefore steer away from providing corporate guarantees and will only do so if it is for a short period, such as for a bridging loan.

o Portfolio valuation policy: The rules for valuation of listed and unlisted portfolio companies would usually be stated in the LPA, especially if the management fee is based on the value of assets managed. We shall review this in Chapter 22: Fund Performance.

o Divestment decisions: The LPA would specify the mechanism and authority for divestment decisions, and also maintain that the GP must complete divestment within say eighteen months of the investee company going IPO. LPs do not want the GP to become a mutual fund manager.

o   Extension of fund life: The life of the fund may be extended beyond ten years, on a year by year basis, up to a maximum of usually three years. Each extension would be subject to the approval of the Advisory Committee or a majority of the LPs. The management fee is often reduced, or sometimes waived completely, for the extended period.

o   Involvement of limited partners: It would be explicitly stated in the LPA that the LPs will not be involved in the management of the fund, particularly in the investment and divestment decisions, so as to protect their tax status.

o   GP's contribution: It is common practice for the GP to commit to invest in the fund, usually one percent of committed capital, and this is captured in the LPA. The one percent amount was mandated by law until it was removed by the 1986 Tax Reform Act, but the practice has remained. The amount may now be lower, or in some cases, especially for smaller funds, the GP may commit up to 2 percent.

o   GP's co-investment: The GP would be allowed to co-invest in the deals done by the fund as it aligns the GP's interest with that of LPs. However, the GP has to co-invest in all deals and not cherry-pick. Its investment will be at the same time and under the same terms as that by the fund, and will also be divested at the same time. The GP may set up a parallel fund for such co-investments, and may allow junior staff to also invest in it. This parallel fund and the main fund will co-invest such amounts that are pro rata to the respective sizes of the funds.

o   Raising new funds: LPs will restrict the GP from raising a new fund until two-thirds or 75 percent of the present fund is invested. This is to prevent dilution of attention to the portfolio of the existing fund. In some cases a new fund may be allowed to be raised earlier if it has a different focus or management team.

o   Significant staffing and staff compensation changes: These changes include replacement and addition of senior partners, reallocation of partnership interests, and redistribution of carried interest to staff. Obviously LPs may be alarmed by such changes, if significant, as staff performance and motivation may be affected, and hence performance of the investments. The LPA will require the GP to inform the Advisory Committee or all LPs of such events, so that the LPs can investigate further if they so choose.

o Regulatory requirements: The LPA would have a clause to ensure that the GP conducts its business without infringing tax regulatory requirements, in particular ERISA and UBTI requirements (discussed in Chapter 4) so that the tax status of LPs will not be adversely affected.

o Default by LPs: If an LP defaults on a capital call, the penalty can be severe, unless it is quickly remedied. The LPA will spell out the recourse which includes forfeiture of the entire holding of the defaulting LP, or forced transfer of its holding to all the other LPs at a discount.

o Limitations of liability and indemnity clauses: These would be standard clauses put in by the GP to limit its liability and to provide for indemnification from the partnership for losses and claims arising from the management services rendered, which are not due to negligence or misconduct.

It might appear that there are many covenants and controls on the GP, but considering that the GPs themselves impose many covenants and controls on investee companies, in addition to having board seats, these would not be surprising.

Conflicts of Interest

There may be occasions when the GP may be in conflict between its own interest and that of the fund. The LPA will spell out rules for such resolution or specify that the matter be put up to the Advisory Committee. Hence the LPA will also specify the formation of an Advisory Committee consisting of the larger LPs. The more common conflict of interest situations would be as follows:

○ New fund investing into portfolio of old fund: This is the most common conflict of interest situation, since VCs manage multiple funds. The LPA would restrict the current fund from investing into any portfolio company of prior funds. This is to prevent the new funds from being used to rescue prior bad investments, or to artificially inflate the value of the investment. If the GP is convinced that such investment is justified, approval would be required from the Advisory Committee or from a super-majority of LPs.

○ New investment by parallel funds: The GP may manage several active funds due to overlapping time periods or due to the need to set up parallel funds with different structures to meet taxation needs of investors. It is common for the active funds to co-invest into a new investment opportunity. The LPA will spell out the rules for such co-investments so as to avoid preferential treatment of one fund over another. Usually the funds will co-invest on the same terms, at the same time, with investment amounts that are pro rated according to their respective fund sizes. If a particular fund does not have sufficient funds for this co-investment or for future follow-ons, its share will be allocated to the other participating funds on a pro rated basis. Divestments will also be at the same time on a pro rated basis.

○ GP's investments: If the fund does not invest in an opportunity, perhaps because it falls outside the fund's charter, the GP may be allowed to invest personally, or through the staff's parallel investment fund. This is usually discouraged by LPs as it distracts the attention of the GP from the fund's interest. Sometimes these investments may compete with future investment opportunities suitable for new funds. If such a situation arises, it would have to be brought to the attention of the Advisory Committee.

○ GP's other business activities: General clauses would be put in the LPA to require disclosure or approval by the Advisory Committee for any other business activity that the partnership or the senior partners personally may wish to undertake, as it would dilute their attention.

Disclosure

A controversy that has arisen recently is the disclosure of confidential partnership information by LPs. Such confidential information includes LPA terms and conditions, as well as performance data of the fund and portfolio companies. Under the U.S. Open Records Act, public organizations such as state pension funds have to comply with requests by the media to reveal such information. Since late 2001 several requests have been made. Some were complied with, to the horror of the GPs, and some were contested in court. Some GPs took legal counteraction to prevent the LPs from releasing the data.

Some states have proposed amendments to the Open Records Act. GPs are taking action to tighten their confidentiality agreements with LPs, or working out arrangements that would limit access to confidential information by the affected LPs. Some GPs have even threatened not to accept certain LPs into their new funds.

Most GPs, but not all, are willing to reveal IRR data of funds on an aggregate basis, but not on individual investments. GPs are unwilling to reveal partnership terms and conditions, other than perhaps fees and carried interest, and certainly not confidential information of investee companies, such as valuations and performance data. The trend is that LPAs will move towards a tightening of disclosure clauses.

Termination

The LPA will have clauses relating to termination of the agreement such as *for-cause* and *no-fault* provisions. For-cause provisions would be termination due to poor performance or breach of fiduciary duties. No-fault provisions would be termination of the fund or removal of the GP without a reason given, which would require a super-majority of LPs. Instead of termination, the LPs may choose to suspend the fund, which means that there will be no more drawdowns of committed capital and no more new investments. Another termination clause would be a *key-person* provision. This allows the LPs to terminate or suspend the fund if one or more of named senior partners leave the firm.

Termination of a fund can be quite troublesome. LPs see such drastic clauses as a means to force quick resolution of issues by the GP. Suspension of a fund is more common, particularly arising from poor performance or the key-person provision.

Chapter Recap

In this chapter we explored the importance of the Limited Partnership Agreement and details of key provisions:

- o The fund-raising closings, capital calls, distributions and investor rights
- o The structures for the GP's management fees and carried interest
- o The imposition of covenants and controls on the GP
- o The resolution of conflict of interest situations
- o The disclosure of confidential information
- o The termination of the agreement

PART III

FINDING & SCREENING DEALS

Sourcing of investment opportunities is the beginning of the VC investment process. It is important for the VC firm to secure a rich supply of deals, so that it can cherry-pick and will not miss good opportunities. How does the VC firm find deals? After finding them, how does it distinguish the good ones from the bad? What system or criteria do the VC firms use to screen the deals?

Chapter 6: DEAL SOURCING describes the approaches used by VC firms to source and generate deals. Chapter 7: DEAL SCREENING describes the initial screening process. A VC firm sources thousands of deal opportunities and a good screening process is necessary, so that subsequent intensive investigation and evaluation work is not wasted on too many deals that would end up being rejected.

6

Deal Sourcing

Looking for deals is the first in the chain of activities in the VC Process. Some VCs may neglect to give it the importance that it deserves. A rich inflow of deal opportunities (called *deal flow*) means that the VC improves its chances that the deals it selects are among the best in the market. A scanty deal flow coupled with pressure to sustain investment rate means temptation to lower criteria and investing in suspect deals.

Merely depending on business plans submitted in the mail does not ensure sufficient high-quality deals as many of these are likely to be rejects. Even if it happens that a quality deal appears in the mail, it is likely to have been sent to several VCs, and there would be intense bidding for the deal, resulting in a high valuation and hence making it less attractive. A bidding situation also usually requires the VC to rush into deciding.

Therefore a proactive deal sourcing effort is necessary to increase the inflow of better quality deals. By getting a foot early into the door, the VC can preempt other VCs to the deal. This allows time for the VC to evaluate the business, develop a relationship with the entrepreneurs, and to help shape the business strategies. All these help to improve the quality of the deals that are pursued. Even if the deal is dropped eventually, the entrepreneurs are likely to appreciate the help and advice.

In this chapter we shall examine the what, where, and how of VC deal sourcing. First the VC firm needs to define what it considers to be a quality deal and the characteristics of a quality deal that its investment staff should look for. We shall then discuss where these characteristics may be found, and how VCs carry out the search. We shall also touch on a couple of related matters: the Confidentiality Agreement or otherwise known as the Non-Disclosure Agreement, which entrepreneurs may require to protect the confidentiality of information submitted by them to VCs, and the setting up of a deal database to support deal sourcing.

What To Look For

A VC should look for the following ingredients in any deal:

- o   A market potential that is large and fast growing
- o   Products or services that have unique value and high entry barriers
- o   A business that is scalable regionally or internationally
- o   Founders and a management team with passion and execution ability
- o   Well-conceived business model and plans
- o   A company valuation that is reasonably low
- o   No intractable exit difficulties

A large and fast-growing market potential provides the growth that is necessary for the company to generate high investment returns for the VC. Such a market also means less competition for market share and opportunities for broadening of product range. Note that the emphasis is on the word "potential." As pointed out by Clayton Christensen[5], a young company with *sustaining innovation* trying to penetrate a large market dominated by existing players will inevitably fail. In this case the market is large, but the *potential* market for the young company is negligible. On the other hand, a young company with *disruptive innovation* may have a large potential market if it can create new markets from present non-consumers, or capture market share through its low-end product features desired by the market. However in these cases, the size of the market potential is unpredictable, but have often turned out to be remarkably rewarding. In any case the VC should look for a large and fast-growing market potential

---

[5] Clayton Christensen and Michael Raynor, *The Innovator's Solution*, Boston: Harvard Business School Press, 2003. This book is a must-read for all VC practitioners, as well as Clayton Christensen, *The Innovator's Dilemma*, Boston: Harvard Business School Press, 1997 and Clayton Christensen, Scott Anthony and Erik Roth, *Seeing What's Next*, Boston: Harvard Business School Press, 2004.

as an essential ingredient in a deal, and can subsequently carry out due diligence to verify the assumptions and projections.

A company that has products or services that have value and are unique will enjoy strong market demand and little competition and hence high profit margins. High entry barriers keep out competitors from entering the market.

A business should be scalable, in order to be attractive to a VC firm. This means that the business can be rapidly grown or duplicated in several market regions or internationally, without losing its competitive advantage. The company will then enjoy economies of scale and will be able to quickly exploit the large market opportunity. As an example, a consultancy business is not readily scalable, as it depends on recruiting and building up groups of experts with requisite domestic market knowledge and networks. While it is possible, and there are examples of successful international consultancies, it takes too long and success in one market may not be replicated in another market. Such deals would fall outside the scope of VC firms.

A team of founders and managers that have passion towards the business and the ability to execute plans and strategies is necessary to exploit the growth opportunities by delivering the products or services into the fast-growing market. The VC then provides the funding to support the effort. It would be ideal if the VC has the qualities and network that can add value to the business.

A well-conceived business model and business plan is an important ingredient. It shows that the founders and management team have the relevant knowledge and experience and have put in the dedicated effort to work out the plans. However, a less than perfect business model and plan may be acceptable provided the founders and managers are amenable to changes that may be required. In any case, early stage companies go through many revisions of plans before finding some direction, and even later stage companies always keep their plans under review. At this deal sourcing stage, the VC is more concerned about the quality of the thinking and the effort behind the plans than the perfection of the plans, which would be subject to later scrutiny and perhaps modification at the due diligence stage.

Despite having all these ingredients, and perhaps because of them, the entry valuation may be too high and the deal may not be doable as the investment return would be too low. The entry valuation would have to be reasonably low relative to the quality of the deal and the potential exit valuation. This is not much different from looking for undervalued listed stocks of a company, which may have underpriced shares due to poor market sentiment or other temporary external factors. In the same way, a private company may be undervalued because of its immaturity and unrecognized potential. Furthermore, the valuation is subject to negotiation, and perhaps the VC can persuade the entrepreneurs of its strengths and potential contributions to the business growth and convince them to lower the valuation. The VC could also structure the deal to provide for an attractive share of the upside gains to the founders. In any case the starting point, at this deal sourcing stage, must be a valuation that is within a reasonable range.

Finally, some VCs view that a necessary ingredient is that the deal must not have intractable difficulties in achieving an exit. This is important in some Asian countries with less developed capital markets, few M&A opportunities or regulatory restrictions on capital repatriation. Difficulties in gaining a timely exit result in forced divestment at low valuation, and hence a low return.

In later chapters we shall discuss how these ingredients are to be further investigated and evaluated.

Where To Look

The important deal ingredients described in the previous section point to the industry sectors that the VC should target, and to the desirable companies and entrepreneurs that operate in those sectors. The VC will then contact them through cold-calling or through introductions by contacts in its network. The VC could also receive referrals from its network of contacts or receive business plans in the mail, and would then search for these desirable ingredients. In the next chapter we shall discuss the undesirable qualities that the VC will look out for to screen off inferior deals.

Looking for Growth Sectors

We have said that a large and fast-growing market potential is a desirable deal ingredient. A VC would be led to think of computers, wireless communications, Internet, nanotechnology, and biotech, as well as their respective sub-sectors, as target growth sectors. While this may be true for the U.S., the list may be different for an Asian country and may vary from one country to another in Asia, depending on the country's stage of economic development and industrial structure.

In Asia, rising affluence means that health care and certain consumer products could be attractive growth industries. Greater industrialization means process plants producing metals, plastics or paper as well as supporting industries producing parts or tooling could be growth industries too. Also, due to different tastes and physiology, food or medicines popular or applicable in the U.S. or Europe may not be suitable in Asia. Therefore, food processing plants or medical products tailored to Asian needs could have huge market potential. Deregulation of telecommunications and power services could also generate growth of these and related services.

The VC's investment managers must be familiar with and be in close touch with industrial developments in their investment territories. Focusing attention on the target growth sectors will lead to the companies that are active and require funds for expansion, as well as emerging companies in the sectors.

Looking for Uniqueness and Value Creation

Within the growth sector, the VC would have to pick a potential winner from among the existing and emerging companies. A differentiating factor would be a company that produces a product or delivers a service that provides unique value or creates value to its customers. It would also be important that the company is able to protect its market share through patents or proprietary know-how.

Examples of value creation in growth sectors are products that offer higher data rate and wider bandwidth in data communications; products that offer greater mobility, accessibility, and convenient communications capability;

services that provide wider customer reach, more efficient, and higher availability features; or enterprise software that increases productivity as well as effectiveness through knowledge management and collaborative systems. Taking the pointers from Clayton Christensen, value can also be created by products that are simpler, cheaper, or more convenient to use, and not necessarily only those that offer more features or are more sophisticated.

W. Chan Kim and Renee Mauborgne, in their book, *Blue Ocean Strategy*,[6] describe concepts and tools to evaluate whether a company is competing in a Red Ocean (bloodied by intense competition) or has found or created a Blue Ocean, a market where companies ignore or find strategically incompatible to their existing businesses. The VC may find it useful to apply the value innovation analytics prescribed in the book to evaluate and perhaps modify the entrepreneur's business model and strategies to differentiate and create value.

Looking for the Best Team

Another desirable ingredient to look for is a team of entrepreneurs and management who have the passion and the ability to execute the business plans. The deal should be chased after if other desirable ingredients are also present. If not, the VC may still want to work with the team to modify the business model and strategies.

A strong team is not easy to find. One way is to look for serial entrepreneurs. They have successfully started up companies previously and want to do so again. Another way is to look through past investments for entrepreneurs who may now have new ideas. Revisiting past rejected deals may turn up companies that have been successfully turned around by a new team and may be now ripe for an investment. We shall later discuss an example deal database that can be set up to store both done and rejected deals. A wide network of successful entrepreneurs and CEOs will be a rich

---

[6] W. Chan Kim and Renee Mauborgne, *Blue Ocean Strategy: How to create uncontested market space and make the competition irrelevant*, Boston: Harvard Business School Publishing, 2005

source of deals as they can more readily pull together strong management teams.

Looking for High Returns

High returns are obviously generated by successful companies in high growth sectors. The pursuit of investments in such companies is likely to result in high returns provided the entry valuation is reasonably low.

However, a company may also experience high growth in a low growth or even declining industry sector. Such growth is possible through increase in market share from acquisitions or from failing competitors as the industry shakes out or consolidates. When an industry declines, product prices are likely to drop, but if the company's increase in revenue is faster than the price decline rate, and if it enjoys economies of scale from the growth, its profitability can increase. A case in point is a company based in Hong Kong called Varitronix Ltd, which gained market share when Japanese companies dropped out of the monochrome liquid crystal displays market in the early 1990s to upgrade their plants to produce color displays. There continued to be a strong market for some years for monochrome displays from handheld electronic games, toys, and simple instrument displays. Admittedly, as the monochrome display market dwindled, Varitronix had to upgrade to small color panels and other related products as well, but the high growth years led it to a successful IPO and satisfactory returns for its VC backers.

Other examples of such opportunistic deals that may generate high returns are those:

- o   Where the VC can add value through its own expertise or its network
- o   Where there is synergy with another portfolio company
- o   Where the target company is grossly undervalued
- o   Where there is an opportunity for higher than usual exit valuation through trade sale, or a merger or acquisition, or a listing in a foreign stock market

These deals are worth following up for further screening and due diligence.

How To Look

Having identified what deals to look for and where to look, the VC needs to know how to go about looking for them. The VC can take an opportunistic approach through networking and cold-calling whenever it comes across possibilities or responds to investment proposals received through the mail. Occasionally, the VC may take a systematic approach through identification of specific industry sectors. A third approach is through the creation of new deals, where it is the VC that initiates the deal. We shall discuss these three approaches in greater detail.

Essential to all approaches is that the VC must have the right investment staff who have some knowledge or experience in the target investment sectors, so that the appropriate networks can be developed, the right companies be spotted, the right approach be taken to ignite their interest in a possible investment by the VC, and proper assessment of the companies can be conducted. By having the right knowledge or experience, the VC can capture the interest of the target company by demonstrating that it understands the business and can add value.

In addition, a VC which has good reputation will attract a strong inflow of deal proposals and engender recognition and attention when cold-calling. In Chapter 23 we describe the attributes that entrepreneurs look for in a VC. VCs gain a reputation through successful investments and enhance their market image through advertising; announcements of deals done and successful IPOs of portfolio companies; and participating at industry and VC conferences by speaking or sponsoring events. Listings in VC directories, having well-designed marketing collateral and an up-to-date Web site are also essential.

Opportunistic Approach

An opportunistic approach is one where there are no specific targets in mind, and the search is left wide and open so that deal opportunities may be seized upon when they are encountered. The VC may passively wait for deal proposals to be received, screen the interesting ones, and pursue them further. The yield from these proposals may not be very high.

Even when taking an opportunistic approach, the VC needs to be proactive to generate better quality deal flow. The VC does this by cold-calling and developing a network of contacts. The cold-calling may be by spotting companies from regular scans of business newspapers and journals, industry directories, company rankings, or by ad-hoc visits to exhibitions, conferences, investment seminars, universities, research institutes, incubators or industry associations. By developing a network of contacts, with companies, CEOs, entrepreneurs, other VCs (for syndications), business angels and angel groups, and professional firms such as accounting, legal, consulting, and financial advisory firms, as well as investment banks and brokers, the VC will receive referrals of deal opportunities. Past and existing portfolio companies and limited partners are also sources of deal flow. Developing wide networks of contacts and constantly tapping them are important for VC work, not only for deal sourcing, but also for due diligence and value adding.

A deal referral fee, which may also be called a finder's fee, may be payable for some sources of deals, usually on success basis. This may range from 1 to 2 percent of the investment amount. The fee may be higher if the broker also helps in due diligence. Sometimes the fee may be staggered, with a higher rate for an initial amount and reducing as the amount of investment increases. Some VCs refuse to pay referral fees, expecting that the broker or adviser would be paid by the client company.

Systematic Approach

Having identified certain growth sectors, the VC may conduct a systematic search for emerging or leading companies in those sectors. The VC may commission a business information service, a corporate database company, an investment advisory company, or an industry consultant company to carry out a search for companies falling within given specifications of industry sector, location, revenue, corporate history, or other parameters. The VC can then follow up by contacting them. When meeting with companies, finding out about competitors will generate leads to more companies in the sector.

Another systematic approach is to forge formal or informal links with organizations that are likely to be deal sources. These are universities and research institutes which may spin off new technologies or discoveries; incubators which may have companies that are ripe for VC funding and business angel groups and a few selected friendly VCs that have similar investment focus. By developing close relationships with these organizations, the VC could be the partner of choice for investment or co-investment opportunities.

Creating Deals

Besides searching opportunistically or systematically for deals, the VC can also generate its own deals. The VC may identify gaps or weaknesses in an industry sector; see a new need arising from new industry developments or market shifts; observe opportunities to consolidate a fragmented industry sector; find opportunities to transplant a technology or business model from one industry to another, or across country borders; or find cross-border M&A opportunities. All these require the initiative of the VC to create investment possibilities out of the identified business opportunities.

The VC would have to identify a suitable entrepreneur or CEO, or an anchor company with a suitable management team to drive the initiative, funded by the VC. Some VCs have an Entrepreneur-In-Residence scheme, where an entrepreneur is brought in and funded with a small investment to carry out a feasibility study or a proof-of-concept project. If this turns out to be satisfactory, the entrepreneur will develop a business plan for VC funding. In the case of consolidations, technology transfers and M&A, the VC would invest in the anchor company which would then acquire other companies, acquire the relevant technology or adopt the new business model.

These types of deals can generate high returns since the VC invests at the ground floor and has full control of the deal initially. However, the VC needs to devote more attention than usual at the initial stage and needs to have an extensive network of CEOs and entrepreneurs to be able to tap into to find the right person at relatively short notice to drive the deal. For some VCs, one of the general partners may take on the role of CEO initially until a suitable person is found.

Non-Disclosure Agreement

Many entrepreneurs are apprehensive that their business concepts or plans may fall into the wrong hands and would insist on the VC signing a Confidentiality Agreement or Non-Disclosure Agreement (NDA) before revealing intimate details of their business. On the other hand, some VCs are apprehensive of the potential legal liability and refuse to sign any document of this sort and would rather not do the deal.

More often, the VC and the entrepreneur would settle with a simple agreement. The entrepreneur would see this as a deterrence and a necessary compromise if the VC is to be sought after as a partner. A simple NDA, especially one limited in time frame, would be acceptable to most VCs.

An example of a simple NDA is given in Appendix 6A on page 119. It would be necessary for the VC to have an in-house standard agreement that can be offered as an alternative to the one produced by the entrepreneur.

Deal Log

The Deal Log is a database of all the deal proposals received by the VC, whether they are actively followed up or not. As soon as a business plan or deal proposal is received, the key details are entered into the database. Fields may be left blank if the information is not provided, and may be filled up later when available.

Useful statistics and information can be mined from the database, such as an analysis of deal flow by month, by industry sector, by how the deal is sourced, by stage of the company, investment mode, or proposed usage of the investment funds. The database may be used to track progress of deals, and details can be printed out for reference during regular internal deal meetings when investment staff discuss the active deals in progress.

The deal database would also be a useful reference for details of deals looked at in the past and reasons for rejection of particular deals. The information would be useful for the handling of similar deals or to serve as learning tools for staff. When the VC is raising a new fund, potential LPs would want to have an analysis of the quantity and quality of deal flow, as part of their due diligence.

An example deal database format is given in Appendix 6B on page 121, showing a suggested list of data fields that can be captured in the database. Note that at the bottom of the example format are suggested links to documents related to the deal. The Deal Alert, which will be discussed in the next chapter, will be produced for every deal that is pursued by the VC. The other documents will be produced if the deal is done and becomes an investment. All these form the knowledge management system for the VC.

Chapter Recap

In this chapter, we discussed deal sourcing from the following aspects:

- o   What are the ingredients of an ideal deal
- o   Where to look for these ingredients
- o   The different approaches to sourcing deals.

We also considered examples of:

- o   A non-disclosure agreement
- o   A deal database format

which are useful and related to deal sourcing.

APPENDIX 6A   NON-DISCLOSURE AGREEMENT

[Date]
[Name of Company]
[Address]

Attn:

Dear Sirs

NON-DISCLOSURE AGREEMENT

In pursuance of our interest to invest in [Name of Company] ("the Company"), we require confidential information relating to the Company ("Confidential Information") for the purpose of evaluating our potential investment.

In consideration of your making Confidential Information available to us, we undertake that such information will be held in confidence, will be for the sole purpose of our staff and advisors to evaluate our potential investment in the Company, and will not be disclosed to any other person or used for any other purpose, without your prior written consent. Our undertaking will continue for a period of six months from the date of this Agreement and all our obligations shall terminate thereafter.

The definition of "Confidential Information" shall <u>not</u> include the following:

(a)   Information which is already publicly available or becomes publicly available other than as a result of a breach of this Agreement by us or our advisors,

(b)   Information that is lawfully in the possession of our staff or advisors prior to the date of this Agreement,

(c)   Information which lawfully comes into our possession from a source other than you or the Company, provided that the source did not obtain the information as a result of a breach of this Agreement by us or our advisors,

(d) Information that is required to be disclosed by any law or government regulation.

In return you undertake that you or any of your staff will not disclose, without our prior written consent, our interest in evaluating the potential investment in the Company, or in having discussions to that effect. Such disclosure includes but is not limited to disclosing our name to the press. This undertaking from you shall continue after the termination of our obligations under this Agreement.

This Agreement shall be governed by and construed in accordance with the laws of [Country]. Kindly sign and return a copy as acceptance of the terms.

Yours faithfully
[VC Firm]

_____
Authorized Signatory

Name:
Designation:

We hereby confirm and accept the terms and conditions in this Agreement.

For and on behalf of
[Name of Company]

_____
Authorized Signatory

Name:
Designation:
Date:

APPENDIX 6B   DEAL LOG

| **DATA FIELD NAME** | **EXPLANATION** |

1. Deal Number — *A serial number provided by the computer system.*

2. Office Location — *For firms with multiple office locations.*
3. Date of Data Update
4. Company Name
5. Company Codename — *A codename may be given for confidentiality.*

6. City/State/Country
7. Industry Sector Code — *A standard industry classification code may be used.*

8. Introduction Code — *Data to compile statistics showing the distribution of sources of deals.*
(a) Direct approach by entrepreneur
(b) Cold-call by us
(c) Personal network
(d) Referral by other VC
(e) Referral by limited partners/sponsors
(f) Referral by financial/professional firms/brokers

9. Business Description — *One sentence description of the business.*

10. Stage of Company — *Data to compile statistics showing the distribution of deals by stage of development of the company.*
(a) Seed/Start-up
(b) Development
(c) Revenue
(d) Profitable
(e) Mature
(f) Special situation

11.	Investment Mode	*Data to compile statistics showing the*
(a)	Sole investor	*distribution of deals by the mode of*
(b)	Lead investor	*investment.*
(c)	Syndicate	
(d)	Joint venture	

12.	Investment Amount	
13.	Pre-Money Valuation	

14.	Use of Funds	*Data to compile statistics showing the*
(a)	Growth	*distribution of deals by the proposed use*
(b)	Reorganization	*of investment funds.*
(c)	Mezzanine	
(d)	Buyout	

15.	Deal Champion's Name	*Name of the investment staff assigned to*
		the deal.

16.	Deal Progress Dates:	*Dates are to be entered to track the*
(a)	First contact	*progress of the deal. Data would be*
(b)	Business plan received	*useful to monitor progress of deals and*
(c)	Deal alert issued	*to compile statistics of lead times for the*
(d)	Term sheet issued	*different stages of the investment process.*
(e)	Investment proposal submitted	
(f)	Investment approved	
(g)	Legal documents signed	
(h)	First disbursement of funds	
(i)	Deal on hold	
(j)	Deal revived	
(k)	Deal declined	

Comments		*Additional information such as reasons*
		for the deal to be put on hold or
		declined.

Links to:

(a)   Deal Alert
(b)   Term Sheet
(c)   Investment Proposal
(d)   Legal Documents
(e)   Investment Status Reports
(f)   Divestment Reports

If there is a Knowledge Management System, hot links can be provided to the important documents relevant to the investment. These would be useful for corporate reference and learning.

7

Deal Screening

In the previous chapter, we described the desirable ingredients of a deal that the VC should look for. In this chapter we shall describe those characteristics of a deal that most VCs would find undesirable, to the extent that the deal would be rejected. Such a screening process is necessary as dozens of business plans are received every week by a VC, and this process saves further time and effort to be spent on investigating and evaluating deals that will be eventually rejected anyway.

On receipt of a deal, the VC will quickly scan through the business plan to understand the business dynamics and to detect the major merits and demerits of the proposals. One or two meetings may be necessary for clarifications and to get a feel of the entrepreneurs and the management team members that may be already on board. A few phone calls to third parties may also be necessary to verify aspects of the business or to check on the backgrounds of the entrepreneurs. A Deal Alert, which is a document capturing essentials of the new deal will be put up. The deal would be brought up for discussion at one of the regular internal deal meetings, to tap the collective knowledge of colleagues and the wisdom of the senior partners.

The deal screening process is a preliminary or condensed form of the due diligence process to quickly detect critical flaws in the proposed deal or business, if any. Therefore the concepts and methodologies involved are the same for both processes. The difference is only in the scale and depth of effort. Therefore the principles of due diligence which will be discussed in the next chapter will also apply here. During this preliminary investigation process, if no major showstoppers emerge, and there are enough merits like those described in the previous chapter, the deal will proceed to the due diligence process stage.

In this chapter we shall describe the VC Deal Meeting, look at a format for the Deal Alert, and then run through the common showstoppers that cause VCs to reject deals at the initial screening stage.

Deal Meeting

The Deal Meeting, usually held weekly, plays an important part in the VC Process. This is an internal meeting of the investment professionals to discuss all aspects of a deal from its initial preliminary assessment stage, through due diligence, deal structuring and negotiation, and continuing to post-investment monitoring and divestment stages.

The discussions give the opportunity for all staff to share knowledge and experience, to view deals from different angles to minimize the likelihood that critical issues are missed; to cross-fertilize ideas and learn from each other; to help each other to assess and verify due diligence issues; and to brainstorm solutions to managing deals or business problems faced by investee companies. Specific valuation, deal structuring issues or negotiation tactics may also be discussed.

Readiness to surface problems; openness and honesty in expressing opinions; desire to help each other; and willingness to reassess a deal based on constructive and valid criticisms from others will make deal meetings productive and improve the quality of deals done. A deal champion should be objective in presenting both the merits and demerits of his deal, and should be prompt in highlighting critical problems faced by an investee company under his charge. Using the deal meeting as a platform to raise and discuss issues will tap the collective wisdom of the investment team. Subsequent follow-up work can then be assigned to specific staff.

Deal Alert

Appendix 7A on page 139 shows a Deal Alert form. As the name implies it is meant to alert other investment staff that a deal is being pursued, so that if any of them has seen a similar deal before, has relevant knowledge or experience of the business, or might know about the entrepreneurs, could immediately contribute information or comments. As stated previously, the Deal Alert is also used at deal meetings to remind details and provide updates of a deal.

The Deal Alert is issued only when a deal is being pursued. On the other hand, the Deal Log, described in the previous chapter, is used to log in each and every deal received, regardless whether it is pursued or not. Hence the Deal Log captures only cryptic essentials of the deal, whereas the Deal Alert has more elaborate information to facilitate preliminary assessments. However, it is still meant to be a brief document, with not more than two or three pages.

It is important that the deal champion diligently records into the Deal Alert, comments and concerns expressed by other partners during deal meetings so that these are not forgotten and are adequately addressed if the deal is taken to the investment proposal stage. Also, if the deal is dropped at any stage, the reasons for dropping should be duly recorded. All Deal Alerts are filed into the VC firm's knowledge management system.

Showstoppers

Our list of possible showstoppers[7] is rather long, but by no means exhaustive. Finding a showstopper does not mean that the deal will be dropped automatically. It does mean that the negative aspect has to be analyzed more thoroughly; ways have to be examined to alleviate it, if possible; and its seriousness assessed and balanced against the merits of the deal. If there are insufficient mitigating or compensating factors, the deal would be dropped.

These showstoppers need not necessarily arise only at the initial screening stage. They may be discovered at the later due diligence stage and may also

---

[7] These showstoppers are from personal experience and also gleaned from industry reports and articles to reflect a more complete picture of the range of screening criteria used in the industry.

result in the deal being rejected. The typical showstoppers may be categorized as shown in Figure 7.1.

FIGURE 7.1   TYPICAL SHOWSTOPPERS

Business Model	Lack of focus
	Cannot scale up
	Slow growth
VC's Policies	Outside fund focus
	Competitor of portfolio company
	Shopped deal
Valuation / Exit	Valuation too high
	No exit
Market	Intense competition
	Price control
	Market acceptance problems
Profitability	Low margins
	High burn rate
Management	No CEO
	Management change
	Execution weakness
Technology	Intellectual property problems
	Commercialization difficulties
Shareholders	Shareholder conflicts
	Shareholder dilution

Lack of Focus

If the entrepreneur proposes to carry out several diverse and unrelated businesses or to develop too many products or services at the same time, the deal may not be worth pursuing. For example, the entrepreneur may want to develop a suite of enterprise software applications right from the start. Such an endeavor would stretch manpower and funding resources. Usually it would be better for the company to concentrate on one or two applications where it has unique solutions that meet pressing customer needs. Or the company could just develop the core application. The product range can be expanded or additional features can be added after revenue is generated. Lack of focus indicates that the entrepreneurs do not know their key strengths or do not understand market needs.

Cannot Scale Up

Another showstopper is a business that cannot scale up, which means that it does not enjoy economies of scale or requires duplication of resources when expanded. Examples are products or services which need to be customized or duplicated in different markets, such as consultancy services which require duplication of talent in multiple offices. While such business may thrive on a small scale, they are not suited for VC investments which require high growth. On the other hand, certain businesses, such as semiconductor wafer fabrication plants and petrochemical plants have minimum economic sizes and thus have high fixed costs and become inefficient if scaled down during industry downturns. Wrong timing of such plants would be a showstopper.

Slow Growth

Those businesses in declining or slow growth markets, or have long gestation periods, will take too long compared to the VC time frame of an average holding period of about five years. Examples of industries with long gestation periods are resource and energy exploration, extraction and processing, infrastructure construction, and satellite communications. Investment opportunities in these industries would not be attractive to a VC. Similarly, entrepreneurs seeking VC funding for companies that are at too early a stage, such as when they are still carrying out basic research, will not be attractive as the gestation period will also be too long.

Outside Fund Focus

A VC sets a focus for its fund and establishes consistent policies and strategies for investments, such as those based on investment size, development stage of the company, industry sector, and geographical territory. Investment proposals falling outside these guidelines would obviously be showstoppers. Also, if a business happens to be one where the VC is unable to add value, it may be rejected, unless other strong merits enable the company to grow on its own steam. Some VCs steer away from businesses involving gambling, tobacco or alcohol.

Competitor of Portfolio Company

A deal which involves a business that competes with that of a portfolio company gives rise to a conflict of interest, and would be avoided by the VC. If there is synergy or a possibility for a merger, the VC would usually let the portfolio company drive the deal.

Shopped Deal

A shopped deal is one that is being or has been shopped around to many VCs. A VC would usually avoid such a deal. Either the entrepreneurs are only interested in getting the highest valuation instead of getting the best partner, or the deal has been rejected by many VCs and hence is of suspect quality. On the other hand, a good deal that is being shopped around is likely to be high priced due to the bidding that arises when many VCs chase after it.

Valuation Too High

High company valuation is frequently a deal breaker. The entrepreneur wants a high valuation because of a biased or overly optimistic view of the potential growth and profitability of the business opportunity. The projected investment return would then be below the VC's target. If due diligence does not support the optimism at all or negotiations do not bring the valuation down to an acceptable value, the VC will drop the deal. In Chapter 13 we shall discuss valuation methods and the expected returns of VCs.

No Exit

An uncertain or difficult exit avenue could also be a showstopper. VCs usually take a minority stake. If the majority shareholders have a change of mind and do not wish to go public, the VC will have no easy exit and would usually find that it has to sell its stake at a low price, often to the majority shareholders. Therefore if the VC is not convinced that the majority shareholders have a sincere intention to go public or to go for a trade sale, it would be a showstopper. In some countries, the stock market may not offer much liquidity, and the absence of strategic buyers or an alternative to list in another country's stock market, would also be a showstopper.

Intense Competition

Businesses that are subject to intense competition are usually avoided by VCs. These are businesses with low entry barriers, a market crowded with many suppliers, or a market dominated by several large entrenched players. Margins would be low and it would be difficult to gain market share. Examples of industry sectors dominated by large corporations are white goods, electronic consumer products, personal computers, printers, digital cameras, displays, electronic media, microprocessors, and various electronic components. Unless the company has discovered a revolutionary new technology, or has disruptive innovations, it would be difficult to compete with similar or me-too products. Alternatively, if a company's business model or strategy can be modified, using the value innovation tools prescribed by W. Chan Kim and Renee Mauborgne[8], to move it away from intense competition in a Red Ocean into a Blue Ocean, the deal may be worth considering.

Price Control

Businesses subject to price controls will have profit margins and growth limited, and face uncertainties of changes in regulations. Examples of industries subject to price control are essential food products, some commodities, and utility services in some countries.

---

[8] W. Chan Kim and Renee Mauborgne, *Blue Ocean Strategy: How to create uncontested market space and make the competition irrelevant*, Boston: Harvard Business School Publishing, 2005

Market Acceptance Problems

A new business concept or process which requires changes in human behavior or in well-ingrained procedures, will likely face slow market acceptance if at all. While it may not be impossible, it is usually too difficult to impose such changes, too costly or takes too long. Similarly, products or processes that are governed by international quality, health, or safety standards may take years to commercialize, if at all, due to the time and effort needed to meet the standards and to secure the approvals. Corporations are also fearful of unproven products and reluctant to be guinea pigs.

In the computer, communications, and consumer electronics worlds, different and often conflicting operating systems exist because the companies want product differentiation and captivity of customers. These companies jealously protect their proprietary systems and it would take a lot of time and effort to achieve compatibility with their systems. On the other hand, end customers demand inter-operability and compatibility. Products with limited inter-operability and compatibility will face market acceptance problems.

Low Margins

Businesses with low margins are those with low entry barriers, little or no technology, and are crowded with competitors, such as small retailing businesses. A low margin means low investment returns, and inability to withstand increased competition.

Often an entrepreneur will claim that the proposed product can be produced at a much lower cost than that of existing producers in the market. The estimations of competitors' costs or margins may be faulty, or the entrepreneur may have underestimated the marketing costs, service support costs, or R&D expenses in the costing of his product. This would be a showstopper requiring more investigation or rejection of the deal.

High Burn Rate

For a start-up or early stage company that has not yet reached cash flow breakeven, the burn rate, which is the rate at which cash is consumed, is an important figure. It is an indicator of the propensity of the management to spend, or on the other hand, its ability to be capital efficient. A high burn rate should ring alarm bells and trigger further investigation. Management may be paying themselves too high salaries, spending on unnecessary or luxurious assets, hiring too early, or not finding more capital efficient alternatives such as leasing or contracting. A high burn rate will require a larger amount of investment, increasing the risks and reducing the returns.

However, it is not always the case that a high burn rate is bad. A management that is too conservative will not generate the fast-growth rate that would be desired by a VC. Ultimately, the VC needs to assess whether the cash is used aggressively and wisely, but not excessively and in unproductive areas.

No CEO

Some VCs may invest in a start-up without a CEO, but having a CTO temporarily acting as CEO. If the VC already has a CEO candidate or is convinced that a suitable CEO can be readily found, this will not be a showstopper. Otherwise, concerns over the recruitment time and effort, compatibility with existing team members or the business, may make the absence of a CEO a showstopper.

Management Change

Unsuitability of the CEO or a critical management team member such as the CTO may be due to character defects such as lack of integrity, or a noncooperative or autocratic attitude; a lack of capability to grow with the business; or a poor track record. Many VCs would prefer changing the CEO or team member before the investment is made, otherwise it could be a showstopper.

Execution Weakness

Concerns over the ability of the management team to execute the business plans could be a showstopper. Such concerns may not necessarily arise from the character or capability weaknesses previously mentioned, but may arise from a misfit between the team's capability and the business demands. The team may otherwise have various strengths but may lack knowledge of the space, or lack ability to grow a company fast, or lack the necessary marketing skills or have other similar weaknesses in areas which are crucial for the success of the business. Another serious concern may arise over the ability of the team to work together, even though each member may be strong individually.

Intellectual Property Problems

A company with little or no intellectual property would find it difficult to differentiate its products and protect its markets. In this case it would usually be a showstopper. In another case, the VC may receive a proposal from an entrepreneur who has left a company to start a venture to develop and produce products similar to those of the previous employer, but claimed to be superior and cheaper. Possibility of infringement of intellectual property rights would usually be a showstopper. If the deal is compelling, the VC would need to find ways to mitigate the concerns, by seeking expert technical and legal advice. In some countries there are laws which protect individuals from being deprived of a livelihood by being barred from using their technical expertise and knowledge, which might mitigate the possibility of a legal suit.

Commercialization Difficulties

In many cases a new technology may look very innovative and superior, but the viability of the implementation and commercialization can be questionable. For example, a biometrics company may have developed superior algorithms for fingerprint identification which win international competitions by being the fastest and the most accurate. The problem faced by the company would be the way to commercialize this. Licensing the algorithms would not generate much revenue or growth, as there are already many of such algorithms in the market and there is no premium for being the fastest and the most accurate, as systems in the market already have acceptable speed and accuracy. Developing security systems incorporating the technology would be a business beyond the capability of entrepreneurs, whose expertise lies in development of the algorithms.

The following mini-case study shows the difficulties that can be encountered.

Mini Case Study: Brightek Inc.

In 2001, Brightek Inc. received VC funding to support its market launch of a software application for sending and receiving handwritten messages via SMS (Short Messaging Service) by mobile phones. The three young and bright Chinese engineers who invented the technology and started the company had no idea of the insurmountable commercialization difficulties that they would face. Unfortunately, neither did the VC.

The market for mobile phones was a rapidly growing and huge market worldwide and particularly in China. SMS was a popular and cheap means of communicating with mobile phones. The three young entrepreneurs developed a compact piece of software that could fit into the limited memory of the mobile phone SIM card, and which could compress each written character into few enough bytes so that several lines of handwritten text could be sent via SMS. No character recognition software was required, as it would be beyond the memory and power of the mobile phone. This capability would enable ideographic languages, such as Chinese, Japanese, Korean, Hindi, Jawi, Hebrew, etc., and even hand-drawn pictures to be transmitted via SMS. It was envisaged that the market for this neat piece of software would be tremendous. The software was verified to work well, using PDAs as the platform.

When Brightek started to talk to the mobile phone companies, it encountered the first hurdle. These companies were worried about standards. SMS was evolving to EMS (Extended Messaging Service) and MMS (Multimedia Messaging Service) was appearing on the horizon. The phone manufacturers wanted tests to be carried out to ensure that the technology complied with SMS and the evolving EMS standards. Brightek also talked to the telecommunication operators (Telcos) as they often dictate the features required in the phones. The Telcos were concerned about interoperability, which also meant compliance with standards.

Brightek had to spend about a year making several presentations and providing test results to the 3GPP, an international standards committee represented by phone manufacturers and operators, to convince the 3GPP to incorporate Brightek's technology into the new EMS standards. The tiny Brightek managed to fend off competition from three corporate giants which also wanted to incorporate their respective graphics technology into EMS, and finally its technology was accepted.

However the catch was that Brightek had to make its technology an open platform, which meant Brightek could not secure any revenue from the use of the platform. Brightek was caught between keeping it a closed platform, which meant that no phone company would want to use it, or to make it open and not enjoy any royalty. Brightek decided to make it open, with the hope that it could garner revenue by helping companies to apply the technology efficiently.

The commercialization effort faced yet another difficulty. A phone that allows handwritten messages has to have a touch screen, like a PDA. At that time such phones were only starting to emerge and remained at the high end of the market. Brightek managed to convince a Chinese phone company to build a small handwriting tablet that can be attached to its phone. The product did not take off as it was regarded as cumbersome. The big phone companies in the West did not have to deal with ideographic languages and were not convinced about the market demand to want to incorporate the technology into their phone models. Brightek languished in the irony that although its technology was accepted and incorporated into world standards, it could not derive any monetary reward for its efforts.

Shareholder Conflicts

Sometimes a deal may come with some of the shareholders being locked in a legal dispute over their respective equity in the company, or perhaps over a matter not related to the company at all. This can hold up the operations of the company as shareholders' resolutions may be blocked or channeled into irrelevant side-issues by the disgruntled shareholders. Such situations will be showstoppers for the deal.

Shareholder Dilution

For start-ups, it is not unusual to have family, friends, business angels, and consultants taking up small stakes. When an institutional investor enters the picture with significant funding, many if not all of these individual shareholders would be unable or unwilling to invest more funds. They may resent being badly diluted, and may insist on a much higher valuation, or delay or even block the funding. Since management's dilution gets compensated by stock options, they may accuse management of selling them out and resent the increased dilution from the stock options. To make matters worse, if the founders, even if they collectively hold the largest stake, are reluctant to force the issue and offend their family, friends, and business associates, it would be difficult to close the deal. The VC would perhaps rather walk away than get entangled in the mess.

Proceeding to Due Diligence

A large majority of deals received, typically about 60 percent, can be rejected through this initial screening process. The actual percentage depends on the quality of the deals received and the screening criteria of the VC. In many cases, the deal is rejected merely after a quick examination of the business plan. In some other cases, perhaps a couple of meetings with the entrepreneurs, some phone calls and internal discussions at deal meetings would uncover showstoppers that cannot be resolved satisfactorily, resulting in rejection. In some cases, the showstopper issue may allow resolution or alleviation and the deal may be allowed to be pursued further. Finally, in some instances, the showstopper issue may not be so serious or so clear that the deal deserves to be instantly rejected, in which case it proceeds on for more intensive investigation under the due diligence process.

The screening process saves unproductive work on deals that would eventually be rejected. Although in this process some good deals may be rejected, it is necessary to weed off the bad deals to allow more time to be spent on evaluating the better ones. If a deal passes through the screening process, it will move on to the proper due diligence process which will be covered in the next few chapters.

Chapter Recap

In this chapter we have discussed a number of the common showstoppers that would screen off a majority of deals received by the VC. These showstoppers can arise from many different aspects of the deal, such as issues relating to the business model, the VC's investment policies, valuation, exit, market, profitability, technology, and existing shareholders of the company.

We also discussed the Deal Meeting, which is an important weekly activity of the VC, during which matters arising from new deals and existing investments are discussed. We also reviewed the Deal Alert form which is filled up for every deal that is pursued, and which serves as a useful tracking form for deal details and opinions expressed, as the deal progresses.

APPENDIX 7A   DEAL ALERT

DEAL ALERT

Date Issued: Deal Champion:
Deal Log #:   Code Name:
Industry: Industry Code:

Name of Company:
Address:

CEO/Contact:
Deal Source:
Company Business:

Company History:

Strengths/Weaknesses:

Management:

Financials: Year   Year   Year   Year   Year
  Turnover:
  Gross Margin
  EBIT:
  PBT
  NPAT:
  Net Tangible Assets:

Amount Sought:
Valuation:
Use of Funds:

Deal Structure:

Exit:

Status of Deal:

Merits/Demerits of the Deal:

Comments or Issues Raised by Partners:

Follow-up Action by Deal Champion:

————————————————————   ————————————————

Deal Champion Signature   Date Revised

PART IV

CONDUCTING DUE DILIGENCE

Due diligence is the investigation work that is conducted on a deal, to verify the claims and projections, as well as to evaluate the merits and risks of making an investment. Such work can be very extensive and intensive, but it is a crucial part of the VC investment process.

How does the VC firm conduct due diligence? What strategies and techniques does it employ to balance between effectiveness and resources? What are the areas that require due diligence? What should the VC firm look for in these areas? After amassing all the data from the due diligence work, how does the VC firm arrive at a conclusion on whether to invest, given that much of the data could be conflicting, incomplete or unclear?

Chapter 8: DUE DILIGENCE BASICS provides a systematic framework and process for the whole due diligence process from the planning stage to arriving at a conclusion. Chapter 9: DUE DILIGENCE OF MANAGEMENT is devoted to the conduct of due diligence of the management of the potential investee company.

Chapter 10: DUE DILIGENCE OF MARKETING & THE MARKET describes the due diligence issues that need to be considered for the market need, potential, characteristics, strategies, and risks. Chapter 11: DUE DILIGENCE OF MANUFACTURING examines the issues that need to be investigated for the manufacturing operations, including issues relating to technology, and in Chapter 12: DUE DILIGENCE OF FINANCIAL & LEGAL ASPECTS, the financial and legal issues affecting the company are discussed.

8

Due Diligence Basics

When a VC makes an investment into a company, it is with the expectation that the business plans will be carried out, targets will be achieved, and investment returns will be realized. There is no guarantee or certainty that all these will happen. The VC therefore has to conduct intensive investigations to assess the probability and risks that they will or will not happen and to understand the factors that contribute to the success or failure of the business. These investigations are called due diligence. The information gathered from the due diligence work will provide an overall risk-reward assessment that will enable the investment decision to be made.

Due diligence work can be very extensive, requiring checks on the management team as well as all aspects of the business, including the product or service, market, technology, operations, financial aspects, legal, environmental, and regulatory factors that can affect the business. Also, the VC has to look into the past and present performance of the company and the future prospects. The VC has to verify the claims made by the founders or management of the company, and secure the feedback of independent third parties such as customers, suppliers, bankers, competitors, ex-employees, and professional associates. The VC has to achieve a reasonable level of understanding of the dynamics and drivers of the business and the market. It is therefore all too easy for the VC to be lost in the quagmire of details.

In the previous chapter we described a multitude of adverse factors that can result in a deal being rejected. If this screening effort to surface critical issues results in the deal being rejected, it will avoid the extensive due diligence effort. However, if the screening did not result in rejection, and if the VC remains interested in the deal, the VC needs to review the business afresh and in greater detail.

A systematic approach is required to ensure efficient and effective due diligence work, and to keep within the time constraints. The scope of the due diligence has to be defined so that work is kept within the set boundaries, and the relative importance of issues to be investigated has to be ranked so that work is carried out according to priorities. To achieve these objectives, I propose that the Plan-Do-Check-Act Cycle (PDCA Cycle) be applied to due diligence. The PDCA Cycle is a proven systematic process in Total Quality Management for problem solving and quality improvement.

In this chapter we shall explain the PDCA Cycle and the stages of Plan, Do, Check, and Act as applied to the due diligence process. In the next several chapters we shall discuss the detailed due diligence of management, marketing, operational, financial, and legal aspects of businesses, using the PDCA approach.

The PDCA Cycle

The PDCA Cycle was originally developed by Walter Shewhart in the 1930s and subsequently promoted by the authority on quality management, Edwards Deming. The four stages are as illustrated in Figure 8.1 which depicts the continuous cyclical process.

When applied to quality improvement, the PDCA Cycle starts with the Plan stage, which consists of analyzing the quality problems, identifying the best solutions, and planning the testing and implementation of the solutions. The Do stage consists of testing the solutions, preferably on a pilot scale and over a limited time period. The Check stage is to monitor and study the results of tests to see whether the solutions were effective in improving quality. If successful, the Act stage implements the solutions on a wider scale and over an extended period or on a permanent basis. If not satisfactory, the Act stage involves deciding on whether to abandon the failed solutions or to modify them. This leads on to the Plan stage, where plans and studies are made for modified or new solutions or if the previous cycle was successful, to look at new problems. The cycle then repeats.

FIGURE 8.1   THE PDCA CYCLE

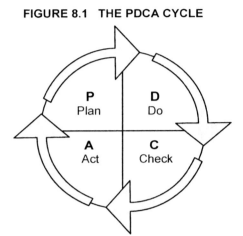

Let us see how these concepts may be applied to the due diligence process.

Plan Stage

At the Plan stage, it is important to start by identifying and analyzing the business issues of the particular deal under consideration, which will lead to defining the scope and setting the priorities for the due diligence exercise. These will then give direction and avoid haphazard and endless due diligence work at the next stage which is the Do stage.

There are certain major issues that are common to every deal. These relate to the quality of the management, the valuation of the present business, and the extent of the investment returns, which have to be investigated regardless of the type of business. Each deal will also have its peculiar set of critical business issues. The following key questions will help to identify these issues:

    o   What is the business or revenue model?
    o   What are the key performance indicators of the business?

o   What gives the business its competitive edge, its unfair advantage?

o   What is the unique selling proposition?

o   What compelling and real market needs are being fulfilled?

o   What are the potential pitfalls in this business?

o   What is required of management to be able to execute the plans?

These questions focus on identifying the issues qualitatively and on a macro basis. It is harmless and in fact may be useful to ask similar questions in different ways in order to examine the business from all angles to bring out all the relevant critical success and failure factors. The VC should give thought to these questions and not simply accept what is told by the founders or management of the company. Deal meetings would be the best occasions to bounce around these questions internally.

Continuing with the systematic approach, a framework will be set up for the ensuing due diligence work, which will be to verify the validity of the identified issues, to quantify as much as possible the degree of seriousness or impact of the specific issues, and perhaps to also uncover new issues. The framework is illustrated in Figure 8.2.

This framework is used to define the scope of the due diligence work according to the critical assumptions used in the business plans; the critical success or failure factors that have been identified to be relevant to the business; the due diligence sources or methods; and also to record the results of the due diligence checks in terms of validity, seriousness of impact, or reasonableness.

The upper section of the framework points to the main areas of the business that need to be investigated: the management, the product or service, the market and marketing strategies, the manufacturing operations (if any), the technology, financial performance, and legal issues. In some cases, environmental factors, such as availability and quality of supporting industries, skilled workers, or infrastructure such as power, transportation, port, and communication services may also need to be investigated.

FIGURE 8.2   DUE DILIGENCE FRAMEWORK

Investigation Area	Critical Assumptions & Success/Failure Factors	Due Diligence Sources	Validity & Seriousness of Impact
Management Product or Service Market and Marketing Strategies Operations Technology Financial Legal			

Investigation Area	Due Diligence Sources or Methods	Reasonableness
Valuation Expected Investment Return Exit Options		

The first step is to consider key questions that will help to identify the critical success and failure factors that impact the business. These are entered into the framework. For example, what gives the company its competitive edge may be its superior technology, and therefore it is critical that the technology works. Thus "Feasibility of technology" may be entered into the row titled "Technology" and in the column titled "Critical Assumptions & Success/Failure Factors." Another example may be that the company has used a sustained market growth of 30 percent per year in its business projections. If this is deemed to be a critical assumption that needs to be verified, "30 percent growth per year" can be entered into the row titled "Market" and in the same column. The description of the issue can be as cryptic or elaborate as desired.

Obviously certain cells will be blank as they refer to issues that are irrelevant or unimportant to the deal under consideration. This is the very purpose of the framework. It focuses attention on the relevant critical assumptions and business issues by cutting out the unimportant ones.

Next, the sources of due diligence information are identified for the respective assumptions or issues. For example, to check the "Feasibility of technology" issue, a research scientist may be named to obtain advice. For "30 percent growth per year," an industry expert or a marketing consultant may be named. More than one source may be identified, depending on the importance of the assumption or issue.

The last column, titled "Validity and Seriousness of Impact" is for the next stage of the process, the Do stage, to enter in the results and information obtained from the conduct of the due diligence.

The lower section of the above framework covers the due diligence on the valuation, expected investment return, and exit options for the deal. The entry valuation, which is the present valuation of the company, has to be reasonable. In Chapter 13 we shall discuss the various valuation concepts and methodologies as well as calculations of investment returns. The due diligence work may be to check valuations of similar companies in terms of business and stage of development that recently secured investments, or to check market valuations of similar listed companies and discounting appropriately for its less mature and unlisted status. The relevant due diligence sources or methods are listed in the next column, and the last column is for results of the reasonableness assessment to be entered during the Do stage. The reasonableness check for expected investment return is to ensure that the expectation is reasonable and within the desired range of the VC. Exit options are covered in Chapter 21. Here, the due diligence is to check for feasibility of the proposed exit strategy and to examine alternative exit strategies if necessary.

Any unique or unusual issue not covered in the above framework may be added in. Color codes may be used to denote the degree of importance or priority of each of the assumptions and issues entered.

In the case of the assumptions used in the business plan projections, these are known and are readily entered into the framework, giving priority to those assumptions that have the greatest impact on the business performance. In the case of critical business issues, it is not necessary to be too ambitious and detailed in the first round of this PDCA cycle in attempting to figure out all the possible issues. As due diligence work progresses, understanding of the business dynamics will increase, requiring additions and deletions as well as changes to the relative importance of the issues to be investigated in a subsequent round. However it is important to include the topmost two or three critical issues, since any failure of these may result in the deal being rejected, saving any further work.

We have now defined the scope and the priorities for the due diligence work. This completes the Plan stage and we progress to the Do stage.

Do Stage

In the Do stage, we execute the plan that we built. We conduct the due diligence following the road map of assumptions and issues to investigate and the sources to seek information that have been identified and built into the framework.

The business issues to be investigated may require drilling down to deeper levels of details than those that may be prompted by the key questions asked in the Plan stage. We shall go through these details in relation to the management, the market and marketing strategies, the production operations and technology, as well as financial and legal aspects, in the next four chapters.

Due diligence information may be sourced from reference materials, knowledgeable persons or ad hoc research. Examples of these sources are:

- o Written information:
  - o Technical papers, market surveys, reports, etc., provided by the company
  - o Industry journals and newsletters, information databases
  - o Internet-sourced corporate and product information, white papers, online reports and articles

- o Knowledgeable persons:
  - o References provided by the company

- o Company's customers, suppliers, bankers, competitors
- o Company's key managers and ex-managers
- o Consultants, academics, industry practitioners, and analysts
- o VC's personal and industry contacts
- o VC's professional staff
- o VC's portfolio companies' executives
- o VC's sponsors and affiliates
- o VC's limited partners
- o Professional staff of friendly VCs

- o Ad hoc or specialized research:
  - o Industry or market research firms
  - o Feasibility studies
  - o Commissioned surveys
  - o Focus groups

Interviews with knowledgeable persons should preferably be conducted through face-to-face meetings, rather than through the phone or e-mails, for better interaction and observation of body language. Questions should be open-ended and phrased to evoke explanation, elaboration, or substantiation. Sometimes, acting dumb or confused encourages more extensive or greater depth of explanation. Intentional moments of silence may provoke the interviewee to say more. Clarifications should be asked to avoid wrong assumptions or jumping to wrong conclusions on what was said. Sometimes what is not said can reveal more than what is said.

Importance should be given to looking into the future, since the investment is in the future prospects of the company. The due diligence should therefore look for trends such as market or price trends; disruptive events such as emergence of new technology, substitute products, or new competitors; and discontinuities such as change of fads or fashions. Assumptions based on simple extrapolations should be questioned and investigated.

Important clues may be secured from due diligence with the company's founders and staff. Missing data, inconsistency in data and answers to queries, delays in getting requested information, claims that could not be substantiated, discomfort shown by body language during questioning, staff turnover, and poor financial records are evidence of possible internal problems which should be noted in the due diligence.

Check Stage

In the Check stage, we assess the due diligence information that has been gathered to date. It is not necessary to wait until all the planned due diligence work is completed before moving on to this stage. Following the priorities that have been set, the topmost critical issues should have reached earlier completion or at least should have soon reached a stage where initial conclusions could be drawn. Remaining due diligence work continues on while the initial assessment is made.

The assessment is on the validity and seriousness of the various identified business assumptions and issues. These assessments will suggest actions that would need to be taken in the next stage, the Act stage.

Thus, very serious issues could suggest rejection of the deal. An issue that has increased in importance arising from due diligence feedback or greater understanding of the business may require further due diligence. Inconsistent answers, insufficient data, or new issues may need more due diligence. Issues found to be irrelevant or unimportant may be discarded. Incorrect assumptions may require the business plans to be revised. The conclusion may be to await more results from the continuing due diligence or to move to the Act stage.

Act Stage

At the Act stage, decisions are made on the follow up actions that are required. Some of these actions are suggested by the assessments in the previous stage: rejection of the deal, further due diligence, modifications to the set of issues, and revision of business plans and projections.

In any due diligence exercise, it is likely that negative feedback and concerns will arise. Obviously the first step would have been to seek verification. Instead of rejecting the deal outright, the VC should consider actions that can help to rectify or alleviate the concerns. Such actions include renegotiating the terms of the deal, such as lowering the valuation, modifying terms to allow greater control or governance, setting new performance targets, or modifying the deal structure to allow greater downside protection. In other situations, the concerns may be alleviated by getting agreement to make management changes or bringing in an industrial partner. It is only when the concerns are serious enough or beyond relief would the VC consider rejecting the deal. On the other hand there may be situations where the due diligence may suggest changes to enhance the business. For example, the due diligence may lead to the discovery that a trade sale may be more lucrative than an IPO in view of the highly technical nature of the product. The VC's action would then perhaps be to seek agreement, before investing, to modify the product features to better fit in with the product ranges or platforms of the target buyers.

The important point here is that due diligence is not merely to seek confirmation of the presence of huge opportunities, the absence of intolerable downside risks or the realism of the business projections. Due diligence also points to existing or potential weaknesses and the actions that might be taken to correct, improve or control them. Such actions would reduce the investment risks and increase the investment returns for the VC. Taking the trouble to consider and work out such concerns at this stage would avoid rejecting an otherwise good deal, or would further improve a good deal.

The Next Cycle

If it is concluded at this stage that further due diligence work is required, the process moves on to the Plan stage to repeat the cycle. Since there are now some early results from the due diligence, and there is greater understanding of the business dynamics, the relative importance of the issues may have changed, new critical issues may have surfaced, and new information sources may be necessitated. The due diligence framework may be modified accordingly, to change color codes to reflect new priorities, to add new issues or information sources, and to delete unimportant ones. With a revised plan in place, the work proceeds to the Do stage. Most if not all the due diligence would likely be completed in two cycles. Even if the work is not entirely complete, sufficient information would have been obtained, understanding reached, and corrective actions identified to enable conclusions to be made on the deal.

Advantages of PDCA Approach

It is perhaps apparent now why the PDCA approach is advantageous for due diligence work. It provides a systematic and directed approach, avoiding being sidetracked or swamped by numerous unimportant issues. The Plan stage forces thought processes to identify critical issues, whether they contribute to failure or success, to set priorities, and to identify assumptions in the projections that have high impact on the business.

Using the suggested framework, due diligence progress and results are tracked and documented to facilitate assessment in the Check stage. The Act stage forces thoughts and strategies for improvements to the business as well as investment terms and returns. Finally, completion of a cycle provides a gate to consider wrapping up the work, or at least to review any continuation in a meaningful way.

Many VCs use a due diligence checklist. At best, a checklist serves as a reminder to avoid missing important checkpoints, but for it to be comprehensive enough it would run into many pages and become impractical to use. More importantly, it might encourage going through the list mechanically, without thought to focusing the due diligence on important issues that are specific to the deal, their relative importance, and corrective actions that might be taken.

Conclusion of Due Diligence

When the due diligence is completed—or more appropriately when due diligence has reached a satisfactory stage since it often seems unending—conclusions have to be drawn to enable a decision on whether to proceed with the deal.

The framework would be filled with copious notes, spilling into many attachments detailing the due diligence findings. The VC would now have to pick out those findings or concerns that affect the go/no go decision, which are the issues confirmed to be serious, have high adverse impact on performance, and are found to be not amenable to the corrective actions that were suggested at the Check stage.

If no serious issues are found, the VC would be lucky indeed, but should step back and honestly assess whether he has fallen in love with the deal, excited by the merits but blind to the demerits, whether enough thought has been given to the critical business issues, or whether the due diligence has been thorough enough. If none of these is the case, the deal may be happily proceeded with.

More likely, some of the issues may be found to be serious enough to warrant reconsideration of whether to proceed further with the deal. If any one of these is as serious as those described in the previous chapter, then the deal would likely be dropped. Otherwise, the VC may add one more dimension to help in the decision making—the element of probability. For each of the serious issues, an estimate is made of the probability of occurrence, graded into low, mid or high probability. The estimation will depend on pure judgment, and perhaps from information gleaned from the due diligence or experience of the VC. A risk grading is also given to each issue, depending on the degree of seriousness or impact on the business. A Risk versus Probability matrix is then drawn up, as illustrated in Figure 8.3. The descriptions of the issues may be as detailed as necessary.

FIGURE 8.3   RISK vs. PROBABILITY MATRIX

RISK		LOW	MID	HIGH
	HIGH			Technology may not work
	MID		Market acceptance	
	LOW		Management execution	
		LOW	MID	HIGH

PROBABILITY

Inspection of the matrix would help the decision process. In the example in Figure 8.3, the management execution issue is rated as low risk, with mid-probability of occurrence. This implies that management execution problems have some likelihood of occurring but these would not seriously affect the business. However, if this issue falls into the mid-risk, high probability cell, for example, the concern could be serious enough to warrant rejection of the deal.

In this particular example, the risk of the technology not working is high and assessed to have a high probability of occurring. Although this would usually lead to a rejection decision, the VC may still want to pursue the deal, because of the exceptionally high returns if the technology works. The benefit of this analysis is that it points to specific measures the VC should take, for example: to minimize its risk exposure by investing in tranches which are subject to milestone achievements; to find ways to alleviate the technology risks by strengthening the company's technical resources; and perhaps to better balance the high risks by structuring the deal to achieve a bigger share of the potential upside gains. All these may help to bring the deal to be within the VC's risk appetite to allow it to proceed to invest. Otherwise the VC may lose the golden opportunity to capture a big winner.

Some VCs may advocate assigning percentage values to the risks and probabilities to calculate weighted averages, but this may be overdoing it, given the degree of judgment involved. The value of this matrix is not to derive a magical numerical solution, but to trigger the thought processes further, to help in deal negotiations and structuring, and investment decision making. This analysis will also be useful in post-investment monitoring and value-adding work by focusing attention on the high risk areas.

Chapter Recap

In this chapter we discussed the basics of due diligence investigation and how the due diligence process can use the concepts of the PDCA Cycle and its stages:

- o   Plan
- o   Do
- o   Check
- o   Act

We noted the advantages of adopting the PDCA approach for due diligence work and discussed how conclusions can be drawn after completion of due diligence.

9

Due Diligence of Management

The management is arguably the most important aspect of any deal and must be inescapably investigated for every deal. It has been said that good management can turn around an initially bad company, but bad management can destroy a good company. It is also said that the three most important things in a venture deal is management, management, and management.

Some VCs argue that size and growth of the addressed market are more important than management. This is likely to be the perspective of VCs that invest in start-ups and early stage companies, where usually the team is incomplete, often lacking a CEO, but where strong market opportunities have been identified. Often the CEO can be hired or replaced later, but usually little can be done to change market forces. In any case, it is undeniable that management is crucial and hence must be given top priority in any due diligence.

When conducting due diligence, we should focus on the key managers, not forgetting founders who may hold less important management positions but may still have influence on decisions, as well as any external management resources or influences, such as board members, advisors, consultants, angel or institutional investors.

There are many management qualities described in countless books and a very long checklist of qualities can be drawn up. It would not be meaningful to mechanically tick items off the list against each management team member. We should first identify the critical factors that contribute to the success or failure of the business, as described in the previous chapter. We should then determine the management qualities that are necessary and important to achieve the success or to mitigate the risks of failure of the business under investigation.

We must be mindful that many management qualities that contribute to the success of larger or more established companies, as well as those that are necessary for long-term growth, may not be entirely applicable to VC ventures. Some management qualities are intrinsically important to any business, while others may be important in relation to the type of business or the stage of development of the company. We should always assess the relevance of the management qualities to the business and the particular ways in which these qualities affect the business, to arrive at conclusions on the relative importance and impact of each quality to the business under investigation. The PDCA approach and framework suggested in the previous chapter will again be useful to guide the due diligence of management.

The PDCA Approach

In the Plan Stage, we ask several key questions to determine the necessary and important management qualities that contribute to the success and mitigate the risks of failure of the business under investigation:

- o   What are the qualities of the CEO required for this business?
- o   What are the management attributes desirable for this business?
- o   What management skills and experience are required to successfully execute the business plans?
- o   Can the management team adjust and grow as the business changes and develops?
- o   Will the team value the relationship with the VC?
- o   Are the management compensation packages appropriate for this business?

The answers to these questions can then be placed in the second column of the framework in Figure 9.1.

FIGURE 9.1   DUE DILIGENCE OF THE MANAGEMENT

Investigation Area	Critical Success/Failure Factors	Due Diligence Sources	Validity & Seriousness of Impact
The CEO Integrity Entrepreneurship Commitment Adaptability Domain expertise Team dynamics Relationship with VC Compensation			

The investigation areas listed in the first column of the above framework are those where major weaknesses in the management team would endanger the success of a VC-backed venture, and hence could give rise to rejection of the deal. The list is not exhaustive. It would be impractical, and certainly is not the intent of this book, to cover all manner of management strengths and weaknesses. We shall focus only on those that are of greater relevance and importance to VC-backed ventures.

Since the CEO plays the prime role, an important part of the due diligence will be focused on him or her. Even if the position were not filled as yet, some thought would have to be given to the CEO qualities that are required for the business. The other investigation areas are for each member of the team, including the CEO, and to the team as a whole.

It is hoped that the framework and process suggested here will facilitate systematic and effective due diligence of the management. The major ingredients provided serve as pointers and may have to be refined for the particular business and management team under investigation.

In the Do stage, we conduct the planned due diligence, delving into the issues prompted by the key questions raised earlier. The VC starts off by obtaining a list of all key employees and potential hires, with their respective resumes, job descriptions, compensation details, employment contracts if any, and an organization chart.

Here the vital due diligence information source would be the direct interviews with each of the key staff. The interview should not be limited to merely finding out or confirming past qualifications, experience, and knowledge. The VC should invite opinions on the company's potential and risks; ask how the staff can contribute to the company; and include open-ended discussions on topics such as business strategies and hypothetical business problems. Provocative questions could test responsiveness and reveal character traits. Obviously, observation of body language is important. The advice on interviews with knowledgeable persons on page 150 of the previous chapter will also be applicable here. Some VCs resort to personality or psychology tests, but this is not frequently done.

Group interviews and participation in company meetings and functions would be useful to observe team interaction. Third party reference checks with past or present bosses, peers, subordinates, and business associates would supplement the direct interviews.

On completion of this Do stage, the process continues with the Check and Act stages, as described in the previous chapter, and the cycle may be repeated if necessary.

In the following sections we shall elaborate on the issues in each of the investigation areas. However, many of these qualities are obvious and well treated in management books, so our focus will be more towards how these qualities are desirable in the context of VC ventures.

The CEO

There are many important qualities that are required of any CEO, regardless of the type of company. These include leadership, decisiveness, communication and organizational skills, execution strength and results orientation, as well as the qualities such as integrity, entrepreneurship, commitment, and adaptability which will be described in the following sections.

The VC needs to consider those specific CEO qualities that are important and have the most impact on the company in question, and ignore those that are unimportant. For example, great visionary ability would probably not be important to an early stage company, where the top priority is to concentrate on the near term successful execution of the business plans. On the other hand, early stage companies are usually weak in marketing, so a CEO with marketing experience will be an asset. Experience working in start-ups and with VCs would also be very useful. The CEO should also be assessed as part of the management team to identify complementarities of skills and character. It would be advantageous if the CEO has past working relationships with some members of the team, or if the CEO balances the skill sets of the others.

Remember that the key question we asked is: "What are the qualities of the CEO required for *this* business?" Here again it would not be meaningful to have a checklist of all the desirable characteristics, qualifications, and experiences of a CEO, and mechanically tick off those that are strong or weak in the CEO in question, and then conclude whether he or she is suitable on the basis of the number of strong points. What is more important is whether the CEO's skills set and other qualities closely match those that are most important to the company in question, given its type of business, stage of development, and its growth and business strategies.

Therefore it is important for the VC to first determine the specific CEO qualities required by the company in question, and rank them by importance according to the impact on the company. The CEO would then be assessed against these requirements and the degree of impact of the weaknesses and strengths are noted in the last column of the framework in Figure 9.1. This assessment will later be taken into account together with other due diligence findings.

Integrity

This is a quality that is important in any staff. It is particularly important in a VC venture because the VC leaves the day-to-day running of the company to the management team. It would not be difficult for a dishonest CEO or management team to defraud investors or siphon off business or funds. Discovery will often be only after irreparable damage to the company. The sense of integrity should extend beyond honesty and truthfulness into being forthcoming enough to surface problems promptly and to admit mistakes made, so that corrective actions can be considered and taken early enough.

The due diligence of this quality involves checking for consistency of answers, detecting any tendency to avoid questions or not giving direct answers, and observing body language, during interviews. When conducting reference checks, it is likely that direct answers will sometimes not be given, but again, judgment can be based on whether there was hesitation, lack of enthusiasm or avoidance of the question versus a prompt, unqualified endorsement. If some uncertainty is detected, probing further could yield enlightenment.

Experience has shown that it is always better to walk away from a deal when there are doubts about the integrity of the key founder or CEO. If there are doubts about the integrity of other founders or managers, the key founder or CEO has to be confronted to investigate the issue further with the possibility of replacing the person in question.

Entrepreneurship

A young and rapidly developing company faces many risks and uncertainties, and needs a management team that is undaunted by these challenges, that continuously seeks new opportunities, and is flexible enough to adapt and adopt new business strategies. The company will frequently be beset by problems and requires the management team to have persistence, resilience, self-confidence, a sense of urgency, and be goal oriented to work out solutions and not give up. These are all entrepreneurial characteristics which are essential in a team managing a VC-backed venture.

In conducting due diligence, the VC will have to search through the past experience of the team members, particularly the CEO, to discover evidence of entrepreneurial spirit and initiatives, whether successful or failed. During the interactions with the CEO, presence or absence of such traits could be detected through open-ended questions on business strategies and approaches to solving business problems.

Commitment

A measure of commitment would be the amount of cash injected by the founders and managers as equity, and the amount of salary cuts they may be willing to sacrifice. Failing such tangible indicators, this quality is not easy to judge during due diligence, since the team members will obviously put on an impression of commitment when interviewed. Questions put to them on their views of the longer-term future of the company as well as their own long-term plans may provide some indication.

Adaptability

A VC-backed venture undergoes frequent modifications and even transformations of business strategies. As it develops through the stages from a start-up to a company mature enough to be listed, the management skills, styles, systems, and processes undergo changes in parallel. The VC has to have confidence that the management team will be able to adapt to the changing demands on their abilities.

As the company grows, the managers have to balance their entrepreneurial spirit with stricter professionalism and increasing emphasis on establishing and complying with policies, procedures, and controls. As a start-up, the emphasis would be on speed of execution, being task-oriented, and achievement of near term goals. At a later stage, the emphasis would shift towards strategy, planning, longer-term goals, and being more people oriented in management skills and policies.

The VC's due diligence will have to identify those key managers who may not have the capacity and potential to grow, and to assess the impact of future changes of staff or roles. A common occurrence of this issue arises in technology oriented start-ups where there is initially no CEO and the CTO takes on this role. If the due diligence shows that the CTO is unsuitable to be the CEO, this would be a due diligence negative, unless the CTO can be convinced that he will later have to surrender the CEO role. Similarly, the CFO or the Marketing VP, for example, may adequately perform their roles in smaller companies, but may have to later report to more senior executives with greater ability to build up and lead larger teams. Proper due diligence will surface these issues prior to investment, so that satisfactory agreement can be reached to resolve them, failing which the issues would be showstoppers.

Domain Expertise

Expertise is the summation of skills, knowledge, and experience. Obviously the ideal would be to have management team members that have strong expertise in their respective professional fields and functional responsibilities, have good business sense, and relevant experience in the business of the company. The due diligence should note any serious inadequacies so that they can be evaluated based on their impact on the future of the company and to consider any corrective actions that may have to be agreed upon prior to investment. On the other hand, a good track record with relevant experience and evidence of good understanding of the company's business, market, competitors, and cost and profit drivers would be noted as positives.

The professional and functional expertise required of the CEO, CTO, CFO, COO, and other key executives are well known, but for the sake of completeness, we shall briefly review them. We have described those for the CEO. For the CTO, due diligence will focus on his technical qualifications and experience in the relevant technologies required by the business. It would be advantageous if he had led R&D or product development teams before. It would be important that he has a sense of balance between product perfection, time to market, and development costs.

For the CFO, besides finance or accounting qualifications, it would be preferable that she has worked in early stage companies previously, set up accounting systems, and established financial controls and procedures. Cash flow management skills would be important for young and fast-growing companies. It would be advantageous if she is comfortable with technology and has some understanding of operations.

The COO, who may not be required initially, should preferably have technical or business qualifications, and relevant operational experience. His skill set would be similar to that of the CEO, except that he would need to be more meticulous in resolving daily internal issues while the CEO would be more focused on external, bigger picture issues.

The chief marketing person may have a business or marketing qualification, and should have experience in building up a marketing team and a marketing support group, as well as establishing marketing and product positioning strategies. Having a good network with relevant channel partners and distributors would be advantageous.

When interviewing a key manager to investigate domain expertise, the VC should find out about specific projects and contributions made in prior jobs. The VC should also take care to look for gaps in employment history which are unaccounted for, and reasons for leaving prior companies. There have also been cases of forgeries of qualifications and work experience. If doubts arise, further investigation will have to be made.

Team Dynamics

Team dynamics is how the members of the management team interact with each other and includes how each of them interact with the CEO and with any founder who may not be in management but may still exercise some influence on decisions. Due diligence to understand the dynamics and to observe any friction or incompatibility is important. This is because the team will be subject to many stresses and strains as the company grows. Interests should be aligned and team members should complement, support, and encourage each other. In particular, the CEO should command respect and loyalty and should be able to hold the team together. It would be an advantage if some of the key managers have worked together in the past.

One of the common failures of start-ups and early stage companies is the breakup of the team, when they succumb to the pressures and problems. While the departure of a less important team member may be a welcome weeding process, it is a serious problem if the whole team breaks down.

Due diligence of this aspect would be by observation at group activities and group interviews. Asking for personal views of colleagues could also reveal the nature of relationships.

Relationship with the VC

Developing rapport with the founders and management team is important for the VC in view of the future close working relationship extending over several years. The team members must share a common goal to build the company successfully towards an IPO and should welcome the help and partnership of the VC to achieve the goal.

Some entrepreneurs are only interested in the VC's funds and consider inquiries from the VC as bothersome, unnecessary, and perhaps even as interference. They may also not appreciate the value of working with and tapping the resources and networks of the VC. Obviously during the deal discussions, the entrepreneurs will hide this attitude and appear to be friendly with the VC. It would take some due diligence to unearth the entrepreneurs' true character, with clever questioning or from reference checks on past relationships with investors.

Compensation

Besides conducting due diligence on management qualities, an important related area to investigate is management compensation. The VC has to check whether the compensation for each of the key managers, including the CEO, is performance-based, adequate, market comparable, and not overly generous. Employee benefits should be commensurate with the size of the company and in line with market practice. If the due diligence investigation finds any of these to be out of line, it should be noted for subsequent discussion to seek agreement on corrective adjustments prior to or at the time of investment.

During due diligence discussions, the VC would have to check whether the key managers have any objection to employment contracts, which would incorporate confidentiality and non-competition provisions. Sometimes tacit agreement may also need to be secured for compensation to be frozen for an agreed upon period, especially for early stage companies prior to revenue generation, and such agreement will be captured in the employment contracts.

Since the motivation of key staff is critical to the success of the venture, the VC must ensure fairness and competitiveness in compensation. On the other hand, if there are cases of overgenerosity, such as high salaries or benefits for the founders, these must be rectified as part of the deal negotiations.

Chapter Recap

In this chapter we reviewed the framework and process for due diligence investigation of the management team. We looked deeper into the due diligence of the CEO and several important qualities that should be investigated for each key manager:

- o Integrity
- o Entrepreneurship
- o Commitment
- o Adaptability
- o Domain expertise

We also discussed the importance of investigating team dynamics, whether the team values the relationship with the VC, and the compensation of the team members.

10

Due Diligence of Marketing & the Market

S ome VCs argue that a large and growing market is more important to a deal than having a strong management team. They argue that without such a market, no company can grow and succeed sufficiently to generate the high returns that they expect from their investments. On the other hand, a weak management team can be strengthened or replaced.

There is no need to debate the relative importance of the management team and the market to a deal. In considering a deal, the VC firm would be failing in its duties if due diligence is not carried out on either the management or the market.

Due diligence of the market aspect of the deal includes investigation of marketing strategies, market characteristics, and market risks. Taking the PDCA approach again, we ask several key questions at the Plan stage. These relate to the important market factors that can contribute to the success or cause the failure of the business under consideration:

- o What market need does the product or service fulfill?
- o What is the size of the market opportunity?
- o How fast is the market growing?
- o What are the characteristics and dynamics of the target markets?
- o What would be the right marketing strategies to capture market share?

o   How can market share be sustained or grown?
o   What are the market risks?

As stated previously, it is all right if the key questions overlap to some extent. It is important, at this stage, to be able to look for potentials and risks from many angles. Depending on the type of business, there may be other key questions that are relevant.

Next, we form the framework for the due diligence, as shown in Figure 10.1.

FIGURE 10.1   DUE DILIGENCE OF THE MARKET

Investigation Area	Critical Success/Failure Factors	Due Diligence Sources	Validity & Seriousness of Impact
Market need Market potential Market characteristics Marketing strategies Market risks			

The investigation areas in the above framework are structured and sequenced to provide a thorough and logical analysis. First the product or service has to be assessed to determine what market need is being fulfilled. Then the market potential in terms of market size and growth rate has to be assessed. If the potential is found to be unattractive, the deal may be dropped without the need to address the other areas. Next, the market characteristics, in terms of structure, trends, and competition, have to be investigated and properly understood. Then the marketing strategies, such as those related to promotion, pricing, product positioning, and distribution channels, can be assessed as to whether they are appropriate and consistent with the market characteristics, or whether there are better alternative strategies.

Even if marketing strategies appear to be appropriate and consistent, due diligence investigation has to be made to assess the market risks that may cause these strategies to fail. These market risks include demand shifts, market downturns, emergence of new competitors or product substitutes. Backup or counter-strategies could then be assessed. Also, if the company is a new entrant into an existing market or an entrant into a new market, there are risks that the company may not gain market traction. Market traction means gaining a foothold in the market, as well as sustaining and growing market share. All these market risks can have dramatic adverse impact on the prospects of the company.

At this point it is worth repeating that thought must be given to the importance and relevance of the issues that are raised to the business under investigation, so that the due diligence can be focused and productive. If there is doubt on the importance or relevance, the issue should be included so that the doubt may be clarified through the due diligence work. The validity and seriousness of the issue to the business would be noted down in the last column of the framework in Figure 10.1.

Sources of due diligence information would be from interviews with the CEO and the chief marketing officer, market consultants, industry experts, existing and potential customers, competitors if possible, trade associations, market surveys, industry reports, and trade statistics. Existing customers are obviously an important source for feedback on relationships, satisfaction with price, delivery, quality, technical support, future orders, market trends, and comparisons with competing companies.

You are by now familiar with the PDCA process, so we shall not go through it again, except to reiterate what is to be done at the important Act stage. Due diligence is not merely to validate and verify claims and assumptions. It should prescribe actions to correct, improve, or control any detected weaknesses through modifications or renegotiations of business concepts and strategies, business projections, or investment terms. These actions serve to reduce investment risks and enhance returns.

We now move on to the issues that may be faced in each of the marketing investigation areas. As this is not a marketing textbook we shall not delve into marketing theory, but shall just focus on marketing issues that the VC may need to consider and to investigate.

Market Need

The VC has to first understand the product or service and what market need is being addressed. A product or service may be acquired for one or more of the following purposes:

- o   As a tool to do a job or solve a problem
- o   As an enabling device or means for a job to be done or done better or for a solution to be applied
- o   As a means to add value by reducing cost, saving time or increasing productivity
- o   As a fulfillment of a physical, emotional or intellectual need

Understanding the nature of the need helps in assessing how real and critical the need is. If the need is real and critical enough, sometimes fancifully called "mission critical," there will be motivation to pay for the product or service, provided the features of the product or service match and satisfy the need. However, the VC should not jump to the conclusion that the company's product or service is inferior simply because it does not fully satisfy the need. This has to be viewed in comparison with competing products or services. The limitation could be technology or costs which would affect all suppliers. Customers will have no alternatives and would still purchase, if the need is critical and the product or service at least solves some of the problems, while waiting for technology or costs to improve. In fact, if the features are more than what is required, customers may not pay any premium for the extras.

If the need is already being met by other companies, the VC would need to investigate how this company's product or service fulfills the need better than others. Due diligence of the entrepreneur's claims of a better mousetrap will have to be carried out. If the need is not presently fulfilled, the VC would have to investigate whether this company's product or service overcomes the economic or practical problems that might have hindered others, unless it is a newly identified need. Examples of economic or practical problems would be exorbitant costs incurred in the manufacture or distribution of the product, or provision of the service, or complexity of the product preventing selling to mass consumers. It may be the case that the company has discovered ways to overcome these problems through new enabling technology, product simplification methods or a low cost business model.

The VC has to investigate whether the proposed business or revenue model is the best among the many that may be possible to fulfill the need. For example, a company may manufacture the product or subcontract the manufacture, or just be a design company, or produce the key components (such as chip sets) to supply to product manufacturers, or license the technology, or enter into a joint venture. The aim would be to choose the most profitable model, taking into consideration constraints such as funding, management capability, and other resources.

Another example of finding the best revenue model is in the provision of an Internet-based service. The revenue models that may be possible could be:

- o Sales of the services combined with annual license fees
- o Subscription fee for the services, on monthly, usage, or transaction value basis
- o Free services, but earning fees from advertisers
- o Free services, building value through a huge users base
- o Licensing of the technology
- o A combination of the above, by suitably packaging the services

Choice of the best model depends on many factors such as the specific type of service, the company's resources, and management capability, but perhaps a good guide would be the extent and strength of the market need, which would turn into the best value for the company.

Not only must there be a real and significant market need, the need must also be continuing and not one-off and must be large or widespread, so that the business can be sustained and grown. In these respects, the VC has to investigate whether the company has a product road map to fulfill the continuing need, and whether the business is scalable to exploit increasing demand.

In summary, the due diligence issues in investigating market need consist of the following:

- o   What is the nature of the market need that is being fulfilled?
- o   Is the market need real and significant enough?
- o   Do the features of the proposed product or service match the need and how well do they satisfy the need?
- o   If the need is fulfilled by others, how does the proposed product or service fulfill the need better?
- o   If the need is not yet fulfilled, has the company overcome the economic or practical problems that might have previously prevented such fulfillment?
- o   Is the proposed business model to fulfill the need the most profitable?
- o   Is it a continuing market need and does the company have a product road map?
- o   Is the market need large or widespread and is the business scalable?

Market Potential

The size and growth rate of the market are not the only indicators of market potential. Other factors such as stability and predictability of market trends, sensitivity to economic or industry cycles, strengths and weaknesses of competitors, barriers to entry, as well as complexities and costs of distribution may color the attractiveness of a market.

However, in the due diligence, the VC should look first at size and growth rate, both at present and in the future. The other factors will arise from the other investigation areas. The VC has to be careful not to rashly dismiss smaller markets or slower growth rates, without considering the other qualifying factors.

For example, a large market may not be that attractive if there are many entrenched incumbent competitors. On the other hand, a slowly growing market may not necessarily be unattractive, if many incumbent high-cost suppliers are dropping out of the target segment and moving towards higher margin segments. The one or two remaining suppliers with low-cost operations would find their market shares growing at a much faster rate than the overall market, and hence could be attractive medium term investment opportunities. An example is the company called Varitronix Ltd, described in Chapter 6.

When proclaiming attractive market potential, entrepreneurs are prone to start off with a huge market base like China's population or the installed base of PCs in the world, quoting market shares of several similar companies in the market and claiming a supposedly conservative smaller share, which still works out to be a large number. The VC should be wary of such arithmetic, and should investigate more appropriate market segmentation methods as part of the due diligence. The VC should also keep in mind that market share is not simply handed on a platter; the company must have the right marketing strategies to capture the share. Such strategies must be crafted to suit the characteristics of the target market segment.

Market Characteristics

Due diligence work on the characteristics of the target market segments is necessary to better understand the real market dynamics and potential and the correctness of the proposed strategies to reap the opportunities. The nature of the business will dictate the areas to investigate, but the following will be inescapable:

- o   Market structure
- o   Competitors and nature of competition
- o   Demand and price trends

The VC would have to investigate characteristics such as whether the target market is structured as a monopoly, an oligopoly or is fragmented; how is the market segmented and the dispersion and characteristics of customers among the segments; whether the market is protected by import tariffs or have price or production restrictions; and whether there are natural entry barriers such as technology, capital costs, special supplier or customer relationships, or imposed barriers such as government licensing or regulatory controls. The VC would also need to look into the structure and costs of distribution channels and the network of strategic marketing partnerships.

When investigating the competitive landscape, the VC would have to know the existing competitors, their products, production capacities, market shares, strengths and weaknesses, strategies and plans; as well as to uncover emerging competitors. The VC would need to appreciate the intensity of competition and the possible reactions of existing companies to market entrants.

The VC would also need to understand the basis of competition, such as product features, quality, reliability, ease of use, customer service, ready availability of products, price, or a combination of these. If the company's strategy is to compete in existing market segments, the VC would have to evaluate how well it can compete on the basis of what the market segments demand. If the company intends to address new market segments, the due diligence would focus on what are the market needs that are unfulfilled by existing suppliers and how well the company will serve those needs.

The VC would need to find out what are the demand and price trends of the products and markets, such as industry cycles, seasonal fluctuations, changing fads, constancy of brands, market windows, sustainability of demand over the next five years or so, price trends, pricing power, cost structures, sales lead times, and factors that affect demand and prices.

With an understanding of the market characteristics, and taking into consideration the stage of development of the company and the resources available to it, the VC can properly assess whether the company's proposed marketing strategies and plans would be appropriate and effective.

Marketing Strategies

Herein we are not discussing the principles and theories of marketing but to provide guidance on the due diligence of the company's marketing strategies. That is, to suggest investigation areas and issues related to the strategies and policies. The key areas to look into would include:

- o   Marketing objectives
- o   Product strategy
- o   Pricing

- Promotion
- Distribution
- Staffing and incentives

Marketing Objectives

The VC has to check that marketing objectives are succinctly stated, with measurable time-based targets. They have to be consistent with the company's overall objectives and resources available. For young companies the objectives must obviously be aimed at generating revenue and not on corporate image or brand building. All the marketing strategies must be based on and support the stated objectives.

Product Strategy

When describing product features, entrepreneurs have the tendency to wax lyrical about superior technology and extra bells and whistles, losing sight of the fact that a product or service is to fulfill a need. The emphasis of the product strategy should be on how well the customer's need is satisfied. The customer does not care whether the technology is superior, only whether it works. Similarly the customer is only interested in those bells and whistles that are relevant and important to his need. The VC's due diligence on the market need, as well as product features, described earlier in this chapter, would be useful here.

Besides product attributes, the VC would have to investigate other elements of the product strategy, such as product positioning and product road map. The VC has to assess whether the product is properly positioned, differentiating it from competing products, so that potential customers do not perceive it as a me-too product. Products may be positioned based on categories of consumers, usage, features, benefits, or combinations of these. The VC has to assess whether the chosen positioning best suits the products under investigation.

Sometimes, especially for software, the product may be tweaked to position it as complementary to the products of entrenched competitors instead of being head-on competing products. Sometimes, as suggested by Clayton

Christensen and Michael Raynor[9], it may be better to reconfigure the product and position it as a low-end disruption when facing established competitors, or as a new-market disruption aimed at existing non-consumers, when faced with established products that are already meeting market needs.

A product road map is important to plan out a consistent long-term product strategy and to achieve growth. The VC should assess whether the product extensions help to deepen the market and whether the product range broadening helps to penetrate new market segments and takes opportunities of new market windows opening up. The VC should also check for consistency between the product pipeline and the projected increases in revenue.

If the company is more established, it would be useful to check the historical product road map to assess the accomplishments of the company and the performance and life cycles of past products.

Pricing

Since VC-backed companies are likely to have a limited product range, many pricing strategies that are more relevant in retailing would not be applicable. Most frequently the company would want to price as high as the target customers would bear, so as to generate the profits to fund the past and continuing product and market development costs. This would be coupled with a discount structure that will allow selective market penetration and maintenance of market traction.

The VC would have to investigate whether the proposed pricing structure is realistic, comparable with competitors, and attractive to potential customers.

Promotion

Typically, VC-backed companies have a limited promotion budget, so the strategy has to be focused, preferring lower cost or no-cost methods (such

---

[9] Clayton Christensen and Michael Raynor, *The Innovator's Solution*, Boston, Harvard Business School Publishing, 2003.

as publicity programs), and aimed at shorter term results. The promotional strategy and content of marketing collateral should be consistent with the product positioning and directed towards selected target market segments. The VC has to assess how consistent, targeted, and cost-effective are the proposed promotion activities and whether sales goals are set for these activities.

Distribution

To get its products to end users, the company may choose between direct or indirect selling, or have a combination of these methods. Direct selling involves having a sales force, working in the field and in the premises. The in-premises sales force would support inquiries or orders via the phone, mail, or Internet. Indirect selling would be through wholesalers, distributors, retailers, multi-level marketers or strategic partners or representatives such as value-added resellers, OEMs (original equipment manufacturers), systems integrators, bundling partners, or marketing agents.

The VC has to assess the suitability and cost-effectiveness of the chosen distribution strategy and the reputation of major channel partners. Important contracts that are entered into with channel partners would have to be examined for sales strategy, targets, exclusivity, if any, commitment of resources, and termination conditions. Benefits of strategic partnerships such as extending the sales network or customer base; exploiting the technology, brand, or product complementarities of the partner; or riding on the customer support or service infrastructure, would also have to be assessed.

The VC also has to have the comfort that the company treats channel partners just as importantly as its own sales staff, providing adequate support and incentives to them and monitoring their performance.

Staffing and Incentives

Though relating more to the company's policies than strategies, investigation of the quality of the sales and marketing staff and their incentive schemes are an important part of the due diligence on the market and marketing strategies. A most attractive market and the best marketing strategies would be worthless without an effective and motivated team.

The due diligence on management would have focused on the senior staff. Here the VC would assess the key sales managers. Firstly, how they are organized, such as by product groups, territories, or types of accounts, would be assessed as to whether it is consistent with the company's marketing strategies and resources. Secondly, the qualities of the key staff and the incentive schemes would be examined to ensure they are aligned with the strategies and sales plans. Finally, the VC would need to ensure that the front line is adequately supported by sales administration and technical support staff, within the budget constraints.

Market Risks

Having investigated the potential and characteristics of the target market, and the company's marketing strategies, the VC needs to investigate and assess the risks of failure to capture market share. Such failure could be due to internal factors such as weaknesses in the marketing team, the strategies and execution of the plans, or external factors such as inability to gain market traction and unanticipated shifts in the market.

Due diligence of the marketing team and marketing strategies will yield many clues to the team's capability to strategize and execute responses to market changes. The VC should also assess the team's ability to work closely with development, engineering, and production teams, by channeling market feedback and customer requirements and jointly developing consistent product and marketing strategies that respond to or even anticipate market changes. It is important that the VC consciously looks for these qualities and does not get caught in arguments over the finer points of the proposed strategies or alternatives. Often strategies and plans have to be put to the test, monitored, and constantly modified. How well these can be done depends on the quality of the marketing team. We shall now turn to market risks caused by external factors.

Market Traction

This risk relates to start-ups that are launching their products into the market or to companies launching new products. Since the products or services are new, market acceptance is uncertain. Without market traction, whatever initial sales will soon dwindle away. Although it involves some speculation, it is important for the VC to assess this risk if the company is launching new products, as market traction failure would lead to business failure.

Market traction failure could be due to:

- o   The business model
- o   Customer issues
- o   Competition
- o   Dependency on standards

If the product cannot be differentiated or the business cannot be scaled, revenue will remain limited and market traction cannot take hold. If the sales cycle or supplier qualification period is so long that funding is exhausted before significant revenues are generated, or marketing budgets are trimmed, this could lead to self-fulfilling market traction failure. If the market is very fragmented, the company's initial range of products may be too limited to gain much traction on a total basis. The VC has to detect such inherent weaknesses in the business model or business characteristics.

Market traction failure is often due to difficulties in securing customer adoption or loyalty. Potential customers may dislike the costs and efforts in extensive education and training required in adopting the product. Worse, if adoption requires change of customer behavior, habits, usage patterns, systems, or procedures, most potential customers would choose another product that does not add such pain. If there are competitors that are more established, customers would rather not be a guinea pig to a market entrant and instead rely on well-proven, although more expensive, suppliers.

Strong reaction from existing suppliers to a new market entrant could preempt market traction. Existing suppliers could reduce price or reconfigure their products to compete head on feature for feature. In some industry sectors, such as mobile phones and high-definition TV, time is required for common standards to be resolved. An application or product that requires compatibility and interoperability will not gain market traction until common standards are accepted. Products that require new legislations or regulations to be imposed will suffer if there are delays in passing them.

These are some common examples of difficulties in gaining market traction that the VC should investigate further if the business under due diligence might face any of them.

Market Shifts

A shift in the market may cause loss of sales which could be deadly to a young company which would likely not have a diversified market base. Many shifts are not anticipated and the VC cannot be faulted if due diligence fails to foresee the event. On the other hand, many shifts are preceded by much industry or market discussion, although somewhat speculative, and in some cases, trends may already be emerging. These could be detected by wider due diligence, provided the VC thinks of the possibility and takes the effort to investigate further.

A market shift could be favorable, providing new or enlarged market opportunities. However, we are concerned here with unfavorable shifts, the likelihood of which has to be thought through and checked by the VC. Such effort would be very worthwhile if an investment is averted in a company that could later suddenly turn for the worse.

Besides the obvious causes such as changes in fashion, prices, the economy, trade patterns and barriers, war and natural disasters, as well as changes in regulatory measures, market shifts faced by VC-backed companies could be caused by changes in technology, emergence of substitutes, or emergence of a formidable competitor, such as Microsoft, in the case of companies developing software applications.

Obviously the VC cannot afford to investigate each and every one of such possibilities, but should concentrate on those that the business at hand is most susceptible to. For example, a precision metal component may be competing on the basis of superior tooling or machining fixture design. If customers require a change of the material or a change in design of the component, the tooling or fixture may be rendered irrelevant. The VC should then concentrate on checking with customers on the possibility of changes in materials or design which might cause the company to lose its competitive advantage.

Chapter Recap

In this chapter we discussed the framework and process for due diligence investigation of the company's marketing function and the market. We started the process by gaining an understanding of the market need that is being fulfilled by the company. We then had to investigate the potential size of the need and growth rate that may be possible in fulfilling the need. Next we had to study the characteristics of the target market and to assess the appropriateness and effectiveness of the company's:

o   Marketing objectives
o   Product strategy
o   Pricing strategy
o   Promotion strategy
o   Distribution strategy
o   Marketing staffing and incentives

We concluded with a discussion on two major risks a company may face in the market:

o   Market traction failure
o   Market shifts

11

Due Diligence of Manufacturing

This chapter describes the due diligence of a company that has a manufacturing facility. Such due diligence will be focused on the capability of the company to produce the products cost-effectively, deliver them on time, and with acceptable quality and reliability.

If the company is at an early stage and does not have a manufacturing facility but instead is still developing its product, the section on due diligence of Research and Development in this chapter would be relevant. If the company does not produce hardware but instead produces software or provides services, only certain sections in this chapter may be applicable. Production of software or provision of services, like manufacture of hardware, has to be carried out cost-effectively, delivered or installed on time, and with acceptable quality and reliability. Due diligence of these aspects would therefore be similar. If the company subcontracts the manufacture of its products, then the due diligence described in this chapter would be applicable to the subcontractors.

The due diligence of a manufacturing operation can be very complicated because of the complex organization of many departments, functions, procedures, and interrelationships. As in previous chapters, we shall use the PDCA approach and develop a framework that will enable a systematic and effective due diligence process.

The five fundamental objectives of a manufacturing operation are to produce:

o   The right product
o   To the right quantity
o   On time
o   At the lowest cost
o   With acceptable quality

Therefore, the due diligence of a manufacturing operation would be to gain good understanding of the manufacturing and supporting processes and to assess the ability of the operation and the difficulties it may face to achieve the objectives of producing the right product to the right quantity—on time, at the lowest cost, and with quality that meets or exceeds customer requirements.

A wide-ranging checklist of questions could help to gain an understanding of a business. However, it would neither be meaningful nor productive to mechanically go through a standard checklist for every different kind of business. Instead, the due diligence work has to focus on the particular business that is being investigated and attempt to thoughtfully elicit all the important positive and negative factors that may contribute to the success or failure of the manufacturing operation in that business. A few key questions can help to unlock these factors.

We follow the PDCA methodology described in previous chapters on due diligence. At the Plan stage of the PDCA cycle, some of the key questions that the VC should ask would be:

o   What can cause failure in any of the five manufacturing objectives?
o   How are the systems set up to prevent such failure?
o   What corrective action would be taken in event of such failure?
o   What programs are in place to improve the systems and processes?

The VC would interview each of the department heads with these questions. The answers, together with the VC's own opinions on these questions, would form the framework for due diligence at the Do stage. Such a framework is illustrated in Figure 11.1.

FIGURE 11.1   DUE DILIGENCE OF THE MANUFACTURING OPERATION

Investigation Area	Critical Success/Failure Factors	Due Diligence Sources	Validity & Seriousness of Impact
Manufacturing: The right product To the right quantity On time At the lowest cost With acceptable quality Preventive measures Corrective actions Improvement programs			

A manufacturing plant usually produces multiple products or different models of a product. It is therefore critical to manage the production so that the correct mix of products or model configurations is produced to the right quantities respectively and to be completed according to the required time schedule. There can be many factors or variables that have to be incorporated in the plans, and well-laid plans are all too often upset. Therefore the operation must have in place measures to prevent or avoid occurrences of failure, and if and when it happens, as it often will, corrective actions can be quickly taken. Any downtime or quality problems can be very costly. The VC has to understand the factors that can cause a failure to produce the right product to the right quantity and on time, and the factors that can help successful achievement of these objectives.

The manufacturing plant also has to ensure that cost targets and customer quality requirements are met, and to continually find ways to reduce cost and improve quality. The VC must find out what actions are taken in these areas. The VC must also be convinced that cost and quality consciousness reside not only in the Finance or Quality Assurance departments but in everyone in the plant, since all departments contribute to and affect cost and quality.

The specific issues that may arise in each of the investigation areas will become clear when we later discuss how the framework is applied to each of the departments of a manufacturing organization. We shall focus on the key departments that have direct impact on the achievement of the objectives of the manufacturing plant: Materials, Production, Manufacturing Engineering, Incoming Quality Control, and Quality Assurance. We shall also discuss the due diligence of the R&D, Finance, and Human Resource departments, which support and have indirect impact on the performance of the plant. In our discussion of the R&D department we shall discuss due diligence of technology, which is important for high-tech companies. The specific names and organization structure of the departments may vary from company to company, but our choice would be representative. For the sake of simplicity, we shall designate the head of each department as a manager, as there are a variety of titles used in practice.

Obviously it would be impossible to anticipate or discuss every eventuality or issue that may arise. We shall only go through several illustrative examples. Again, our desire is not to look for set answers but to understand the framework and the process so that they can be usefully applied in any given due diligence situation.

The due diligence of a manufacturing operation is not complete without a plant tour, or several tours, to inspect and verify the systems and processes established by the department heads and described by them during the interviews. We end the chapter with a description of what are some of the good practices and weaknesses that may be revealed through careful observation and questioning during the tour.

Materials

The first question that the VC would fire at the materials manager would be: What issue in the Materials Department would cause failure to produce the right product, or the right quantity, or on time, or at the lowest cost or with acceptable quality? Most likely the answer would be: materials shortage, which affects product configurations, production quantity, timeliness of output, production cost, and sometimes quality. If the company has a high volume manufacturing operation, a disruption can be very costly.

Poor planning of materials supply by the Materials Department is only one of the many possible causes of a component shortage situation. A supplier may suddenly face a production problem and cannot deliver. A supplier delivery may be rejected due to a quality problem. A significant change, at short notice, of finished product delivery schedule or product mix might cause a mismatch between component availability and requirement. A particular lot of materials in the stores, previously accepted by Incoming Quality Control, may be found to be unusable on the production line, due to quality deterioration during storage or other reasons. Another reason may be an Engineering Change Notification (ECN) issued by the Engineering Department requiring a change in specifications of a component or the addition of a new component. These are typical examples of causes of a component shortage situation in a manufacturing plant.

The VC, in questioning the materials manager, must first find out what processes are in place in the Materials Department to provide for the timely availability of components; what measures are in place to prevent component shortages; what corrective actions would be taken if a shortage occurs; and what programs, if any, are in progress or planned, to improve the situation.

For example, the materials manager may reply that the materials planners use a sophisticated Material Requirements Planning (MRP) system; that there is double sourcing of critical components and components with long lead times; that if the shortage is due to a supplier problem, alternate approved sources will be quickly located and a SWAT team of purchasing staff and incoming quality engineers would immediately visit the guilty supplier; and that there is no improvement program needed as present systems and efforts are adequate.

Based on these answers, the VC would note down that in the Do stage of the due diligence, he would check the frequency of materials shortages and how serious were the events. He would also verify how well the processes cited by the materials manager are actually carried out. For example, it often happens that a young company that has recently installed a computerized MRP system may have materials planners that are still furtively using spreadsheets and doing manual calculations, instead of solely relying on the computer reports. They do not trust the new system and indeed errors can be generated because input data such as bills of materials are not kept updated.

Besides verifying compliance and adequacy of systems, the VC may also test the materials manager by asking for or making suggestions for improvements, such as implementing a supplier performance rating system and rating suppliers in terms of cost, quality, and delivery. Such a system will progressively improve the quality of the company's supplier base, which in turn helps the company's cost, quality, and delivery performance.

The VC would note down the responses to his questions, which will indicate the quality and attitude of the materials manager. If the VC finds out that the company has been plagued by frequent parts shortages, or the VC has doubts about the reliability of suppliers, he may need to go deeper into the due diligence, such as visiting the suppliers of single-sourced and critical parts to check their quality and reliability, or perhaps to check whether there are important suppliers disgruntled by price reductions or reduced orders. If he suspects that the problems are internal, he may need to interview materials planners, purchasing staff, and product engineers in charge of bills of materials to assess how well the internal systems and procedures are operating, and perhaps even interview finance staff, who would perhaps be more open and objective, being independent from the materials department.

These examples show how the application of the framework leads to the identification of issues at different levels that are relevant to the business and have impact on the success or failure of the business. How deep and detailed the investigation should be depends on the VC's assessment of the seriousness of the issues.

Another important issue that could arise from the discussion with the materials manager is inventory control. It would reflect poorly on the materials manager if he does not bring this up as an issue that is important to him. On one hand the materials manager has to ensure adequate and prompt supply of materials to the production lines, on the other hand he cannot excessively overstock and has to periodically purge the stores of old, non-moving, unusable, or obsolete materials. At the same time he has to ensure accurate accounting of every single piece of inventory in the stores, which means accurate recording and tracking of receipts and issues of inventory items.

Improper inventory control could result in parts shortages, increased financing costs, and inventory write-offs. The VC would need to ask about the inventory management process, what preventive measures are in place against excessive inventory and inventory write-offs, what corrective actions may be taken when an excess inventory situation occurs, and what programs are there to improve inventory management.

As an example, the materials manager may reply that his department uses a computerized inventory control system linked to the MRP system and that he has regular review meetings with his purchasing and materials planning staff, including engineering and finance staff, to find ways to use or dispose of any excess inventory. He may also be working with the incoming QC manager to initiate a Just-In-Time (JIT) program with key suppliers, so that parts are delivered only when needed, resulting in minimizing inventory levels.

Further due diligence may be required for issues that the VC thinks would be important enough to require verification, or for issues where the replies from the materials manager are not entirely satisfactory. For example, the VC may need to go deeper by asking for relevant information such as inventory turns, frequency of cycle counts, physical stock-takes, past write-offs, economic order quantities, and safety stock levels. Besides having data to evaluate, the responsiveness and ready availability of the information, or otherwise, will be good indicators of the quality of the systems and processes in place.

Production

The Production Department is another important department for due diligence as innumerable issues may arise that can impact the company's ability to produce the right configuration of products, at the right quantities, on time, and with acceptable quality. Again, the framework recommended in this chapter may be applied to identify and zero in on the critical issues that are relevant to the manufacturing operation under investigation.

Issues that could arise would likely relate to:

o   Production Control: How effective is the production planning and control system in ensuring that the right product configurations are produced to the right quantities and according to the required delivery schedules?

o   Shop Floor Control: Is there a shop floor control system to track the work in progress (WIP), to help manage configuration mix, as well as to report outputs, yields, and cycle times at key production and test stations?

o   Process Control: Is there a statistical process control (SPC) system to acquire data, analyze them, and report on process variability and process capability?

o   Quality Management: Does the plant practice Total Quality Management (TQM), involving production employees and all other employees?

o   Quality Standards: Has the manufacturing plant achieved GMP (Good Manufacturing Practice) or relevant ISO 9000 standards?

Besides the above questions, the VC may also enquire whether the company has six sigma or zero defect programs. Many of these systems and processes may be integrated into an Enterprise Resource Planning (ERP) System. Implementation of these systems and processes is what one would expect in a world-class manufacturing operation. Of course that would be too much to expect from a young or newly established manufacturing operation. In such a case, the VC may have to scale down the expectations, but use such standards as benchmarks to measure the company's current operation. Commencement of initiatives in these areas would be a good sign, even though early attempts may rely on manual systems and may be limited in scope.

The answers given by the production manager will reveal the ability of the production operation to produce the right product configurations, to the right quantities, on time, at lowest cost and acceptable quality, the ability to prevent production problems and take corrective actions when needed, and the extent of improvement programs in place. The answers will also reveal the knowledge and capability of the manufacturing staff to build the operation to world-class standards, which should be the expectation and aspiration of management.

The follow-up due diligence effort will be focused on verifying the strengths and weaknesses, and assessment of the seriousness of their impact on the success or failure of the business.

Even plants that have installed the most sophisticated systems can have instances of non-compliance, lapses in controls, and ad-hoc production problems, which can only be detected by inspection of the shop floor. They will not be revealed by inspection of nicely written policies and procedures or by merely interviewing the production manager. We shall discuss the important observations that can be made on the shop floor in the section on the Plant Tour.

Manufacturing Engineering

This department supports the manufacturing operation and may have several sections such as Line Engineering, which develops and maintains machinery, tooling, and assembly fixtures for the line; Test Engineering, which develops and maintains the test equipment and software; Product Engineering, which is responsible for the specifications of all the product configurations including the respective bills of materials; Document Control, which controls archiving, updating, and release of all technical documents; and Facilities, which maintains all plant facilities. There may be some variation in the organization and naming of sections from company to company.

It would be useful for the VC to go through the department's organization structure with the manufacturing engineering manager, as the lack of a functional section may reveal weakness in the management of that function. For example, the lack of a Document Control section should prompt the VC to question how engineering drawings and specification sheets are controlled and updated, and whether there is a formal engineering change notification (ECN) process. Improper control of documents will result in departments having different versions of drawings and specifications and documents that are not updated, which will lead to wrong configurations and poor quality of products being produced.

Similarly if weakness is detected in the Facilities section, the VC should be prompted to dig deeper in the due diligence, such as finding out the age of the building, air-conditioning plant and other facilities, preventive maintenance schedules, and history of breakdowns. Downtime due to breakdown of plant equipment or facilities can be costly and a history of such events would reflect poor management, or management trying to cut corners.

A positive sign would be the existence of a Value Engineering section, which would be responsible for seeking improvements in the products, processes or manufacturing equipment and tooling, to reduce cost, improve quality or increase performance. Successful efforts by this group would help sustain competitiveness of products.

Incoming Quality Control

Issues that may arise in and from the Incoming Quality Control (IQC) department that may affect the plant's ability to produce the right products to the right quantities, on time, at the lowest cost and with acceptable quality, could be categorized under supplier quality issues and materials quality issues.

Quality problems faced by suppliers would lead to disruption of materials supply, resulting in production downtime, increased cost, and if serious enough, cancellation of orders by customers. Preventive measures would be to have a formalized supplier qualification program, monitoring of suppliers onsite by IQC inspectors, and tracking of the quality of shipments from the suppliers. Good communication between the company and suppliers is important, with the company alerting suppliers of quality trends and any impending changes of specifications, and the supplier alerting the company of production problems and changes of tooling or processes. In event of a quality problem, IQC has to react fast and the supplier has to be cooperative. The VC would have to look for such qualities in IQC and in critical suppliers as part of the due diligence.

Quality improvement programs would include a supplier zero defect program and a supplier rating program which could include other factors such as timeliness of delivery and cost performance, besides quality. A ship-to-stock program with suppliers which have reached a reliable quality level would reduce IQC manpower and costs. The VC would have to inquire about the existence of, or plans for, such programs.

If quality problems are not detected at the supplier, the bad materials would be received by the company, but IQC should be able to screen them off. This requires IQC to have sampling plans based on the quality history of the supplier or part, and well-equipped inspection equipment that are kept calibrated to appropriate measurement standards. Nonconforming parts would have to be stored in a clearly marked off area for return to the supplier, for rework by a contractor, or for in-house rework, as determined by a Material Review Board chaired by the IQC Manager, with appropriate representatives from purchasing, materials planning, and engineering.

Quality Assurance

The Quality Assurance (QA) department is concerned with in-house and customer quality issues. QA may be viewed as the customers' representative in the company, championing their requirements and expediting resolution of their problems, if any. Thus QA should be in close touch with customers, constantly receiving feedback.

In-house, the QA department drives the Total Quality programs encompassing every single employee; audits practices, processes, documents, equipment and products; and drives process and product quality improvement programs, including process capability studies, product failure analyses, product life, stress or other reliability tests, GMP or ISO 9000 implementation and certification. The VC should check for the presence and depth of implementation of these activities which would be indicators of the quality consciousness of the organization.

Research & Development

This department is the source of intellectual property of the company. Intellectual property can be in the form of novel or new materials, processes and devices which may be patented, and may be defined to include the designs, drawings, descriptions, and specifications related to the inventions. These form the know-how or technology possessed by the company. Intellectual property also includes unique trademarks, brand names, copyrights, software algorithms, and domain names created by the company, which has the sole right to use them.

In an early stage company, the intellectual property would be the only significant asset. Hence the due diligence of start-ups and early stage companies would be focused heavily on the value of the intellectual property, besides the quality of management and the business strategies. For later stage companies, the R&D department would have the added role of supporting manufacturing for deep-seated technical problems that may require changes to product designs or specifications, which would be outside the responsibility of manufacturing engineering. In such cases, the R&D department would have impact on reducing production cost, improving product quality, reducing process cycle times, and enhancing product marketability through improved product designs and functionality. Therefore the VC has to direct the due diligence appropriately, depending on the company's stage of development.

The legal aspects of intellectual property will be discussed in the next chapter. Here we shall concern ourselves with the due diligence investigation of the quality of the intellectual property and the capability of the R&D department.

For an early stage company, the VC needs to assess how well the technology works and how quickly it can be commercialized. The VC has to go through the proof of concept and feasibility studies, and examine any product prototype or mock-up. The VC may need the assistance of experts or potential customers to observe or advise and to make sure the studies or demonstrations are not faked or rigged. If necessary, additional demonstrations may have to be set up according to the specifications of the expert or potential customer.

Even if the VC is satisfied that the technology works, investigations have to be made on whether the derived product can gain market traction, and if so, how long it would take and how difficult it would be, which translate into time to market and costs. We discussed these issues in the previous chapter.

For a later stage company, the due diligence of the R&D activity would be focused on the ability to create follow-on products and to support the manufacture of existing products by resolving design or production problems, or by enhancing product price-performance. Due diligence effort should be focused on studying the R&D team's ability to design with optimum product cost, manufacturability, maintainability and reliability considerations, and completing working designs within the prescribed schedules. Applying Design For Manufacturability concepts is important, as the major part of the product cost and quality is determined at the design stage rather than the production stage.

The VC would have to query the R&D manager on these issues and examine track records of past successful and unsuccessful product introductions to assess the capability. Since a common concern is the R&D engineer's desire to achieve technical perfection, the VC also has to assess the R&D manager's ability to balance the commercial priorities of time to market with the desire for design perfection. Another investigation area the VC needs to review with the R&D manager is whether the staffing is adequate to encompass the technical disciplines that are required to complete development of the product. If not, what are the plans for hiring or tapping of resources from appropriate consultants or research organizations? Delays in product introductions can be costly.

Finally, here are a few reminders for the VC to keep in mind when carrying out due diligence of technology. The VC must not be so enraptured by the technology that other due diligence findings are disregarded. Technology is only one factor in the success formula; without a capable management team with well thought out strategies to exploit it, the technology would not be worth investing in. Furthermore, it is not always that the best technology wins, as marketing clout can turn the tables. The due diligence may show no competing technologies, but competing companies may be in stealth mode and may suddenly emerge. Deeper due diligence may unearth them, or expert observers may advise on the impending shifts in technology trends. Application of a new technology in products that are governed by safety, quality or regulatory standards may be hampered by compliance requirements or approval processes. All these have to be considered in the due diligence work.

Finance & Human Resource

In the due diligence of the manufacturing operation, the VC should not forget the importance of the Finance and Human Resource departments in supporting the manufacturing objectives. The Finance department can help to control and reduce costs and inventory levels, by providing timely and relevant reports to the other departments. In carrying out due diligence of the Finance department, the VC should ask for financial policies and procedures, internal audit reports, and management reports of external auditors, to determine adequacy of controls and to detect any compliance problems. The VC should also check the promptness of the Finance department in producing financial reports and test the accuracy and consistency of financial data to detect any weaknesses in the department.

The Human Resource department helps by instituting worker training and certification programs. World-class plants would only allow operators to man stations that they are certified for. Training and workstation certification supplemented by welfare and motivation programs will enhance worker productivity and quality. Operators that are cross-trained would allow flexibility in reassigning work when needed. It would be useful for the VC to also meet with the finance and HR managers as part of the due diligence, to review how they help the manufacturing operation to achieve its objectives.

Plant Tour

The tour of the plant is an essential part of the due diligence. If the VC does not have relevant experience, he would need to bring along a colleague who has manufacturing experience. The tour must not be rushed through. The VC should pause frequently, to talk to shop floor managers, engineers, and even production operators; to read notices and posters on the walls; to watch some of the operations to observe work flow. He may also need to stray away from the designated tour path to look for rubbish such as disposables, scrap, broken machinery or tools, or product rejects hidden in remote corners. When asking questions during the tour, the VC should also immediately ask for substantiating evidence, if he doubts the claims or replies given. A vivid personal example was a claim made by a factory manager while touring the plant. When asked about a large crate in a corner some distance away, he claimed it was a new machine that has just arrived, not expecting his word to be doubted. On walking to the crate and examining the labels, it was revealed to be another type of machine, which was obviously wrongly ordered.

From my experience of inspecting scores of manufacturing plants in many countries, ranging from labor intensive garment factories in Indonesia to automated automobile assembly plants in Japan and advanced semiconductor wafer fabrication facilities in the U.S., there is no doubt that keen observation and probing questioning during a plant tour can reveal intangible qualities in the shop floor, such as the levels of controls, discipline, systems compliance, corporate culture, quality consciousness, and even worker motivation and happiness levels.

Starting with the production floor, the VC should observe whether the line layout is systematic, with work in progress flowing smoothly through. He can see the age and state of repair of equipment and plant facilities. He should observe whether the shop floor is clean and tidy, with work areas and passageways clearly marked out, and without materials or waste overflowing into walkways. He should watch out for piling up of work in progress, which indicates production problems or bottlenecks due to line imbalance. He should inspect rework areas to see the amount and nature of rework being done, which are indications of quality problems.

He should stand at certain stations to count the percentage of rejects and should ask the production manager on the spot to explain the reasons for rejection and what happens to the rejects. Walking along the lines, he should observe whether work procedures and instructions are posted up at each station, and whether operators are certified for their respective stations. Plants that are handling semiconductor devices require workers to wear grounded wrist straps for electrostatic discharge control. In such cases the VC should observe any noncompliance that indicates lack of worker discipline and supervision.

He should watch out for charts on pillars or walls, such as production rates, quality levels, and process capability plots, as well as programs and activities for employees such as training and social programs, safety and healthcare notices, quality circles notices, and work reports. The types of charts displayed and whether they are updated and well drawn up would be evidence of the types of management, quality, process, or production control systems that are implemented, and the amount of feedback provided to the production floor.

All these observations will help the VC to form an impression of the efficiency of the plant and its productivity and quality levels, and to detect production problems that may not be evident from reports and discussions.

An important stop on the tour is the IQC department. Here the VC should go through randomly selected supplier qualification and quality reports and sampling plans; look at the inspection equipment, tools, and gauges; and look for the dates when these were calibrated and to what standards. He should ask to see the MRB (Material Review Board) area, to check whether the area is fenced off and locked, and whether there is an inordinate amount of rejected material pending disposition or scrap pending disposal.

At the materials and finished goods stores, he should observe any slackness in security and whether storage racks are well laid out and items neatly stacked. He may randomly select a stock card, locate the item, and verify consistency of the parts identification and storage location data. He may ask the stores manager for records of cycle counts and physical stock takes and identification of obsolete and slow-moving items.

The remainder of the tour would be to walk through the offices of QA, Manufacturing Engineering, R&D, and Materials departments to verify the equipment and systems that are in use, study the experiments and projects underway, and to look at some of the reports that are generated. These may include, for example, failure analysis and reliability tests, value engineering studies, low cost automation projects, samples of engineering change notifications, stop orders issued by QA, if any, MRP printouts, and samples of purchase orders. These are to verify the claims made by the respective department managers of the equipment, systems, and projects that they have, and to detect lapses and noncompliance.

Chapter Recap

In this chapter we discussed the due diligence of a manufacturing operation, whose fundamental objectives are to produce the right product configurations to the right quantities, on time, at the lowest cost, and with acceptable quality. The due diligence focuses on the key departments: Materials, Production, Manufacturing Engineering, Incoming Quality Control, and Quality Assurance, with regard to:

- o   how they impact the manufacturing objectives
- o   what measure are there to prevent failure
- o   what corrective actions may be taken in event of failure
- o   what improvement programs are in place or planned

We also discussed the due diligence of the Research & Development department, focusing on due diligence of technology, and the Finance and Human Resource departments. Finally, we ran through a tour of the manufacturing plant, highlighting some of the important observations and queries that may be made.

12

Due Diligence of Financial & Legal Aspects

This chapter deals with the remaining due diligence that needs to be carried out, which are on financial and legal issues. Financial due diligence, in this context, is distinct from due diligence of the Finance department. Financial due diligence is the investigation of the financial performance of the company, as well as the financial returns and risks. Due diligence of the Finance department is the investigation of the financial procedures, systems, controls, compliance, and reports that are set up and managed by the Finance department. We have touched on this in the previous chapter. In this chapter, we shall focus on due diligence of financial performance and legal issues that may affect the business.

Financial Due Diligence

We again follow the PCDA cycle approach described in Chapter 8. In the Plan stage of the financial due diligence of the company, the VC will examine the past and current financial statements, and the financial projections in the business plan. Examination of past and current financial statements may surface issues that occurred or are occurring that may have impact on the future business, and these would be noted down for due diligence work at the Do stage, to assess the validity and seriousness of each discovered issue. At the Do stage, besides number crunching, interviews with the finance manager may be needed for clarifications or supporting information.

Examination of the financial projections will involve checking for accuracy of calculations, and more importantly, for validity and realism of the assumptions used. Issues of concern, such as assumptions that appear to be overly optimistic, or those factors that have high impact on profitability, will be noted down for work at the Do stage. At the Do stage, earlier due diligence work on the management, the market, marketing strategies, manufacturing operations, and technology will be heavily drawn upon as inputs for the assessment. Any serious issues surfaced in the examination of past and current financial statements will also be inputs here, to assess whether history will repeat. Supplementary due diligence may be conducted if necessary.

In parallel with the due diligence of past, present, and future financial performance, the VC would have to investigate the financial returns and financial risks of the proposed investment. While these may be inherently captured in much of all the other due diligence work done, financial returns and risks are important enough for specific analysis and thought.

Based on these considerations, the key questions to raise would be:

o   Were there past financial lapses that might recur in future?
o   How were previous financing rounds structured?
o   What is the current burn rate, and is it reasonable and controlled?
o   What is the funding required, and how will the funds be used?
o   How valid and realistic are the key assumptions used in the projections?
o   What are the risks of significantly missing the projections?
o   What will be the investment return, using realistic projections?

As stated previously these are examples and the VC may think of more questions relevant to the business under investigation. Also, it does not matter if the questions overlap with each other or with previous due diligence. The purpose is to examine the business from as many financial angles as possible.

The issues surfaced from these questions are entered into the framework in Figure 12.1 to guide the subsequent due diligence work.

FIGURE 12.1   FINANCIAL DUE DILIGENCE

Investigation Area	Critical Success/Failure Factors	Due Diligence Sources	Validity & Seriousness of Impact
Past performance			
Present performance			
Future performance			
Risks			
Returns			

Past Performance

The VC should perform standard ratio analysis of past financials, with year to year comparisons and comparisons with other similar companies. The VC should watch out for and ask the reasons for any uneven growth, seasonality of revenues, unprofitable years, significant write-offs, major capital expenditures, payment of dividends, changes in shareholdings or shareholding structure, terms of shareholders' or directors' loans, changes in depreciation policies, changes in fiscal years, and trends such as building up of inventory or accounts receivable and declining margins. If the company has multiple product lines, breakdowns of revenues and profit margins by product line and market segment and the reasons for changes in product mixes and market segments would be required. If the company has bank borrowings, any changes in the terms and limits may indicate the bank's level of confidence in the business. Concerns raised in any of these issues would require further due diligence investigation. While past good performance is no assurance of future potential, past financial lapses have a tendency to recur.

If there were past financing rounds, the VC needs to have the terms of each round, such as the valuation, conversion or ratchet terms, capitalization table, preferential rights granted to investors, and any issue of warrants or employee stock options. Past actions in these areas may affect or prohibit some of the terms and conditions that may need to be imposed on the deal. This part of the due diligence may also reveal disgruntled or tired investors who may not wish to continue supporting the company, or worse, may hinder future corporate actions.

Present Performance

It is important that the VC secures the company's latest current financial statements, albeit unaudited. The mere fact of how current are the financial statements is an indication of the financial health of the company, or at least the health of its finance department. The VC should also carry out ratio analysis to detect any of the changes as described previously that might have occurred recently.

The due diligence should provide good understanding of current status and trend of revenues and profitability. The current quality of the assets and status of liabilities and contingencies may have to await a special audit to be conducted after there is some certainty that an investment will be made, due to confidentiality and costs involved. The special financial audit is described in Chapter 18.

For early stage companies, the current monthly expenses, called the burn rate, is of importance since insufficient cash flow is the downfall of many young companies. The VC needs to investigate the reasons for high burn rate, such as high salaries or benefits paid to founders, hiring staff too early, too much rented space, luxurious office furniture and fittings, or an inordinate amount of travel and entertainment expenses. These may need to be corrected or alleviated as part of the investment conditions.

Future Performance

The due diligence of the future performance will be focused on the profit and loss as well as cash flow projections, which should preferably be for the next five years. Such projections should be on a monthly basis for the more immediate two years and on a quarterly basis thereafter. Assumptions used should be clearly stated.

Besides checking the accuracy of calculations and for consistency between the profit and loss statements, balance sheets and cash flow statements, the VC needs to pay a lot of attention on the projections because the investment is in the future of the company. This means checking the validity and realism of assumptions used.

Due diligence of assumptions used in the pro forma profit and loss statements include checking that pricing structures and unit prices of products are competitive against competing or substitute products in the market and that there may be a need to project declining prices arising from competition and customer insistence. Quantities of units sold have to be consistent with market size and realistic market share.

For start-ups, the timing of first sales has to recognize typical sales cycles for the type of products sold, which may be six months or longer in many cases. Too optimistic projection of commencement of sales may lead to cash flow problems. The sales growth rate should also be realistic. If the projections show constant growth rate year to year, the VC should ask for more details or substantiation to show that the number is not conveniently plucked from the air.

Due diligence of unit costs may require reference to development costs for software products or bills of materials for manufactured products. Gross margins should be significant enough to provide a healthy net margin after all other costs and a buffer for price erosion. Young companies have a tendency to underestimate marketing costs, which should be commensurate with the distribution channels used and the marketing strategies mapped out, and warranty costs should not be forgotten. Direct costs may show decline due to economies of scale and cost reduction efforts, but overhead costs may increase to reflect inflation. However, headcount should be under control and compensation structures should be reasonable. R&D costs should trend lower as the company progresses to more product enhancement or development and less research. There should also be appropriate provisions for tax.

Due diligence of assumptions used in the balance sheets should include checking on the nature of and justifications for major capital expenditures. For young companies with cash constraints, leasing of capital equipment and renting of facilities would usually be desirable. Other balance sheet items to check for reasonableness are amortization rate for start-up costs, depreciation rates, and inventory levels. For a later stage company with bank borrowings, any repayment of loans built into the projections should be queried. The VC's investments should be used to grow the business and not to bail out the bank, unless future cash generation is sufficient.

Due diligence of the cash flow statements should include checking the assumptions of sales credit terms and payment cycles of accounts payable for reasonableness and conformity with industry practice. The proposed financing rounds to meet funding requirements until cash breakeven is reached have to be checked to ensure that timing and amounts to be raised are well conceived, facilitated by achievement of major milestones with sufficient allowance for time required for fund-raising. Without any significant progress after a round of financing, it would be difficult to raise the next round. The earlier round may then require a larger amount to be raised, resulting in greater dilution, or the later round may have to be delayed, requiring funds to be stretched.

Besides due diligence of the projections and assumptions used, the VC should also check the proposed use of the investment funds, which should be to grow the company, whether through expansion or new business activities or acquisitions. Sometimes the funds may be used to restructure a failed or failing company, to effect a management buyout or buy-in. There should be no bailing out of lenders or shareholders, although in some cases the VC may agree with partial liquidity for shareholders or to buy out minority shareholders who do not contribute to the company. The VC should also ask whether fees are to be paid to consultants and financial advisors helping in the fund-raising. If significant, the VC may want to account for this in the company's valuation. The VC should also ensure that the company does not celebrate successful fund-raising by raising salaries and benefits for supposedly long-suffering staff. The VC may need to make a note to expressly forbid such unauthorized usage of the investment funds in the investment agreements.

Finally, the VC may have to revise the projections, and in fact usually does so, taking into account the findings from the due diligence carried out. In addition, the VC may also carry out sensitivity analysis by changing various assumptions to see the impact on cash flow and profitability.

Risks

The due diligence of the future performance described in the previous section is to bring the assumptions and projections to valid and realistic levels. Entrepreneurs naturally tend to be overly optimistic in their enthusiasm over the business potential. However, even after rationalizing the projections, there are risks that may endanger or hinder achievement of the realistic projections. In this part of the due diligence, the VC examines these risks. Understanding the potential pitfalls in the financial projections will help the VC to further assess the deal, to incorporate relevant downside protection if possible, or to negotiate better investment terms so that the returns would still be attractive should an adverse eventuality occur. Of course, it may be difficult to incorporate perfect or comprehensive protective measures, as the entrepreneur may then not want to do the deal. On the other hand, if the higher risks cannot be satisfactorily alleviated by modifying the business strategies and plans, or by tougher investment terms, the VC may not want to do the deal either.

In other words, the due diligence on past, present, and future financial performance is to establish a base case for the projections. By considering the risks here, we are trying to establish some worst-case scenarios. Such a task should not be done mechanically, by merely scaling down revenues or profits by a certain percentage and then looking at the results. With the understanding of the business and the assessments made in all the due diligence work done on the management, market, marketing strategies, manufacturing, and financial aspects, we can work out a list of the more probable downside risks faced by this business.

For example, if we conclude that the management team is not top rate in terms of execution, we may then have a scenario where the rollout and ramp up of the business would not be as fast as the base case plans. Another example would be that if we conclude that the business is in a highly competitive industry, we may have a scenario where prices may decline faster than the base case projections and unit sales may not be as high.

The VC would have to make his judgments on where the pitfalls are and how serious could be the impact. Basically the causes of failure could be from the management, the market, marketing strategies, or manufacturing operations, which could then perhaps result in problems such as delays, market traction problems, slower growth rate, reduced gross margins, uncontrolled burn rate or calling of loans, if the company has bank debt.

It may also happen that some upside potentials may be uncovered in the due diligence. The financial projections for the optimistic scenarios may also be worked out. The respective returns for the base, pessimistic, and optimistic scenarios can then be calculated.

Returns

The financial return on an investment is measured by the internal rate of return (IRR) and the return multiple derived from the investment. The following is an example of the calculations involved.

The VC invests $2 million at a post-money valuation of $10 million, thus securing a 20 percent shareholding in the company. Five years later the company goes IPO, issuing 20 percent new shares to the public at a valuation of $100 million. The VC's shareholding is hence diluted to 0.8 × 20 = 16 percent and this is worth $16 million. By the next year the VC is able to dispose all its shares in the market at an average price that is 10 percent higher than the IPO price, due to run-up in the share price. The VC therefore derives total proceeds of $16 × 1.1 = $17.6 million. Thus an outlay of $2 million generates an income of $17.6 million after six years. The IRR is 44 percent, and the return multiple is 8.8 times.

We shall discuss more examples in the next chapter on Valuation, including those that take into account additional rounds of financing prior to IPO. The VC would perform these calculations using the projections that have been revised based on the due diligence conducted.

VCs typically require an IRR of at least 30 percent to make their effort worthwhile. Such investments would be lower risk ones such as companies that are in their third or fourth round of financing, and are about a year or so from IPO. Companies that are younger have higher risks. Those that are raising second or third rounds of financing may need to promise IRRs of 40 percent to 60 percent and from 30 percent to 50 percent respectively. Companies in the start-up stage would need to promise IRRs of 50 to 70 percent and those in the seed stage would have to promise 80 percent or more.

These are guidelines, as the risks and attractiveness of an investment depend not only on the stage of development of the company, but on a host of factors that are the subject of due diligence discussed in this and the previous chapters. The guidelines are useful because they can trigger alarm bells. If an investment opportunity looks attractive at first, but on revision after due diligence looks way below par in terms of investment return, the VC would have to either give up on the opportunity, conduct further investigation, or renegotiate the investment terms.

Return multiple is an important measure to use together with IRR. An investment of $2 million that generates $3 million proceeds after six months gives an IRR of 100 percent. However a second investment of $2 million that generates $40 million after five years gives an IRR of 82 percent. The second investment is far more attractive although the IRR is lower. The return multiple of one and a half and twenty times respectively show the difference in absolute dollars generated between the two investments. As a rule, VC funds do not reinvest the proceeds from an investment (with only rare and justified exceptions). Therefore a quick and small harvest is not as good as a later but bigger harvest.

The returns calculations for the base, pessimistic, and optimistic scenarios will serve as inputs, together with all other due diligence results, to help arrive at an investment decision. If a composite returns value is desired, probabilities of occurrence can be estimated for each scenario and a weighted average can be calculated. An example is shown in Figure 12.2.

A weighted average for the return multiple may similarly be calculated. If the calculated weighted average return (whether IRR or return multiple) falls too far below expectations, the deal may be rejected. Otherwise, it may be used as a decision input.

FIGURE 12.2   WEIGHTED AVERAGE CALCULATION

Scenario	Probability	IRR	Weighted IRR
Optimistic	10%	100%	10%
Base	70%	40%	28%
Pessimistic	20%	25%	5%
Total	100%		43%

Care should be taken that a likely pessimistic scenario is not masked out by an optimistic scenario with an exceedingly high return. The pessimistic scenario may have to be studied further. Therefore it would be advisable to keep the scenarios separate. Furthermore, inspection of the separate returns may indicate the financial quality of the business potential, and may also point towards an appropriate deal structure.

For example, the returns in Figure 12.2 show that the business has some downside potential, but the investment return in that event is still marginally acceptable. However, the upside promises a very high return. The business may therefore be considered to be financially attractive. The VC should structure the deal with some downside protection and with a good share of returns on the upside.

Legal Due Diligence

Much of the legal due diligence may have to be conducted after agreement is reached on the investment terms and prior to completion of the investment documentation. This is because the due diligence involves sighting of confidential documents such as sales contracts, supplier terms, patent filings, and employment contracts, which the company may not wish to open for examination unless there is confidence that an investment will be made, even though the VC may have signed a nondisclosure agreement. Therefore the VC would have to depend on partial disclosures and verbal assurances for the time being. Besides taking sight of the relevant documents at a later stage, the VC and its lawyers may include many of the legal concerns into the representations and warranties document that will form part of the set of legal documents that will be signed on completion of the investment. The company will then be responsible for making the appropriate disclosures.

The legal due diligence is more mechanical in nature, consisting of ensuring that certain legal documents exist and that the terms and conditions therein are not unduly unfavorable. Checklists would be useful in this case, and we shall now go through the items in a typical checklist for legal due diligence.

Corporate Documents

The target company has to be appropriately incorporated, with limited liability and allowing for issue of shares to investors. Sometimes the target company may be established as a proprietorship, partnership, limited partnership or an S corporation (which in the U.S. is structured as a corporation but taxed as a partnership). Such companies will have to be reincorporated as a C (or normal) corporation. Also, the place of incorporation may have to be chosen. For example, certain states in the U.S. and certain countries in Asia have more progressive corporate laws and favorable tax regimes. In some countries in Asia, such as India or China, an investment holding company formed outside the country of incorporation of the target company may better facilitate eventual exit through IPO or trade sale.

It may also be useful for the VC to go through recent board minutes and board resolutions to see the recent issues discussed and decisions or commitments made by the company.

Commercial Agreements

The VC may need to examine commercial contracts entered into by the company with customers, distributors, resellers, dealers, or suppliers to be assured that commitments made are reasonable; as well as tenancy or mortgage agreements, to be assured that terms are reasonable and that necessary renewals are planned for. A seemingly unimportant matter such as an office lease agreement can suddenly be costly if it is shortly due for renewal but the landlord wishes to take back the space, or if the company wishes to move to more suitable premises but faces a huge lease cancellation charge.

If the company has joint ventures, obtained marketing or technology licensing arrangements, or secured bank loans or capital equipment leases, the VC should inspect the agreements to be assured that the terms are fair and reasonable. The VC also has to be assured that the company does not wittingly or unwittingly breach the terms or covenants of these agreements.

Intellectual Property

Intellectual property is a valuable asset that provides competitive advantage through superior products or lower costs. In early stage companies, it is probably the second most important resource after the people. It is therefore important that intellectual property be protected by patent filings, which may also form entry barriers against competitors. The VC needs to obtain copies of patent filings and trademark and copyright registrations. Sometimes the patents may be filed under the name of a founder. The VC has to ensure that the rights are transferred or assigned to the company. If the patents are filed domestically but not in other target markets, steps would have to be taken to do so. If the company had previously chosen less experienced patent lawyers, probably for economic reasons, the VC may need to assist in hiring lawyers who have better knowledge of the different country patent laws and conventions to improve the extent of coverage and protection, both technically and geographically.

The VC should find out whether the company has a repository for its intellectual property and agreements, with proper access authorization and controls, as well as records of any disclosures made to individuals or companies, and corresponding nondisclosure agreements signed.

Staff

Any existing staff employment contracts, confidentiality agreements, and non-compete agreements should be examined. Sometimes an improperly drafted employment contract may bind the company to exorbitant termination compensation to a founder or a key manager. The VC may require this to be renegotiated prior to the investment. The VC may also need to interview the key staff to have assurance that they are not in breach of employment contracts or non-compete agreements with previous employers or infringing on the intellectual property of previous employers. As added assurance, this may be included in the representations and warranties document. The VC would also need details of any company loans extended to staff or directors.

Legal Actions

The VC will require the company to disclose any pending or potential lawsuits faced by the company, or liabilities arising from product warranties, as well as disclosures of any legal, pecuniary, criminal, or regulatory actions in the past, in progress or pending with any director or management staff. Conflicts of interest or related party transactions or relationships in significant contracts will also have to be disclosed.

Issue of Stock

It is important that the VC obtains all agreements of prior financing rounds to check the rights given to previous investors. Prior rights may make the present investment void if they were breached, or may trigger increases in the shareholdings of prior investors. Certain prior rights may also hinder actions by the board or shareholders. The VC would need to ensure that such prior rights are cancelled, waived, or subsumed, as appropriate, as part of the conditions of the current round. On the other hand, obligations agreed upon by previous shareholders may be carried on into the new investment agreements. In some cases, the company may be slack in documenting prior investment agreements which could give rise to future claims or lawsuits by shareholders.

Regulatory Requirements

Another area for legal due diligence is to ensure that the company has secured all necessary government licenses and permits, complied with all regulatory requirements and are current with payments of corporate and sales taxes. In some countries and some industries, there may be government imposed price, production, export or import controls or quotas, or strict safety or health standards. Some industries such as those with polluting effluents may be subject to environmental controls. The company may also have been awarded tax concessions, incentives, or cash grants, which may be subject to certain conditions.

Some countries may have strict labor laws or active worker unions. Some may have restrictions on corporate ownership, repatriation of capital or profits or exchange controls. The VC has to be aware of all these requirements as they may affect the conduct of the business and compliance may add to operating costs.

Chapter Recap

In this chapter we discussed financial and legal due diligence. For financial due diligence we reviewed a framework for investigation into the past and the present and future projected financial performance of the company so as to establish a base case for the projections that use valid and realistic assumptions. The due diligence has to include consideration of risks of not meeting projections so as to establish worst-case scenarios. Finally, the projected investment returns are calculated as inputs, together with all other due diligence, to make the final investment decision.

For legal due diligence we went through a checklist of legal documents and matters that need to be examined and the possible issues that may arise from them.

PART V

MAKING THE DEAL

While the due diligence work is in progress, and if it continues to be satisfactory, the VC firm needs to work out the terms for the potential investment. In structuring the deal, the VC firm has a few key issues to consider and decisions to make: What is the amount to invest? What should be the valuation of the company? What investment security should be used? What should be the rights and obligations attached to the security? What forms of control and protection mechanisms should be incorporated into the investment agreement? What exit options are there?

The two most critical issues are the valuation and the rights attached to the security. These are considered in Chapter 13: VALUATION and in Chapter 14: INVESTMENT SECURITIES. Next, Chapter 15: DEAL STRUCTURING looks at the deal structuring issues and objectives in totality.

Having considered the issues and arrived at the terms and conditions for the investment, these have to be documented. Chapter 16: TERM SHEET describes the important document capturing the key investment terms, which is the basis for negotiations before the closing of the deal.

13

Valuation

I t has often been said that valuation is partly an art and not an exact science, since many of the factors affecting the valuation of a company, especially one at its early stage of development, are subjective and unclear. However, the VC practitioner can make it more of a science than an art through understanding of the factors that affect a company's valuation, the concepts and techniques of valuation, and certain methods to verify and validate the valuation made.

In this chapter we shall discuss these factors and concepts to gain a deeper understanding of valuation, which is perhaps the central and most important part of the VC investment process. We shall also review various methods of valuation, concentrating on the most commonly used method in the VC industry, not surprisingly called the Venture Capital Method.[10] We shall also see how this method works and why it works for VC deals.

Valuation Factors

There are a multitude of factors that affect the value of a company at a given point in time. These may be listed as follows:

---

[10] See William Sahlman, *A Method For Valuing High-Risk, Long-Term Investments – The "Venture Capital Method,"* Boston: Harvard Business School Publishing, 1987, Note 9-288-006 revised August 12, 2003, for a comprehensive discussion on the Venture Capital Method.

o   Company specific: Such as management, development stage, track record, intellectual property, technology, market traction, etc.

o   Industry or market specific: Such as market size and growth rate, industry structure and trend, competition, pricing and distribution structure, etc.

o   Financial market specific: Such as market P-E ratios, IPO market, VC funding demand/supply cycle, competition for the deal, exit opportunities, etc.

o   Economic or environmental specific: Such as level of economic and industrial development of the region, the regulatory and taxation environment, etc.

o   Investor specific: Such as industry familiarity, availability and quality of alternative deals, the VC's fund availability, and performance, etc.

o   Investment specific: Such as investment amount, majority control, investment terms such as covenants and controls, ratchets, etc.

o   Negotiation: Such as alternative funding available to the entrepreneur, negotiating power, negotiation skills, etc.

o   Subjective: Such as chemistry between the parties, eagerness to consummate the deal, etc.

There is no magic formula that combines all these factors together to arrive at a single valuation number. Many of these factors can only be assessed on a qualitative and not quantitative basis. Furthermore the company's present value is affected by its future prospects which entail uncertainty and risks. Finally there is some information asymmetry between the entrepreneur and the investor on the company's status and potential.

It is therefore clear that at best the VC could only arrive at a valuation that is within the ballpark. However, it is important for the VC to also ensure that its due diligence is exhaustive enough to detect and account for or eliminate surprise factors that may throw the valuation way off the mark. Surprise factors that provide upside to the valuation would be welcome, but should not be depended upon. Those that could cause a drop in value should be identified as far as possible and examined closely.

Some Valuation Concepts

Pre-money and Post-money Valuation

The amount to be invested divided by the number of shares in the company that this amount will purchase gives the price per share to be paid by the investor. This purchase price per share multiplied by the total number of existing shares in the company results in the *pre-money valuation* of the company. It is the value of the company prior to the investment.

Sometimes the investee company may have some stock options, warrants, or convertible securities that could be exercised or converted into shares but have not been exercised or converted yet. If all such options, warrants, and convertibles are assumed to be exercised and converted, the resultant number of shares multiplied by the investor's proposed price per share will result in the *fully diluted pre-money valuation*. The fully diluted valuation gives a more accurate reflection of the value placed on the company than on a non-diluted basis.

After the investment has been made, the shares issued to the investor would have enlarged the number of shares issued by the company. This enlarged number of shares multiplied by the investor's price per share will result in the *post-money valuation* of the company. If the investor had invested in the form of convertible securities, one would assume the conversion had taken place in the calculation.

In dollar terms, the pre-money valuation added to the amount invested would equal the post-money valuation. For example, if the pre-money value of the company is $10 million and the VC injects $2 million cash into new shares, the value will immediately rise up to $12 million (i.e., the post-investment or post-money value goes up to $12 million).

If a portion of the investment goes towards purchase of old shares (i.e., shares from another shareholder), this portion should not be counted into the post-money valuation as the funds do not go to the company and hence does not increase its value. In the prior example, if the $2 million investment does not buy all new shares, but consists of $1.5 million for new shares and $0.5 million for old shares, the post-money valuation would be $11.5 million.

In some cases, the investor may agree, as part of the investment terms, that a certain number of stock options will be awarded to founder managers on attaining specified milestones, or that an employee stock option plan will be put in place. As and when these options are awarded, they have the potential to dilute the investor's stake, if the options are exercised. Thus it would be important to work out the *fully diluted post-money valuation*.

Example

A VC intends to invest $5 million into a company for 20 percent, thus valuing it at $25 million post-money (5/0.20 = 25), or $20 million pre-money (25 − 5 = 20). However, the founders had put into the company shareholders' loans amounting to one million which can be converted into common shares. The VC therefore negotiates that the shareholders should not take out money from the company, but should convert the loan into shares. But the VC insists that it should not be diluted by such conversion; it should still get 20 percent stake for its $5 million.

Therefore the loan conversion has to take place prior to the VC investment. The pre-money valuation was then $19 million, which increased to $20 million after the conversion of the one million loan. The valuation is further increased to $25 million after the investment of $5 million. At the end of the day, the VC's post-money valuation is still $25 million, and the fully diluted pre-money valuation was $20 million.

As part of the deal, the investor has promised to give stock options amounting to 5 percent of the company if the founders were to meet a certain milestone and has also agreed to set up an employee stock option plan, allocating 15 percent of the company to the plan. Assuming these were all awarded, there will be additional 20 percent new shares in the company and thus the investor's 20 percent stake will be diluted down to 80 percent of 20 percent, which is 16 percent. Thus the investor actually would have got 16 percent stake for its $5 million and hence the fully diluted post-money valuation would be 5/0.16 = $31.25 million versus $25 million on an undiluted basis. Thus the investor actually paid a higher price arising from the dilution.

Sometimes, especially at times when VC funding is hard to get, the VC may be tougher and insist on setting aside the shares for the options prior to its funding, so that its $5 million investment will still result in a 20 percent stake on full dilution.

This example shows the difference between pre and post-money as well as dilution effects. Pre-money valuation is a useful figure as it is the value placed on the company prior to the investment. In this example, the VC would have to ask: is the company presently worth $19 million? Post-money valuation is a useful figure for the VC when it looks into the future for future financing rounds or for exit. The VC may ask: if the company grows without further financing into one worth $150 million at IPO, what would be my return? The return would be quite different depending on whether the VC uses $25 million or $31.25 million as the value it paid for. If all the options were awarded and exercised, the correct figure would be $31.25 million. It would only be $25 million if none of the options were awarded. It would be somewhere in between if a portion of the options was awarded and exercised.

Step-up and Step-down in Valuation

In Chapter 2 we introduced the term *step-up* in valuation, which we repeat here for the sake of completeness. As a company raises one round of financing after another, there should be a step-up in valuation at each round, if the company is progressing well. The valuation of the company rises progressively, and the accumulation of increased value is reflected in an incremental jump in value at the next round of financing. A young company typically raises each round after about eighteen months and the step-up in valuation is typically about two times, but these are not hard and fast rules.

If the company encounters problems and delays, its value declines, and this could be reflected in a step-down in valuation at the next round of financing, which is then called a down round.

Entry and Exit Valuation

The VC's *entry valuation* is the valuation of the company at which the VC enters as a shareholder of the company. This would equal the post-money valuation. If there was no additional investment made by the VC into the company, this figure remains constant. If the VC makes a subsequent investment, the *average entry valuation* would be calculated as follows:

Average Entry Valuation = Total Investment/Total Shareholding

Note that the average entry valuation is a measurement at a given point in time, as the value may change with each round of financing.

For example, if a VC invests $5 million into a company at a first round pre-money valuation of $20 million, it would have 20 percent of the company. The post-money valuation would be $25 million and the VC's entry valuation is $25 million. If in a second round of financing, the VC invests another $2 million at a post-money valuation of $40 million, it would acquire another 5 percent of the company. We should be careful not to add 20 percent to 5 percent and say that the VC now owns 25 percent of the company. The second round causes dilution of the shareholdings of first round investors. If there are no other investors in the second round, the dilution would be 5 percent. If another VC also invested $2 million in the second round, the total dilution would be 10 percent.

Assuming a 10 percent dilution, the VC's first round shareholding becomes 18 percent instead of 20 percent. Adding the 5 percent acquired in the second round, its total shareholding would be 23 percent. This is from a total investment of $7 million. Hence the VC's average entry valuation is 7/ 0.23 = $30.43 million.

The VC's total shareholding can also change due to dilution arising from exercise of options or warrants, or other investors investing into the company. Hence the average entry valuation changes due to dilution. Let us use the staging of investments in Ideal Inc, shown in Figure 2.8, and reproduced in Figure 13.1, as an example.

Figure 13.1 shows the change in the VC's average entry valuation at each financing round. Average entry valuation is a useful concept as it is a measure of the VC's "cost" of the investment. When this cost increases, the VC needs a corresponding increase in the value of the company to maintain its investment return. Fortunately, in this example, the valuation increased at a faster rate, and hence the VC's notional return multiple increased with each round. For example, if the VC was able to exit soon after the second round, it would have received $9 million (36 percent of $25 million), which is 1.8 times return multiple.

FIGURE 13.1   CHANGES IN ENTRY VALUATION

($ million)

Financing Round	Seed	1st	2nd	3rd	IPO
Pre-money Valuation	2	6	15	60	250
Amount Raised	1	4	10	20	50
Post-money Valuation	3	10	25	80	300
% Share Offered	33%	40%	40%	25%	17%
Founders' Share	67%	40%	24%	18%	15%
Founders' Share Value	2	4	6	14	45
1. VC's Investment Amount	1	5	5	5	5
2. VC's Shareholding	33.3%	60.0%	36.0%	27.0%	22.5%
3. VC's Average Entry Valuation (3 = 1/2)	3.0	8.3	13.9	18.5	22.2
4. Company Valuation	3	10	25	80	300
5. VC's Return Multiple (5 = 4/3)	1.0	1.2	1.8	4.3	13.5

(Refer to Figure 2.8)

Exit valuation is the valuation of the company at which the VC exits from the investee company, which could be through an IPO or a trade sale. In Figure 13.1, if the VC divested completely at the IPO valuation, the exit valuation would have been $300 million, and the return multiple would have been 13.5 times. Thus:

Return Multiple = Exit Valuation/Average Entry Valuation

Average entry valuation and exit valuation are not commonly used, but are useful concepts when considering exit alternatives. Using the above example again, if after the second round financing, the company were to receive a trade sale offer, the VC knows that the company has to be valued higher than 4 × 13.9 = $55.6 million if the desired return multiple is at least four times.

The average entry valuation also shows the impact of dilution on the VC's investment cost. This is why VCs are always concerned about dilution of its shareholding.

Valuation Methods

The most common methods of calculating valuation of companies fall into the categories shown in Figure 13.2.

FIGURE 13.2 VALUATION METHODS

Earnings Based	Price-Earnings Ratio
	EBITDA Multiple
	Venture Capital Method
Assets Based	Net Tangible Assets
	Net Worth
	Breakup Value
Cash Flow Based	Discounted Free Cash Flow
VC Industry Averages	VC Industry Valuations
Other Methods	Revenue Multiple
	Subscribers Multiple
	Cost to Create

The Venture Capital Method, as the name implies, is the most commonly used method in the VC industry. Price Earnings Ratio is also frequently used, and VC industry averages are often used as benchmarks. The other methods are used for specific special cases. Sometimes it may be advisable to use several methods to countercheck the results and to derive a range of valuations that may be useful for negotiation purposes. We shall focus our discussion on Price-Earnings Ratio and the Venture Capital Method, and briefly discuss the other methods.

Price-Earnings Ratio Method

The Price-Earnings Ratio is the ratio of price per share to earnings per share. P-E Ratio, which may be further shortened to PER, is used to measure the value of listed securities and may be used for private companies which are later stage and hence have an earnings track record. It goes without saying that this method would not be directly applicable to a start-up or a company that is not profitable. An adjustment would normally be applied for the fact that the company is not listed and hence not as mature and its shares lack liquidity. This adjustment is called the private market discount.

As an example, if the earnings per share of a company is $1.00 and its market price is $15.00, the PER is fifteen times. It is typical that PERs for listed companies with low growth prospects range between six and ten times, those with medium growth rates would be between 10 to 15 times, and those with high growth would be between fifteen and twenty times. If in addition to high growth prospects, the company is a clear market leader, the PER could be between twenty and thirty times. An example of such a company would be Intel, a dominant market leader in the high growth semiconductor industry.

The overall market PERs could be weighted down during an economic downturn, or boosted during an economic boom. The market price of a specific company may also be boosted during a period of high sectorial growth or speculative interest, or lowered due to poor performance of competitors within the same industry sector or lack of liquidity of the stock. There is also some variance in market PERs from one country to another, depending on the maturity of capital markets, the investor interest in particular sectors, and the degree of speculation. It is therefore important to relate the PER being applied to a company to those of companies in a similar industry sector in the same country.

The PER is usually a multiple of after-tax profits forecasted for the current or next fiscal period. Projected PBT (profits before tax) or EBITDA (earnings before interest, tax, depreciation, and amortization) may also be used, with appropriate adjustments to the ratios.

The private market discount varies, depending on the maturity of the company. If the company is less than a year from IPO, the discount may be 10 percent to 20 percent. VCs are unlikely to invest in such mature companies as the return may not be attractive enough. If the company is some years away from IPO, the discount may be 50 percent or more. Thus if the private company shows earnings after tax of $2 million for the current or next fiscal year, and typical public market PER for similar companies is fifteen times, the private company may be valued at $14 million, applying a PER of seven times.

When taking a basket of similar listed companies for comparison, the VC has to be careful of short-term distortions affecting companies in the sector. Volatile sectors would have a wider range of PERs. For example, technology stocks may temporarily zoom to PERs of fifty times and sometimes more than a hundred times. Similarly a company within a basket that exhibits a widely different PER, whether on the low or high side, should be removed from the basket to avoid distortion.

On the other hand, the VC should also be careful that the earnings forecasted by the private company are real and sustainable, and conduct the necessary due diligence to verify these. This is to avoid placing a valuation based on earnings that may be inflated by write-backs of charges or provisions, or other exceptional and extraordinary items. The VC should also ensure that depreciation and inventory valuations have been properly accounted for.

The VC Method

Over the years, the VC industry has developed a relatively simple method to value companies, and it is so commonly used that it is now called the VC Method. This method is particularly suited to VC deals involving young companies, where there is no profit track record as yet, hence the PER method cannot be applied to value the company. Furthermore the method rightly focuses on the proceeds on divestment, which is the VC's main reward from the investment.

In the VC Method, a future valuation of the company is determined at the time of the VC's exit, called the *terminal year*. This valuation may be called the *exit valuation*. The exit valuation is determined by applying a PER to the earnings of the company in the terminal year. Depending on the nature of the anticipated exit, such as an IPO or trade sale, and by referencing typical PERs of similar listed companies, an appropriate PER is used.

The exit valuation is then discounted back from the terminal year to the present year at a rate which is the desired rate of return for the VC. The result is the deemed present valuation of the company or the *entry valuation*. The amount to be invested divided by the entry valuation results in the shareholding to be purchased by the investment.

We can explain this method by looking at it on the basis of moving forward instead of backward in time. The VC Method enables the calculation of the present valuation, or entry valuation of the company, so that the investment amount will purchase the required shareholding that will provide the desired rate of return when the investment is divested at the anticipated exit valuation in the terminal year.

VC-backed companies typically go through more than one round of financing and usually establish an employee stock option plan. These result in the dilution of the VC's shareholding after the investment is made. This means that the VC would need to have a larger shareholding initially. The VC Method allows for calculations to take into account dilution effects.

Appendix 13A shows the derivation of formulas that are used in the VC Method and introduces the terms Dilution %, Retention %, Pre-dilution Shareholding and Post-dilution Shareholding, which are used in these formulas. Let us look at a few examples to understand the methodology and the application of the formulas.

An illustrative spreadsheet model to calculate the valuation using the VC Method is given in Appendix 13B. This model may be easily adapted to a specific case, and was in fact used for the following examples. If you use a calculator, your numbers may differ slightly due to rounding off errors.

In view of the importance and prevalence of use of the VC Method, the reader may have to bear with rather detailed explanations and some repetition in the following examples.

Case A: One Round to IPO

Ideal Inc is looking for a $5 million investment which will take it through to positive cash flow. Therefore it does not require any further funding until its planned IPO in three years, in 2007. Ideal projects that it will achieve an after-tax profit of $5 million in 2007 to support an IPO valuation of $75 million, anticipating an IPO PER of fifteen times. The company plans to raise $15 million in its IPO. The VC has evaluated the business plans and verified through extensive due diligence that the plans are achievable. The VC wants to have at least 40 percent IRR on this deal. What percentage of the company should be purchased by the $5 million investment?

The VC first determines the terminal year to be 2008, on the basis that it would take some time to fully divest after IPO. She feels more comfortable in being a little conservative. She also notes that similar listed companies have an average PER of twenty times. Since the IPO will be priced a notch below market, she is comfortable with the company's projection of fifteen times. She then determines that her exit valuation is $60 million, which is the pre-money valuation at IPO ($75 million post-money less the $15 million raised). Again, being conservative, she is not factoring any post-IPO run up in the share price.

Her next step is to discount the exit valuation of $60 million in 2008 to the present 2004 (which is four years), at a discount rate of 40 percent. She uses the Discounting Formula:

Entry Valuation = Exit Valuation/$[(1 + r)^n]$
where r = 0.40 and n = 4, to derive an entry valuation of $15.6 million.

The $5 million investment hence purchases 5/15.6 = 32% of the company. The pre-money valuation of the company would hence be 15.6 − 5 = $10.6 million.

In the above calculation we took the IPO pre-money valuation, and therefore did not have to account for the IPO dilution. Let us see how the calculation works out if we take the IPO post-money valuation of $75 million. Since $15 million is to be raised on IPO, the dilution is 15/75 = 20 percent dilution. Using the exit valuation of $75 million and discounting at 40 percent over four years, the entry valuation would be $19.5 million. Her $5 million investment should buy 5/19.5 = 25.6 percent of the company. Due to the 20 percent IPO dilution, this shareholding has to be grossed up to 25.6/(1 − 0.20) = 32%. This is the same result as the previous calculation.

The steps involved in this case were:

1. Determine the Terminal Year to be 2008 (one year after IPO to allow time for full divestment).
2. Determine the Exit Valuation, which is the value of the company at the Terminal Year, using the PER Method. This is determined to be $60 million.
3. Discount the Exit Valuation to the present year (2004), using the expected IRR. Using 40 percent discount rate, the $60 million when discounted to 2004 is $15.6 million. The Entry Valuation is hence $15.6 million.
4. Determine the required shareholding. An investment of $5 million at a valuation of $15.6 million secures 32 percent of the company.
5. Optional: Check that this valuation provides IRR of 40 percent.

If we take the IPO post-money valuation of $75 million, we have to apply the Dilution Formula. The steps would have been:

1. Determine the Terminal Year to be 2008.
2. Determine the Exit Valuation, which we now take as $75 million.
3. Discount the Exit Valuation to the present year (2004), using the expected IRR. Using 40 percent discount rate, the $75 million discounted to 2004 is $19.5 million. This is the Entry Valuation before considering the dilution effect.
4. Determine the required post-dilution shareholding. An investment of $5 million at a valuation of $19.5 million secures 25.6 percent of the company.
5. Apply the Dilution Formula to determine the pre-dilution shareholding:

IPO Dilution % = 20%
Post-dilution shareholding = 25.6%

Therefore:
Pre-dilution shareholding = Post-dilution shareholding/(1 −
Dilution %) = 25.6/(1 − 0.20) = 32%

6. Calculate the Entry Valuation. An investment of $5 million for 32 percent implies a post-money entry valuation of 5/0.32 = $15.6 million.
7. Optional: Check that this investment provides IRR of 40 percent.

Case B: Two Rounds to a Trade Sale

Ideal2 Inc is also looking for $5 million of funds, but expects to need another $8 million in two years. This is because Ideal2 has aggressive plans to ramp up fast. It hopes to be bought over by Microsoft in 2008 (four years from now) at a valuation of $100 million.

The VC requires 50 percent IRR on its initial investment of $5 million. Assume that the VC will invest additional $3 million in the next round and expects 40 percent IRR for this follow-on investment. What percentages of the company should be purchased by these two investments?

The VC has verified, through her due diligence, that the management team members have track records of successfully building software companies rapidly and the company has a good chance of achieving its plans. She has also verified that large software companies like Microsoft are interested in such enabling software. A trade sale would be more feasible as an exit, due to the technical nature of the product, which would not be fully appreciated by the investing public. The VC determines that the terminal year is 2008. Being a trade sale, the full proceeds will be received at the time of the sale, and there would be no dilution. The exit valuation would therefore be $100 million. Discounting at 50 percent from 2008 to the present 2004, the calculation would be:

$$\text{Entry Valuation} = \text{Exit Valuation}/(1 + r)^n$$
$$= 100/(1 + 0.5)^4$$
$$= 19.75$$

Thus the entry valuation would be $19.75 million, assuming no subsequent dilution. Her $5 million investment would purchase $5/19.75 = 25.3\%$ of the company. She concurs with the company that another $8 million would be needed in 2006. The VC believes that her firm would be unlikely to fully fund this amount. She believes that she would follow-on with $3 million and would bring in a new investor for $5 million. She believes that the co-investor would perhaps be satisfied with an IRR of 35 percent, since the company would be more mature and hence the investment risks would be lower. However she decides to use 40 percent instead to be conservative again. This means that the entry valuation for the co-investor would be:

$$\text{Entry Valuation} = \text{Exit Valuation}/(1 + r)^n$$
$$= 100/(1+ 0.40)^2$$
$$= 51.0$$

Hence the co-investor's required entry valuation would be $51 million and the shareholding would be $5/51 = 9.8\%$. The VC chooses to also use 40 percent discount rate for her follow-on (although she could justifiably use 50 percent), since the risks would be lower than her initial investment. Her follow-on entry valuation would then be $51 million and her $3 million follow-on would purchase $3/51 = 5.9\%$. There would therefore be a total dilution of 15.7 percent from the financing round in 2006. The VC therefore realizes that her originally calculated initial shareholding of 25.3 percent would have to be grossed up to cater for the subsequent 15.7 percent dilution. The result would be $25.3/(1 - 0.157) = 30.0\%$.

Thus the initial investment of $5 million should purchase 30.0 percent of the company to generate 50 percent IRR, and the follow-on investment of $3 million should purchase 5.9 percent to generate 40 percent IRR upon the trade sale.

Checking her calculation, the VC notes that her initial 30 percent ownership gets diluted by the second round financing which takes away 15.7 percent, thus causing an 84.3 percent dilution to her 30 percent, resulting in 25.3 percent. Therefore the proceeds from the trade sale in 2008 would be 25.3 percent of $100 million which equals $25.3 million. Proceeds of $25.3 million from an investment of $5 million over four years indeed result in an IRR of 50 percent. If you use a similar calculation for her follow-on investment of $3 million which purchased an additional 5.9 percent, you will find that the return for the follow-on investment would be 40 percent.

Note that at the time of initial investment, the VC's entry valuation is actually 5/0.30 = $16.7 million. In the second round, the VC invests $3 million for 5.9 percent, making a total investment of $8 million and a total shareholding of 5.9 + 25.3 = 31.2% (since the original 30.0 percent is diluted to 25.3 percent). Thus the average entry valuation for the VC after the second round is 8/0.312 = $25.6 million. The total divestment proceeds is 25.3 + 5.9 = $31.2 million, giving a return multiple of 3.9 times to the VC.

The steps involved in this case were:

1. Determine the Terminal Year, which is 2008.
2. Determine the Exit Valuation, which is $100 million, through a trade sale.
3. Discount the Exit Valuation to the present year. Using 50 percent expected IRR as the discount rate, $100 million in 2008 discounted to the present is $19.75 million. This is the Entry Valuation before considering any dilution effect.
4. Determine the required shareholding. Five million investment at valuation of $19.75 million buys 25.3 percent. This is the required post-dilution shareholding.
5. Work backwards from the Terminal Year and determine the dilution events and respective dilution effects, as in the following steps.
   a. On exit there is no dilution as it is a trade sale.
   b. In the round before the sale, a co-investor in 2006 would require 9.8 percent for a $5 million investment, given the expected IRR of 40 percent upon exit.
   c. With the same assumptions, the VC would require 5.9 percent for $3 million follow-on.
   d. Total Dilution % in this round is hence 15.7 percent. Applying the Dilution Formula:

   Pre-dilution shareholding = Post-dilution shareholding/(1 − Dilution %)= 25.3/(1 − 0.157) = 30.0%

6. Calculate the Entry Valuation. The initial investment of $5 million for 30 percent of the company means an Entry Valuation of $16.7 million.

7. Optional: Check that the initial investment of $5 million gives the expected IRR of 50 percent and the follow-on of $3 million gives 40 percent IRR.

Case C: Two Rounds to IPO with an Employee Stock Option Scheme

If the exit for Case B is an IPO in 2007, and full divestment in 2008, the VC will have a second dilution and will need to gross up accordingly. Say the company is expected to be worth $100 million post-IPO with an issue of 25 percent new shares. As in Case B, discounting $100 million from 2008 to 2004 at 50 percent, the entry value would be $19.75 million, and $5 million would buy 25.3 percent, on an undiluted basis.

The co-investor's entry valuation would be $51.0 million, upon which $5 million will buy 9.8 percent, but this needs to be grossed up due to the IPO dilution of 25 percent. The co-investor's shareholding should be 9.8/(1 − 0.25) = 13.07%. The VC's follow-on investment of $3 million would also need to be modified to 5.9/(1 − 0.25) = 7.87%. The total dilution from the second round is hence 13.07 + 7.87 = 20.9%. The VC's first round investment faces this second round dilution of 20.9 percent and the IPO dilution of 25 percent. Hence the undiluted shareholding of 25.3 percent needs to be grossed up to 25.3/(1 − 0.209)(1 − 0.25) = 42.7%. The VC would therefore ask for 42.7 percent for her investment of $5 million, which means a valuation of $11.7 million.

Thus the additional IPO dilution has resulted in the VC requiring 42.7 percent for her initial $5 million and 7.87 percent for her follow-on of $3 million. This compares with 30.0 percent and 5.9 percent respectively in Case B.

Assume that along the way, an employee stock option scheme is to be established with a pool amounting to 20 percent of shareholding. Therefore there would yet be another dilution.

The VC's first round shareholding will have to be further grossed up to 42.7/(1 − 0.20) = 53.3%. If the scheme is established before the second round financing, the second round shareholding percentages do not need to be grossed up.

The steps in this case were:

1. Determine the Terminal Year, which is 2008 (one year after IPO).
2. Determine the Exit Valuation, which is $100 million (post-money).
3. Discount the Exit Valuation to the present year. Using 50 percent expected IRR as the discount rate, $100 million in 2008 discounted to the present is $19.75 million. This is the Entry Valuation before considering any dilution effect.
4. Determine the required shareholding. Five million investment at valuation of $19.75 million buys 25.3 percent. This is the required post-dilution shareholding.
5. Work backwards from the Terminal Year and determine the dilution events and respective dilution effects.
    a. On exit there is the IPO dilution of 25 percent.
    b. In the second round financing, a co-investor in 2006 would require (before IPO dilution) 9.8 percent for a $5 million investment, given the expected IRR of 40 percent and Exit Valuation of $100 million. His actual required % shareholding would be:

    Pre-dilution shareholding = Post-dilution shareholding/(1 – Dilution %)
    $$= 9.8/(1 - 0.25) = 13.07\%$$

    c. With the same assumptions, the VC would require:

    Pre-dilution shareholding = $5.9/(1 - 0.25) = 7.87\%$

    d. Total dilution in this round is hence 13.07 + 7.87 = 20.9%.
6. Apply the Dilution Formula to the initial investment, considering the second round dilution of 20.9 percent and the IPO dilution of 25 percent:

    Pre-dilution shareholding = $25.3/(1 - 0.209)(1 - 0.25) = 42.7\%$

7. Calculate the pre-dilution Entry Valuation. Five million for 42.7 percent means a post-money valuation of $11.7 million.
8. Optional: Check that the $5 million investment provides IRR of 50 percent, taking into consideration the two dilution events.

If there is a third dilution event such as a 20 percent ESOS, the calculation would be:

$$\text{Pre-dilution shareholding} = 25.3/[(1 - 0.209)(1 - 0.25)(1 - 0.20)]$$
$$= 53.3\%$$

Case D: Three Rounds to IPO

Ideal3 Inc is a recent start-up with one million founders' shares, and requires $2 million investment. It projects going IPO in five years (2009), at a valuation of $100 million and raising $20 million. From the company's cash flow, which the VC has reworked using realistic assumptions drawn from extensive due diligence, the company needs to raise $4 million in 2006 and a pre-IPO round of $8 million in 2008. The VC requires 60 percent IRR, which is commensurate with the high risks of a start-up. What percentage of the company should the $2 million purchase? What number of shares should be issued to the VC?

The VC makes her calculations as follows:

Terminal Year = 2009, this time assuming full divestment to be within 2009

Exit Valuation = $100 million post-money

Required IRR = 60%

Entry Valuation before dilution effect = Exit Valuation$/(1 + r)^n$
$$= 100/(1 + 0.60)^5$$
$$= \$9.54 \text{ million}$$

Investment Amount = $2 million

Therefore Required 1st Round Post-dilution shareholding = 2/9.54
$$= 21.0\%$$

Impact of 3rd Round (pre-IPO Round) in 2008:

Assume required IRR = 30%

Post-dilution Entry Valuation for 3rd Round Investors = $100/(1 + 0.30)^1$
$$= \$76.92 \text{ million}$$

Investment Amount = $8 million

Required Post-dilution shareholding = 8/76.92 = 10.4%

IPO Dilution = 20%
Required Pre-dilution shareholding = Post-dilution shareholding/(1 – Dilution %)
$$= 10.4/(1 - 0.20) = 13.0\%$$
Therefore 3rd Round Dilution = 13.0%

Impact of 2nd Round in 2006:
Assume required IRR = 40%
Post-dilution Entry Valuation for 2nd Round Investors = $100/(1 + 0.40)^3$
$$= \$36.44 \text{ million}$$
Investment Amount = $4 million
Required Post-dilution shareholding = 4/36.44 = 11.0%
IPO Dilution = 20% and 3rd Round Dilution = 13.0%
Required Pre-dilution shareholding = Post-dilution shareholding/$(1 - D_1)(1 - D_2)$ = $11.0/(1 - 0.20)(1 - 0.130) = 15.8\%$
Therefore 2nd Round Dilution = 15.8%

Therefore required 1st Round Pre-dilution shareholding

$$= \text{Post-dilution shareholding}/(1 - D_1)(1 - D_2)(1 - D_3)$$
$$= 21.0/[(1 - 0.20)(1 - 0.130)(1 - 0.158)]$$
$$= 35.8\%$$

Therefore Pre-dilution Entry Valuation = 2/0.358 = $5.59 million

Therefore the VC's initial investment of $2 million is at a post-money valuation of $5.59 million, which is 35.8 percent of the company. This means the pre-money valuation is $3.59 million. Since there are one million shares outstanding, each existing share is priced at $3.59. The VC's $2 million will therefore buy 0.56 million new shares. The total number of shares outstanding after the first round would be 1.56 million shares.

She may also use the Share Issue Formula (see Appendix 13A):

New shares to be issued: $N = [C/(1 - C)] \times S_1$
$$= [0.358/(1 - 0.358)] \times 1,000,000 = 0.56 \text{ million}$$

After getting her answers, the VC does some checking of the numbers as follows:

In the 2nd Round:
>Investors invest \$4 million for 15.8%
>
>2nd Round post-money valuation = 4/0.158 = \$25.36 million
>
>2nd Round pre-money valuation = 25.36 – 4 = \$21.36 million
>
>Price of each of 1.56 million existing shares = 21.36/1.56 = \$13.72
>
>New shares to be issued = 4/13.72 = 0.29 million shares
>
>Total shares outstanding after 2nd Round = 1.56 + 0.29 = 1.85 million shares

In the 3rd Round:
>Investors invest \$8 million for 13.0%
>
>3rd Round post-money valuation = 8/0.130 = \$61.54 million
>
>3rd Round pre-money valuation = 61.54 – 8 = \$53.54 million
>
>Price of each of 1.85 million existing shares = 53.54/1.85 = \$28.96
>
>New shares to be issued = 8/28.96 = 0.28 million shares
>
>Total shares outstanding after 3rd Round = 1.85 + 0.28 = 2.12 million shares

At IPO:
>IPO pre-money valuation = $100 \times (1 – 0.20)$ = \$80 million
>
>Price of each of 2.12 million existing shares = 80/2.12 = \$37.65

IRR of 1st Round Investor $= (37.65/3.59)^{1/5} – 1 = 60\%$

IRR of 2nd Round Investor $= (37.65/13.72)^{1/3} – 1 = 40\%$

IRR of 3rd Round Investor $= (37.65/28.96) – 1 = 30\%$

These are indeed the expected return rates for the respective financing rounds.

Discount Rate

The discount rates that are used in the VC Method correspond to the stage of development of the company and hence the inherent risk of the investment. Refer to Figure 2.3 in Chapter 2 which shows the different rounds of financing. At the seed financing stage, VCs would use a discount rate as high as 80 percent or more, and often invest at par with the founders. For companies at the start-up stage or having their first round of financing, the discount rate may range from 50 to 70 percent. Companies having their second and third rounds may have discount rates from 40 to 60 percent and from 30 to 50 percent respectively. Those at the mezzanine or pre-IPO stage may have a discount rate of 20 to 40 percent.

It would appear that VCs are asking for exceedingly high returns. A 20 percent IRR over an average holding period of five years translates to a return multiple of 2.5 times. Many VCs will consider such an investment to be an average performer. A 60 percent IRR over five years is 10.5 times return multiple. VCs will consider those investments giving ten times or higher return multiple to be star performers. The desirable range for a VC is hence between 2.5 to above ten times return multiple. Due to the high risks and hence high failure rates, these successful investments need to provide sufficient return to cover the failures and still provide the return that limited partners expect, which is around 20 percent IRR over the life of the fund, ranging from the high teens to the high twenties.

Besides justifying the desired returns as being commensurate with the risks, VCs also take into account the value that they add to their investments and the illiquid nature of the investments, when compared against listed securities. Some VCs use a higher discount rate to compensate against the tendency for entrepreneurs to inflate their projections. However, this should not be a substitute for careful due diligence to assess how realistic are the projections and to make appropriate adjustments upon which the valuation should be calculated. Whether the higher or lower end of the range of discount values appropriate to the company's stage of development is used should be based on the assessed risks of attaining the realistic projections and not on the risks of attaining the inflated projections.

Terminal Year and Terminal Value

The terminal value or exit valuation should be based on the adjusted realistic projections, based on due diligence findings, and not simply on the entrepreneur's projections which are likely to be optimistic. An appropriate P-E Ratio arrived at after taking into consideration the issues discussed in the previous section on the P-E Ratio Method should be applied on the adjusted earning in the terminal year. However, since it involves looking a few years into the future, some thought must be given to capital market cycles and industry cycles to have some level of confidence that the exit can be achieved in the designated year.

It is not mandatory that the terminal year must be the year in which the IPO occurs. Some VCs prefer to add a safety margin of one more year to allow for possible delay in the IPO and for the time taken to fully divest the shares. In this case it is usual to be conservative and assume that there is no run up in the market price post-IPO.

It should be remembered that exit is not always through IPO. Sometimes a trade sale could be an easier and more profitable exit, especially where the product or service is not fashionable or easily understood by public investors. The P-E Ratio would have to be adjusted accordingly. Also, the terminal value need not always be based on earnings. In some industries it may be more appropriate to take a multiple of revenue, such as in the retail trade or a value per subscriber, such as for cable TV operators or MSOs (multiple-system operators), Internet subscription services or magazine publishers.

Financing Rounds

Some VCs make the mistake of not considering any further financing round prior to exit, when calculating investment returns. As seen from the examples, the dilution effect of subsequent rounds can be quite significant. It is therefore important to carefully estimate the timing, size, and valuation of intervening financing rounds prior to the terminal year. The VC has to ensure that the timing of each round coincides with the achievement of significant milestones, otherwise it would be difficult to raise the round. The size of a round (i.e., the investment amount required) should not be too large as that will cause unnecessary dilution. It should not be too little or there will not be sufficient funds to last till the next milestone and the next financing round. Allowance should also be given for probable delay in reaching the next milestone or in closing the next round. The VC therefore has to examine the cash flow projections and the underlying assumptions carefully.

The valuation of each intervening financing round also presents challenges. The VC Method applies the desired return rate to discount the terminal value to the year of the financing round in question to arrive at a desired valuation and hence the desired ownership percentage. The VC has to verify that the desired valuation is reasonable for the performance and stage of development of the company at that point in time. Furthermore, the valuation for a round needs to be compared with that for a prior round to verify that the step-up in valuation is reasonable and justified. Adjustments have to be made if these were not the case.

Conclusion

The accuracy of the VC Method depends on the decisions on discount rates, the terminal year, and terminal value (which requires proper choice of the P-E Ratio and verification of the projected earnings in the terminal year, or other methods of determining value), as well as assessment of the timing, size, and valuation of each intermediate financing round. Therefore it is important that the VC Method is not applied in a robotic fashion. Reasonableness checks must be made, not only on the values of the variables used, but also on the intermediate results derived, as well as the financial projections upon which the calculations are based.

The most difficult decisions will be on the discount rates. Some VCs are concerned that the calculated valuation may be too high, if too low a discount rate is used. On the other hand, using too high a discount rate will make it difficult to justify to the entrepreneur. Once the decisions are made, the calculations are mechanical, and easy with the help of a spreadsheet. Use of a spreadsheet also eases working out what-ifs by tweaking the numbers such as the discount rates.

VC Perspectives on Valuation

We now see why valuation is both a science and an art. The P-E Ratio and the VC Method, as well as the other methods described in this chapter, are all based on financial projections and calculations. These are largely the "science" aspects of valuation, although there are elements of judgment and forecasting. But we saw in the section on Valuation Factors at the beginning of this chapter that there are innumerable factors affecting the value of the company, many of which are non-financial and some are external to the company. Most of these are not quantifiable and often change with time. One of the most important factors for the success of a venture—the capabilities of the management team—cannot be quantified into a multiplier to be applied to the financial valuation. These are the "art" aspects of valuation.

Given that the most scientific financial calculations only provide an estimate of value, and that there are many other qualitative variables, the VC's common attitude towards valuation is, at best, to seek simple calculations that will derive a reasonable range of values that will be starting points for negotiations. Precision is not required. At worst, some VCs decry the calculations on the grounds that any valuation figure can be produced by varying the assumptions. They prefer to use rules of thumb or prevailing industry averages. They also argue that the valuation derived from hours of meticulous calculations can be simply changed through minutes of negotiations. Some VCs therefore pursue the simple strategy of negotiating for as low a valuation as possible, recognizing that for any given investment the lowest entry valuation means the highest return possible for them. After stretching the entrepreneur to the limit, the VC would then decide whether the negotiated valuation is acceptable or not.

VCs also stress the importance of understanding the fundamentals of the business and carrying out proper due diligence to verify the assumptions in the projections and the credentials of the management. VCs also embed adjustments and protective measures into the investment terms, such as ratchets, milestones, and anti-dilution terms, to cater for overestimation of value or unexpected mishaps. However, all these are important and necessary parts of the investment process and should not relieve the VC from careful consideration of the valuation.

The practice of deriving valuation by a logical method, using carefully considered assumptions, honed through experience, inculcates a consistent and disciplined approach among VC professionals and should help to convince and achieve credibility with the entrepreneur in the negotiations.

Other Valuation Methods

We shall briefly review other valuation methods that are interesting and may be occasionally used by VCs.

EBITDA Multiple

EBITDA is the earnings before interest, tax, depreciation, and amortization costs. It is the operational earnings, and reflects the ability of the company's operations to generate cash. The EBITDA Multiple is the ratio of the Enterprise Value (EV) to EBITDA. The EV is the market value (i.e., the valuation) of the company plus debt minus cash. Thus the two formulas are:

Enterprise Value = EBITDA Multiple × EBITDA
Enterprise Value = Valuation – Cash + Debt

EV measures the net amount of funds needed to buy the company and pay off all debt, netting off cash remaining in the company. Thus the ratio of EV to EBITDA may be simply seen as the number of years for the company to operationally pay back its operational value.

Using EBITDA instead of after-tax earnings separates out distortions caused by different financing, tax, and capital expense structures. These can then be looked at separately. This method allows more accurate comparisons between companies.

The valuation of a company is hence derived by first applying the EBITDA multiple of comparable companies to the EBITDA of the target company, and then adding the cash and deducting the debt in the company:

Valuation = EBITDA Multiple × EBITDA + Cash – Debt

If the EBITDA multiple is derived from listed companies, a discount should be applied to the target private company, just as in the use of the P-E Ratio.

Net Tangible Assets Multiple

Net Tangible Assets (NTA) or Book Value is defined as the total assets less all liabilities and less any intangible assets (such as goodwill, patents, trademarks, copyrights, computer software, permits, licenses, franchises, and capitalized start-up costs). It is useful to separate out the intangible asset value as this often involves rather subjective valuation and requires further evaluation or revaluation, if it is significant in value.

NTA is also useful for companies that are not profitable and hence the PER method cannot be applied. The NTA is calculated based on the financial statements and the negotiation is usually focused on the value of the intangible assets that should be added back to NTA. The company is therefore valued as a multiple of its NTA:

Net Tangible Assets = Total Assets – Total Liabilities – Intangible Assets
Valuation = (1 + Premium %) × NTA

For more traditional businesses the premium for intangible assets may be 25 or 50 percent over the NTA. Therefore the value of the company may be 1.25 times NTA or 1.5 times NTA. For companies with strong intellectual property such as patents, the company may be valued at two times NTA. These multiples are indicative and validation would have to be from comparison with companies in similar businesses or with similar intellectual property. For software companies it would not be meaningful to use NTA as almost all the value will be in the intellectual property.

Net Worth

The Net Worth is the amount by which total assets exceed total liabilities. It is also known as the Net Assets or Shareholders' Equity. This is a readily and easily calculated number and is usually used as a rough reference point for the valuation derived by other means, since a more accurate comparison of companies would require closer examination of the assets and liabilities such as depreciation and asset valuation policies and debt structures to ensure proper valuation of assets and liabilities.

Breakup Value

Breakup Value is the aggregate market value of those parts of the company that can be operated separately or that can be sold off. This method to derive the value of a company is useful for conglomerates (i.e., companies with several businesses). The conglomerate does not derive full value from some of its businesses because they are not fully developed or operating sub-optimally, or they are burdened by the other businesses. The conglomerate is thus valued at below its breakup value and this discount is referred to as the conglomerate discount. Corporate raiders have found it profitable to buy and break up such companies. The VC may also find it profitable to invest and take control of such a conglomerate, sell off non-core businesses, and further develop the core business. In this case the valuation that the VC would pay for would be derived from:

Breakup Value = Sum of Market Values of separate businesses
Valuation = Breakup Value – Conglomerate Discount

Liquidation Value

The Liquidation Value of a company is the net proceeds that can be realized from the sale of all assets and after payment of all debts when a company goes out of business. Since the company is to be liquidated, all the accumulated goodwill will be worthless. Hence the Liquidation Value is defined as the value of the company as a going-concern less the goodwill value. However, certain of the other intangible assets, such as software or patents, may not be entirely worthless and may be sold. On the other hand, some of the hard assets such as plant and equipment may not realize their book value if dismantled.

The Liquidation Value may be used to set the minimum value of a company in a turnaround situation. However, the valuation could be lower than the Liquidation Value if the seller gets a share of future gains in value of the company if the turnaround is successful. Assuming this is not the case, the valuation would be:

Valuation = Going-concern Value – Goodwill

Discounted Free Cash Flow

This valuation model defines the operating value of a company as consisting of two parts—the value to equity providers and to debt providers—which together provide the capital to the company. The operating value is calculated from the free cash flow, which is the net operating profit after tax (tax being adjusted for the depreciation tax shield), adding back depreciation and amortization, and deducting capital expenditures and changes in working capital. The Operating Value is the net present value (NPV) of all future free cash flows.

Equity providers derive value from the flow of dividends and any repurchase of shares. The Equity Value is hence the NPV of all such cash flows to the equity providers. Debt providers derive value from the flow of interest and loan capital repayments. The Debt Value is hence the NPV of the cash flows to the debt providers. Since the Operating Value is the sum of the Equity Value (the valuation of the company) and Debt Value, we can derive the valuation as follows:

Valuation = Operating Value – Debt Value

The model prescribes the appropriate rates to discount the free cash flows and the debt. The free cash flows are discounted by a weighted average of the cost of equity and the cost of debt, called the Weighted Average Cost of Capital (WACC). The debt cash flows are discounted by the prevailing market interest rate for debt with similar terms and conditions. Unlike debt which has a limited life based on the repayment terms, the free cash flows can go on forever; hence the model prescribes a method to take a chosen initial forecast period of a number of years, and estimating the Continuing Value after that period. We shall not get into the details of the calculation of WACC and Continuing Value and refinements to the model.

Financial economists consider this model to be based on sound principles to calculate the valuation of companies. This model, with refinements, is used in Economic Value Added (EVA) and Value-Based Management (VBM) theories, which are gaining increasing acceptance among companies for performance measurement, management compensation, and strategic planning. However, VCs find the calculations complex, requiring some variables which are hard to determine for private companies. As explained previously, VCs seek simplicity and do not need high precision. This method has not gained much acceptance among VCs.

VC Industry Averages

VC industry publications and database services, such as VentureOne and Venture Economics, annually survey VC done deals and compile average valuations of companies under different categories such as stage of development, round of financing, and industry sector. These are valuable benchmarks. There is some variation from year to year depending on the state of the VC industry, the prevailing capital markets, and health or hype of the particular industry sector.

Not counting the wild valuations during the dot-com craze, typical valuations, culled from various publications, at different stages of development are as shown in Figure 13.3.

It should be stressed again that there can be wide fluctuations in valuations. For example, a company in the development stage, given sufficient hype and VCs bidding to invest, may be valued as high as $80 million. Valuations can vary from company to company, from industry sector to sector, from one industry to another, and one country to another. This reinforces the VC's mentality that attempting to fine tune the calculation of valuation would be a waste of time.

FIGURE 13.3   TYPICAL VC VALUATIONS

($million)

	Pre-money	Investment Amount	Post-money
Seed	2 to 3	1 to 2	3 to 5
Start-up	4 to 5	2 to 3	6 to 8
Development	8 to 15	5 to 8	13 to 23
Revenue	12 to 20	7 to 9	19 to 29
Profitable	15 to 30	5 to 10	20 to 40

Revenue Multiple

Sometimes it may be more appropriate to use a Revenue Multiple instead of an earnings multiple. For retailers, food outlets, and some Internet-based companies, market traction and market share are indicators of growth prospects. Technology companies in new emerging markets may need to pursue a price penetration strategy so that future benefits can be reaped when the customer base and distribution channels are established. In this effort to establish markets, companies may also face high customer acquisition or advertising costs, and hence may not have the earnings to which a P-E Ratio may be applied. Hence a multiple of net revenues would be a better measure of value. Valuation is thus obtained by:

Valuation = Revenue Multiple × Net Revenues

The Revenue Multiple is usually within the range of half to three times and occasionally may fall outside the range. Earlier stage companies will be around 0.5 to 1.5 times, while later stage companies may be around two to three times. The Revenue Multiple may also be used for profitable companies as a useful check against the valuation obtained by the P-E Ratio.

Subscribers Multiple

In certain industries, especially service providers, the revenues and cash flows have strong correlation to the number of subscribers or members that are signed on. Examples are cable TV operators or multiple system operators (MSOs), telephone service operators, Internet service providers (ISPs), online and private data network service providers, and health maintenance organizations (HMOs). For these types of companies, the average revenue per subscriber and average cost of infrastructure per subscriber, together with the growth potential, can be determined and used as benchmarks. Sometimes, recent acquisitions of such companies will provide the ratio of valuation per subscriber, which may be called the Subscribers Multiple. Hence:

Valuation = Subscribers Multiple × Number of subscribers

It should be noted that the Subscribers Multiple may not necessarily be the same from one geographical region or one country to another. For example, the average value per subscriber for an MSO in the U.S. is different from one in Taiwan. This is attributable to different service offerings and charges, expenditure levels, and usage patterns which give rise to a different revenue level per subscriber. Different infrastructure construction costs also make a difference in the valuation of such companies.

Cost to Create

This method is usually applied to start-ups and other early stage companies. The value of the company is based on the costs that would have to be incurred if the investor were to set up the business himself and reach the same stage of development as the company. A premium would then be added, since time would need to be incurred to set up the business all over again. Hence:

Valuation = Start-up Costs + Premium

For example the investor may estimate that it would cost him $2 million and one year to set up the business and reach the same level of product development or the same level of revenues. He could value the company at $2.5 million, thus placing a premium of $0.5 million on being able to be in the market one year earlier and avoiding the risks of incurring higher costs due to start-up problems he might encounter. The target company itself might have actually incurred more or less than $2 million or may have taken more or less than one year, and therefore may have to accept the loss or gain of valuation accordingly.

Effect of Cash or Debt

It should be noted that a company is usually valued free of cash or debt. An early stage company is unlikely to have any significant amount of cash, which is the reason for its fund-raising. Neither is it likely to be able to secure any bank borrowings. Therefore this would usually be irrelevant in the valuation of an early stage company. However, there may be occasions when a VC may invest in a later stage company. The company may have cash, but may wish to partner with the VC to tap its network and other value-add opportunities. On the other hand, the company may be in debt and may need to be restructured. In such cases, the cash or debt would be added to or deducted from the valuation.

Using Scenarios

The VC Method or other methods can be enhanced by working out the valuations based on different scenarios and then calculating the weighted average valuation, using the estimated probability for each scenario as weights.

The choice of scenarios may vary from investment to investment. Examples of scenarios are:

o   Base Case: This is based on realistic assumptions and appropriate adjustments to the entrepreneur's projections as determined by due diligence.

o   Optimistic Case: This could be based on the entrepreneur's projections, or based on the more optimistic assumptions and projections determined by due diligence.

o   Pessimistic Case: This would factor in lower growth, possible delays, greater competition, a lower P-E Ratio on exit, or other risks and pitfalls as determined by due diligence.

o   Liquidation: This would be a future failure of the business, but may assume that the VC would still be able to recover part of the investment.

o   Total Loss: This would be a total loss of the investment.

There could be refinements in between, such as a Less Optimistic Case, or a Less Pessimistic Case. It is advisable to limit the number of scenarios to four or five of the most probable cases. The choice of the probability for each case would be based on the key factors that are critical to the business. For example, a strong management team and a fast-growing and large market will increase the probability for the optimistic case. Obviously, the sum of the probabilities for the chosen scenarios should be 100 percent.

It is important that all the scenarios be derived from the ground up from the adjusted basic assumptions, as determined or indicated by due diligence. For example, it is not advisable to merely assume that for the Pessimistic Case the terminal year valuation will be 50 percent of that for the Base Case, and that the valuation for the Optimistic Case will be 150 percent of that for the Base Case. The factors that drive up the business or put the business at risk should be assessed and appropriate values put into the business model to derive the terminal year profits.

After working out the terminal year valuations of the various scenarios, the respective probabilities of the scenarios occurring are applied, and the weighted average valuation could be calculated. An example is shown in Figure 13.4.

In this example the weighted average terminal valuation is $116 million and this figure would be used for discounting to derive the present value of the company.

FIGURE 13.4   WEIGHTED AVERAGE CALCULATION

Scenario	Probability	Terminal Year Valuation	Weighted Valuation
Optimistic	20%	$200	$40
Base	55%	$120	$66
Pessimistic	15%	$60	$9
Liquidation	10%	$10	$1
Total	100%		$116

Chapter Recap

In this chapter we reviewed different aspects of valuation of a private company:

- o   The factors that affect valuation
- o   Certain valuation concepts, such as:
  - o   pre-money and post-money valuation
  - o   step-up and step-down in valuation
  - o   entry and exit valuation
- o   Valuation methods, in particular:
  - o   the Price-Earnings Ratio Method
  - o   the VC Method
- o   VC perspectives on valuation
- o   Other valuation methods, such as:
  - o   EBITDA multiple
  - o   net tangible assets multiple
  - o   net worth
  - o   breakup value
  - o   liquidation value
  - o   discounted free cash flow
  - o   VC industry averages
  - o   revenue multiple
  - o   subscribers multiple
  - o   cost to create
- o   Using scenarios in calculating valuation

APPENDIX 13A

The Venture Capital Method: Derivation of Formulas

There are three essential formulas in the VC Method to determine valuation of companies. The names adopted for them in this book may not be widely used, but they serve as convenient references. The three formulas are:

1. The Discounting Formula
2. The Dilution Formula
3. The Share Issue Formula

We shall discuss how these formulas are derived. From these formulas, we can calculate the required ownership percentage and price per share for the VC and the valuation of the company. We shall also touch on the definitions of Retention % and Dilution %. Finally an illustrative spreadsheet model to calculate valuation using the VC Method is presented.

The Discounting Formula

The discounting process is the reverse of the compounding process. The future value FV of a present value PV earning compound interest at the rate r% over n periods of time is calculated as:

$$FV = PV \times (1 + r)^n$$

Hence: $PV = FV/(1 + r)^n$

Thus $100 earned five years from now, discounted at a rate of 20 percent is equivalent to a present value $PV = 100/(1 + 0.20)^5 = \$40.19$. We shall call this the Discounting Formula.

The Dilution Formula

When new shares are issued by a company, all the existing shareholders will have their shareholding percentages reduced, or diluted.

Let: a   = number of shares held by existing Shareholder A
       S_1 = total number of existing shares in the company
       N   = number of new shares to be issued
       S_2 = enlarged number of shares in the company

Then: S_2 $= S_1 + N$

Let: D   = Dilution %
           = % to be issued
           $= N/S_2$

(We shall later look at the alternate definition of D, where $d = N/S_1$. See the section "Basis of New Shares to be Issued" later in this Appendix.)

Let: Pr_a = Pre-dilution shareholding of Shareholder A
           $= a/S_1$

Let: Po_a = Post-dilution shareholding of Shareholder A
           $= a/S_2$

Therefore:

$$Po_a/Pr_a = (a/S_2) \times (S_1/a)$$
$$= S_1/S_2$$
$$= (S_2 - N)/S_2 \qquad \text{since } S_1 = S_2 - N$$
$$= 1 - N/S_2$$
$$= 1 - D \qquad \text{since } D = N/S_2$$

Thus: $Po_a = Pr_a \times (1 - D)$

Therefore the shareholding of existing Shareholder A is diluted from Pr_a to Po_a by a factor of $(1 - D)$. The general formula would be:

Post-dilution shareholding = Pre-dilution shareholding $\times$ (1 – Dilution %)

This may be called the Dilution Formula. Taking the inverse form:

Pre-dilution shareholding = Post-dilution shareholding / (1 – Dilution %)

You may interpret this formula as saying that the post-dilution shareholding has to be grossed up by the dilution factor, $(1 - D)$, to obtain the pre-dilution shareholding.

What if there are multiple rounds of dilution?

Let: Pr_1 = 1st Round Pre-dilution shareholding
         Po_1 = 1st Round Post-dilution shareholding
         D_1 = 1st Round Dilution %
         Pr_2 = 2nd Round Pre-dilution shareholding
         Po_2 = 2nd Round Post-dilution shareholding
         D_2 = 2nd Round Dilution %
         Pr_3 = 3rd Round Pre-dilution shareholding
         … and so on

Since: $Po_1 = Pr_1 \times (1 - D_1)$
And the Post-dilution shareholding after the First Round is the same as the Pre-dilution shareholding before the Second Round (i.e. $Pr_2 = Po_1$)

Thus: $Pr_2 = Pr_1 \times (1 - D_1)$

Since: $Po_2 = Pr_2 \times (1 - D_2)$
Thus: $Po_2 = Pr_1 \times (1 - D_1) \times (1 - D_2)$

Similarly:

         $Po_3 = Pr_3 \times (1 - D_3)$ and $Pr_3 = Po_2$
So: $Po_3 = Pr_1 \times (1 - D_1) \times (1 - D_2) \times (1 - D_3)$

For n number of rounds of dilution:

         $Po_n = Pr_1 \times (1 - D_1) (1 - D_2) (1 - D_3) \ldots (1 - D_n)$

Thus the generalized Dilution Formula for a multiple of n rounds of dilution is:

Post-dilution shareholding = Pre-dilution shareholding $\times [(1 - D_1)(1 - D_2)\ldots(1 - D_n)]$

The inverse form is:

Pre-dilution shareholding = Post-dilution shareholding / $[(1 - D_1)(1 - D_2)...(1 - D_n)]$

Let us look at a couple of examples to show the application of the Dilution Formula.

Example A: Calculating the Post-dilution Shareholding

An existing shareholder owns thirty shares in a company with a total of a hundred existing shares. The company issues fifty new shares. Therefore:

> Pre-dilution shareholding = 30/100 = 30%
> S_1 = 100
> N = 50
> S_2 = 100 + 50 = 150

The % being issued, on a post-money basis, is 50/150 = 33.3%. In other words, the Dilution %:

> $D = N/S_2 = 33.3\%$

Therefore:

Post-dilution shareholding= Pre-dilution shareholding $\times$ (1 − Dilution %)= $0.30 \times (1 - 0.333) = 20\%$

Thus the 33.3 percent dilution effect results in the shareholder's original 30 percent shareholding being decreased to 20 percent. This calculation is for illustrative purposes. The simple direct calculation is to divide the number of shares owned by the new total number of shares (i.e., 30/150 = 20%).

Example B: Calculating the Pre-dilution Shareholding

There are one million existing shares in a company. The investor expects the company to IPO in a few years at a valuation of $50 million with the issue of 25 percent new shares in the enlarged capital. The investor wants its shares to be worth $10 million on IPO. What should be its current % shareholding in order to achieve this?

To secure $10 million from the IPO, the investor must own $10/50 = 20\%$ of the company, after the IPO dilution. Hence:

> Post-dilution shareholding = 20%
> IPO Dilution % = 25%

Therefore:
> Pre-dilution shareholding = Post-dilution shareholding $/(1 -$
> Dilution %)
> $$= 0.20/(1 - 0.25)$$
> $$= 0.20/0.75 = 26.7\%$$

Thus the required current ownership must be 26.7 percent so that the ownership after the IPO dilution of 25 percent would be 20 percent.

As a check:
Post-dilution shareholding= Pre-dilution shareholding $\times$ (1 − Dilution %)= $0.267 \times (1 - 0.25) = 20\%$.

The Share Issue Formula

In the VC Method we work backwards by firstly determining the terminal value and discounting this back to derive the present value. We adjust this present value for dilution effects to arrive at the current shareholding that should be acquired. We now need to calculate the number of new shares to be issued to secure this required current shareholding.

Let: C = current % shareholding required (or acquired) by investor
      S_1 = total number of existing shares in the company
      N = number of new shares to be issued to investor
      S_2 = enlarged number of shares in the company

Then: N $= C \times S_2$
           $= C \times (S_1 + N)$
           $= C \times S_1 + C \times N$
        $N - C \times N = C \times S_1$
        $N \times (1 - C) = C \times S_1$

So: $N = [C/(1 - C)] \times S_1$

This is referred to as the Share Issue Formula in this book. The price per share that the investor pays is then simply the investment amount divided by the number of shares issued to the investor:

$$\text{Price per share} = \text{Investment Amount}/N$$

The valuation is commonly on a post-money basis, (i.e., the price per share multiplied by the total number of outstanding shares. Thus:

$$\text{Post-money Valuation} = (\text{Investment Amount}/N) \times S_2$$
$$= \text{Investment Amount}/(N/S_2)$$

Thus:

$$\text{Post-money Valuation} = \text{Investment Amount}/C$$

Example C: Price Per Share and Valuation

To finish Example B above, the number of shares to be issued to the investor so that it gets the required 26.7 percent shareholding is N = [(0.267 /(1 − 0.267)] × one million = 363,636 shares.

If the Investor invests one million, the price per share is 1,000,000/363,636 = $2.75. The current post-money valuation of the company is hence 1/ 0.267 million = $3.75 million.

Retention %

Some VCs use Retention % instead of Dilution %. Retention % is the percentage shareholding that is retained by existing shareholders after the dilution event. Dilution % is the percentage shareholding that is sold away to a new investor. Therefore Retention % + Dilution % = 100 %.

$$
\begin{aligned}
\text{Let:} \quad R &= \text{Retention \%} \\
&= 1 - D \\
&= 1 - N/S_2 \\
&= (S_2 - N)/S_2 \\
&= S_1/S_2 \qquad \text{since } S_2 - N = S_1
\end{aligned}
$$

Thus: Retention % = (Number of existing shares)/(Enlarged number of shares)

The Dilution Formula may be recast using Retention % instead of Dilution %, by merely substituting $R = 1 - D$:

Post-dilution shareholding = Pre-dilution shareholding × Retention % or
Pre-dilution shareholding = Post-dilution shareholding/Retention %

Basis of New Shares to be Issued

When stating that x% of new shares will be issued, one has to be careful whether the percentage is based on the existing shareholding (S_1) or based on the enlarged shareholding (S_2). For example, a company having eighty existing shares and issuing twenty new shares is issuing 25 percent (= 20/80) of its existing shareholding which is the same as 20 percent (= 20/100) of its enlarged shareholding.

Simply stating that the company (say with existing eighty shares) is issuing 20 percent new shares is ambiguous as it either means it is issuing sixteen new shares (based on *existing* shareholding) or twenty new shares (based on *enlarged* shareholding).

In this book we have used the basis to be the enlarged shareholding. This is the more common definition. When a VC firm says it wants 30 percent of a company, it usually means that the 30 percent is based on the enlarged shareholding. Likewise, if a company wishes to establish an Employee Stock Options Scheme, by setting aside 20 percent of its shareholding, it usually means 20 percent of the enlarged shareholding, unless otherwise stated. If a company goes IPO with an issue of 25 percent new shares, it usually means 25 percent of the enlarged share capital. Hence we use, and many VCs prefer, D = Dilution % = (% to be issued) and Retention % = (1 – % to be issued) or Retention % = (1 – Dilution %), all based on the *enlarged* shareholding.

If the new issue is based on *existing* shareholding, the Dilution Formula will have to be modified.

Let: S_1 = total number of existing shares in the company
       N   = number of new shares to be issued
       S_2 = enlarged number of shares in the company

Then: S_2 = S_1 + N

Let: d   = Dilution %
           = % to be issued (based on *existing* shareholding)
           = N/S_1 (Note: S_1 and not S_2)

As before:

$$Po_a/Pr_a = S_1/S_2$$
$$= S_1/(S_1 + N) = 1/[(S_1 + N)/S_1]$$
$$= 1/(1 + d)$$

Hence the Dilution Formula becomes:

Post-dilution shareholding = Pre-dilution shareholding$/(1 + d)$ or
Pre-dilution shareholding = Post-dilution shareholding $\times (1 + d)$

By definition, R = Retention %
                    = S_1/S_2
From: $Po_a/Pr_a = S_1/S_2 = R$

Since: $Po_a/Pr_a = R = 1/(1 + d)$
$$R = 1/(1 + d)$$
And: $d = (1/R) - 1$

The Dilution Formula in terms of Retention % is therefore:

Post-dilution shareholding = Pre-dilution shareholding × Retention % or
Pre-dilution shareholding = Post-dilution shareholding / Retention %

It is interesting to note that the different basis used for the percentage of new shares to be issued changes the definition of the Dilution % and hence changes the Dilution Formula when expressed in terms of Dilution. However the definition of Retention % is not changed, since the issue of new shares does not affect the number of old shares, and hence the Dilution Formula expressed in terms of Retention % is unchanged.

If we define $d = N/S_1$ and $D = N/S_2$, we can prove that the Dilution Formula:

Post-dilution shareholding = Pre-dilution shareholding$/(1 + d)$

reverts back to:

Post-dilution shareholding = Pre-dilution shareholding × $(1 - D)$.

The reader may wish to do this little exercise.

Summary

In summary, using the same variables defined earlier in this Appendix:

The Discounting Formula is:
$$PV = FV/(1 + r)^n$$

The Dilution Formula is:
Post-dilution shareholding = Pre-dilution shareholding × $(1 - D)$
where D is the Dilution %

Dilution % is:

$D = N/S_2$ where N is the number of new shares to be issued and S_2 is the post-investment enlarged number of shares

Retention % is:

$R = 1 - D = S_1/S_2$ where S_1 is the pre-investment number of shares

The Share Issue Formula is:

$N = [C/(1 - C)] \times S_1$ where C is the current % shareholding required (or acquired) by the Investor

Price per Share is:

Price per share = Investment Amount/N

Post-money Valuation is:

Post-money Valuation = Investment Amount/C

Note:

If Dilution % is defined as $d = N/S_1$ (i.e., based on existing number of shares) then:

Post-dilution shareholding = Pre-dilution shareholding/$(1 + d)$

APPENDIX 13B

A SPREADSHEET MODEL FOR THE VENTURE CAPITAL METHOD

A spreadsheet model for Case D on page 237 is on the next page. An Employee Stock Option Scheme is added in Year One to have a more complete picture. Changing the 0 percent for ESOS to say 15 percent will show the resulting changes. This model can be readily adapted to other situations.

All the user needs to do is to enter the investment amounts in the different years, the exit valuation, the dilution at exit, if any, the ESOS percentage, the required IRR for the different rounds, and the present number of shares outstanding in the company.

For each round of financing, the model provides answers for the entry valuation, the required pre-dilution percentage shareholding, the number of new shares to be issued, and the price per share. The last row provides a check against data or model errors.

If there are several investors in a round, the numbers can be prorated. This model will also be useful for studying what-if scenarios for different investment amounts or required IRRs.

ILLUSTRATIVE MODEL FOR THE VENTURE CAPITAL METHOD

	A	B	C	D	E	F	G
1	Year	0	1	2	3	4	5
2	Investment ($m)	2	0	4	0	8	
3	Exit Valuation ($m)						100
4	Exit Dilution						20%
5	ESOS		0%				
6	Required IRR	60%		40%		30%	
7							
8	Non-diluted Valuation ($m)	9.54		36.44		76.92	
9	Post-dilution Shareholding	21.0%		11.0%		10.4%	
10	Pre-dilution Shareholding	35.8%		15.8%		13.0%	
11							
12	Entry Valuation ($m)	5.59		25.36		61.54	
13							
14	Beginning No. of Shares (m)	1.00	1.56	1.56		1.85	2.12
15	No. of New Shares (m)	0.56	0.00	0.29		0.28	
16	Price / Share ($)	3.59		13.72		28.96	37.65
17	Ending No. of Shares (m)	1.56	1.56	1.85		2.12	
18							
19	IRR	60.0%		40.0%		30.0%	

	A	B	C	D	E	F	G
1	Year	0	1	2	3	4	5
2	Investment ($m)	2	0	4	0	8	
3	Exit Valuation ($m)						100
4	Exit Dilution						0.2
5	ESOS		0				
6	Required IRR	0.6		0.4		0.3	
7							
8	Non-diluted Valuation ($m)	=G3/(1+B6)^(G1-B1)		=G3/(1+D6)^(G1-D1)		=G3/(1+F6)^(G1-F1)	
9	Post-dilution Shareholding	=B2/B8		=D2/D8		=F2/F8	
10	Pre-dilution Shareholding	=B9/((1-C5)*(1-D10)*(1-F10)*(1-G4))		=D9/((1-G4)*(1-F10))		=F9/(1-G4)	
11							
12	Entry Valuation ($m)	=B2/B10		=D2/D10		=F2/F10	
13							
14	Beginning No. of Shares (m)	1	=B17	=C17		=D17	
15	No. of New Shares (m)	=B10/((1-B10)*B14	=C5/(1-C5)*C14	=D10/((1-D10)*D14		=F10/((1-F10)*F14	
16	Price / Share ($)	=(B12-B2)/B14		=(D12-D2)/D14		=(F12-F2)/F14	
17	Ending No. of Shares (m)	=B15+B14	=C15+C14	=D15+D14		=F15+F14	=F17
18							
19	IRR	=(G16/B16)^(1/(G1-B1)) -1		=(G16/D16)^(1/(G1-D1)) -1		=(G16/F16)^(1/(G1-F1)) -1	=G3*(1-G4)/G14

(Note: Shaded cells are for data entry)

14

Investment Securities

VCs may invest in companies through a variety of investment securities. These could be in the form of stocks (common or preferred), options (or warrants), or loans (convertible or non-convertible). VCs could also employ a combination of these. A non-convertible or straight loan is not used by itself, as the interest received is too low a return to the VC. The VC may provide a straight loan in combination with another investment security to provide bridging finance to the investee company prior to obtaining a bank loan or another round of financing. When the loan is repaid, the VC may use the funds for another investment.

Each type of security entails differing degrees of commitment in the company, and hence takes on different degrees of risk in the company. Therefore the type of security and the attached features and rights chosen by the VC depend on the investment risks as perceived by the VC. The higher the perceived risks, the weaker will be the commitment, so that it would be easier for the VC to bail out with minimum loss. On the other hand, the entrepreneur wants the VC to have as firm a commitment and as much risk sharing as possible, with the minimum of rights to be given away to the VC.

Figure 14.1 shows the common investment securities ranked from one with the highest commitment and sharing of risk to that with the least commitment from the investor.

FIGURE 14.1   COMMON INVESTMENT SECURITIES

Common Shares	Highest risk of ownership
Preferred Shares	Lower risk, more rights than common shares
Convertible Loan	Ranked higher than shareholders, option to convert to shares
Warrants or Options	Lowest risk, no upfront capital

Common shares, which are held by the founders, rank last to receive liquidation proceeds and have the least rights. Hence they represent the highest risk of ownership of the company. Preferred stock is most commonly used by the VC, as it allows specification of any number of rights to be attached to the stock. These rights give the shareholders preference over common shareholders and therefore reduce the risks of ownership. A loan ranks higher in a liquidation and is usually collateralized. The lender has the choice to convert to shares at a later date when the company's performance is more certain, or to be repaid on maturity if the future is uncertain. Having warrants or options entails the least risk, as there is no up-front payment, and the warrant or option is exercised at a later date when the prospects of the company are more clear.

While obviously the VC would want the least risks and the most rights, the tussle between the VC and the founders of the investee company have resulted in the most common solution of the VC taking preferred shares, sometimes combined with some convertible debt or some warrants. However, the VC negotiates into the deal many special or preferential rights attached to its preferred shares. A plethora of such rights has been created and accumulated over the years, such as convertibility to common stocks, redemption, and participation in dividends, as well as certain voting, anti-dilution rights, liquidation, and registration rights.

In this chapter we shall review the features of each type of security and will focus on the various preferential rights that VCs usually ask for.

Types of Securities

Common Shares

Common stock, or ordinary shares, confers no other rights except those that relate to ownership, such as entitlement to dividends and certain voting rights. In a liquidation, common shareholders will rank last to receive liquidation proceeds. The founders of the company would normally have common shares. Passive investors also take common shares as they merely share in the risk without adding value. Angel investors may take common shares although sometimes they may have preferred shares with limited rights such as liquidation preference.

Preferred Shares

Preferred shares may also be called preference shares. This is the most common type of security for VC deals, as it offers great flexibility. As the name implies, a preferred share can be conferred preferential rights which need not be conferred on common stock. As an example, the preferred share would typically have *liquidation preference*, which gives it a higher ranking than common shares in terms of entitlement to proceeds from the liquidation of the company, if such an event occurs. These and other preferential rights will be discussed in the next section.

It is interesting to see why a simple right such as liquidation preference is important to the VC. Suppose a VC invests one million for 25 percent of a start-up company with nothing except an entrepreneur with a bright idea and some capability to develop the idea into a product. Assume the VC invested in common shares, which means that the VC has only voting rights, which do not amount to much since the entrepreneur can outvote the VC whenever he chooses. What happens if soon after the money went in, the entrepreneur has a heart attack and could no longer work? The company is wound up, and the proceeds is the one million cash. However, the VC firm gets only 25 percent, which is $250,000, compared with the one million it disbursed.

Another situation may be that soon after the VC's investment, the entrepreneur gets an offer from a large corporation to buy 100 percent of the company for $2 million. The entrepreneur accepts the offer, seeing that this means that 75 percent of the $2 million, which is $1.5 million, goes into his pocket; he gets to work in a subsidiary of the large corporation that can provide the support to build up the company; and he would personally get perhaps 10 percent stock options. The VC cannot stop the transaction and gets 25 percent of $2 million, which means a loss of $500,000.

Thus it has become standard practice that the VC would insist on liquidation preference, so that in a liquidation or sale of the company, the VC would get its investment back first. Thus its shares would no longer be common shares because of the preferential right, but are called, not surprisingly, preferred shares.

In both the above examples, if the VC had a simple liquidation preference right, it would receive one million first, and the rest of the proceeds, if any, would be distributed to common shareholders. We shall see in a later section in this chapter, where we discuss liquidation preference, that this simple right can be modified to lean more in the favor of the VC.

The price per share of the preferred shares would typically be higher than that for common shares, which would be held by the founders and angel investors. The structure of having preferred shares for investors and common shares for founders and employees allows not only different rights, but also different pricing for the shares. Common shares are usually priced at a low price to give founders a significant stake for a small outlay.

For example a start-up may issue 500,000 common shares priced at $0.10 each to the founders. They may then raise a first round of financing by issuing 1,000,000 preferred shares at $2.00 each. Thus the founders will own one-third of the company for an outlay of $50,000 while the investors will own two-thirds for an outlay of $2,000,000. As future rounds of financing are raised, the founders and the first round investors will be diluted. However the founders, if they are active in the company, will have their stake increased through the employee stock option plan, so that they remain motivated. The first round investors can participate in future rounds to reduce dilution, or might remain content that their shares have increased in value, even though they may end up with a smaller percentage in the company.

In subsequent rounds of financing, the price and rights attached to the shares are likely to be different from those in the first round, and hence the first round preferred shares are identified as Preferred A shares, the next round as Preferred B shares, and so on.

It is likely that later round investors will want to have at least all the rights of prior round investors. It is also possible that later round investors will require changes in the rights of earlier round investors, if the later round investors believe that they will be disadvantaged by earlier round terms. The earlier round investors will have to agree to give away certain of their rights if the later round investors are needed to support the company. How much is given or taken away result from the investment negotiation process.

Convertible Loan

The convertible loan is a loan that gives the lender the right to convert the loan into shares of the company at a pre-determined formula or calculation method. To the investor this is like having his cake and eating it. As a lender he could ask for collateral as security and he would rank above shareholders in a liquidation. Yet he would be able to enjoy the upside from an increased valuation should the company do well, by converting the loan into shares. Usually entrepreneurs do not like this type of security. There is a cost to the financing arising from the interest charged. The company will be in a more difficult position to borrow from banks as its assets would be already pledged and its gearing would have been increased by the convertible loan. However, the VC may have to agree to have the loan subordinated, in which case the bank may treat this as equity and be prepared to offer debt facilities to the company.

The entrepreneur would prefer to have an investor with a stronger commitment and greater preparedness to share in the business risk. He would also prefer not to have a constant threat that the investor may call the loan, putting the company into sudden cash flow problems.

A convertible loan would therefore be used more frequently alongside an equity investment. The investor keeps the entrepreneur happy by taking some equity risks, but limits his exposure by investing partly in the form of a convertible loan. A corporate investor would often choose this method because it wants to limit its initial ownership so as to avoid having a significant adverse impact on its own financial results. For example, the local corporate laws may require the parent company to *equity account*, if its ownership is 20 percent or more, and to *consolidate* the daughter company's accounts if its ownership is more than 50 percent. If the daughter company is not making profits, the parent may choose to hold only 19 percent, which then allows it to treat the daughter as merely an associate. If the daughter requires a larger amount of funding, the remaining amount can be invested in the form of a convertible loan, which can be converted when the daughter becomes profitable.

Similarly, if the corporate investor does not wish to consolidate the daughter company's accounts, it may invest just up to 49 percent. If the VC wishes to bring in a corporate co-investor, it has to recognize these concerns when structuring the deal.

In situations where the VC views the investment as having high risks, yet promising very high returns, the VC may insist on a convertible loan instead of taking preferred shares. If the company later makes satisfactory progress, the VC will convert the loan to preferred shares, otherwise it will call the loan at maturity or earlier. The VC may be able to get away with a convertible loan instead of preferred shares if it has exceptional bargaining power or if entrepreneurs are finding VC funding hard to come by.

A convertible loan may charge a simple interest, or may have the interest accrued and be convertible together with the principal amount. Accruing the interest reduces the cash flow burden of the investee company and provides more upside to the investor.

Bond Plus Warrants

In a situation where the previous round valuation had to be preserved in spite of a decline in performance, perhaps an amenable structure would be to invest in the form of a convertible bond with warrants. The bond will be convertible at the previous round pricing. The warrants will be convertible to common shares at a nominal price, say at one-third the previous round price. Management can argue to existing shareholders that the bond preserves the valuation, in spite of the decline in performance, and the warrants are awarded as an incentive to attract the latest investor to help rescue the company.

Loan with Detached Warrants

Warrants are options to buy the company's shares under certain terms and conditions. Such warrants may be free or at a nominal cost to the investor. The exercise price of the warrants may be at a predetermined price or at market price. For example, the investor may be sold 100,000 warrants at a nominal price of $1.00, which give him the right, but not the obligation, to purchase 100,000 shares at $10 each within a specified time period. Obviously he will exercise the warrants only if the value per share goes above $10. If the value does not increase above $10 within the life of the warrant, he does not exercise and he does not lose anything (other than $1.00).

A loan with detached warrants is such that the warrants are not affected by decisions relating to the loan. The warrants are independent and hence are called detached from the loan. This gives the advantage to the lender that he has the freedom to take actions on the loan, such as restructuring or withdrawing it, without being forced to convert to equity or losing the right to convert, as in the case of a convertible loan. Such a form of investment is not typical for VCs but frequent for banks and mezzanine funds. The detached warrants give the bank or mezzanine fund the equity upside that adds to its returns from the interest charged.

Senior or Subordinated Debt

This would be in the form of a term loan usually secured by assets of the company. This is not used by a VC as the return derived from the interest earned is less than 20 percent, which is too low to satisfy the fund investors.

Preferential Rights

Figure 14.2 shows the common preferential rights that a VC usually asks for. Just one look at this table is enough to appreciate the confusion and bewilderment that can arise in an entrepreneur when confronted with a term sheet that spells out these rights in all their myriad variations and combinations.

It would be useful to reiterate that these preferential rights, as the name implies, accrue to the preferred shareholders only, and not to common shareholders. Each series of preferred shares, Series A, Series B, Series C, Series D, etc., has its own set of preferential rights. We are distinguishing these preferential rights from standard shareholders' rights, such as right of first refusal, tag along rights, and drag along rights, which are applicable to both common and preferred shareholders.

The rest of this chapter will be devoted to discussions on the preferential rights listed in Figure 14.2.

FIGURE 14.2 PREFERENTIAL RIGHTS

Preferred Dividend	with	Guaranteed cumulative dividend,
	or	Non-cumulative preferred dividend
Liquidation Preference	with	Simple preference,
	or	Multiple preference,
	or	Participating preference,
	or	Participating multiple preference
Conversion	with	Conversion at 1:1 or other fixed ratio,
	or	Based on a ratchet formula
Redemption	with	Redemption premium,
	or	Without
	with	Redemption on the company,
	or	Put option on the Founders
Anti-Dilution	with	Full ratchet formula,
	or	Broad-based weighted average formula,
	or	Narrow-based weighted average formula
	with	Pay-or-play provision,
	or	Without
	with	Preemption provision,
	or	Without
Registration	with	Demand registration,
	and	S-3 registration,
	and	Piggyback registration

Preferred Dividend

The VC's preferred shares may carry the right to an annual dividend in preference to the common shares. Such a *preferred dividend* helps to boost the VC's return when it exits at a future date. If the company is a total loss, this dividend provides at least some return on the VC's investment.

How this dividend right is structured depends on how favorable the VC wants to make it for itself. A very favorable form would be a *guaranteed cumulative dividend* rate of say 15 percent per annum. This requires the company to annually pay a dividend to the preferred shareholders equal to 15 percent of the investment made. If in any year the funds are insufficient, the company will have to make up in subsequent years. No dividends may be paid to common shareholders for as long as any dividend is outstanding to preferred shareholders.

A less strict provision would be a *non-cumulative preferred dividend*, which means that if a dividend is not declared in any year, it would not be necessary to make up in subsequent years. However, it still means that if the company wishes to declare a dividend to common shareholders, it must have sufficient profits and cash to pay the dividend to preferred shareholders first.

The VC may choose to agree that the dividends be accrued, so that the company's cash flow is not impaired, and have the option to convert the accrued dividends to preferred shares with the same rights and at the same price as those it has invested in.

Some VCs take the view that they would prefer the company to reinvest its profits to further grow the company and hence would not require such a dividend right. They would rather achieve their return from the capital gain when they divest. This would more likely be the case where the VC is the sole investor, besides the founders, and hence does not need to possess this right to help gain a more advantageous position than earlier round investors. In such a case the provision would merely be to entitle the preferred shares to participate in dividends together with common stock on an as-converted basis.

Liquidation Preference

To give added protection to the VC, it has become a standard practice to provide for preferential treatment when the company is liquidated, or sold, or merged with another company, or undergoes a change in control affecting a specified majority, say 75 percent, of the shareholders' votes in the company. In such situations, the preferred shares have *liquidation preference*—i.e., the net proceeds from the liquidation or sale (after settling with creditors and employees' salaries) will first go to repaying the investment made by the VC before dividing out to the other shareholders, who would be holding common shares or holding preferred shares which rank lower (*senior* preferred shares versus *junior* preferred shares).

This *simple liquidation preference* has morphed over the years. At times when VC funding was tight, VCs were able to create more favorable versions of this right. One version allows the VC to not only get its investment back, but also a certain yield from it. This would not make any difference if the investee company had gone under and the liquidation proceeds would not have been enough to return the investment amount in any case. However, there could be instances where the investee company is acquired or merged with another company, with the investee company being valued at a price close to or even below that at which the VC paid for, even though the real value could be higher. The founders may not object to the low valuation as they may be rewarded with rich stock options by the new owner.

To protect itself from such situations, the VC may insist on a certain annual yield attached to its liquidation preference, taking care to define liquidation to include mergers and effective acquisitions. A typical yield arrived at after negotiations may be 20 percent, which would be inadequate compensation against the VC's desired IRR of at least 30 percent from an investment, but may still be satisfactory under the circumstances. This type of liquidation preference may be called a *liquidation preference with a yield.*

After the severe dot-com crash in early 2000, many companies were able to raise more funds only in a *down round* (i.e., a financing round at a lower valuation than the previous round). More onerous terms were imposed on investee companies. The liquidation preference right morphed further. The yield became a multiple instead. A 20 percent annual yield is about two times after four years and 2.5 times after five years. The multiples that were specified became as high as five times, which represents 38 percent IRR over five years.

Thus a *multiple liquidation preference*, as it was called, means that on liquidation or on a deemed liquidation such as a merger or a trade sale, the proceeds would first be paid to the VC firm until it gets back the specified multiple of its investment amount, ahead of other shareholders. If the VC had invested one million with a five times multiple liquidation preference, the net proceeds from the liquidation will first go to paying the VC $5 million and the remaining amount, if any, will be paid to other shareholders.

Due to the quick merger or trade sale of many dot-com companies, VCs felt that specifying a multiple would be more advantageous than an annual yield. Thus, for example, assuming that there are sufficient proceeds from the liquidation or deemed liquidation, a 20 percent yield will mean 20 percent IRR regardless of the time period. On the other hand, a two times multiple will be equivalent to 20 percent if the liquidation occurred after four years but if it occurred after two years instead, the IRR to the VC will be about 40 percent.

To make it even more favorable, some VCs asked for the remaining amount to be paid to all shareholders on a pro rata basis (proportional to shareholding, with preferred shares treated on an as-converted basis). Thus the VC not only gets a large first bite of the proceeds, it also gets a prorated second bite of the remaining amount. Such a preference is called a *participating liquidation preference*. This is also known as *double dipping*, since the VC takes two bites of the pie. If this is combined with a multiple liquidation preference, it would be called a *participating multiple liquidation preference*.

Let us look at some examples to clarify. Assume a VC had invested $3 million in a company two years ago, resulting in the shareholding structure given in Figure 14.3. Also assume that the company is now sold for $12 million.

FIGURE 14.3   SHAREHOLDINGS OF Example Inc

	Type of Shares	No. of Shares	
Founders	Common	5,000,000	50%
Angels	Common	2,000,000	20%
VC	Preferred	3,000,000	30%
Total		10,000,000	100%

Case A: VC has simple liquidation preference

A simple or straight liquidation preference only gives the VC the first bite of the liquidation proceeds. The VC therefore would take $3 million out from the $12 million proceeds. The remaining $9 million would be shared by the founders and angels on a pro rata basis. The founders would get 5/7 × 9 = $6.4 million and the angels 2/7 × 9 = $2.6 million. However, in this case, this would not be the preferred route for the VC.

In this case, the VC should not deem this to be a liquidation event and would be better off taking its 30 percent share, which is pro rata the shareholding. This amounts to $3.6 million, which is higher than $3 million. The liquidation preference right should be worded such that the VC would have the higher of its investment amount or the prorated share. Alternatively, the VC could convert its preferred shares to common shares prior to liquidation and be entitled to 30 percent share of proceeds.

Thus in this case, if the proceeds were less than $3 million, the VC would simply exercise its liquidation preference. The VC will take the whole proceeds and the other shareholders get nothing. If the proceeds were between $3 million and $10 million, the VC would still be better off to exercise its liquidation preference. If the proceeds were more than $10 million, the VC would be better off to take its 30 percent share instead.

Case B: VC has simple liquidation preference with a 20 percent annual yield

The $3 million investment would have yielded about $4.3 million after two years, at 20 percent compounding. Thus the VC will be paid $4.3 million and the remaining $7.7 million will be distributed to the other shareholders.

Case C: VC has participating liquidation preference

The VC takes $3 million first. The remaining $9 million is shared by all shareholders on a pro rata basis: the founders, angels, and the VC get $4.5 million, $1.8 million, and $2.7 million respectively. Thus the VC receives in total $5.7 million.

This is the case where the VC has a *double-dip* into the proceeds. Compare this with Case A where the VC gets only a single dip, with a choice of either taking back its investment amount *or* its pro rata share.

Case D: VC has multiple liquidation preference of three times

The VC takes three times its investment amount (i.e., $3 \times 3 = \$9$ million). The remaining $3 million is shared by the other shareholders. The founders get $5/7 \times 3 = \$2.1$ million and the angels receive $2/7 \times 3 = \$0.9$ million.

Again it is interesting to note here that if the company was sold for more than $30 million, which is entirely possible, it would have been better for the VC to take the 30 percent prorated share instead of the three times multiple. Thus it would be advisable for the liquidation preference clause to be worded so that the VC has the choice of the higher of the two.

Case E: VC has participating multiple liquidation preference of three times

Here, like Case C, the VC takes a double dip into the proceeds, but with the first dip magnified by the liquidation multiple, which in this case is three times.

The VC first takes three times its investment amount or $3 \times 3 = \$9$ million. The remaining $3 million is shared pro rata by all the shareholders, including the VC. The founders get $1.5 million, the angels $0.6 million and the VC gets $0.9 million. In total the VC gets $9.9 million.

The participating multiple liquidation preference is *always* higher than the prorated share, so there is no need to ask for the higher of the two. This can be worked out algebraically. Or it can be reasoned out logically as follows. Although the second bite is shared on a pro rata basis, the VC has all of the first bite to itself. On a pro rata basis, the first bite would also have to be shared, thus would always be less.

These examples show how the various forms of liquidation preference can increase the VC's return, albeit at the expense of the other shareholders. In Case E, the VC takes $9.9 million out of the $12 million proceeds, an 82.5 percent share. It has the effect of increasing the VC's shareholding from 30 percent to 82.5 percent.

The practice of asking for multiple liquidation preference became common during the dot-com days when start-up and early stage companies were sold or went IPO within a short time. If the VC invested say $10 million into a dot-com company at a valuation of $100 million and the company was sold for $120 million after a year, the VC would not have been satisfied with its 20 percent return for the risks involved. A 1.5 liquidation multiple would have been satisfactory if the company was indeed sold for $120 million after a year. But if it took two years, the return would have been about 22 percent. The multiple ballooned to two or three times, and in the frenzy of those days, went to as high as five times.

This practice started to wane off in mid-2002, after the crash and after investors found that it only promoted an inhospitable feeling from the entrepreneurs and other earlier investors. However, the financing environment continued to remain difficult and investors continued to insist on participating multiple liquidation preference, although frequently at the reduced rate of one and a half to two times the investment amount. Three times or more became rare.

Many VCs hold the position that a two or three times multiple is fair. A two and a half times return over five years translates to about 20 percent compounded annual rate of return, which after deducting the VC's management fees will be insufficient to achieve the better than 20 percent IRR required by limited partners. Unlike the dot-com days when a liquidation event can occur as soon as six months after a VC's investment round, the investment holding period has now fallen back to the usual three to seven years time frame.

When the VC market becomes hot again, with many VCs chasing after a deal, it is probably unlikely that the liquidation multiple will revert to three to five times, after the lessons learned from the dot-com days. Many VCs will likely revert to the original straight preference, with or without a yield. In the case of start-ups and other early stage companies, because of the higher risks, and the greater likelihood of a trade sale, the VC may ask for participating liquidation preference with a multiple of say one and a half or two times.

Conversion Rights

The preferred shares that are issued to the VC are usually convertible to common shares at a later stage. The shares are hence called *Convertible Preferred Shares* or CPS in short form. This convertibility enables the VC's shares to be listed when the company goes IPO. Therefore there is usually a provision for the preferred shares to be automatically converted to common shares prior to an IPO. The conversion may also be on a voluntary basis—for example, to facilitate the sale of the company.

Typically the preferential shares held by the VC will convert to common shares on a one-to-one basis, which means one common share for each preferred share. However, VCs have found that the conversion ratio is a convenient way to make an adjustment to its investment price if the company does not meet projections by a significant margin. If the company underperforms it is unlikely to be able to return money to the VC to effect a lower price for the shares purchased. Thus the alternative is to issue more shares to the VC. This can be done by adjusting the conversion ratio, so that more common shares can be issued for each converted preferred share. The alternative way is for the company to keep an amount of shares in escrow (in reserve). The escrowed shares will then be issued to the VC if the company underperforms by a specified measure. The conversion ratio formula allows for greater flexibility in varying the investment price, whereas the escrowed shares arrangement is a single point adjustment.

Such an adjustment mechanism is called a *ratchet* mechanism. A ratchet is actually a mechanical device that allows a wheel to be turned only one way, when it is set. A financial ratchet, in this case, is a formula by which the investment price may be adjusted downwards if the company underperforms after the investment is made. However, the original meaning has since been lost, as the financial ratchet can now be turned either way. Entrepreneurs have successfully negotiated for the investment price to be increased should the company perform above plan. Therefore some VCs do not like to impose ratchets, as the entrepreneur will ask for the ratchet to turn the other way, too.

Conversion Terms

If the preferred shares are to be convertible to common shares not on the basis of one to one but based on a formula, a typical conversion formula may be as follows:

$$N2 = N1 \times P1/P2$$

Where $N1$ = Number of preferred shares held
$N2$ = Number of common shares to be issued
$P1$ = Target performance measure (e.g. NPAT, revenue, etc)
$P2$ = Actual performance

Thus if the VC held one million preferred shares and if the actual NPAT was $0.8 million for the target year, versus a targeted one million NPAT, then the number of common shares to be issued will be $1 \times 1/0.8 = 1.25$ million. Since the company's performance is below expectations, the VC is compensated by an additional 0.25 million shares, so that its price per share is averaged down and the entry valuation is lowered.

In practice, the entrepreneur often tries to negotiate a two-way ratchet, so that if the company's performance were to exceed projections, the VC would get fewer shares. Using the above formula, if $N1 = 1$ million preferred shares, $P1 = \$1$ million, $P2 = \$1.25$ million, then $N2 = 1 \times 1/1.25 = 0.8$ or 800,000 common shares.

The VC may stand firm and insist that the formula applies only if $P2$ is less than $P1$. On the other hand, the VC may give in, particularly if the VC feels that the projections are so optimistic that the ratchet is much more likely to move down (worse than projected) than to move up.

Obviously there are countless ways to structure the ratchet formula or to use different performance measures or a combination of measures in the formula. It is also possible to specify an average of two years as a target or a series of years as targets to reduce the ability by the management to manipulate the numbers for a single target year by bringing forward revenues or postponing expenses.

Depending on how the ratchet formula is structured, it may happen that the VC ends up having a large majority or even the whole company. Driven by such fears, the entrepreneur may ask for a floor to the ratchet. Thus he may insist that there will be a floor to the value of $P2$—for example, to deem that $P2 = \$0.5$ million—even if the company's actual NPAT for the target year drops below this. Thus the maximum conversion ratio will be two in this case. In response the investor may insist on a ceiling to the ratchet, in case the investee company derives windfall profits in the target year that will not be repeated.

The VC needs to remember to exclude extraordinary income, and not to allow changes to financial policies such as depreciation rates, provisions for inventory obsolescence or other accounting policies that might artificially inflate earnings.

In view of all these to-and-fro tactics, some VCs do not like to use a ratchet. The school of thought here is to work out realistic projections and to invest at a valuation based on the realistic projections. If the entrepreneur demands a valuation that is higher, the VC will just walk away instead of giving in and incorporating a ratchet for downside protection.

Some VCs take the downside protection to the other extreme, by structuring the investment in the form of a convertible loan, which converts into convertible preferred shares upon the company hitting specified milestones. These convertible preferred shares may then be converted to common shares upon other milestones being reached. Ratchets are built into the respective conversion ratios. These VCs may get away with such terms when the market is turned against investees, such as after the dot-com crash.

Redemption Rights

Preferred shares can carry rights for redemption, which means the shareholder has the right to return the shares and get repaid in cash. The stock is called *Redeemable Preferred Shares*. Unlike convertibility, which is normally a given, redemption right is optional. If both redemption and convertibility are incorporated, the stock is called *Redeemable Convertible Preferred Shares* or RCPS in short.

The redemption feature provides an escape mechanism for the investor to exit if the company is not performing to expectations. However, under such circumstances the company is unlikely to have the cash to pay for the shares being redeemed. Sometimes the company may be raising another round of financing and may have the cash, but the new investor would most likely object to the funds being used to bail out a prior investor. Although the value and enforceability of this feature is arguable, VCs nevertheless often ask for it.

The redemption may be at the option of the VC or at the option of the company. The VC wants to have the option to redeem so that it gets its money back if it thinks that the investee company is going nowhere. The founders of the investee company want to have the option to redeem the shares, so that they will have a larger stake in the company, should the company be successful and generate sufficient cash to pay back the investor. Usually the VC will want such redemption to be solely at its option, because if the company were successful, it would want to retain its shareholding. However the VC should realize that if the company is not successful, it will not have the cash to make the repayment, and may trigger liquidation. Such a provision would usually be useful for *living dead* investments. These are companies that have not made much progress and the VC will likely get its investment back with little or no return. Since a VC manages funds which have finite lifetimes, it has to divest from all its investments towards the end of life of the particular fund. Thus it has no choice but to redeem its investment even if the return is not favorable, rather than to distribute the shares of the company to limited partners. The limited partners would be rather unhappy to receive shares of an unlisted company, and worse, a company that is not doing well.

Often the investor requires a return on its investment on redemption through a redemption premium, or through the provision of an interest or dividend that may be payable annually or accrued to be payable on redemption. This works like the liquidation premium. The redemption provision may be made very favorable to the VC by providing for a large premium. In some cases the premium can be as high as twice the invested amount, thus the total amount payable by the company can be three times the investment made. It would be most probable that the company would be unable to make such a hefty payment in one lump sum, so there is usually a provision for installment payments. Again, the extent to which the VC may impose such a condition depends on the prevailing VC market conditions and the relative bargaining positions of the VC and the investee company.

Anti-Dilution Rights

One of the greatest fears of a VC is that it has paid too high a price for its investment. This could have been due to an overestimation of the value, especially during hot markets, or as often is the case, the company did not perform to its projections. When the company raises a subsequent round of financing, the pre-money valuation could be lower than the post-money valuation of the prior round. Such a situation is called a *down round*. The VC will find that its investment value has dropped (i.e., its investment has been diluted). Thus VCs frequently insert a clause which requires the company to issue more shares to the VC to compensate for the dilution in value. This is called an *anti-dilution right*.

For example, the VC may have invested $5 million for 20 percent of a company. It was issued 5 million shares at $1.00 each out of the outstanding

25 million shares. The post-money valuation was therefore $25 million. If the company raises a subsequent round at a pre-money valuation of $20 million, it would be down round. Say it raises $2 million by issuing an additional 2.5 million shares at $0.80 each. The VC's investment value has been diluted to $4 million (5 million shares at $0.80 each). If the price per share were $0.80 when the VC invested, it would have got 6.25 million shares instead of the 5 million. Thus the VC will need to be compensated with an additional 1.25 million shares, if it had an anti-dilution right.

In practice the conversion price or the conversion ratio for the preferred share would be adjusted. In our example, the conversion price would have been $1.00 and the conversion ratio would have been one common share for every preferred share. With the anti-dilution adjustment, the conversion price will become $0.80 instead of $1.00, and the conversion ratio will become 1.25 instead of 1. Such an adjustment is called a *full ratchet* as the adjustment fully compensates the VC, as if it had invested in the previous round at the price of $0.80.

Again in practice, the VC may not get away with such a heavy protection. In a down round situation, the new investor is obviously in a stronger bargaining position and when it finds out that prior investors have a fully ratcheted anti-dilution clause, it may demand that this clause be rescinded or at least be reduced in effect, or else it will not invest. This is because the new investor itself gets diluted when the anti-dilution clause is effected. Thus in the foregoing example, the new investor would have got 2.5 million shares out of the enlarged shareholding of 27.5 million shares, or 9.1 percent. When the anti-dilution clause is effected, the total outstanding shares get increased to 28.75 million shares through the issue of additional 1.25 million compensating shares. The new investor gets diluted down to 8.7 percent of the company.

If the new investor insists on having 9.1 percent shareholding, and the old investor refuses to waive or change the anti-dilution clause, an iterative calculation will have to be made. This is because effecting the anti-dilution results in diluting the new investor. Then by increasing the shares for the new investor to his desired percentage, the old investor gets further diluted, and his anti-dilution adjustment has to be recalculated. This iterative calculation can be done manually using a spreadsheet or by solving algebraic equations.

In the example given, this results in the new investor paying $0.75 per share. He invests $2 million for 2,666,667 shares, which is 9.1 percent of the company. The old investor gets adjusted to 6,666,667 shares, which results in a price of $0.75 per share for his $5 million investment.

Figure 14.4 shows the shareholding structures before and after the new investment.

FIGURE 14.4   SHAREHOLDING STRUCTURE

(A) BEFORE INVESTMENT

	Amount Invested	No. of Shares	Shareholding	Price per Share
Founders		20,000,000	80.0%	
Old Investor	$5,000,000	5,000,000	20.0%	$1.00
Total		25,000,000		

(B) AFTER NEW INVESTMENT, BEFORE ANTI-DILUTION ADJUSTMENT

	Amount Invested	No. of Shares	Shareholding	Price per Share
Founders		20,000,000	72.7%	
Old Investor	$5,000,000	5,000,000	18.2%	$1.00
New Investor	$2,000,000	2,500,000	9.1%	$0.80
Total		27,500,000		

(C) AFTER NEW INVESTMENT AND ANTI-DILUTION ADJUSTMENT

	Amount Invested	No. of Shares	Shareholding	Price per Share
Founders		20,000,000	68.2%	
Old Investor	$5,000,000	6,666,667	22.7%	$0.75
New Investor	$2,000,000	2,666,667	9.1%	$0.75
Total		29,333,334		

Notice that the founders who are common shareholders and do not have anti-dilution rights, have been diluted from what would have been 72.7 percent to 68.2 percent shareholding after the adjustment. If there had been several rounds of VC financing, and each round had anti-dilution rights, a subsequent down round can result in very substantial dilution to the founders, because of the many adjustments. In such a case, the new investor would likely ask for the employee stock options pool to be increased, or the founders be given incentive stock options, to be awarded based on performance. If there were angel investors who took common shares, they would not be granted such incentive options and they would be severely diluted. If any of the VC investors did not have anti-dilution rights, it would be similarly severely diluted.

Adding employee stock options can also have a dilutive effect. Figure 14.5 shows the impact of adding 4 million shares for an employee stock options plan into the given example.

FIGURE 14.5   AFTER NEW INVESTMENT, ANTI-DILUTION ADJUSTMENT AND ADDING STOCK OPTIONS

	Amount Invested	No. of Shares	Shareholding	Price per Share
Founders		20,000,000	56.8%	
Old Investor	$5,000,000	8,000,000	22.7%	$0.625
New Investor	$2,000,000	3,200,000	9.1%	$0.625
Options		4,000,000	11.4%	
Total		35,200,000		

The founders are further diluted down to 56.8 percent, but they may participate in the stock options plan. The new investor gets more shares to maintain his 9.1 percent shareholding, resulting in a price of $0.625 per share. The old investor's conversion ratio gets adjusted such that when his shares are converted he will get more shares to match the price of $0.625.

Compare Figure 14.4(C) with Figure 14.5. The founders would end up being rather unhappy, as the 11.4 percent for the stock options are actually taken away from them, to be given back to them only if they perform. This would not be the case if there are other shareholders without anti-dilution rights, such as angel investors.

In any case, Figure 14.5 is for illustrative purposes, as it is unlikely to occur. Anti-dilution is normally not triggered by issuance of employee stock options. Furthermore, the old investors' anti-dilution right is likely to be cut down or removed, on the insistence of the new investor.

A less severe implementation of the anti-dilution right is a *weighted average* formula instead of a full ratchet. There are two ways of taking the weighting. They are known as *broad-based weighted average anti-dilution* and *narrow-based weighted average anti-dilution*. If the term sheet does not specify which method of weighting is to be used, it is more likely to be broad-based.

The broad-based weighted average method works as follows:

New conversion price = Old conversion price × T1/T2

Where   T1 = Total outstanding number of shares if the new investor
                invested at the old investor's price
            T2 = Total outstanding number of shares based on the new
                investor's price

Thus using the foregoing example (without the options), where the old investor invested $5 million for 5 million shares and the new investor invested $2 million for 2.5 million shares:

T1 = 25 million + 2 million = 27 million, since the new investor would
           have received 2 million shares if it invested at the old investor's
           price of $1.00 per share
T2 = 25 million + 2.5 million = 27.5 million

New conversion price = $1.00 × 27 / 27.5 = $0.98

Compare this with the new conversion price of $0.80 for the fully ratcheted case. Without the weighting of the outstanding shares, the ratio T1/T2 would have simply been 2/2.5 = 0.8. Since the impact is less severe on the new investor, it may accept the continuation of this provision after its investment, or it may use this to leverage for more favorable positions on other terms.

Usually the weighting will be against the fully diluted capital of the company (i.e., assuming conversion of all convertible loans, preferred stock, options, and warrants taken together with all outstanding common stock). In some cases the weighting may be against only outstanding stock (i.e., ignoring unconverted securities). This will mean a smaller base and hence greater dilution.

In the case of narrow-based weighted average anti-dilution, the adjustment factor is calculated as follows:

A1 = Amount raised in the old investor's round
A2 = Amount raised in the new investor's round
N1 = Number of shares issued in the old investor's round
N2 = Number of shares issued in the new investor's round

New conversion price = Old conversion price × (A1 + A2)/(N1 + N2)

Using the foregoing example, the calculations will be as follows:

A1 = $5 million
A2 = $2 million
N1 = 5 million
N2 = 2.5 million

New conversion price = $1.00 × (5 + 2)/(5 + 2.5) = $1.00 × 7/7.5 = $0.93

This calculation takes the average price per share of the two financing rounds combined as the weighting factor to be applied to derive the new conversion price.

Unlike the commonly accepted method to calculate broad-based anti-dilution using the fully diluted quantity, there can be variations in the calculation method for narrow-based anti-dilution, depending on whether options are included or excluded.

In the above example, all options are excluded. Another calculation method may include options that are issued and yet another calculation may include issued options as well as those set aside for but are not yet issued. The fewer the number of options included, the less severe the anti-dilution adjustment.

The full ratchet is most severe to the other shareholders and the broad-based method is the least severe. The narrow-based methods fall in between. Most probably the narrow-based methods were dreamed up by creative VCs to arrive at different degrees of compromise between broad-based and full ratchet anti-dilution.

In general, the anti-dilution clause also covers other changes to the shareholding structure such as stock splits, stock dividends (bonus shares), and recapitalizations. If, for example, the number of outstanding shares is split from 25 million to 50 million, the conversion price will have to be halved to $0.50, since the value of each share has been halved.

The anti-dilution clause may also have certain exemptions where it would not be triggered—for example, the issuance of stock under the company's employee stock option plan, or issuance of warrants to a bank for a credit facility.

Pay-or-Play Provision

Sometimes the entrepreneur may negotiate a qualification to the anti-dilution clause whereby the VC would have to participate in a down round in order for the anti-dilution to be triggered. The rationale is that a new investor would not like to see that the VC benefits from a price adjustment without contributing further to the company. It would be more difficult to raise the down round if there are many severe anti-dilution adjustments. At the least, the round may be protracted by negotiations to water down or remove the adjustments.

Such a provision is called a *pay-or-play provision* as it is meant to penalize an investor by the loss or reduction of anti-dilution rights (pay) if it does not participate in a down round (play). Confusingly, this is sometimes called a *pay-to-play provision*, which means the same, but the name implies that the investor has to participate (pay) in order to continue enjoying the rights (play).

The VC may strenuously reject such a provision, if proposed by the founders. The VC would argue that the down round is a result of the founders not meeting their targets and hence the VC had paid too high a price and should be compensated with more stock, regardless of whether it participates in the down round or not. The whole issue of anti-dilution could be the subject of difficult negotiations.

The examples on dilution given here are known as price-based dilutions as the issue of new shares affects the price of the investment and the intent is to preserve the ownership price. Note that price-based anti-dilution usually applies in a down-round situation. Another form of dilution is percentage-based dilution, which arises from the issue of new shares that affects the ownership percentage and the intent is to preserve such percentage. This right to preserve ownership percentage when new shares are issued is called a *preemptive right*.

Preemptive Right

This gives an existing shareholder the right to participate in a future financing round under the same terms as the new investors, so as to maintain his shareholding percentage. If any shareholder waives his preemptive right, partially or wholly, the stake not taken up will be available to the other shareholders of the same series of preferred shares.

Besides a future financing round, a percentage-based anti-dilution clause may be applied to a special situation. This is in the case of a technology provider (e.g., a research institute) that may be given 5 percent ownership in a company in return for continuing technology support. Given that the company will have further rounds of financing, the research institute will find its ownership diminishing to a negligible amount. In such a case it may demand that its ownership will be adjusted back to 5 percent after each round of financing, without any funds to be contributed since it is contributing technical know-how on a continuing basis. If the technology support is considered valuable and the royalty fees that may be charged are considered reasonable, the new investors may agree to such an anti-dilution clause being applied. A provision may be included whereby the anti-dilution clause will cease to apply when the technology support is no longer provided.

The name preemptive right is often used interchangeably with *right of first refusal*, although more often preemptive right refers to the intended sale of shares by the company at a financing round, whereas right of first refusal refers to the intended sale of shares by an existing shareholder to a third party. Both rights entitle existing shareholders to preempt the sale by taking up their respective pro rata share of the shares.

The preemptive right (when it refers to an intended financing round) is an anti-dilution measure, as it enables a shareholder to preserve his shareholding percentage in the company. The right of first refusal (when it refers to sale by an existing shareholder) relates to control over transfer of shares by existing shareholders, to enable the other shareholders to increase their respective stakes or to block out an unwelcome party from being a shareholder, if they wish. Right of first refusal is a shareholder right, and will be further discussed on page 336.

Registration Rights

Registration rights arise from U.S. securities and exchange laws and are hence relevant only to U.S. companies. The registration rights that VCs ask from investee companies usually consist of three types: *Demand Registration Right, S-3 Registration Right,* and *Piggyback Registration Right.* These rights facilitate avenues for the VC to exit from an investee company after it has gone public. These rights will be explained together with Rule 144 regulations as they also affect the exit of the VC.

For the sake of clarity, it should be noted that the registration rights belong to the shareholders of the preferred shares, but the registration is for those common shares that are issued when the preferred shares are converted.

After the IPO, the VC would hold only common shares, but it would still have the registration rights for those shares.

Registration rights have been for a long time a bone of contention in U.S. venture investments, but fortunately by now they are widely accepted with certain built-in qualifications, such as restrictions on the timing and frequency of exercising such rights and cost-sharing arrangements, to reduce the inconvenience and cost to the company.

The following is a simplified explanation of SEC registration rights and Rule 144 requirements, capturing the more common scenarios, so that the picture is not complicated by extraneous variations and exceptions.

When a VC invests in a U.S. private company, the shares issued to the VC are usually "restricted" shares. Such shares can be resold only under certain conditions or exemptions spelled out in the USA Securities Act of 1933. A private sale to sophisticated ("accredited") investors or corporations may be made under specified conditions and would be exempted from SEC registration.

A sale to the public would obviously come under more stringent requirements. The public sale has to be registered with the SEC, unless it is made under certain exemptions (which include the Rule 144 exemption) spelled out in the Securities Act. This is to ensure full and fair disclosure, which would have to be provided in the registration statement. The form to be submitted to the SEC by a company issuing shares to the public for the first time—its initial public offering (IPO), is usually Form S-1, which is prescribed in the Act.

Prior to the IPO, all preferred shares are converted to common shares to facilitate eventual disposal of the VC's shares, and also because public investors subscribing to common shares in the IPO would feel disadvantaged if there were shareholders with preferential benefits such as preferred dividends. (However, the registration rights are retained by the preferred shareholders). In the IPO, a certain number of common shares are registered for public sale. Only these shares are freely tradeable. All other shares remain restricted and can only be sold under Rule 144 or other exemption rules, or through another registered offering. If the sale qualifies under the exemption requirements, a registration statement need not be filed.

A VC firm which wants to dispose its shares in the IPO would ask the company and its investment bank to include its shares in the offering. Such shares are known as secondary shares, while the new shares issued by the company for sale are known as primary shares. There would be a limit to the number of shares the VC can sell since there are other existing shareholders who may also want to divest, and too many secondary shares will reduce the amount of funds the company can raise and give the impression that existing shareholders are bailing out. How the primary and secondary shares are to be allocated will have to be agreed upon prior to the IPO, among the shareholders, the company, and the underwriters. The VC will almost always find that it will not be able to sell all its shares, and often none at all, in the IPO.

After the IPO, the VC would have to patiently wait out the lockup (or "hold-back") period, which is typically 90 or 180 days, or sometimes longer, during which existing shareholders are not allowed to sell their shares. This is imposed by the underwriters to ensure good aftermarket price performance. If existing shareholders dump shares soon after IPO, the price will crash.

After the expiry of the lockup period, the VC may want to start selling, but since the shares are restricted they have to be registered first before they can be sold publicly, or the sales have to meet Rule 144 exemption requirements. If the VC requests the company to register its shares with the SEC, the company may refuse to do so, since the registration process, which is tantamount to another IPO, entails costs and management time, requires the company to make disclosures that may affect its competitive position, exposes the management and directors to liability risks, and restricts the company from certain corporate actions while going through the process.

Therefore when the VC first invested in the company it would have asked for the right to demand the company to undertake a registration exercise. Such a right is known as a **Demand Registration Right**. Knowing the costs and disadvantages, the company would negotiate for limits and conditions under which the right can be exercised. If the VC exercises such a right and meets the conditions for it, the company has no choice but to comply.

A typical registration rights agreement would not allow a demand registration until some time (say six months) after the IPO, so that the VC cannot force the company to undertake another offering too soon after the IPO. The company would also limit the VC to demand registration only twice, and each time the company will accede only if the offering is sizeable enough. This could be defined such that shareholders holding at least a certain percentage (say 30 percent) of a particular series of shares (say Series A Preferred) make the demand, and/or the aggregate proceeds from the offering will amount to more than $10 million or some other specified amount. It will also be specified whether the expenses would be paid by the company or shared.

Even if the VC were to have Demand Registration Rights, whether a demand can be met in practice also depends on the VC's influence in the company, the influence of the underwriter, the state of the financial markets and the demand for the company's shares, and to a less extent, the cost of the registration exercise. It would not be advisable to force an offering, incur the costs and effort, and then fail.

However, if the IPO was very hot, and there is fresh and significant demand for the company's shares, the company may accede to the registration and make a secondary offering, perhaps several months after the IPO. This also provides an opportunity for the founders themselves to have some liquidity, as they would likely to have been prevented from selling their shares in the IPO.

If it were not possible to carry out a demand registration, the VC would have to consider disposing shares under Rule 144 exemption.

Rule 144 is a provision in the U.S. Securities Act that allows sales of restricted shares (without a registration statement) if certain conditions are met. Any restricted shares bought within one year cannot be sold publicly other than through a registration statement filing. After the first year, the shares may be sold publicly without registration, but such sales is subject to volume restrictions related to the company's total outstanding shares and the volume of trade of its shares. If the restricted shares were held for at least two years, there is no volume restriction.

The volume restriction is such that in any three-month period, the VC cannot sell more than the greater of one percent of the outstanding shares of the company or one week's average trading volume, such average being calculated over the four weeks immediately prior to the sale, excluding the VC's own sales. If the VC is considered an affiliate (for example if it has a board seat or has a significant shareholding), there are further restrictions—limiting the sales to certain non-sensitive time periods before and after announcement of the company's quarterly results.

The one-year holding period is usually not a problem, since the VC is likely to have invested earlier than one year prior to the intended sale. The volume restriction could be a problem if the VC owns a substantial number of shares and if the volume of trade is relatively low. If the VC has a board seat, it should give up the seat. The VC may still be considered an affiliate if it has a significant shareholding (not defined in the regulations, but usually interpreted to be 10 percent or more). Nevertheless, some VCs have successfully dribbled out their shareholding while meeting all these restrictions. Besides dribbling into the market, the VC could also make private placements to institutional investors to sell large blocks of shares, albeit with some discount. The VC could seek advice and assistance from brokers who have expertise in selling stocks under Rule 144.

There is yet another way for the VC to dispose its restricted shares. This is through an S-3 Registration, which refers to the Form S-3 used for such filing. This form is shorter than Form S-1, as information can be provided by merely referring to the financial statements and other reports that have been periodically filed with the SEC as requirements of a listed company. S-3 filing is hence less onerous than S-1 filing. (Demand Registration Right refers to Form S-1 Registration).

Form S-3 Registration, otherwise known as a **Shelf Registration**, may be used when a listed company issues shares to make an acquisition. As part of the acquisition agreement, the seller would want the shares that he receives to be tradeable. The company would therefore make an S-3 filing for the shares that are issued to the seller. S-3 Registration may also be used to cover shares issued when employee stock options are exercised. S-3 registrations are relatively inexpensive, incur little or no restrictions on the number of shares, volumes or price limits, the registration can be kept open indefinitely, and the shares may be sold through brokers, whose fees are lower than underwriters. However, an S-3 registration can only be made after at least one year after IPO, since a requirement is that the company must have made filings to SEC for at least twelve months.

Since an S-3 registration can be made only by the company, the VC has to request the company to do so. The company may not agree, as such a registration may create a negative overhang which could depress the stock price, since such shares are sold from time to time over a period of time, which could be months. This is unlike an underwritten offering where the shares are quickly sold. This gives rise to the **S-3 Registration Right** that is asked for by VCs at the time of the investment. Since S-3 registrations are relatively easy, there is usually agreement to give the VC unlimited number of registrations, provided each offering is of a specified minimum size. Expenses may be paid by the company or the VC, or shared.

Finally, the VC would want one more registration right in its investment terms, known as a **Piggyback Registration Right**. In contrast to the Demand Registration Right which demands the company to initiate registration of shares, a Piggyback Registration Right comes into play when the company itself initiates the registration of its shares for its own benefit (such as an offering to raise funds for an acquisition) or for benefit of other shareholders (who may have exercised their demand rights). In such a case, a shareholder with Piggyback Rights who is not included in the registration could demand to piggyback on the action, to have at least a portion of its shares to be registered as well. In this case, unlike demand rights, the company would be more willing to accede, since there is only marginal cost and effort to include the additional shares. Expenses in this case will be borne by the company.

Note that although registration rights are really meant for post-IPO use, they can theoretically be used before the company goes IPO (unless specifically prevented from doing so in the agreement). However, in practice it is almost never done, since it does not make sense to force a company to IPO if no underwriter is willing to support it. If a reliable underwriter is willing to support it, then it is unlikely that the company will not go IPO.

Impact on Returns

As a footnote it should be remembered that when calculating returns from an investment, the exercise of some of the preferential rights, such as convertibility and anti-dilution rights and enforcement of ratchets, affects the VC's ownership percentage and investment entry price, as shown by examples in this chapter. In working out scenarios based on different performance achievements of the investee company, one should consider whether ratchets would be triggered to ensure the correct returns would be calculated.

Chapter Recap

In this chapter, we went through the following:

- o The common equity investment securities
- o The preferential rights that may be attached to preferred shares:
    - o Preferred dividend
    - o Liquidation preference
    - o Conversion
    - o Redemption
    - o Anti-dilution
    - o Registration
- o The common variations in definition and application of these rights

15

Deal Structuring

D eal structuring refers to the construction of the main terms of the deal, such as the amount of investment, the valuation, type of security and preferential rights. In a wider sense, deal structuring may refer to all the terms and conditions of the deal. We shall use the narrower sense and separate the deal terms as shown in Figure 15.1.

FIGURE 15.1 DEAL TERMS & CONDITIONS

DEAL STRUCTURE	OTHER KEY TERMS
Amount of Investment	Management Control
Valuation of the Company	Management Incentives
Type of Security	Shareholder Rights
Preferential Rights	Exit Provisions
	Miscellaneous Terms

The deal structure is the more important part of the set of deal terms. The VC and the entrepreneur will focus attention and negotiate hard on these terms. If there is no agreement on the deal structure, the other terms are irrelevant.

In working out the deal structure, the VC aims to maximize returns and minimize risks of the investment. In this chapter we shall examine the elements of the deal structure and see how the VC firm constructs these elements to achieve its aims. We shall also discuss some deal structure related issues and the structuring of later stage investments and special situations such as recapitalizations, privatizations, buyouts, management buy-ins, industry consolidations, and turnarounds.

Deal Structure Elements

As we go through the deal structure elements (amount of investment, valuation, type of security, and preferential rights), we shall consider how they may be designed to achieve maximum returns on the investment and to minimize risks of loss of the investment.

Amount of Investment

The amount of investment required is determined by the cash flow of the company, based on its burn rate, capital expenditures, and debt servicing needs if any. If the company is going to take some time to reach cash breakeven and hence would require a large investment, the VC would consider breaking up the funding into several smaller rounds to reduce the risks.

These rounds would have to be marked by milestones that are significant enough to show real progress to enable the company to raise each round of financing. The VC would then invest enough for the company to reach its next milestone, with provision for some contingency. Good judgment would have to be exercised to ensure that the company would not run out of funds prematurely or have excessive funds that may encourage laxity in spending control. The VC therefore has to verify the assumptions in the projections and often may need to bring down the burn rate, including salaries and benefits, as most entrepreneurs tend to be generous on such expenses. On the other hand, delays are inevitable, so the VC has to factor in such contingencies into the funding amount to provide some additional runway for overruns.

We saw in Chapter 2: VC Financing how the staging of investments maximizes returns and reduces risks. Hence structuring the investment to allow for staging to match milestone achievements is a well-accepted and proven VC practice. However during the dot-com days, VCs raised mega-funds resulting in pressure to invest large amounts quickly. "Give the company sufficient runway" became the catchphrase and rationale for fully funding a company from start-up or early stage right through to cash-flow breakeven or even through to IPO. Raising $20 million or more in a Series A or B Round became common. It may be argued that in those days, it took only eighteen months or two years from start-up to IPO, therefore it did not make sense to have several intervening rounds of financing. The view then was that relieving management from more rounds of fund-raising enabled concentrated effort to race towards IPO. VCs have returned to the practice of investment staging, which reduces financial exposure, provides pressure on management to perform and meet milestones, and necessitates mid-stream progress review and adjustment of business strategies.

Valuation of the Company

Obviously the more the investee company grows successfully, the higher will be its valuation and hence the investment return. But the VC's return will be even higher if the investment was made at a lower valuation. Low entry valuation is crucial to achieving a high return. However, a low entry valuation, or for that matter, great deal structuring, does not make a bad investment turn into a good one. Low entry valuation makes a good investment give a better return, and proper deal structuring can enhance returns, minimize losses, and reduce risks.

Low entry valuation may be achieved through hard negotiation. Often, the VC has to do his homework to rework the entrepreneur's projections based on his knowledge and due diligence of the business to convince the entrepreneur that the projections are too optimistic and hence the valuation too high. If the entrepreneur refuses to be convinced and the VC wishes to pursue the deal, he may have to resort to negotiating a ratchet or some sort of profit guarantee.

Another way would be to compromise or horse-trade on other terms of the deal in return for the lower valuation. One way would be to increase the stock options pool. Another way would be to offer free shares if milestones are achieved. The argument here is that more stock options or free shares are dilutive to the VC, which means the VC ends up paying for a higher valuation. However, if milestones are indeed achieved, the VC would not mind the higher valuation. This is similar to a ratchet, but may be viewed better by the entrepreneur since it is a reward in nature whereas a ratchet may be viewed as punitive. If despite all efforts the valuation remains too high, the VC would have to walk away from the deal.

Type of Security

What type of investment security should the VC choose to maximize returns and minimize risks? A straight loan with collateral or guarantees is with minimum risk, but the return from the interest charged would be below the desired return for the VC. A convertible loan allows the VC to have his cake and eat it. If the company performs, he can convert to equity to enjoy higher returns. If the company does not perform, he recalls the loan. However the entrepreneur does not like an investor that can pull out at the first sign of trouble. He would want much more commitment.

We saw in Chapter 14: Investment Securities, that warrants or options represent even less commitment than a convertible loan as they do not even require an upfront outlay of capital. The warrant holder may choose to exercise the warrant only when the company's performance gives him the confidence to do so, or if the prospects do not turn out to be as good as anticipated, the warrant may be allowed to lapse, with no loss to the holder. Obviously this is totally unacceptable to the entrepreneur as his purpose is to raise funds for the company. Warrants are therefore used in conjunction with other investment securities to provide more upside to the investment with no added risk.

Investing in common shares would represent the highest commitment and hence degree of risk for the VC. Since the VC has some bargaining power, he does not need to plunge in to that extent. The VC's investment security of choice is therefore the preferred share, which ranks higher than the common share and can be conferred a host of preferential rights. It offers the VC tremendous flexibility to pick the desired combination from a wide variety of rights, giving him the choice to modify and weight each of them appropriately to suit the deal. He can even create a special right that has never been used before, but usually there is no need to do so, since a sufficient menu has already been created over the years.

Another advantage of preferred shares is that they allow differential pricing versus common shares, so that founders, management, and employees can have cheaper shares to motivate them. Also, the preferred shares issued at different rounds of financing can be priced differently to reflect the changing valuation of the company.

Preferred shares provide the balance of commitment and risks that are acceptable to both the VC and the entrepreneur.

Preferential Rights

Let us review how the preferential rights work in maximizing returns and reducing risks for the VC. Reference may be made to the section on Preferential Rights in Chapter 14 and the discussion below acts as a summary focusing on the risk and return features.

- o Preferred Dividend: This enhances the returns to the VC. The VC can choose between not having a preferred dividend, having a non-cumulative dividend or the highest payoff of a cumulative dividend. For early stage companies it may be wiser for the VC to choose not having a dividend as the money ploughed back into the company can bring higher returns. For investee companies that will be generating strong cash flow, the VC is likely to invest at a higher valuation and hence may need to enhance returns with a preferred dividend.

- o Liquidation Preference: This preference reduces downside risks compared to common shares, by having a higher ranking in the distribution of liquidation proceeds. This preference has been modified to take on returns enhancing characteristics as well, by giving the holder the right to receive more than its pro rata share according to shareholding percentage. This type of share can be defined as simple preference (just a higher ranking), preference with a yield, participating preference (double-dipping), preference with liquidation multiple (receiving a multiple of the investment), participating multiple liquidation preference (receiving a multiple and participating in the remainder). Liquidation events are defined to include mergers and acquisitions. More and more, young technology companies are sold off to large corporations, and VCs have this liquidation preference to provide it the returns that it feels it deserves, comparable to that from an IPO.

o   Conversion: This preference was originally simply to allow conversion to common shares prior to an IPO. Again this right has taken on more features by incorporating a conversion formula that acts as a ratchet, which protects the downside risks of the company underperforming and restores the returns to the VC, at least partially if not fully. Here the VC has free choice to craft the appropriate formula to increase the number of common shares on conversion, according to the degree of underperformance.

o   Redemption: This preference is a risk protection feature. It provides the effect of a convertible loan by allowing the preferred shares to be redeemed for cash, if the company does not perform. Obviously this right should be at the VC's option. If it is at the company's option, the VC may be denied the upside from the investment. Typical of VCs, some may squeeze a little more from this right by adding on an interest charge on redemption to at least secure some yield from the investment.

o   Anti-Dilution: This is a risk and return protection feature in a situation where the company does not perform, or market valuations drop substantially so that a subsequent financing round is at a lower valuation than what the VC paid for. Here the VC can choose different strengths of protection, ranging from a full ratchet for full protection, or a broad-based or narrow-based weighted average formula.

o   Registration: These do not affect the risk or return of the investment, but facilitate the divestment process for the VC.

Balancing Factors

So far we have merely considered the choices open to the VC on how he can work the deal structure to maximize returns and reduce risks. Obviously he will want to make those choices that can deliver the highest returns and give the best protection of risks. However, his decisions do not depend entirely on his own objective for returns and concerns for risks. The entrepreneur also has his objectives and concerns which often run counter to those of the VC. Influencing these are the prevailing VC market conditions which set the range of options acceptable at that time. We shall discuss these factors in Chapter 17: Deal Negotiation.

It should also be noted that the deal structure is not the only means by which the VC can maximize returns and minimize risks. Indeed, it is also not only the deal structure and all the other terms and conditions of the deal, such as management control and incentives. It is the total management of the deal. From the pre-investment stage of working out and negotiating the terms, to the post-investment monitoring, value adding and finding the best exit option. At every instance, the VC should be mindful of how returns can be maximized and risks minimized.

Deal Structure Related Issues

Besides the deal structure elements, there are related issues that the VC has to consider when structuring the deal. We shall now discuss those issues.

Investment Tranches

Staging investments into financing rounds is a way to maximize returns and minimize risks. Staging may be worked a step further by breaking up an investment round into several tranches. For example the VC may commit to invest $5 million which would bring the company to a significant milestone for the next financing round. However, instead of investing the whole amount at once, the VC may break up the amount into two tranches; the first amounting to $3 million and the second tranche for $2 million. The second tranche could be conditioned on certain targets being achieved, or on satisfactory review of progress made. Investment tranches are usually spread three or six months apart, whereas financing rounds are usually a year or more apart.

Tranching is like staging in that it also maximizes returns and minimizes risks, except that in tranching the VC has made conditional commitment to the next tranche or tranches. Tranching allows reevaluation of the company's financial and operational progress and prospects, review of achievement of targets or milestones, maintains performance pressure on entrepreneurs and managers, and allows the periodic realignment of interests with them.

On the other hand, such short-term targets can prove to be a distraction to the entrepreneurs and managers, and may create unnecessary dispute. Such dispute may arise over interpretation of targets, over small shortfalls, or over adverse events beyond the control of management. The management may also be tempted to mask or delay revelation of problems. The entrepreneurs may also feel that the VC had been unfair, in that the later tranches should be at the same valuation as the first tranche.

Use of Funds

Typically, a start-up company raises funds to develop a product or service and a later stage company raises funds to support its growth, such as purchasing capital equipment, adding facilities, making acquisitions, launching new products, venturing into new markets, increasing working capital, hiring new staff, etc. The successful growth increases the value of the company and hence provides the investment return to the VC. Therefore the VC would normally not want to purchase shares from existing shareholders as this means that the funds do not go into the company. An exception would be a recapitalization situation, which is discussed in the next section of this chapter. The VC should also refuse to allow the investment to be used to pay off shareholders' loans. Such loans should be converted to equity, or be restructured to be paid off when the company has positive cash flow.

Syndication

If the amount of funding required is too large for the appetite of the VC, or if the VC wants to spread its risks, the VC would have to structure the deal to be syndicated to co-investors. The added advantages would be that there would be more investors to share the monitoring effort and to add value. A strategic investor in the same or compatible industry could also be a co-investor to add business knowledge, synergy, and perhaps management support. A brand name financial or strategic investor could lend credibility to the company. A side benefit to the VC is that it could receive quid-pro-quo treatment and be invited to the deals of co-investors.

It is very important that a syndicated deal should have properly chosen lead investor and co-investors. The lead investor is not necessarily the one who found the deal or even the one who negotiated investment terms. If there is an investor who can better monitor and add value to the deal, leadership should be passed on after the deal is done. A clearly identified lead investor is necessary for accountability and reporting of progress of the investment. The co-investors must also be properly chosen so that there is alignment of understanding and interest. They must have agreement on how the company is to be directed and be able to reach consensus on follow-ons and exit strategies. Investments have been driven to failure through delays in or inadequate follow-on funding, or missed exits, because of an unreasonably dissenting shareholder or board representative.

Controlled Investments

For early stage companies where the valuation is low, the investors usually end up with a majority stake initially. Therefore syndicating the deal is also a means to spread out the ownership so that none of the investors have a majority stake, which may carry with it undue corporate responsibilities and liabilities. However, should the VC still desire to structure the deal towards a majority stake, he should be aware of the implications. In some countries, a controlled investment is not just defined by a controlling stake. Having control of the board or having the power to change management may also define control of the company and incur the ensuing responsibilities. If necessary the deal may be syndicated, or the investment structured as part equity and part convertible loan to avoid majority ownership.

Corporate Structure

Often the structuring of the deal has to take into consideration corporate restructuring for a variety of reasons such as corporate tax, capital gains tax, withholding tax, intellectual property protection, ownership structure, corporate legal requirements, IPO listing requirements and liquidity, licensing, marketing, etc. This would be particularly true in Asia, where companies conduct business across countries with different corporate laws, tax laws, and capital markets. The VC has to work out the optimum corporate structure and hence structure the investment accordingly.

If the investment is to be into a company operating in a country that requires local ownership, a foreign investment holding may be formed, which then enters into a joint venture with the local party. This is a common example for investments in China. The foreign holding company could also be listed in a country that has a more developed capital market so as to enjoy higher valuation and better liquidity. Certain bilateral tax treaties may make it more tax efficient to invest into a country through a holding company incorporated in another country that has a favorable tax treaty.

Companies with intellectual property may need to transfer intellectual property rights to a holding company in a country with better patent protection. Sometimes it would make sense to transfer intellectual property or other intangible asset out from a country with high capital gains tax, at an early stage when the asset value and hence the tax is low, to a country where the capital gains tax is nil or low. When the asset has increased in value and is sold, the company would not need to pay high taxes. Licensing of technology and know-how may also require proper corporate structures to optimize on taxes on royalty payments.

These are just some examples where deal structuring through creative and intelligent corporate structures can lead to better returns. Also, doing this upfront could save inconvenience and costs of later corporate restructuring.

Existing Investors

Sometimes structuring a deal may require thought on how existing investors in the company are to be handled, especially if they do not wish to participate in the current round. Buying out inactive investors is an alternative as mentioned previously. The VC may also structure the deal as a *cram-down* round by pricing the deal at a very low valuation so that non-participating investors get badly diluted. The understanding with the founders is that they would be compensated by the award of stock options. If there is a pay-or-play provision, which is explained in Chapter 14: Investment Securities, it may be enforced as part of the deal. Even in the absence of such a provision, the VC may still structure the deal so that earlier investors lose benefits and rights such as anti-dilution and veto rights, or may be forced to convert to common shares, if the VC has sufficient bargaining power.

Keeping It Simple

VCs are well advised to keep deal structures and investment terms simple. Particularly in Asia, the entrepreneur is more likely to be financially unsophisticated and unfamiliar with much of the common terminology and practices in the financial world. In such a case, the entrepreneur might harbor the suspicion that the VC is incorporating complications into the deal to hide some clever tricks to take undue advantage of him. Also, the entrepreneur may lack understanding or appreciation of the full impact of ratchet terms or convertibility terms that come into effect later. When they get enforced, the entrepreneur might be shocked by the result. Such fears might make the entrepreneur walk away from the deal or create distrust of the VC.

Besides mistrust of confusing and complex deal structures, the entrepreneur has other concerns which we shall discuss in Chapter 17. In any case, it would be to the benefit of both the VC and the entrepreneur to keep deal structure and deal terms simple.

Structuring Later Stage Deals

Besides early stage investment opportunities such as seed deals, start-ups, and companies that have just started to generate revenue, the VC will come across later stage deals where companies that are more mature require equity funding. This is especially the case in Asia, where there are typically more later stage deals than start-ups that are attractive investment opportunities. Many of them are experiencing growth or seeing growth opportunities that require funding exceeding their internally generated funds. They need funding for plant expansion, market development, and making acquisitions, many of which would be cross-border and require VCs that have regional presence or experience to provide both funding and practical assistance.

The structuring of deals to fund growth would normally follow the principles as explained earlier in this chapter. However there are other types of later stage deals and special situations that require more than the straightforward direct investment into the company. Figure 15.2 shows the various types of later stage deals. Many of these deals, especially the larger ones, would be more appropriately classified as private equity deals. Our discussion shall focus on those that would likely fall within the scope of a VC.

FIGURE 15.2   LATER STAGE DEALS

Growth
Recapitalization
Privatization
Management Buyout (MBO)
Leveraged Buyout (LBO)
Management Buy-In (MBI)
Consolidation
Turnaround

In general, being later stage deals, the VC needs to obtain appropriate representations and warranties from the other shareholders, the management, and the company, on past corporate actions and transactions, default remedies and indemnifications. These could include exercising of warrants, enforcement of ratchets, increased dividend rate if applicable, taking over board control, accelerated redemption, or rescission of investments made. The VC should obtain tag along rights as an insurance that the founders may later bail out. The VC should also seek tax advice on the proposed transaction, where necessary.

Recapitalization

As the name implies, a recapitalization deal is one in which the capital structure has to be changed to facilitate the VC's investment. The reason for recapitalizing may be one or more of the following:

o   Non-supportive or inactive shareholders
o   Aging or tired shareholders
o   Shareholders in financial difficulties
o   Management needing revitalization
o   VC wanting a larger stake without diluting other shareholders

The company may have major shareholders who are unwilling or unable to continue supporting the company through further capital injections. Some may not have any interest in the company and are purely passive shareholders. The other shareholders may want them out so that they do not hinder financing rounds out of fear of dilution. At the very least, it would be easier to manage fewer shareholders. The opinion may also be that these non-supportive shareholders should not benefit from the future growth of the company.

Another situation may be that the shareholders themselves wish to exit because they are aging and want to retire. In this case, the VC has to investigate to ensure that they are not bailing out due to fears that the company is failing. A similar situation would be a VC investor that has to exit because its fund life is expiring soon, or a major shareholder may be selling his stake because of personal financial difficulties or financial difficulties in another company within his group.

In many of such cases, shareholders are losing interest because the management lacks motivation and hence the company's performance is lackluster. The recapitalization would usually include the setting up of an Employee Stock Option Plan, strengthening of the management team, and changes to the board of directors.

Buying old shares enables the VC to increase its stake without diluting the other existing shareholders, while also achieving other objectives as mentioned above.

We shall now look at a case study of a recapitalization deal, which considers whether, and how, a different deal structure affects the return to the VC.

Case Study: Stamptek Pte Ltd

(Currency in Singapore $)

In 1976, four brothers set up a small stamping shop called Stamptek Pte Ltd. in Singapore to supply metal parts to the increasing number of multinational companies that were setting up manufacturing plants to produce consumer electronic products and sub-assemblies for export to world markets. In the early years Stamptek had to struggle to meet the customers' high quality standards, and there were recession years when the company sustained losses due to reduced revenue and high inventory cost of steel coils and sheets. Nevertheless, the company survived and the sons of two of the brothers joined the company in 1996.

By 1999, the company was essentially managed by the two young cousins, while their fathers and uncles were at different stages of retirement. Unlike the four founder brothers, the two cousins, being educated in the U.S., were more open to having a professionally run company. They hired a CEO who drew up a plan to expand into China. He saw that the company's business was starting to decline as their customers moved operations to China. The company had to set up a plant in China to protect and to expand its business. With a plant in China, Stamptek would make a good IPO story. The two cousins and the CEO approached a VC who had offices in Shanghai and Guangdong that could help them work with the Chinese authorities and set up the plant.

The four brothers each held 20 percent of the company. The cousins were given 10 percent each. The brothers saw this fund-raising as an opportunity to partially cash out to enjoy their retirement after all the years of hard work. They also wanted to retain a stake in the company as they realized that there could be upside from the IPO. The CEO himself wanted to buy a stake in the company. The company wanted to raise $3.2 million. It did not accumulate much cash as dividends had been paid out regularly.

The VC valued the company at $16 million. With one million shares, each share was valued at $16. The following was the structure before and after the investment by the VC:

FIGURE 15.3   STAMPTEK CAPITALIZATION TABLE

	Before	After the VC's Investment		
	No. of Shares	No. of Shares	% Held	Amount Invested
4 Brothers	800,000	400,000	26.7%	
2 Cousins	200,000	200,000	13.3%	
CEO (old shares)		100,000	6.7%	$1,600,000
VC (old shares)		300,000	20.0%	$4,800,000
VC (new shares)		200,000	13.3%	$3,200,000
ESOP		300,000	20.0%	
Total	1,000,000	1,500,000		

The company set aside 20 percent or 300,000 shares for an Employee Stock Option Plan for management staff including the CEO and the two cousins. The investment was made in 2000, and $700,000 was used to upgrade the Singapore plant while the remaining $2.5 million together with another $2.5 million of bank borrowings were used to set up the China plant in leased facilities. The China plant produced high volume lower cost parts, such as those for audio and video equipment, while the Singapore plant upgraded to sophisticated metal parts for disk drives and television picture tubes. In 2003, Stamptek was listed on the Stock Exchange of Singapore after splitting its 1.5 million shares to 60 million shares and offering 15 million new shares and 3.75 million vendor shares, with each share priced at $1.00. The company was therefore valued at $75 million on its IPO.

The VC's 33.3 percent shareholding is 20 percent diluted by the IPO to 26.7 percent (33.3% × 0.8 = 26.7%). The VC's 20 million shares were disposed after the lockup period at an average price of $1.20. The investment of $8 million gave a return of $24 million after three years, or an IRR of about 44 percent. The return multiple was three times.

Questions: VCs do not like existing shareholders to cash out. Would you have insisted on investing only $3.2 million in new shares? How would the returns compare with the actual case? What are the pros and cons of this alternative? Assume that the CEO buys 100,000 old shares from the brothers, and a 20 percent ESOP is established.

Privatization

In this situation, a public company is taken private so that it would be easier to restructure and grow the company again for another listing or a trade sale. Usually the company is grossly undervalued because the public does not understand or has no interest in its business, the company is not followed by analysts, or it could just merely be poor market sentiment. There were such opportunities in Thailand and other countries in Asia in the months after the Asian financial crisis which started in mid-1997.

Being public companies, the deals are usually sizeable and more suited to private equity funds or strategic buyers than VCs. However, the VC may wish to join a consortium to take control of the company. The consortium would normally work with financial advisers or merchant banks to structure the deal, ensuring compliance with securities laws and takeover regulations. However the VC should be concerned not only with the terms of the deal, but also on the business plans post privatization. The VC's investment horizon would likely be shorter than the other investors, and it would need to be convinced that there will be viable exits within its time frame. The VC needs to know how the character of the company will be changed to assure much better liquidity if it is to be re-listed, or that it would become attractive enough for a strategic buyer.

Management Buyout and Leveraged Buyout

A management buyout (MBO) is a situation where a business or a company is acquired by the incumbent management team, or part of the team, financed by investors such as a VC. The target company may be a division or a subsidiary of a large company that may be spinning off non-core businesses; a family business where the shareholders are aging and without heirs to take over, or in financial difficulties; or an undervalued listed company. A management buyout is initiated by the management team, while a recapitalization or a privatization deal would be initiated by existing owners of the target company.

If the target company has a high valuation, the deal may be partly financed by bank and perhaps mezzanine financing, in which case the deal would be called a Leveraged Buyout (LBO). The structuring of an MBO or LBO consists of three parts. First is the negotiation of the acquisition price and other terms. The VC would usually remain behind the scenes, since it is likely that the management would secure a better price for the company, as they know the strengths and weaknesses of the company better than anyone else. If the existing owners know that an established investor is involved in the acquisition, they may raise the price.

If the seller wants to open up the sale of the company to bidders, the management may be caught in a conflict of interest, since their responsibility is to secure the best value for shareholders, while at the same time they want the company at the lowest price. If the management knows of the intention to sell early enough, they may preempt a bidding situation by quickly arriving at a satisfactory deal. The owners may prefer selling to the management if they desire to continue to off-take products for a period of time, or has some sympathy towards the management, provided the price is reasonable.

The second part of the transaction is the negotiation of the debt financing. Here the VC will play an active part, since it is more likely to secure better terms than the management team. The bank would provide senior debt, and subordinated debt may be secured from mezzanine financiers, at higher interest and usually with an equity kicker. Sometimes the bank may also want an equity kicker. The VC will not provide corporate guarantees as this will require them to set aside funds that will not be invested and hence not generating returns.

The third part is the structuring of the equity investments, allocating between the VC, the management team, and the debt providers. The VC expects the management team to invest a relatively significant sum, and would be happier if they show commitment by mortgaging properties or securing personal loans to do so. Management often contributes at least 10 percent of the equity. Sometimes the sellers may want to retain a small equity, but they will be passive investors. Besides the allocation of equity, the VC has to structure the appropriate securities and rights to the different equity holders. A generous performance based stock option scheme will be structured for management.

The equity and the debt should be sufficient to pay the acquisition price and provide working capital for the acquired business. To reduce the funding required, the VC may negotiate with the seller to accept a partial payment in the form of a note with installment payments, or to retain a part of the equity with put and call options.

The typical corporate structure for an LBO would be to form a HoldCo into which the VC, management, and lenders inject funds which are used to acquire the target, and to inject working capital funds into the target after the acquisition, as shown in the left diagram of Figure 15.4. The lenders' collateral will be Holdco's shares of the target. In such a structure, if the target goes into liquidation, the lenders will rank below that of target's creditors, since the lenders hold shares. Without any corporate guarantee from the VC, the lenders may not be satisfied. An alternative structure is to form a NewCo to buy the assets of the target as shown in the right diagram of Figure 15.4.

FIGURE 15.4 ALTERNATIVE STRUCTURES FOR LBO

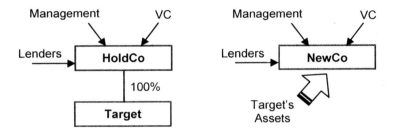

NewCo becomes an operating company, and the lenders will be secured by the assets. In such a structure, the seller may now become the unhappy party, depending on the tax regulations. The seller may face double taxation, once on the profits made by the target on the sale of assets, and again on the proceeds of liquidation of the target. LBOs often end up in convoluted structures because of the many parties involved, their different interests, tax, and other issues.

Management Buy-in

Management Buy-In (MBI) is a situation where a new management team is brought into the acquired company or business. Typically, core members of the team identify an acquisition opportunity, convince a VC to support, and persuade other members of the team to join. The target company or business is likely to be one where there are growth opportunities that the existing management is unwilling or unable to see or exploit. The existing shareholders may sell out if they also do not appreciate the opportunity or are unable to support the effort. The transaction may be structured as an MBO or a LBO, except that it is a new management team instead of an existing one.

In its due diligence, the obvious issue that the VC should look into is the advantages and disadvantages of such an acquisition versus starting up a new company with the MBI team. The existing business infrastructure, brand recognition, and customer base is to be balanced by the liabilities, any negative corporate image, and deep-seated undesirable corporate cultures and practices. The VC also has to assess the MBI team's capability and fit with the acquired business.

Industry Consolidation

In certain fragmented industry sectors, with many small companies and without any one company dominating the market, the VC may see an opportunity to consolidate several of the players to form a significant sized company. Such a consolidation can be within a particular sector, across related sectors or across geographical boundaries. The consolidated company can either be brought public or be sold to a large corporation in a related industry sector. The VC would be able to achieve a good return since the investment cost of each of the small companies would be low, and the consolidated company can be worth more than the combined values due to synergies and economies of scale.

The VC would have to identify the company that has the strongest management team to be the platform company to acquire other companies and to build new related businesses. Often, these companies have to be upgraded in various ways, such as the technology, equipment, operations, and product packaging, and savings can also be achieved through consolidation of purchases, rationalization of product lines, and joint marketing. The biggest problems to overcome in such efforts lie in the ability of the platform company management to merge corporate cultures and exploit synergies.

Turnaround

A financially distressed company may be the target company for an MBO, LBO, or MBI. The VC has to be convinced that there is a real opportunity for a turnaround with various measures such as cost-cutting, downsizing, sales of non-core assets, restructuring debt, additional equity, as well as ways to regenerate sales, revitalize management, and improve morale. Often it makes more sense to start a new company or find another target that may be in less dire straights or may have better chances of being turned around. The VC also has to keep in mind its investment time horizon, since turning around a company and rebuilding it to a reasonable size may take too long.

Acquisition of a distressed company requires compliance with bankruptcy laws. Although the usual way is to structure the transaction as an acquisition of just the assets and not the liabilities, the transaction may still be affected if the seller of the assets is subsequently wound up. The transaction may be deemed to be void, depending on the timing and value of the transaction, and whether unfair preference was given to the buyer. The VC has to be aware of such laws and make this part of its due diligence.

Chapter Recap

In this chapter, we studied how VC deals are structured, by considering:

- The deal structure elements, such as:
    - Amount of investment
    - Valuation of the company
    - Type of security
    - Preferential rights
- Deal structure related issues, such as:
    - Investment tranches
    - Use of funds
    - Syndication
    - Controlled investments
    - Corporate structure
    - Existing investors
    - Keeping it simple
- The structuring of later stage deals and special situations:
    - Recapitalization
    - Privatization
    - Management Buyout
    - Leveraged Buyout
    - Management Buy-in
    - Industry consolidation
    - Turnaround
- A case study of a recapitalization deal

16

Term Sheet

The Term Sheet is a letter of intent given by the VC to a potential investee company stating the terms and conditions of the proposed investment. By this time, the VC would have carried out its initial evaluation of the business and the prospects, and verified much of the assumptions and projections through due diligence checks. Initial discussions with the entrepreneur would have indicated that key terms, such as the valuation of the company and the proposed deal structure were within the ballpark for negotiation.

The intent of the Term Sheet is for the VC to lay out on paper the deal structure and all other proposed terms for the investment so that these are clear to both parties and further clarifications or negotiations can be carried out. It also shows the seriousness of the VC to pursue the investment opportunity. Resulting from the negotiations, the Term Sheet may be revised, sometimes several times.

When agreement is reached, the Term Sheet is signed, which becomes the basis for the legal documents. Although the Term Sheet is not legally binding, once it is signed it signifies the commitment on both sides to complete the investment in good faith under the agreed terms. Such a commitment is important as much time, effort, and costs have to be expended by both parties to prepare for the investment.

In this chapter we shall look at how the Term Sheet is constructed and go through its key clauses. In doing so, we shall integrate the knowledge from previous chapters on Valuation, Investment Securities, and Deal Structure, together with all the remaining clauses to form a total picture of the Term Sheet.

Organization of the Term Sheet

There are perhaps as many variations of the Term Sheet as there are VCs and corporate lawyers. A comprehensive list of most, if not all, of the key clauses in Term Sheets, organized into categories, is shown in Figure 16.1. In practice a Term Sheet may not necessarily incorporate all the clauses listed. The VC may pick and choose those relevant and important to the deal.

An example of a comprehensive Term Sheet is given in Appendix 16A on page 343. Admittedly, this is a rather detailed and lengthy Term Sheet, but it is chosen to illustrate as many of the terms as possible. Some VCs prefer a much more concise version amounting to two or three pages for working purposes. It is preferable to have a more complete Term Sheet to avoid misunderstanding with the founders or management of the investee company. After signing the Term Sheet, the legal documentation will be prepared, and important issues that may be missed in the Term Sheet will be brought up, which will delay the process, or worse, may create ill will between the parties.

Preamble

The Term Sheet is written in a somewhat legal format. The preamble section may have a title, the date, name of the company issuing the stock, and an introduction to the intended transaction.

For companies that are into their second or subsequent rounds of financing, there will be a description of the securities that have been issued, giving the type and number of each class of stock, including employee stock options, if any. This serves as a confirmatory record.

FIGURE 16.1   ORGANIZATION OF THE TERM SHEET

Preamble	Title, date, etc
Deal Structure	Amount of investment Type of security Company valuation Capitalization table Use of funds
Preferential Rights	Preferred dividend (if any) Liquidation preference Conversion Redemption Anti-dilution Registration Changes to rights
Conditions Precedent	Actions by investor Actions by investee
Management Controls	Voting rights Board representation Operational controls Minority protection Key person insurance
Management Incentives	Incentive shares Employee stock options
Shareholder Rights	Right of first refusal Exempt share transfers Tag along rights Drag along rights Management share transfers Information rights
Exit Provisions	IPO conditions Automatic conversion Buy-back rights
Miscellaneous	Representations and warranties Confidentiality VC internal approval Expenses Governing law
Exclusivity	Exclusivity period

Deal Structure

This group of terms and conditions, as we saw in the previous chapter, relate to how the investment is to be made, such as the amount of funding, the type of security, the price of the security or the company valuation, the number of shares, shareholding percentage, and the use of the funds.

Amount of Investment

The amount of investment required is determined by the cash flow of the company, based on its burn rate, capital expenditures, and debt servicing needs if any, until the next round of financing or until the company reaches cash breakeven, with some provision for contingencies. The VC needs to verify the assumptions and often may need to query and bring down the burn rate, including salaries and benefits. These should have been largely ironed out by the time the Term Sheet is issued, although fine tuning may continue, which would usually not affect the amount of funding.

Often for start-ups, the VC may wish to limit risks and exposure by breaking up the investment amount into tranches and set milestones. The amount and timing for each tranche will be determined by the cash flow and should be set at reasonable intervals and at milestones that can be readily measured. This can involve quite lengthy negotiations on the tranche amounts, timing, and milestones.

The amount to be invested may have to be adjusted depending on the negotiations on the use of funds. For example, the VC may refuse to allow the company to pay off existing shareholders loans and require them to convert the loans to equity. The VC may then either reduce the amount of funding or may maintain the amount to provide more runway to the company.

If the amount of funding required is too large for the appetite of the VC, or if the VC wants to spread its risks, the VC would have to syndicate the deal to co-investors.

Type of Security

In Chapter 14, we discussed the various types of securities that may be used in an equity investment. The most common security used in venture-backed companies is preferred shares, while common shares are issued to founders and often to angel investors. The most common type of preferred share is one with a convertibility feature, as it is expected that the company will eventually IPO. The preferred shares will then be converted to common shares under the agreed-upon terms.

Company Valuation

We discussed valuation methodologies in Chapter 13. The Term Sheet merely states the valuation at which the investment is to be made, without the need to state how it is derived. It would be more convenient to state the pre-money valuation as the amount to be raised may be stated as a range.

The valuation of the company is obviously of great concern to the entrepreneur as it determines the dilution he suffers as a result of the investment. Negotiations are made more difficult because of the variety of methodologies and the uncertainties of assumptions and projections. Usually each party postulates its methodology and assumptions, and some debate may ensue about the validity of methodology, assumptions, and projections used, and after that it becomes a matter of pure negotiations to arrive at a mutually agreed number, or not.

Capitalization Table

The percentage shareholding in the company is derived from the amount to be invested and the company valuation. For the sake of confirmation and to avoid misunderstanding, both the number of shares to be issued and the percentage shareholding may be stated. For completeness, a post-closing capitalization table may be drawn up and attached to the Term Sheet. This shows the respective quantities of outstanding shares, options, warrants, or rights to shares that will be held by each shareholder or groups of shareholders, after the investment is made. An example was given in Figure 2.13, and another is shown here in Figure 16.2.

FIGURE 16.2   CAPITALIZATION TABLE

	No. of Shares	Investment Amount	Price per Share	% Owned
Common Shareholders				
Founders	1,000,000	$10,000	$0.01	20%
Management	400,000	8,000	0.02	8%
Directors' Options	200,000		0.02	4%
ESOS Reserved	800,000			16%
Series A Preferred Shares				
Investor 1	1,600,000	$3,200,000	$2.00	32%
Investor 2	1,000,000	2,000,000	2.00	20%
Total	5,000,000			100%

The capitalization table may also be more clearly drawn up to show the shareholdings before and after the investment, and in some cases also indicate the preferential rights that are attached to the respective groups of shares.

Use of Funds

The specific uses of the funds invested are stated to ensure that the funds are used by the investee company accordingly. The VC would want the invested funds to be used to grow and add value to the company. The VC would not want the company to use the money to bail out another shareholder, to repay bank debt or to redeem shareholders' loans, unless there is prior agreement that part of the investment will be used for this purpose.

Preferential Rights

This section captures all the preferential rights that the VC wants to be attached to the series of preferred shares in which it will invest. As discussed in Chapter 14, these include preferred dividend, liquidation preference, conversion, redemption, anti-dilution and registration rights, in all their various shapes and forms that have been agreed upon, or are being proposed by the VC. Other than preferred dividend, all the other rights are almost always included in one form or another.

Changes to Rights

Also included in the Term Sheet is a provision to protect the preferential rights by requiring a majority (either simple majority or two-thirds) of the present class of shareholders to agree before their rights and privileges can be changed by future rounds of financing, or be made subordinate to a new class of shares.

If a previous class of shareholders has rights that may deter new investors, such as full ratchet anti-dilution rights, the investors often require the waiver or amendment of such rights as a condition for their investment.

Conditions Precedent

"Conditions Precedent" is a legal term, referring to specific conditions that must be met by the respective parties to the investment agreement prior to legal completion and funding of the investment. This section itemizes the actions that need to be taken to satisfy these conditions.

Actions by Investor

The actions by the VC include completion of due diligence to its satisfaction and obtaining internal approval for the investment. It will also be stated that a condition prior to funding is the signing of legal documents by both parties.

Actions by Investee

The actions required from the investee company include passing the appropriate board resolutions and making amendments to its articles of incorporation if necessary, and sometimes a restructuring of its shareholdings or transfer of legal titles to assets and intellectual property.

The investee will have to produce the appropriate documents to substantiate such actions prior to or at the closing.

These will be discussed in greater detail in Chapter 18: Conditions Precedent.

Management Controls

This group of terms and conditions relate to how the authority and responsibility for the control and management of the company is to be shared between the investor, other shareholders, the board, and the management. Most of these are standard clauses developed to provide protection to minority shareholders. They specify the corporate actions that require the permission or consensus of the VC or minority shareholders.

Voting Rights

This is a long list of actions by the company that requires approval by the investor. It may be worded such that specific approval is required from the investor or its board representative, or it may be worded such that a supermajority vote in the board may need to be taken. A supermajority vote is a favorable vote by a large majority of the board members, such as those representing 75 percent of the shareholding of the company. Thus, in this case, if the VC owns more than 25 percent of the company, it would effectively have a veto right.

Board Representation

Usually the number of board seats that the VC gets in relation to the total number of seats will be pro rata its shareholding in the company. Thus if the VC owns 40 percent of the company, they should have two out of a total of five board seats. It is usual to have just three, five, or seven board members. Too large a board will entail administrative difficulties in organizing board meetings. The odd number is to avoid a voting deadlock. However if it is unavoidable to have an even number of directors, the chairman will get a casting vote. In such a case, the VC may insist on having the chair, or an independent director could be appointed.

To protect its interests, the VC usually has a requirement that its board representative must be present to form a quorum for board meetings. To allay fears from the entrepreneur that this condition permits the VC to prevent the holding of any board meeting, the condition may be modified such that if a quorum is not attained, the postponed board meeting will not require the presence of the VC representative to form a quorum.

Operational Controls

The VC should ensure that included in the list of operational controls is a clause that relates to appointment or dismissal of key personnel, as well as any change to their terms of appointment. The VC would not want the management to jack up their own salaries or give themselves perks immediately after the investment. Such increases should of course be after achievement of targeted performance.

For some investees, particularly start-ups, the VC may want to be a signatory for checks above a certain amount to ensure strict financial control. It is also good practice to enforce a requirement for two signatures in all checks, one of which may or may not be a representative of the investor, depending on the size of the check and the degree of control required.

Minority Protection

Since the VC usually takes a minority stake and does not get involved in day-to-day management, these minority protection rights ensure that his concurrence is secured prior to any major action affecting the company. These actions relate to any change of business direction, acquisition or disposal of interests in other businesses, purchase or sale of major assets or entering into mortgage of such assets, changes in shareholding structure, amendments of articles of incorporation, restructuring or dissolution of the company, incurring major financial commitments or investments, change of auditors, adoption of accounts, distribution of dividends, employee share option schemes, related party transactions, intellectual property transactions, or entering into legal actions. The lawyers will readily produce a boilerplate of such minority protection rights. Refer to Clause 11.2 of Appendix 16A for examples.

Key Person Insurance

The VC may insist that the investee company takes up life insurance for key staff, with the company as beneficiary. This is particularly in the case of a founder who possesses the knowledge for the unique technology of the company, without whom the company would be of little value.

Management Incentives

Incentive Shares

Particularly in seed deals and start-ups, the founders may have a small percentage of the shareholding since the valuation would be low and the VC's investment will take up a majority share. In such a case, the VC may agree that new common shares be issued to founders at the founders' price provided specified milestones are met. The founders will be more motivated with a more significant stake in the company.

Employee Stock Options

The VC would usually set up an Employee Stock Options Plan (ESOP) or Scheme (ESOS). This is to reward key staff, and perhaps other junior staff as well, for achieving targets or milestones. This provides incentives and aligns the interest of the staff to that of investors. Start-ups, smaller companies, and companies in high technology are viewed as having high risks, and will require an ESOP to attract and retain capable and experienced senior management staff. Often they can be less generous with the cash component of the compensation to maintain a lean salary structure and conserve much-needed cash.

The VC has to be cognizant of the dilutive effect of an ESOP. It is not unusual that the VC would insist that shares be set aside for an ESOP prior to its investment, so that it will not suffer dilution.

As it is usually left to the board of directors to set up and administer the scheme, it may suffice to record in the Term Sheet that there is mutual agreement for such a scheme to be set up. In some cases, the main terms of the scheme may be specified, such as the maximum amount of shares to be set aside, the vesting period, and eligibility conditions.

We shall take the opportunity to discuss the ESOP at this juncture, even though it may not be detailed in a Term Sheet. A summary of the main terms of an ESOP is given in Figure 16.3.

The number of options, and hence the number of shares to be set aside for conversion of the options, typically accounts for 15 to 20 percent of the total outstanding shares. It may be as high as 25 percent for early stage companies. Some companies extend the eligibility to all staff, but only those who are confirmed after one year of service. Board directors, members of an advisory board, if any, and consultants may be awarded options as well.

Since the ESOP is to promote loyalty and performance, the options may be awarded according to these criteria. The company may choose to award part of the options based on the overall performance of the company, in which case the awards may be equal to all staff or according to rank. Part of the options may be awarded based on individual or team performance. The company may also have ad hoc special awards to encourage outstanding achievements.

A token payment of $1 is paid for the options that are granted. Option holders are given five or ten years from the date of award to exercise the options, failing which the options will lapse. The exercise price is heavily discounted for private companies. The price could be somewhere between the founders' price for their initial shares and that for the most recent financing round. Often it would be 10 or 20 percent of the price of the most recent round. After the company is listed, a new ESOP is usually set up with less generous terms in view of the interest of public shareholders. The exercise price may then be at market price or discounted by 10 or 20 percent from market price at the time of award.

Options are vested progressively to promote loyalty of service. The vesting period for the options is usually three to five years. A typical vesting method would be to divide the number of options equally between the years of vesting. Another formula would be to vest 25 percent of the amount awarded after confirmation of employment in six months or one year, and then 2 percent every month thereafter. The award would be fully vested after about four years. For directors, advisors, and consultants, the options usually vest immediately.

FIGURE 16.3   MAIN TERMS OF AN EMPLOYEE STOCK OPTION PLAN

Size		Usually 15 to 20% of total shareholding
Eligibility	Key staff Sometimes all staff	After one year of service
	Directors, advisors and consultants	Based on contribution
Basis for Award	Loyalty	Length of service
	Company Performance	Usually across the board award
	Staff Performance	Individualized amounts
	Special Awards	Special contributions
Option Terms	Option Life	Up to ten years
	Exercise Price	Discounted from most recent financing round price
	Vesting Period	From 3 to 5 years Typically 25% after 1 year, then 2% per month
	Anti-Dilution	Provision for adjustments
	Forfeiture	On departure from company, unless already vested
	Other Terms	Limited voting rights Restrictions on resale
Administration	Compensation Committee	External directors
	Offer Procedures	Proper offer and acceptance procedures and documents
	Tax	Borne by option holders
	Amendments	By resolution of the Compensation Committee
	Termination	By resolution of the Compensation Committee or shareholders

In the event of a merger or acquisition exercise, resulting in a change of control of the company, or an IPO, vesting will be accelerated to allow option holders to exercise all or part of all vested and unvested options prior to the exercise.

Anti-dilution provisions in the ESOP are limited to stock splits, consolidations, or capitalization of reserves. The price and number of stock options already issued are not adjusted for share cancellations through buy-backs or for dilution due to issue of shares for acquisitions or new investors. However the ESOP as a whole may be revised to increase the size of the options pool, if there is significant dilution due to a new financing round.

If employment is terminated with cause, all unexercised and unvested options will lapse. Otherwise, on termination or resignation, a period of, say, thirty days is given for any vested options to be exercised, failing which they will lapse. Non-vested options are either forfeited or bought back by the company at cost (the token amount) and absorbed into the options pool. In some cases, the company may vest all unvested options and allow a period of, say, thirty days for the options to be exercised, failing which they will lapse.

Usually shares converted from options have no or limited voting rights until the company goes IPO, upon which all the common shares rank pari passu. This is to limit control of the company to the founders and investors. Similarly, prior to IPO, options and converted shares cannot be sold or assigned, except back to the company, so that shares do not fall into the wrong hands.

The company should have a properly written and documented ESOP so as to avoid misunderstanding by staff. The scheme should be administered by a Compensation Committee, appointed and authorized by the board, consisting of non-executive directors, with the participation of the CEO except when her options are being considered. There should be proper offer and acceptance procedures and documents for the option awards, as well as forms for the exercise of options. Taxes should be borne by the option holders and not the company.

The Compensation Committee would decide on the frequency of awards. Those options tied to loyalty may be awarded based on the length of service while those based on performance would be timed to completion of financial results or performance appraisal.

The ESOP may be modified by the Compensation Committee, except that such modification should not have any adverse retrospective effect. The scheme may be terminated by the Committee or by resolution of shareholders, except that such termination would not affect options already granted.

It should be noted that many VCs require that stock options awarded to their representatives on the board have to be turned in to the VC firm and cannot be kept by the individuals. The LPs consider that board membership is part of the VC's services and added value given to investee companies and compensation for such services should accrue to the fund. However in the case of public listed companies, the individual may be allowed to keep the options, as the view is that there are personal responsibilities and liabilities assumed by the individual.

Shareholder Rights

This group of clauses provides for the rights of the investor as a shareholder of the company. These are distinct from preferential rights which accrue only to the preferred shares held, whereas shareholder rights would normally apply to all shareholders, whether preferred or common, unless otherwise specifically provided for.

Right of First Refusal

The right of first refusal entitles the existing shareholders to purchase the shares that any shareholder may wish to sell to a third party, under the same terms. The other shareholders are allocated such shares pro rata to their shareholdings and if any shareholder does not take up the offer, the others have pro rata right to acquire them. Any remaining shares may then be sold to the third party. Sometimes such right of first refusal is not given by the VC to the other shareholders as it may prohibit the sale of its entire block of shares to a third party. Often the third party wants the entire block and nothing less. As a compromise, the agreement may be worded such that the right of first refusal can be exercised only if the entire block of shares is taken up by the other shareholders. This allows the VC to fully divest, whether to a third party or to the other existing shareholders.

Exempt Transfer of Shares

This clause gives the right to the investor to transfer or sell its shares to an affiliated or associated company, without triggering the preemption or right of first refusal clause. This will be applicable to a corporate VC or a corporate investor, which may undergo a restructuring of its investment vehicles, thus requiring some investment holdings to be transferred from one vehicle to another. Such Exempt Transfer of Shares may also be given to founders for transfers up to a limit, say up to 25 percent of his holdings or for transfers to immediate family members.

Tag Along Rights

If the founders wish to sell to a third party, the investor would have the right to tag along, or join in the sale under the same terms. This is to prevent the founders from bailing out and leaving the investor in the lurch with an unknown new shareholder. Sometimes such Tag Along Rights would be triggered only if controlling interest is acquired by the third party.

Drag Along Rights

If the investor sells all its shares and exercises this right, all other shareholders, including founders, are forced to sell alongside. This is to facilitate selling to a buyer that wants 100 percent of a company, as it does not want to contend with dealing with minority shareholders who may be troublesome. To incentivize the management, the buyer may set up an Employee Stock Option Scheme subsequent to the purchase of the company. Tag Along and Drag Along Rights are generally referred to as Co-Sale Rights. In some cases, the VC may be given more powers than just drag along rights to sell out the company. These would then be captured together as Sell-Out Rights.

Management Share Transfers

It is obvious that the VC will want to restrict the sale of shares by the key managers, which would reduce their commitment and would be a sign that something is amiss in the company. In a situation where the VC is the sole investor having a minority stake and the founder-managers own the majority, the VC will require that the founder-managers maintain their majority shareholding. Should the founders sell down to less than say 51 percent shareholding, a default event will be triggered which may result in redemption of the VC's shares.

In a situation where a key manager resigns from employment, it is usual to require that he sells his shares back to the company. In those countries which do not allow a company to purchase its own shares, the shares would be sold to the other managers or founders. This is to avoid having a troublemaking shareholder who may hinder corporate actions. It is also fair that a departed employee who no longer contributes to the company should not enjoy the benefits of the company's growth while also enabling the staying managers to have a larger stake, or enabling his shares to be awarded to his replacement, if necessary.

Information Rights

These clauses define the scope of the corporate information that the investor is entitled to receive or request for. These usually relate to financial information. If the scope is expanded to include other information, it could trigger fears from the company that it may have to reveal trade secrets or other confidential information.

Exit Provisions

The next group of terms and conditions in the Term Sheet relate to mechanisms that affect how the investor may exit or divest from the investee company.

IPO Conditions

The IPO of the investee company is the typical means for divestment by the VC. However it is not necessarily an easy means. If the IPO raises a small amount of money, the stock may be thinly traded and the stock price may not perform well. Therefore VCs will typically set certain conditions to require a minimum level of profitability or a minimum valuation before an IPO can be proceeded with. For example, the VC may require the company to be valued at a minimum of $150 million or to achieve a minimum of $5 million profits before it can go IPO, or to be able to raise at least $20 million in its IPO.

Some VCs may not require such a condition at all and simply put in a statement that the parties will jointly work together in good faith towards an IPO. This will be the case where the VC controls the board, which then in any case controls the decision on IPO.

Automatic Conversion

It is usual to require that all preferred shares be automatically converted into common shares on IPO. The special rights accorded to the preferred shares would not be acceptable to public holders of the common shares. However, the automatic conversion may be subject to a certain minimum offering price per share or a minimum total offering amount. This condition ensures that the company is of a significant enough size at its IPO, so that the VC derives a satisfactory return. However if the VC is anxious to exit, it can still agree to convert even though the condition is not met.

The company may also ask that if shareholders holding at least half or two-thirds of the company's outstanding preferred stock decide to convert to common shares, all (or a prorated number) of the rest of the preferred shares will be automatically converted to common shares. This is to facilitate an intended sale of the company. The buyer, which is likely to be a strategic buyer, would want to have majority control, or perhaps 100 percent of the company.

In some cases, the entrepreneur may insist on a clause to force automatic conversion of preferred shares to common shares, if a preferred shareholder refuses to participate in a down round. This would ensure support of existing shareholders if the company has to face a down round, and those shareholders who do not participate would lose many if not all of their preferential rights, which would help to facilitate the offering of shares and rights to the new investor.

Buy-Back Rights

In some cases, the VC may want a means to exit by selling its stake to the founders, or the founders themselves may want to have the right to buy back the VC's shares. This could be done through a put option on the founders by the VC, or a call option on the VC by the founders. The options may be set at a price that gives a specified IRR to the VC. Buy-back rights for the founders are not common, as they limit the upside for the VC. They may perhaps be applied in a case where the VC purchases mostly old shares from the founders. They may also be applied if the founders have high net worth and act as guarantors to the VC's investment. Such an arrangement is better than a redemption feature, since the company would likely be unable to redeem the shares if it does not perform to expectations.

Miscellaneous Terms

Representations and Warranties

These are legal written assurances given by the investee company and its directors and management that the business has been conducted properly; that all assets were in good order; that all liabilities, including contingent liabilities, have been disclosed; and that all material information about the business and prospects have been disclosed, and were correct.

Lawyers will readily produce a boilerplate list of representations and warranties to great detail at the final documentation stage. The Term Sheet would merely carry a statement that standard representations and warranties will be provided to the investor by the company, founders, and directors. Therefore this will not be a contentious issue at this stage, but could be so when the final documentation is prepared.

Confidentiality

This clause is to ensure that confidentiality is respected and is a standard condition.

VC Internal Approval

This clause is to state that the investment is subject to the VC obtaining its internal approval for the investment. This is to allow for the rare instance when such approval is not secured, which would release the VC from any obligations in the Term Sheet.

Expenses

It is common to have the investor's expenses incurred for legal documentation and financial audit to be reimbursed by the investee company. If the deal is aborted by the investor, for whatever reason, the expenses may be shared. How the expenses are split depend on the negotiations. The investor's expenses incurred to date may be shared equally with the investee, or each party may bear its own expenses. If the deal is aborted by the investee, the investor may insist that its expenses will have to borne by the investee.

In cases where the investor has to pay a finder's fee, it may require the investee to reimburse this amount.

Governing Law

The governing law is usually that of the domicile of the company. If the VC is domiciled in another country, it may require arbitration to be in its domicile country or in a neutral country or by an international Arbitration Court.

Exclusivity

This clause states the starting date and the period during which the investee company may not approach another party or have discussions with another party on an investment into the company. This quiet period, typically one or two months, gives the exclusivity to the VC to conduct final due diligence, decide on the investment, and proceed with legal documentation.

Chapter Recap

In this chapter, we have reviewed the following:

- o   The organization of the Term Sheet
- o   The principal clauses relating to:
  - o   Deal Structure
  - o   Preferential Rights
  - o   Conditions Precedent
  - o   Management Controls
  - o   Management Incentives
  - o   Shareholder Rights
  - o   Exit Provisions
  - o   Exclusivity

APPENDIX 16A

TERM SHEET
Sale of Series B Preferred Stock
of Fantasy Inc

July 5, 2002

This Term Sheet summarizes the principal terms and conditions of the proposed private placement of equity securities in Fantasy Inc (the "Company") to Singular Ventures (the "Investor"). It is subject to the Investor's satisfactory due diligence, approval by its investment committee and final documentation on terms acceptable to the Investor being executed.

TYPE OF SECURITY

1.1   The investment shall be in Series B Redeemable Convertible Preferred Shares ("BRCPS").

PRICE

2.1   The Company shall issue to the Investor 2,000,000 BRCPS at an issue price of $2,000,000 in aggregate ("Total Subscription Price"), which if fully converted on the basis of one BRCPS to one Common Share, represents a shareholding of 20% in the Company. Such conversion shall be subject to the terms stated herein.

USE OF PROCEEDS

3.1   The proceeds shall be used to continue development of the Company's Super Platform software and derivative products, and sales and marketing of such products.

CONDITIONS PRECEDENT

4.1   The Investor's subscription to the BRCPS shall be subject to the following:

a)   All business, financial and legal due diligence by the Investor has been satisfactorily completed;

b) The Investor is satisfied that:

   (i) no petition has been presented or resolution passed for the winding up of the Company;

   (ii) the Company is not in the process of being liquidated, restructured or amalgamated;

   (iii) the Company is not subject to any legal proceedings or claims; and

   (iv) there has been no material deterioration of the Company's business, operations, financial condition or prospects;

c) There has been no breach of any warranties and representations or other terms contained in the Investment Agreement, Shareholders Agreement and related documents;

d) An agreement for the assignment and/or transfer to the Company of all Intellectual Property Rights owned or developed by the founders, whose names are listed in Annex I herein ("Founders"), has been executed and delivered;

e) The Company has entered into employment contracts on terms acceptable to the Investor with key employees as listed in Annex II herein ("Key Employees");

f) The business of the Company has been carried on in a satisfactory and ordinary manner and the Company has not disposed of any material assets or assumed or incurred any material liabilities (including contingent liabilities);

g) All approvals and consents for the transactions under the Investment Agreement and the Shareholders Agreement have been obtained, and not withdrawn or amended;

h) No event which constitutes a Default Redemption Event has occurred.

MILESTONES

5.1   The subscription of the BRCPS by the Investor shall be in two tranches as follows:

a)   The first tranche of 1,000,000 BRCPS at a subscription amount of $1,000,000 upon the fulfillment of the conditions precedent stated herein; and

b)   The second tranche of 1,000,000 BRCPS at a subscription amount of $1,000,000 upon the Company signing its first customer contract exceeding $1,000,000 in value.

CONVERSION RIGHTS

6.1   The BRCPS may be converted fully or partially into Common Shares at any time, at the option and sole discretion of the Investor. However, the BRCPS shall be automatically converted into Common Shares:

a)   upon the Company obtaining approval to list its shares on a Stock Exchange acceptable to the Board and the Investor (an "Approved Stock Exchange"); or

b)   at the election of holders of at least 75% of the BRCPS then outstanding; or

c)   in the event that all shares in the capital of the Company are being sold.

6.2   The ratio of the number of BRCPS to be converted divided by the number of Common Shares to be issued ("Conversion Ratio"), shall be determined as follows:

a)   if conversion occurs in FY03 (Fiscal Year Ending June 30, 2003), the Conversion Ratio shall be one (1);

b)   if conversion occurs after FY03 but before FY07, the Conversion Ratio shall be equal to N1 divided by N2 where:

(i)   N1 is the audited actual NPAT of the prior fiscal year; and

(ii) N2 is the projected NPAT of the prior fiscal year, given that the projected NPAT for FY03, FY04 and FY05 are $2 million, $4 million and $6 million respectively;

provided that the ratio shall be always not less than half (0.5) nor more than one and a half (1.5); and

c)   if conversion occurs in or after FY07, the Conversion Ratio shall be calculated as if conversion took place in FY06.

LIQUIDATION PREFERENCE

7.1   In the event of a consolidation, merger, stock sale, change of control of the Company, sale of all or substantially all of the Company's assets or a liquidation, dissolution or winding up of the Company ("Liquidation Event"), the Investor shall be entitled to be paid first from the proceeds of any such event, the higher of:

a)   two times the Total Subscription Price, plus any accrued and unpaid dividends, or

b)   the proceeds due to the Investor (on the occurrence of any Liquidation Event) on an as-converted basis.

If this amount is not received in full by the Investor, no assets or other distribution shall be given or made to the shareholders until the Investor has received from the Company such assets so that the Investor shall have been paid this amount in full. Thereafter remaining assets of the Company shall be distributed pro rata amongst all the shareholders of the Company, based on the amount paid up on their shares.

7.2   The above provisions shall be without prejudice to the Investor's veto and supermajority voting rights as set out in this Term Sheet.

ANTI-DILUTION

8.1   In the event of any share splits, share dividends, bonus issues or consolidations or other capital restructuring, an adjustment shall be made such that the Investor shall hold the same relative equity interest and/or percentage shareholding after such action as it had immediately prior to such action.

8.2   In the event that, prior to the conversion of the BRCPS to Common Shares, the Company issues additional equity securities including, but not limited to, options (except pursuant to an Employee Share Option Plan), warrants or convertible securities at a lower valuation, the Conversion Ratio shall be adjusted according to the following weighted average formula:

$$\text{Adjusted Conversion Ratio} = \text{Original Conversion Ratio} \times \frac{T+A}{T+B}$$

where:

T = total number of issued shares immediately prior to the issuance of new securities;

A = total number of shares that the total consideration for the new securities would purchase based on the original Conversion Ratio of the BRCPS; and

B = total number of shares underlying the new securities.

REDEMPTION

9.1   The Investor is entitled to require redemption of all or part of the respective tranche of BRCPS issued to the Investor after one year from the respective subscription dates.

9.2   The Investor shall also have the right to require redemption of all or part of the BRCPS at any time on or after the occurrence of a Default Redemption Event, which shall be any one of the following:

a)   Any of the Founders directly or indirectly sells, transfers or disposes any of their respective interests in their Common Shares without complying with the Rights of First Refusal set out in Clause 18 and the Transfer of Shares set out in Clause 17 herein; or

b)   There is a material breach of any of the representations, warranties and undertakings in the Investment Agreement and Shareholders

Agreement by the Company or Founders which (if rectifiable) is not rectified within a period of 30 days from the occurrence of such breach; or

c) The Company takes any steps towards entering or enters into any compromise or arrangement between it and its creditors and/or any of its creditors; or

d) Any action for the winding-up or administration of the Company, or legal proceedings for the dissolution of the Company or for the appointment of a receiver, manager, trustee, or similar officer of the Company or its assets, or an action to take possession of all or any part of the business or assets of the Company, or distress or execution shall be levied or enforced upon or sued against any of its properties or assets and shall not be discharged or stayed or in good faith contested by action within fourteen (14) days thereafter; or

e) The Company becomes insolvent or is unable to pay its debts as and when they fall due.

9.3   The Redemption Amount payable by the Company upon the redemption of the BRCPS shall be the aggregate subscription price of the BRCPS to be redeemed plus dividends at the rate of 8% of the aggregate subscription amount (compounded annually), accruing from the date of issue of the relevant BRCPS to be redeemed to the date of redemption of the BRCPS, which shall be exclusive of any dividends declared by the Company.

9.4   Provided always that the Company shall ensure that it is able to comply with all requisite requirements to give full effect to the rights of the Investor, with the understanding that the Company shall not be required to hold in liquid assets an amount sufficient to redeem the BRCPS, at any time prior to the redemption of the BRCPS.

DIVIDENDS

10.1   The Investor shall be entitled to receive dividends at 8% per annum of the Total Subscription Price in preference to any dividend on the Common Shares, if and when declared by the Board.

VOTING RIGHTS / VETO RIGHTS

11.1   The holder of each BRCPS shall have the same right as holders of Common Shares to receive notices of and attend meetings and to vote that number of votes equal to the number of BRCPS held. The holders of BRCPS shall vote together with the holders of Common Shares on all matters as a single class except as required by law or as set forth herein.

11.2   The approval of the Investor or its nominee director(s) shall be required to approve any of the following actions by the Company:

a)   Cease to conduct or carry on its business substantially as now conducted and/or acquire or dispose of or dilute any substantial interest in any other business or company;

b)   Purchase, sell, mortgage or charge any asset or property or any interest therein or sell or dispose of the whole or a substantial part of the undertaking and goodwill of the Company, in the aggregate amount exceeding $200,000 per transaction;

c)   Increase, reduce, sub-divide, change the authorized or issued share capital of the Company or issue or grant any option (except pursuant to an Employee Share Option Plan) over the unissued share capital of the Company or list any of the shares of the Company on any stock exchange;

d)   Amend its Articles of Incorporation or such other constitutive documents or part thereof;

e)   Undertake any merger, reconstruction or liquidation exercise;

f)   Resolve to voluntarily wind up or dissolve the Company;

g) Change the auditors of the Company or adopt any policy on financial matters such as significant accounting practices, depreciation practices and directors' fees and remuneration;

h) Incur any financial commitment (including capital commitment, creation or issue of any debenture or charge on any of the undertaking, assets or rights of the Company and granting of loans and guarantees) in excess of an aggregate of $200,000 in any one financial year unless specifically provided for in the approved budget of the Company;

i) Adopt its audited accounts or its annual budget;

j) Appoint, dismiss, settle or adjust the terms of appointment of any key appointment holders such as the Chief Executive Officer, Chief Financial Officer, Chief Technical Officer and Chief Operating Officer;

k) Make any distribution of profits amongst its shareholders by way of dividend, capitalization of reserves or otherwise;

l) Approve any transaction or enter into any contract, agreement or arrangement with any shareholder or any company or business in which any of the Shareholders has financial interest;

m) Settle the terms of and any increase or decrease in the number of new shares to be issued under any employee share option or share participation scheme;

n) Grant any license in respect of any distributorship, agency, reselling arrangement, franchise or intellectual property right to any party (other than in the ordinary course of business);

o) Institute, withdraw or settle any legal action or proceedings in excess or anticipated in excess of $200,000 (except for collection of debts in the ordinary course of business of the Company); and

p) Any investment by way of subscribing for shares or other similar equities in a company or fund.

BOARD OF DIRECTORS

12.1   The Investor shall be entitled to be proportionately represented on the Board of Directors of the Company.

12.2   The directors designated by the Investor shall have the right to be a member of any executive, audit and/or compensation committee of the Board, when they are established.

12.3   The quorum for any board meeting shall always require the presence of at least one nominee director of the Investor. If a quorum is not present, the meeting shall be postponed to a date not earlier than seven (7) days after the original meeting and the quorum for the reconvened meeting need not include a nominee director of the Investor, as long as such nominee director has been informed of the reconvened meeting.

INVESTMENT AGREEMENT

13.1   The investment shall be made pursuant to an Investment Agreement and other documentation reasonably acceptable to the Company and the Investor, which Investment Agreement shall contain, among other things, appropriate representations and warranties of the Company, covenants of the Company reflecting the provisions set forth herein, and appropriate conditions of closing which shall include, among other things, the filing of amendments to the Company's Articles of Incorporation or equivalent constitutive documents to authorize the investment.

EXPENSES

14.1   The Company shall reimburse the Investor for its expenses in connection with the proposed investment, including but not limited to legal and financial due diligence expenses.

14.2   If the Investor decides for any reason whatsoever not to proceed with the subscription (which reason is not due to a lack of good faith on the part of the Company to adhere to the provisions herein or to an unsatisfactory due diligence report), the Investor and the Company shall bear the expenses incurred equally.

RIGHTS TO FINANCIAL INFORMATION

15.1   The Investor shall receive monthly, quarterly, and audited annual financial statements and have standard inspection rights.

15.2   The Investor shall be entitled to, at any time, appoint its own auditor to inspect and review the financial records and information of the Company, and the Company shall allow all access to such auditor.

RIGHT OF FIRST OFFER

16.1   The Investor shall have a 20 (twenty) business days' right of first offer to purchase its pro rata share of offerings of new securities at each subsequent round of financing.

TRANSFER OF SHARES

17.1   The Investor may transfer its shares to affiliated investment holding companies without offering a Right of First Refusal to the other shareholders of the Company, provided that the transfer is in compliance with the relevant securities laws. A transfer of shares by the investor to any of its affiliated institutions shall not be deemed to be an acquisition, merger, consolidation, or change of control.

17.2   The Founders and Key Employees shall not be entitled to sell, transfer, encumber, grant security over or otherwise dispose of or deal with any of the shares in the Company without the Investor's prior written consent, for so long as the Investor shall hold any shares in the Company.

17.3   Should a Founder or Key Employee leave the employment of the Company, he must either sell his shares to the remaining Founders and/or Key Employees at a mutually agreed price, or he may retain his shares, provided he assigns his voting rights by proxy to the remaining Founders or Key Employees.

RIGHTS OF FIRST REFUSAL

18.1   Founders and Key Employees may transfer their shares between themselves only after offering a Right of First Refusal to other shareholders of the Company, Founders, and Key Employees. Except in the event of a listing of the Company's shares on an Approved Stock Exchange or with the Investor's prior written consent, Founders and Key Employees may not at any time transfer their shares to entities not associated with the Company.

18.2   Other holders of Common Shares and BRCPS may transfer their shares only after offering the other shareholders of the Company a Right of First Refusal.

TAG ALONG RIGHTS

19.1   If holders of at least 25% of the voting rights propose to sell their shares, then all other shareholders shall have a right to tag along with the sale by way of pro rata apportionment among selling shareholders of the shares being purchased by the third party.

DRAG ALONG RIGHTS

20.1   Holders of at least 75% of voting rights (on an as-converted basis, whether held by way of BRCPS or Common Shares) in issue shall be able to require a sale of all the shares in the Company.

EMPLOYEE SHARE OPTION PLAN

21.1   The Company shall implement an employee stock option with an initial allocation of Common Shares equal to 20% of the equity of the Company on terms to be agreed by the Board.

EMPLOYMENT AGREEMENTS

22.1   Each of the Company's key management shall enter into a standard form of employment agreement, which shall be in a form acceptable to the Investor, including terms relating to proprietary information, non-competition, customary restraint of trade, assignment of inventions and intellectual property rights. Each director, officer, and employee shall have made appropriate representations and warranties as to no-conflict with prior employers.

WARRANTIES

23.1   The standard representations and warranties shall be given to the Investor by the Company and the Founders.

CONFIDENTIALITY

24.1   The terms of the investment are confidential and the Investor and the Company agree that they shall not disclose or divulge such terms unless otherwise required by law or otherwise mutually agreed.

EXCLUSIVITY

25.1   The execution by the parties of this Term Sheet indicates their commitment to proceed in good faith towards the execution of definitive documentation containing these terms as soon as possible. By accepting this Term Sheet, the Company agrees to refrain from solicitation, consideration, or acceptance of any alternative proposals to finance, invest in, or sell the Company or its business and/or assets for a period of thirty (30) days from the date of this Term Sheet.

NON-LEGAL OBLIGATION

26.1   Except for the provisions relating to indemnification, confidentiality, exclusivity, governing law and jurisdiction, this Term Sheet is intended solely as an outline of general terms and the basis for further discussion. It is not intended to be and does not constitute a legally binding obligation or commitment, any fiduciary relationship, partnership or joint venture between the parties. No legally binding obligation or commitment shall be created, implied or inferred until the authorization, execution and delivery of final legal documentation satisfactory to the parties and their respective legal counsel and the satisfaction of any conditions precedent, including the satisfactory completion of all legal and business due diligence.

GOVERNING LAW AND JURISDICTION

27.1   This term sheet shall be governed by and construed in accordance with the laws of [country].

_____

Mr. Brian Capitalist
President
SINGULAR VENTURES
Date:

_____

To: Singular Ventures

I, as authorized signatory for and on behalf of Fantasy Inc, accept the terms and conditions of the investment as set out in the Term Sheet above.

_____

Mr. Fabulous
as President for and on behalf of
FANTASY INC
Date:

PART VI

CLOSING THE DEAL

Concurrent with the drafting of the Term Sheet, negotiations on the terms of investment will be carried on with the founders or management of the potential investee company. How should the VC conduct these negotiations so that agreement is reached smoothly and satisfactorily to both parties? Once agreement is reached, what is the process by which the VC firm secures internal approval to proceed with the investment? What matters may be required to be cleared up and what conditions need to be met prior to the investment?

The final step in the closing of the deal is the drafting and signing of legal documents. What are these documents? What are the key terms in these documents that the VC firm should pay attention to? What are some of the terms that might cause the deal to break down?

Chapter 17: DEAL NEGOTIATION lays out the approach to the negotiations that the VC firm should take and the key issues that should be kept in mind. Chapter 18: CONDITIONS PRECEDENT describes the issues that may need to be settled prior to the investment closing. Chapter 19: INVESTMENT DOCUMENTATION presents the typical legal documents for a VC investment and their respective important features.

17

Deal Negotiation

This chapter is not on the art of negotiation. The VC can learn negotiation skills and techniques from countless books and courses. However the proper application of the skills and techniques requires understanding of the respective concerns and desires of the VC and the entrepreneurs or founders of the company, the prevailing conditions of the VC market, the attractiveness and pitfalls of the deal, and whether there are other VCs bidding for the deal. These factors are shown in Figure 17.1.

Sun Tzu, the famous Chinese military strategist, wrote in his book *The Art of War*:

"Know your enemy, know yourself, and your victory will not be threatened. Know the terrain, know the weather, and your victory will be complete."

Although the VC's aim is not to annihilate the entrepreneur, the analogy is clear. The VC must understand himself, the entrepreneur, the deal, and the VC market climate. Then he would be able to have the deal terms properly crafted, negotiated, and concluded, and the deal successfully closed quickly and smoothly.

In this chapter we shall go through all these factors and discuss the best approach that the VC and the entrepreneur should take towards the negotiation, and limit ourselves to just some tips on negotiation techniques relevant to VC deals.

FIGURE 17.1   FACTORS INFLUENCING DEAL TERMS

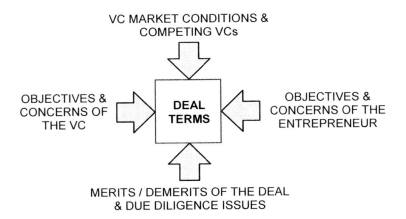

VC MARKET CONDITIONS &
COMPETING VCs

OBJECTIVES &
CONCERNS OF
THE VC

DEAL TERMS

OBJECTIVES &
CONCERNS OF THE
ENTREPRENEUR

MERITS / DEMERITS OF THE DEAL
& DUE DILIGENCE ISSUES

Negotiation Factors

As pointed out earlier, the factors affecting the deal terms are:

o   the objectives and concerns of the VC
o   the objectives and concerns of the entrepreneur
o   the prevailing VC market and competition for deals
o   the merits and demerits of the deal

These affect the inclusion or exclusion of certain terms and conditions, and the extent of their severity or generosity. We shall go through each of these factors.

VC's Objectives and Concerns

The VC's overarching objective for a deal is to achieve the highest return. Before the VC enters into a deal, his greatest concerns are therefore whether he can achieve the expected high return, whether he has sufficient post-investment control to steer the company in this direction, and whether he has enough safeguards to protect his investment and interests. He also acknowledges that the other parties involved, the entrepreneur and the management, must also pull in the same direction. The VC's objectives and concerns when doing a deal are therefore those listed in Figure 17.2.

FIGURE 17.2   VC'S OBJECTIVES & CONCERNS
IN DEAL MAKING

Maximizing investment returns

Minimizing risks of loss of investment

Providing for exits

Exercising management control as needed

Setting management targets and incentives

Achieving a win-win partnership

Every VC has his share of astounding successes and dismal failures, whether directly from his own experience or indirectly through the experience of colleagues. The psychology of the VC when he enters into a deal is therefore like a schizophrenic with simultaneous high hopes and morbid fears. His fears are grounded on the probability of poor returns and business failure. More specifically his fears relate to:

- Achieving too low a return (valuation too high)
- Being too optimistic on the business plans
- Resolving management team weaknesses
- Having control over management decisions and business strategies
- Having sufficient downside protection and redress
- Facing investment exit difficulties
- Having poor rapport and difficulties working with the entrepreneur
- Tarnishing the VC firm's track record and reputation

The VC knows that there are no simple solutions for his concerns. However it is only with knowledge of what are his objectives and concerns, will he be able to address them. But he can only address each of them as best as he can, and at the end of the day he has to make an overall judgment and decide whether the negotiated deal is worth proceeding with.

For example, there is no simple way to address his concern that the company's valuation may be too high, since valuation is not an exact science. At best, he can just negotiate for the lowest valuation he can get without chasing the entrepreneur away. Yet if the entrepreneur gives in to his hard bargaining, he may suspect that there is something inherently wrong with the company. Having determined the best valuation he can get, the VC can calculate the potential return, after adjustments to the company's projections based on due diligence, to see whether this could be a deal breaker.

In the same fashion, the VC can address his other concerns by imposing relevant conditions and negotiating harder on those issues that concern him more and perhaps relenting on the lesser ones. Thus if he believes that the business plans are overly optimistic, he can substantiate this to the entrepreneur by producing due diligence evidence and negotiating for a lower valuation. He may also ask that modifications be made to the business strategies.

If the VC perceives weaknesses in the management team, he could negotiate with the entrepreneur for an undertaking to make appropriate changes prior to or after the investment. He would also impose conditions to exert greater influence over management decisions and strategies and to provide more controls over the operations of the company. Examples would be to put himself as a check signatory, or to set up an Executive Committee, of which he would be a member, to supplement the board.

He will also negotiate for terms that alleviate his risks and allow him to step in at times of trouble and to secure as much redress from losses as possible, even to the extent of imposing conditions that put him in a much more advantageous position than other shareholders.

Exiting from the investment is another important concern to the VC in view of the limited life of VC funds. For those deals where an IPO may not be so feasible within the VC's time frame, he would want to ensure that there are terms that would facilitate a trade sale. If his doubts are even stronger, he may also want to negotiate a buy-back arrangement.

Acknowledging the importance of having incentives to motivate the entrepreneur and his management team, the VC will be willing to provide for stock purchase and stock options schemes. Yet he has to ensure that the shop is not given away. He has to ensure compensation packages are adequate and fair but not too generous. At times he may even ask for salary reductions.

Throughout the whole negotiation process, the VC also has to keep in mind that he is entering into a partnership with the entrepreneur and his team, and so hard bargaining should be tempered by friendliness and reasonableness, and perhaps a touch of humor. The VC also has to keep in mind that doing good deals and achieving good returns are crucial to establishing a track record for his firm. A good reputation is necessary to attract more good deals and a strong track record is necessary to raise the next fund. Therefore while he should negotiate the hardest to get the most out of a deal to help the track record, he needs to conduct the negotiations professionally to enhance the firm's reputation.

With good knowledge of his own concerns, and their relative importance, the VC will not only be able to address them properly and achieve his objectives, but will also be better able to respond to negotiations by the entrepreneur. He will know which terms are less significant to him and so can be horse-traded for stronger terms on important issues. He will also know how the wording of a clause may be redrafted to accommodate the entrepreneur, while maintaining his desired level of control or protection, and arrive at a conclusion speedily and fruitfully.

Entrepreneur's Objectives and Concerns

The entrepreneur's objective is obviously to secure the funding and perhaps also valuable future assistance from the VC. However, his overarching concern is that he might be giving away too much. Specifically, his concerns are chiefly:

- o   Losing management control
- o   Losing too much ownership (valuation too low)
- o   Getting adequate funding
- o   Gaining back a larger stake in the company later

o   Gaining the VC's value add and networking support
o   Having rapport with the VC
o   Building a personal reputation for success

The entrepreneur is convinced that he alone knows how to make the company successful. He is afraid that a new investor will interfere with the way the company is run and the direction it will take, resulting in failure of the company. He is also afraid that he is giving away too much of the company for the amount that will be invested. In other words, he is afraid that his company is being valued too low by the VC.

The entrepreneur wants to be assured that the funding is adequate, taking care of possible contingencies, at least until the next round of financing or IPO. He is afraid he will be left in the lurch and his company may have to be aborted on the verge of success. He wants to know how well he will be rewarded for working hard to grow the pie, and how the VC will contribute in this effort.

He is also concerned about being able to get along with the VC and he wants this whole effort to be more than just being financially rewarding; he has pride in his own reputation and wants to build upon it through the success of this venture.

By understanding the entrepreneur's concerns, the VC knows why he takes a certain position and how much he can be shifted from it. The VC will then be better able to arrive at agreements on specific issues.

The VC should note that a concern shown by the entrepreneur may not entirely be his own. It may be from other founders, other shareholders, or senior managers of the company. Many deals have fallen apart because of recalcitrant decisions or positions taken due to the influence of these people. The VC may need to face them directly to address the issues and overcome such hurdles.

VC Market

Market conditions in the VC industry can fluctuate between those favoring the VC and those favoring the entrepreneur. The VC industry goes through boom and bust cycles like most other relatively young industries. When there is a boom, huge venture funds are raised, leading to a situation of a lot of money chasing after few good deals. The VCs are then willing to loosen their terms, demanding less for their money. When there is a bust, VCs find difficulty in raising new funds and thus become cautious in investing. There will be less competition for deals and VCs will be able to get lower valuations and more stringent conditions imposed on the entrepreneur.

The VC industry is relatively small and close knit. VC firms have a tendency to form syndicates to invest together into a deal. Hence, shifting trends in the tightness of investment terms and conditions become known quickly. VCs have to keep pace with such trends to remain competitive in getting deals done.

For example, prior to the hot dot-com days, the liquidation preference was just a one-time multiple. Just before the bubble burst, VCs were asking for as high as five times multiple. Soon after, it settled back to two or three times participating liquidation preference. Even though terms can vary from one deal to another depending on the perceived attractiveness of the deal to the respective parties, the terms generally lie within the prevailing market ranges. The VC therefore has to know the position of the VC market pendulum when he crafts the term sheet and negotiates terms with the entrepreneur.

While the VC market in the U.S. moves with the cycles, the market in Asia responds more sluggishly. For example, when the industry in the U.S. had moved to imposing several times liquidation multiple, the industry in Asia as a whole did not catch on. Although some VCs, especially those linked to the U.S., tried to impose consistent terms, entrepreneurs were able to find other VCs that were not yet aware of the change or were unwilling to change. Thus the faster moving VCs had to fall back on past practices or may get away with a compromised less severe condition. Thus generally, the Asian VC market tends to fluctuate less severely in terms of valuations and investment terms, but also faces the same boom-bust cycles in terms of availability of funding. The trend towards greater globalization of the industry, consolidation towards fewer players, and the setting up of more global funds will tighten the linkage between the industries in different parts of the world and hence there will be increased consistency in terms and conditions, although there will always be some local exceptions and variances.

Deal Issues

The merits and demerits of the deal as perceived by the VC will affect his attitude towards the deal terms. The more merits there are, the more eager the VC will be and hence the more lenient he may be towards the terms. The demerits of the deal, arising from his evaluation or those that may be surfaced by his due diligence checks, will make the VC more stubborn on those terms relating to the demerits. For example, due diligence investigations may show that the key technologist in the team, although a brilliant engineer, has a tendency to miss development schedules. In this case, the VC may incorporate tighter milestone targets into the terms. Or the due diligence may indicate that the market growth and size may not be as big as claimed in the business plans, in which case the VC would impose ratchet conditions, unless the entrepreneur backs down and agrees to a lower valuation.

Negotiation Approach

It is important to take a balanced approach in the crafting of the term sheet. This must be matched by a balanced approach in the deal negotiations as well. This applies to both sides. The objective of both the VC and the entrepreneur must be to reach a win-win conclusion, arriving at a balance satisfactory to both sides, taking into account their respective objectives and concerns, the attractiveness and risks in the deal, and the prevailing VC market conditions.

It would be a short-lived victory if the VC forces a one-sided deal, by exploiting the entrepreneur's desperate need for funds. The entrepreneur will find ways to get even later, resulting in loss of focus on the business and harming the relationship. The VC's returns must come from the growth and success of the business, and not from taking away a disproportionate share from the entrepreneur. If the business cannot generate returns satisfactory to the VC, the VC should not do the deal. The business and the deal must also generate satisfactory returns to the entrepreneur and his team for them to be motivated to build the business.

How each side approaches and conducts the negotiations sets the tone for their future relationship. Entrepreneurs have found many younger VCs to be rather arrogant. This may arise from overzealousness in negotiations or from the way questions are posed, giving an appearance that the VC knows the business better than the entrepreneur. The VC should therefore be conscious of his behavior at all times. It would also be instructive for the VC to observe the entrepreneur's behavior as well. It is during intensive debate and heated arguments that the entrepreneur would show his temperament, character, persuasive skills, passion, and belief in his business.

Sometimes the VC walks away from a deal not because of disagreement over the terms but by the revelation of character weaknesses in the entrepreneurs. This may be evidenced by behavior such as constant shifts in negotiating positions, obstinate adherence to unreasonable demands, and nitpicking on unimportant details while losing sight of the big picture.

The VC must ensure that the entrepreneur understands all the important terms, otherwise he should take the trouble to explain them clearly. This is especially so in Asia where entrepreneurs are less familiar with VC practices and terminology. This open attitude will build a sense of trust and understanding.

Finally, the VC should avoid negotiating a part of the term sheet at a time. He should go through the whole term sheet with the entrepreneur and gather all the concerns and proposed amendments together. This prevents the entrepreneur from whittling away the VC's position and saves time in the negotiation process.

Useful Negotiation Techniques

- *Knowledge.* Understand the VC deal negotiation factors described in this chapter.
- *Substantiate.* Back up arguments with substantiation, especially for valuation, which can be the most difficult to negotiate, as it is not an exact science and is most critical to both sides. Explain the methodology to calculate valuation and substantiate with due diligence findings.

- *Listen*: Listen carefully to the entrepreneur and watch his body language.
- *Ask for information*: Phrase the question to elicit details, rather than just a yes-no reply.
- *Ask for clarification*: You may be surprised by the answer that comes back, which could be very different from what you expect. Do not make presumptions or jump to conclusions.
- *Occasional silence*: (a) Helps to cool heated situations, (b) allows listening, reflection and observation, (c) allows thinking of alternatives, and (d) might make the other party uncomfortable enough to blurt out information he did not intend to reveal.
- *Walk-away alternative*: Be ready to walk away from the deal. At the same time, try to detect whether the entrepreneur genuinely has this alternative also.
- *Horse trading*: Let the entrepreneur persuade you for what you are already willing to give away, and exaggerate its importance. When the entrepreneur gives something away, emphasize it is a win-win solution.
- *Judo tactics*: Use the entrepreneur's strengths to your advantage. If the entrepreneur swears that his wildly optimistic projections are achievable, suggest a ratchet based on targets or a profit guarantee.
- *Alternative solutions*: Have alternative solutions to sticky issues.
- *Disintegrate*: Break up sticky issues into separate parts to facilitate solutions.
- *Qualifying phrases*: Have an armory of qualifying phrases such as "to the best of knowledge" or "reasonably determine".
- *Non-negotiable can be negotiable*: Probe to understand why the entrepreneur takes a non-negotiable stance on an issue. Often it arises from misperception, and clarification will allow further negotiation.
- *Good cop, bad cop*: This technique still works and often reflects the true situation. The Investment Committee is the bad cop, and the VC deal champion has to convince the Committee that the deal is worth doing and meet its requirements to secure deal approval.
- *Speed*: Time is of essence. Delay may lose the deal and loss of time may impair the company's time to market.

Chapter Recap

In this chapter, we have reviewed:

- The negotiation factors affecting the terms in a VC deal:
    - the VC's objectives and concerns
    - the entrepreneur's objectives and concerns
    - the VC market conditions
    - the merits and demerits of the deal
- The negotiation approaches that the VC should take
- Some useful negotiation techniques for VC deals

18

Conditions Precedent

After the Term Sheet has been agreed upon and signed, the lawyers will be tasked with drafting the legal documents which would typically take four to eight weeks depending on the complexity of the deal and the time consumed by clarifications or negotiations on the wording of certain clauses. During this period, both the VC firm and the potential investee company have to make their respective preparations for the legal completion of the investment.

Matters to be taken care of by the VC prior to the investment include the following:

- o Obtaining internal investment approval
- o Finalizing syndication partners, if the deal is to be syndicated
- o Conducting final due diligence and special audits

Matters to be taken care of by the potential investee company may include:

- o Ceasing further fund-raising effort
- o Corporate restructuring, if necessary
- o Effecting employment contracts
- o Passing corporate resolutions
- o Establishing an employee stock options plan
- o Ensuring no adverse changes in the business
- o Complying with representations and warranties

Other matters to be taken by both parties would be:

- o   Appointing and briefing lawyers, if not done already
- o   Finalizing and signing investment agreements

Most, if not all of these matters would have been captured in the Term Sheet under a section called Conditions Precedent. We mentioned Conditions Precedent in Chapter 16 when we discussed the Term Sheet. These are specific conditions that must be met by the respective parties prior to legal completion and funding of the investment. If any of these conditions are not met, the legal completion may be delayed until there is satisfaction, or waiver of the condition in question, or in the worst case, the proposed investment will be called off.

A Completion Date is usually specified in the investment agreements, on which date all the conditions precedent are to be met, the shares are to be issued to the investors, and the disbursement of the investment is to be made.

In this chapter we shall discuss these preparatory matters, particularly those carried out by the VC, leading to the Completion Date and funding of the investment, and in the next chapter we shall go through the investment agreements in detail.

Investment Approval

Once the Term Sheet has been accepted and signed by the authorized signatory of the potential investee company, the VC would start its process of obtaining internal approval of the proposed investment. There are two important components in this process—the Investment Proposal and the Investment Committee.

Investment Proposal

The Investment Proposal (IP) is the paper put up by the deal champion to the Investment Committee to seek formal approval of the investment. Even though the Investment Committee members may have been kept appraised of issues through e-mails and deal meetings as the deal progressed, the IP should be complete in capturing all the critical issues and presenting all the important merits or potentials, as well as the demerits or risks, in a balanced way.

The IP should also be balanced in terms of length. It should not be weighted down by extraneous information burying critical issues, or merely regurgitated data without assessment or analysis. On the other hand it should not be too brief, glossing over critical issues and without providing possible solutions or mitigation of these issues.

The IP should also avoid the tendency to mix up opinions, claims, and assessments made by the entrepreneur, the deal champion, and third parties. It is important to distinguish between the following:

- o The entrepreneur's assumptions and claims in his business plan
- o The VC's assessments and modifications of the business plan
- o The VC's risk-reward assessment of the proposed investment
- o The opinions and assessments of third parties from due diligence

Many of the entrepreneur's assumptions and claims are likely to be overly optimistic. The VC would have to pick these out, modify them based on knowledge, judgment, and due diligence work. The business plan, after such modification, should be a realistic, middle-of-the-road plan. The VC's risk-reward assessment would be based on this realistic plan, presenting the realistic outcomes, the upside potentials, and the downside risks. It would not be worthwhile to base the risk-reward assessment on the entrepreneur's raw business plan.

Therefore a workable format for an IP would be as shown in Figure 18.1. Each VC firm develops and eventually settles on its own version. Whatever the resulting format, it would be wise to bear in mind the above points on the content of the IP.

Referring to Figure 18.1, the Summary of the Business Plan section should succinctly describe the business, management team, product, technology, market, competition, and financial highlights and relevant environmental factors, if any. Details and supporting data should be in annexes. Projections should be based on realistic assumptions as determined or judged by the VC.

The Deal Structure and Terms section should provide a summary of the deal terms, valuation, type of security and rights attached to it, as well as critical covenants and management controls imposed. The signed Term Sheet and Capitalization Tables should be in annexes. The Returns and Exit section should describe the exit options and the investment returns, giving the assumptions used.

FIGURE 18.1   INVESTMENT PROPOSAL FORMAT

Part I	Summary of Business Plan
	Deal Structure and Terms
	Returns and Exit
Part II	Attractive Aspects
	Critical Issues
	Financial Assessment
	Risk-Reward Assessment
	Conclusion
Appendices	Entrepreneur's Business Plan
	Term Sheet
	Due Diligence Reports

While Part I concentrates on as much of the factual aspects as possible, Part II provides the VC's opinions and assessments of the business and the deal. In the Attractive Aspects section, the merits of the deal are highlighted, such as the unique value of the product or service, the high profit margins, the huge and fast growing market, the proven management team, and the reasonable valuation. Sustainability of profit and scalability of the business are also attractive factors.

The Critical Issues section should list out all the relevant issues raised during deal discussions or by investment committee members, and surfaced by the analysis and due diligence work. The seriousness of these issues and how they may be addressed should be highlighted, for example, by adjusting the business strategies or projections, by imposing appropriate deal terms or structure, as well as actions such as strengthening the management team or bringing in a strategic partner. Here the deal champion has to be open and not avoid or downplay critical issues.

In the Financial Assessment section, common critical issues such as burn rate, cash flow, margins, and cost factors should be addressed. Assessment should be given on the company's ability to control burn rate and to meet top and bottom-line projections. Any financial peculiarities of the business, such as the need for high inventories or unusual credit terms, should be highlighted. The deal champion would need to work out a financial model, in order to modify the financial projections based on more realistic assumptions.

The Risk-Reward Assessment section provides what-if scenarios, looking at most probable, most optimistic, and most pessimistic outcomes for the investment. Short-cut methods by merely taking percentage scale-ups or scale-downs of revenue or profit should not be used. Instead, the what-if calculations should be based on varying basic factors such as performance drivers of the business as well as market and competition shifts in strength. Probabilities may be assigned to the what-if scenarios and a composite weighted result may be derived for the investment returns.

The entrepreneur's business plan need not be circulated to the Investment Committee but should be attached to the archived IP to make a complete record. The signed Term Sheet and due diligence reports consisting of verbatim transcripts of interviews, extracts from relevant business texts, technical papers, or market surveys should also be attached for completeness.

It should be noted that the IP can serve as an important document for post-mortem purposes and as a learning tool for investment staff to review what went right or wrong with a particular investment.

Investment Committee

The Investment Committee is usually formed by several or all of the senior general partners of the VC. Participation may be increased to foster greater team effort and to share commitment to all investments made, and hence to share the successes and failures.

It is important that the Investment Committee makes decisions expeditiously and not hinder the investment process. The Committee members should be brought into the picture early in the deal, as soon as it becomes apparent that the deal is being actively pursued. This will usually be when investment terms are being negotiated and a term sheet is being drafted. This gives an opportunity to Committee members to express their views and concerns, so that appropriate due diligence can be carried out at an early stage to address the concerns, instead of doing so when the deal comes up for approval. Committee members could also contribute to the progress of the deal by assisting in due diligence through their own knowledge and contacts.

Involvement of the Investment Committee members through the final stages of the deal expedites the formal decision process, but does not guarantee approval. Members still have the right to finally reject the deal, particularly if it was not possible to fully address due diligence concerns to their satisfaction, or if the finally negotiated deal terms were not that attractive, or if members felt that with all things considered, the deal was marginal.

The VC firm may set different approval levels based on the size of the investment. For example, smaller investments may be approved by several selected members of the Investment Committee, while larger investments may require unanimous consent of all Committee members. This will reduce the workload of members, allowing them to devote more attention to each investment under consideration.

Syndication

If the VC firm had planned to syndicate the deal, it would have consulted potential co-investors on the Term Sheet, and now would require them to make a firm commitment, so that the respective investment amount can be properly allocated to each investor, and written into the investment agreements. The co-investors would have to complete their own investment approvals and have the amounts ready for disbursement on the Completion Date.

Final Due Diligence and Special Audits

In parallel with securing internal investment approval, the VC would have to carry out its final due diligence checks and special legal or financial audits, if necessary. The VC may not have been able to carry out such checks and audits until after the signing of the Term Sheet because of confidentiality or costs. The company may have been unwilling to disclose certain important or proprietary information until it is sure that there is a deal. Costs would also have to be incurred to carry out a legal or financial audit. Also, the VC's Investment Committee may have raised some new concerns requiring last minute due diligence. All these would have to be completed prior to legal completion.

A legal audit may be required if there are uncertainties over the legal position of the company with respect to its legal or organizational structure; its legal assets or liabilities such as patents or contracts; legal obligations to or claims by shareholders or other parties; pending or potential litigations; outstanding regulatory filings; validity of any licenses or permits; government restrictions on ownership, if any; etc. These would have been investigated at the due diligence stage, as described in Chapter 12, but may require final inspection of documents which may not have been made available by the company until the deal is committed. Such inspection will enable the lawyers to firm up their legal opinions on the issues under consideration.

The VC may also want to appoint an audit firm, which is not the company's auditor, to carry out an independent special audit. Concerns may arise because of doubts over the company's financial assets or liabilities, or the accounting standards of the company and its auditors. In some developing countries, the accounting standards may not be up to international standards.

The VC will need to discuss with the audit firm the scope of the work, the approach to be taken, the time frame, and the costs. The following are examples of the scope of work that may be carried out:

- o Fixed assets
  - o Sighting of fixed assets and titles
  - o Review of controls over purchases, monitoring and sales of fixed assets
  - o Review of depreciation rates
  - o Review of liens or restrictions on titles, if any

- o Intangible assets
  - o Review appropriateness of valuations
  - o Review of amortization rates

- o Inventories
  - o Review of latest physical stock takes and reconciliations
  - o Review of stock valuations
  - o Review of provisions for obsolete, damaged or aged stocks
  - o Review of controls of raw materials, work in progress and finished goods

- o Debtors
  - o Review of aging and reconciliations of debtors
  - o Review recoverability of outstanding debts, deposits and prepayments
  - o Review controls of overdue debt and credit limits
  - o Review the basis for and the recoverability of directors' debts, if any

- o Creditors
  - o Review reconciliations of creditors
  - o Review accuracy and updated status of creditor liabilities

- o Banking facilities
  - o Ascertain existing banking and financing facilities
  - o Review financing covenants
  - o Review bank reconciliations

- o Regulatory filings
  - o Review tax filings, tax provisions and any tax issues

- Review other statutory filings, records, registers and minutes
- Ascertain possession of necessary licenses, and review validity and restrictions

- Contingencies
  - Review outstanding capital or other financial commitments
  - Ascertain any contingent or unrecorded liabilities or financial obligations

Obviously, for an early stage company, the audit will be limited in scope and may not be necessary at all.

Significant issues uncovered by such final due diligence or special legal or financial audits may require renegotiation of valuation or deal terms, or in the worst case, abandonment of the deal.

Investee Company Matters

Ceasing Fund-Raising Effort

On the signing of the Term Sheet, the potential investee company has to refrain from further fund-raising efforts. Although this is obvious, the VC may include this as one of the conditions precedent to ensure compliance and to provide an exit from the deal if it is not complied with.

Corporate Restructuring

In some cases, the company's shareholding may have to be restructured prior to the investment. For example, carrying out a reverse stock split, conversion of senior preferred shares of prior financing rounds to junior preferred shares or converting them to common shares, conversion of shareholders' loans to equity, forming a holding company for minority shareholders to facilitate ease of corporate actions, selling unwanted assets or group companies, etc. These actions would have been part and parcel of the particular deal structuring by the VC.

Effecting Employment Contracts

Prior to its investment, the VC would require the company to enter into employment contracts with key employees. Incorporated into these contracts would be requirements to maintain confidentiality of the company's proprietary information, to assign all intellectual property rights to the company, and to prohibit entering into competition with the company.

Passing Corporate Resolutions

Corporate resolutions would have to be passed by the board and the shareholders to facilitate the investment, such as authorizing the issue of new shares, authorizing signatories to the investment agreements, and may include modifying certain corporate articles.

Establishing an Employee Stock Options Plan

The VC may require the company to set up an Employee Stock Options Plan (ESOP) and to specify the number of ordinary shares to be allocated to the ESOP under terms agreed with the VC. In this way, the VC avoids dilution of its shareholding, which would occur if the shares were allocated after its investment.

Ensuring No Adverse Changes

A standard condition precedent is that the company has to ensure that its business will continue to be carried out in an ordinary manner, during the interim period up till the legal completion date. Any significant adverse change will obviously warrant a reconsideration of the proposed investment. The condition precedent would state that there will be no adverse change in the company's operational or financial conditions or prospects of its business and that there will be no disposal of material assets or incurrence of material or contingent liabilities other than those in the company's ordinary course of business.

Complying with Representations and Warranties

A list of representations and warranties will be required from the company and the founders. They would have to confirm the accuracy of and compliance with these representations and warranties prior to the investment, or make appropriate disclosures of non-compliance. Representations and warranties will be discussed in the next chapter.

Lawyers

Usually both parties would have appointed their respective lawyers to review and to help negotiate the terms and conditions in the Term Sheet. The VC would now have to send a copy of the signed Term Sheet to its lawyers to prepare the legal documents.

Sometimes the VC may ask the lawyers to start work on the legal documents, even though the deal has not yet been approved, to save time. To foster good relations, the lawyers will assume the risk that the deal may be aborted. They will not charge for the initial work, which may consist of reviewing the signed term sheet to make sure there are no glaring problems, and perhaps to also make simple changes to some boilerplate terms. Once the deal is approved by the VC, the lawyers can proceed expeditiously.

Investment Agreements

A condition precedent spelt out in the Term Sheet is the completion of legal documentation for the investment. There have been cases where the deal broke down at this late stage due to intractable disagreement over a clause in or an issue arising from the legal documents. If all goes well the legal documents will be signed but the legal completion and the funding may be at a later date, pending satisfaction of all the other conditions precedent. We shall discuss the legal documents in the next chapter.

Chapter Recap

In this chapter we examined the various conditions precedent that must be satisfied prior to the investment. In particular, we discussed the investment approval process of the VC and the special legal and financial audits that may be required at this stage.

We also discussed a number of actions required by the potential investee company to prepare for the investment.

19

Investment Documentation

The investment documentation captures the investment terms and conditions that are agreed among the parties concerned, and spells out the working relationships between them with respect to the investment. Furthermore, the documentation has to provide sufficient insight into the intent behind the investment terms so as to facilitate resolution of conflicts, if they occur. It has to also anticipate the growth and changes in the company which may affect the investment terms and the relationships of shareholders, and be able to accommodate these changes.

A simple example is to ensure that certain terms and conditions are worded such that if the company later forms subsidiaries, the terms will apply to the subsidiaries as well. Another example is to incorporate terms and conditions that will be activated should the company be acquired by or merged with another company at a future date.

The VC is therefore well advised to work with a legal firm with experience of VC investments. The lawyer is likely to start with a template that already incorporates most of the standard terms typically found in VC investment documentation. He would then use the term sheet to modify the template supplemented by verbal briefings by the VC where needed. An experienced legal counsel will speed up the process, reduce the cost, and require less work by the VC. Often, the legal counsel could point out weaknesses and provide improvements to the terms and conditions spelt out in the term sheet.

At the same time, an experienced VC firm could reduce legal fees and expedite the process if it internally reviews the documents incorporating past experience and requirements of prior deals. In particular, the VC firm should be clear where it stands on business and commercial issues related to the deal, as these fall outside the domain of legal counsel, although they may sometimes be able to advise, using experience from other deals. The legal firm would be best utilized to concentrate on the adequacy, consistency, and applicability of the legal aspects of the deal.

Most of the sensitive and relevant terms should have been ironed out and incorporated in the term sheet by the time it is signed. If the term sheet was not well worked out initially, major revisions would be required by the lawyers, and this could require further protracted negotiations by the parties concerned.

The VC should offer to produce the first draft of the legal documents, as there is a strategic advantage in doing so. The legal counsel for the VC can make sure that all the interests and concerns of the VC are captured and relevant clauses are phrased in the VC's favor. The onus is then on the other party or parties to balance that as well as to originate clauses that are solely to their interests.

As the documents get worked on by the lawyers, the VC should keep close track of amendments to ensure that the process is not delayed by argument over minor legal technicalities by overzealous lawyers. The VC should also be prepared to take over from the lawyers any commercial issues so that these can be directly settled with the entrepreneur.

There are basically two legal documents that are necessary—the Investment Agreement and the Shareholders Agreement. The Investment Agreement describes the type of security being purchased, the terms and conditions relating to the purchase, disclosures about the past operation of the company, and management authority for the future operation of the company. The Shareholders Agreement is an agreement between the new investors and existing shareholders, relating to their respective roles, rights, and obligations.

The Investment Agreement may also be known as the Securities or Stock Purchase Agreement, which is more relevant for purchase of existing stock from a shareholder, or the Share Subscription Agreement, which is more relevant for purchase of new stock issued by the company.

Since these agreements can get to be quite thick and complicated, it has become common to spin off certain parts into supplementary or separate agreements, which will also enable better focus on those subparts. Thus in addition to the Investment Agreement, there could be separate agreements such as the Non-Competition Agreement, Confidentiality Agreement, and Intellectual Property Rights Agreement. Usually there would be separate Employment Contracts for the key managers.

Some of the subparts may be grouped in different ways; for example, there may be just one Confidentiality and Intellectual Property Rights Agreement, and there may not be a Non-Competition Agreement as the relevant clauses could be incorporated into the respective Employment Contracts.

Some legal counsel may prefer to have a separate Registration Rights Agreement to enable focus on the rights and also because they survive after the VC's preferred shares are converted to common shares on IPO. If the investment transaction includes the purchase of warrants, there will be a separate Warrant Purchase Agreement, detailing the terms and conditions for the purchase, exercise, and expiry of the warrants.

The Shareholders Agreement is relatively simpler, but may still have some parts separated out. A supplementary agreement may be an Exit Rights Agreement to state the respective rights of the shareholders during an exit from the investment and defining the various exit situations, such as trade sale, whether partially or completely, merger, or liquidation. Another possible supplementary agreement is a Co-Sale Agreement, relating to the transfer or sale of shares by shareholders. In some cases there may be a Put Agreement or a Buy-Back Agreement to enable the investor to exit through selling back to the founders. Sometimes, the Shareholders Agreement itself may be considered ancillary to the Investment Agreement.

In addition to the various agreements, legal opinions may be necessary, if there is a complex legal issue involved or if there is a party to the transaction that resides in another jurisdiction. The opinions may cover the legality or tax status of the securities to be issued, the compliance of the transaction and the parties with the governing jurisdiction and the jurisdictions of the respective parties, or the status and assessment of critical patent filings. Finally, ancillary documents such as resolutions to change the corporate articles and board resolution authorizing the agreements would be required to complete the investment transaction.

Such a plethora of legal documents can be bewildering to the neophyte VC, not to mention the entrepreneur. An understanding of the functions of respective parts of the documentation will help to relate them together to form the total picture. It can be dangerous if the VC gets overwhelmed and abandons all attention on the documentation, leaving everything to their lawyers. A good understanding of the functions of the respective terms and conditions is required to enable the VC to focus on the critical ones and to leave the standard and less important ones to the lawyers.

We shall now look more closely into the investment documents to help with such understanding and to highlight some of the issues that may arise. Preferably, the VC should have anticipated them and would have brought them up during the Term Sheet negotiations. In this way, the VC will not lose credibility with the entrepreneur and appear to sneak in important issues into the legal documents. However if a lapse should genuinely occur, or if what seems to be an unimportant issue to the VC turns out to be burning to the entrepreneur, it has to be handled carefully, as there have been many instances when the deal is broken at the documentation stage.

Investment Agreement

The structure of the Investment Agreement is shown in Figure 19.1.

The nomenclature and ordering of the sections listed may vary, and as stated previously, sometimes some of them may be captured in separate agreements.

FIGURE 19.1 INVESTMENT AGREEMENT

Preamble and Definitions

Conditions Precedent

Type of Security and Terms for the Purchase

Capitalization

Completion Terms

Representations and Warranties

Use of Proceeds

Company Operations

Employee Stock Ownership Scheme

Employee Stock Options Scheme

Confidentiality and Non-Competition

Intellectual Property Rights

Defaults, Remedies and Termination

Expenses

Governing Law and Arbitration

The **Preamble** lists the contracting parties and the rationale for entering into the agreement. The **Definitions** section lists those terms that have the specific meanings as described. **Conditions Precedent** were described in the previous chapter.

The **Type of Security** and the **Terms for the Purchase** would have been thoroughly negotiated and agreed upon signing of the Term Sheet and should not be an issue anymore at this stage, unless the entrepreneur has second thoughts or new concerns surfaced by the documents. This happens occasionally and has to be managed by the VC.

The Type of Security section would capture all the rights attached to the security. These would include dividend rights, liquidation preference, voting rights, conversion terms, anti-dilution provisions, and registration rights, which were described in Chapter 16 on the Term Sheet. Sometimes, for the sake of clarity, such rights and terms may be put in a separate schedule in the Investment Agreement or be in a separate agreement. In some other cases the registration rights and all other rights of the investor are put into one Investor's Rights Agreement, for convenience.

The **Capitalization** section is to capture the capitalization structure of the company immediately prior to and following the closing of the investment. Schedules will be drawn up to show the authorized and issued number of all types of stock, the number, if any, of reserved stock, warrants, options (including employee options) or convertible securities, as well as any rights to the company's securities that may be pledged or committed. Examples of capitalization tables are given in Figures 2.13A to 2.13C in Chapter 2: VC Financing and Figure 16.2 in Chapter 16: Term Sheet.

Completion Terms specify the time and place for completion and the required corporate actions such as holding of the first board meeting; holding an extraordinary shareholders meeting to approve the issue and allotment of shares; adoption of new corporate articles; and execution of those agreements that are subsequent to the investment such as Employment Contracts. There would also be a clause to ensure that during the period from the signing of the agreement to the date of completion, the company's business will be carried on as usual and that there will be no major change that would affect the investment decision, or require the terms of investment to be changed. The operation of the company prior to the signing of the agreement would be covered under representations and warranties provided in the agreement.

Representations and Warranties are undertakings by the founders and the company (and if necessary the management, directors and other shareholders as well), that the business has been conducted properly; that all assets were in good order; all liabilities, including contingent liabilities, have been disclosed; and all material information about the business and prospects have been disclosed, and were correct.

More specifically, they have to undertake that they have at all times complied with the law; disclosed contracts, litigations, and conflicts of interest; possess proper legal titles, insured and properly maintained all relevant assets and intellectual property; provided true, complete, and accurate financial, corporate, and taxation information, as well as employee contracts and commitments; that all inventories are usable and accounts receivables are collectible; that there are no outstanding lawsuits, violations, tax and warranty claims, contract breaches and contingent liabilities, known or unknown, unless disclosed; and that the necessary approvals and consents for the investment transaction have been obtained.

If the VC is purchasing shares from existing shareholders as part of the transaction, the VC has to ensure that proper representation and warranty are provided that the shareholders have legal title and that the shares are not pledged or otherwise encumbered.

Legal counsel would have an exhaustive menu of carefully worded paragraphs that the VC can pick from or modify accordingly. Such representations and warranties should not be taken by the VC as substitutes for due diligence. They are important due to the following reasons:

o   They force disclosure of material facts that might cause harm to the business. The entrepreneur may have either willfully or forgetfully concealed the facts.

o   Disclosure of such facts would prompt the VC to investigate further and review whether they justify renegotiation of the valuation, walking away from the deal or other appropriate action.

o   They also provide legal recourse if material facts were not disclosed and were uncovered subsequently. Such recourse could be through indemnification or other forms of redress, or if it is substantial enough may cause the rescission of the investment.

Therefore these clauses should not be taken lightly and objections from the founders would be a clue that would require further investigation or reconsideration by the VC. Founders who have not seen investment documentation before will likely be flabbergasted by the number and scope of the representations and warranties. They have to be reassured that these are standard and they can choose to make appropriate disclosures in a disclosure letter to protect themselves.

Shareholders who are not founders or involved in the management of the company would typically object to being included in providing such representations and warranties. A compromise would be for legal counsel and the VC to determine which warranty applies to which group among the founders, managers, company, and existing shareholders, and the relevant groups be held liable jointly, instead of holding all of them liable jointly and severally, as is usually the case.

Sometimes the warranty providers may ask for a limit to the time duration. They will obviously seek to have the representations and warranties expire on closing of the deal, whereas the VC will want them to hold forever. The compromise may be between six months to two years from closing. Another compromise is to cap the amount of indemnification for any inadvertent breach of a warranty, or inadvertent lack of disclosure. Or certain representations may be qualified that they are "to the best of knowledge." The VC should discuss with his lawyers and may agree if the clauses concerned are not deemed to be material. However, materiality is also subjective, so the VC may need to exercise some business judgment, coupled with advice from the lawyers and senior partners in the VC firm.

Use of Proceeds is to ensure that the company uses the funds according to its business plan and to provide recourse if it does not do so. It is important to the VC to specify this, as there have been cases where the investment funds have been diverted to other uses.

Obviously the VC would be concerned about the **Company Operations** after the investment and would put in many affirmative and negative covenants to control or at least influence management actions and directions, yet allowing some degree of freedom for daily operations and decisions in the ordinary course of business. This concern would be stronger if the VC (and its co-investors, if any), do not own majority or have board or management control of the company. Many if not all of these covenants may be placed in the Shareholders Agreement, as they relate to board decisions or board authority over management decisions.

Affirmative covenants relate to those actions that the management and the company should undertake and the desired results that they should achieve. Typical affirmative covenants are those actions necessary for prudent financial management, preparation and approval of budgets, and the continuance of the business such as payment of taxes, insurance, leases, compliance with laws and regulations, maintenance of property, audit and submission of accounts to authorities, and protection of intellectual property rights. If not included elsewhere, board composition and use of proceeds may be covered here. Other affirmative covenants in this section would be the VC's **information rights** such as availability of financial statements and reasonable access to the company operations, as well as a declaration to work towards a public listing.

Negative covenants, which are of greater concern to the VC, relate to those corporate actions that require specific approval of the VC, or at least approval at a board meeting in which the VC representative is present. Since these covenants would be seen to impede or limit management's flexibility and authority, there is likely to be dispute over some of them.

These negative covenants may also be referred to as **minority protection rights** as they are meant to protect the interests of the VC, being a minority shareholder in most cases. If the VC does not have control of the board, the company can effect such changes without its permission, hence the need to have an exceptions list of actions that require its approval. Again, an experienced legal counsel will readily provide a long checklist of negative covenants for the VC to pick from.

Typical negative covenants relate to changes that have major impact on the business. These include starting of a new business or change in the business direction, investment into, acquisition of or mergers with other businesses, sale or purchase of major assets, issuance of securities, guarantees or loans, entering into debt or pledges, and change in accounting policies or practices.

A sensitive issue would be a covenant requiring the VC's approval in the appointment of key managers and in the setting or change of remuneration and employment terms (including benefits and award of stock options) for them. If the VC is not careful, it may find a sudden increase in salaries and benefits soon after the investment. The VC may also want to set check signatory authority policies and amount limits, and for early stage companies, the VC board representative may also be a required check signatory for checks above a specified amount.

These sensitive negative covenants should be included in the Term Sheet, or at least be brought up during negotiations. However, if the VC (with its co-investors) controls the board, then many of the negative covenants may be left out.

The **Employee Stock Ownership Scheme** is distinct from the Employee Stock Option Scheme. The Ownership Scheme allows the outright sale of shares to employees at a favorable price. One use of this scheme is to allow the founders to increase their stake, which may have been highly diluted by the VC's investment. The scheme will provide for the sale of nominally priced shares to founders based on the performance of the founders and the company. Specific milestone targets for the company would have been agreed upon with the VC.

Another use of the Employee Stock Ownership Scheme is to promote loyalty to the company. In this case, the purchase of shares at a discounted price will be open to all employees, with the provision that if employment is terminated the shares have to be sold back to the company or returned to a pool kept by the company.

The issue and sale of shares under this scheme would have to be exempt from the preemptive rights and anti-dilution provisions.

The details of the **Employee Stock Options Scheme** may not be spelled out in the Investment Agreement. Usually broad principles and policies of the scheme may be outlined, and it would be left to the board to establish and administer the scheme. The key features of an Employee Stock Options Scheme were described in Chapter 16: Term Sheet.

Confidentiality clauses require the parties to the agreement to observe the confidentiality of the company's proprietary information. These are standard and usually not sensitive clauses. For many VC investments, the main asset, and perhaps the only significant asset, is the intellectual property and certain proprietary know-how, processes or formulations. Maintaining confidentiality is therefore important. Such clauses are usually not contentious as they are in line with the desires of the founders.

The **Non-Competition** clauses may sometimes be of concern to the founders, as their future careers may be affected. They may require a clearer and narrower definition of the types of businesses that would be considered competing, and shortening of the duration of the restriction may be a compromise. In many jurisdictions, the enforceability of such restrictions is questionable as they could deprive the person from earning a living by the fact that his qualifications and experience do not give him the choice to seek alternative employment. The VC may see the non-competition clauses as deterrents and hence may still insist on having them, despite doubts on enforceability.

On the other hand, the VC should avoid the application of such clauses on itself, since the firm may invest in related businesses. Sometimes the VC may have to accept such a clause if the entrepreneur insists. The VC would then narrow the definition of a competing business to be one that competes head-on.

The section on **Intellectual Property (IP) Rights** provides for the transfer and assignment of the rights for any existing and new or novel inventions and improvements or discoveries to the company. As stated earlier, the IP of a company is of paramount importance, particularly for technology companies, hence the VC will need to ensure that the company has proper ownership of existing IP (that may have been registered in the name of one of the founders), and any new IP developed by the company.

This section will also provide undertakings by the founders that the company will not infringe the IP of other companies and that the company will protect and defend its own IP.

A **Default** section may be necessary to define breaches of the agreement, which would trigger certain actions by the investor, unless remedies as specified are taken by the company or founders. Actions triggered may be redemption of the investment or loan and in extreme cases may trigger rescission rights, which means the withdrawal of the investment and termination of the agreement.

This section may also have **indemnification** provisions, where the founders and top management may be required to indemnify the company or the investor for any breaches of the representations and warranties, such as any costs incurred as a result of infringement of intellectual property rights. Such indemnification provisions force proper disclosure by the founders and managers, but are often vehemently opposed by them. A compromise would be to limit the time period for such an obligation to one or two years, instead of being indefinite. Another solution would be to differentiate the seriousness of such breaches and allow indemnification, or recourse through rescission of the investment, or appropriate adjustment to the valuation of the company, as appropriate. The founders may also request some of the representations and warranties to be watered down to the extent that they are given to the best of their knowledge or with such similar qualification. The VC has to resist watering down those potential breaches that will have serious impact on its investment decision or the company's business.

It is common for the VC to charge its legal fees, and audit fees if any, incurred as a result of the investment, to the company. This will be spelt out in the **Expenses** clause and may require some negotiation. The founders may negotiate for the costs to be shared equally or to impose a limit on such expenses to be borne by the company.

The **Governing Law** is usually that of the domicile of the company. If the VC is domiciled in another country, it may require the specification of an acceptable Arbitration Court.

This coverage is not exhaustive, but captures the salient points of most investment agreements. There are other miscellaneous terms (such as assignability, release, notices, signing in counterparts) that would not be of much concern to the VC. If the contracting parties desire, many of the sections can be simplified and certain clauses left out to arrive at a simpler agreement.

Shareholders Agreement

The Shareholders Agreement spells out the respective rights and obligations pertaining to being shareholders of the company, in respect to the control and authority over the company's management and affairs, the conduct of board and general meetings, as well as issue and transfer of shares. A typical agreement would have the sections as shown in Figure 19.2.

FIGURE 19.2 SHAREHOLDERS AGREEMENT

Preamble and Definitions

Board Meetings

General Meetings

Sale and Transfer of Shares

Employee Stock Options

Default

Deadlock

Expenses

Governing Law and Arbitration

The **Preamble** lists the contracting parties and the rationale for the agreement and references the Investment Agreement. The **Definitions** section lists the terms used that have specific meanings ascribed to them.

The section on **Board Meetings** describes the board composition, rights relating to appointment and removal of directors, alternates, and sometimes observers also, as well as appointment of the chairman. It would state whether the chairman has a casting vote, the notice period, and quorum for board meetings and the voting of resolutions. Board composition can be a contentious issue. Usually the shareholders will be represented pro rata to their respective shareholding, or as closely as possible.

The VC would like to have board control, which would be possible if together with co-investors a majority stake is held. If not, the VC would usually require mandatory presence of its representative to form a board quorum. As the intent is not for the VC to block board proceedings by continually being absent, there will be a provision for the board meeting to be adjourned if the VC's representative is absent, and that such adjourned meeting shall not require the VC's representative to form a quorum.

If not already spelt out in the Investment Agreement, there will be a list of affirmative and negative covenants governing management and board actions and decisions that require the involvement of the VC. These are described under Company Operations in the section on Investment Agreement in this chapter.

The section on **General Meetings** is less contentious as it is usually standard and has less impact on management. This section sets out the conduct, notice, quorum, adjournment, and resolution requirements for annual and extraordinary general meetings. If the VC does not have majority shareholding, there will be a list of negative covenants on actions that fall under the purview of shareholders. Such actions will usually require a super-majority vote, which means that a large majority of the number of shares held (usually between two-thirds and 90 percent) vote in favor. Thus if the VC owns 30 percent, and if the super-majority is specified to be 75 percent, as is commonly the case, the VC can block the action.

The negative covenants cover changes to corporate articles, declaration of dividends, changes to authorized capital or capital structure, restructuring of the company, winding up or liquidation, approval of annual accounts, appointment of auditors, and issue of shares or other securities or rights.

Restrictions on the **Sale and Transfer of Shares** by any shareholder are to ensure stability of ownership and some control over the admission of new shareholders. Such rights and restrictions are right of first refusal, tag along right, drag along right, as well as exempt transfers such as transfers to affiliates in the case of investors and transfers to relatives in the case of founders. These rights were described in Chapter 16 on the Term Sheet.

If not already included in the Investment Agreement, a clause stating the intent to establish an **Employee Stock Option Scheme** may be put in here.

The **Default** section will list those events, such as material breach of the agreement, liquidation, or bankruptcy, which will require the defaulting party to either take remedial action, if possible, failing which its shares will be offered for sale to the other shareholders. The valuation for such sale may be determined by an independent valuer, or may be specified in the agreement.

The **Deadlock** section provides for the rare possibility of a board matter that cannot be decided upon by the board, and is similarly deadlocked when raised to a shareholders meeting. In such a situation, and within a prescribed period for negotiations, either the VC or the existing shareholders can offer to purchase the other party's shares on stated terms and conditions. Within the prescribed offer period, the party receiving the offer may either accept the purchase offer or force the reverse transaction, which is to require the offeror to sell its shares instead, on the same terms. Such a mechanism ensures fair transaction terms and discourages frivolous offers.

The **Expenses** and **Governing Law** sections are similar to those in the Investment Agreement.

Employment Contracts

The Employee Contracts for the key staff such as the CEO, COO, CFO, and CTO, capture their terms and conditions of employment, including salaries and benefits, and termination. There will be non-competition, confidentiality, and intellectual property clauses, as described above, which would survive for a period after termination of service.

The VC has to be careful to include provisions for reassignment of duties, as determined by the board, since it is not uncommon to switch or re-designate jobs, including that of the CEO, in a growing company. The VC also has to ensure that the termination clauses are properly worded so that the termination of a senior staff does not entail onerous difficulties or require unduly high compensation by the company.

Legal Completion

When all the legal documents are agreed upon and finalized by the lawyers, a date will be set for the signing of the documents. Another date, typically a week later or such other date that the parties may mutually agree upon, will be set for the legal completion, called the Completion Date. The later date is to allow time for all the actions and obligations listed in the Conditions Precedent section of the investment agreement, as described in Chapter 18, to be performed or fulfilled satisfactorily by the respective parties.

If this is the case, on the Completion Date the company will issue the share certificates to the investors and provide certified copies of resolutions passed by its board of directors and by its shareholders approving the issue of shares and authorizing the investment. The founders and the company will also provide letters confirming the accuracy of and their compliance with the representations and warranties spelt out in the agreements. The investors will disburse the funds for the investment to the company.

Chapter Recap

In this chapter, we have reviewed the main clauses of the typical VC investment documents:

- o   The Investment Agreement
- o   The Shareholders Agreement

and discussed the issues that may arise from them.

PART VII

NURTURING & HARVESTING THE INVESTMENT

The signing of the investment papers and the disbursement of investment funds mark the beginning of several years of working in partnership with the founders and management of the investee company to build the business. How does the VC firm keep tabs of progress and ensures that it is alerted of potential problems? How could the VC firm help to grow the business? How could the VC firm help at times of trouble?

When is the best time for the VC firm to divest the investment? What are the alternatives available for divestment and their respective merits? How can the VC firm work towards achieving the best returns on divesting?

These questions are answered in Chapter 20: MONITORING & ADDING VALUE, and Chapter 21: REALIZING & RECOVERING VALUE.

The completion of divestment marks the end of an investment and completes the VC investment process for that investment.

20

Monitoring & Adding Value

The closing of the investment marks the beginning of years of effort of working with the founders and management to grow the company. For the VC, a major part of this post-investment effort is to continually and closely monitor the progress of the company. The objectives of maintaining such close monitoring are:

o To have intimate and current knowledge of the status of the business
o To be promptly alerted of potential or impending problems
o To find ways to assist and add value
o To ensure proper corporate governance
o To enforce investment conditions when necessary
o To be able to explore avenues for exit

Achieving the first objective is a prerequisite to meeting the other objectives. Without keeping in close touch, the VC may not know of problems until it is too late or too costly to rectify. Without sufficient and up-to-date knowledge of the company's affairs and plans, it would not be possible for the VC to effectively assist or add value to the company. By keeping a watchful eye, the VC is better able to detect corporate misdeeds committed willfully or to point out those committed unwittingly. The close monitoring also enables the VC to identify suitable buyers or merger opportunities to facilitate an exit that could be more attractive than an uncertain future IPO. We shall elaborate later in this chapter.

If the VC has good rapport with the founders and management, and they in turn view the VC as a valuable partner, the VC's post-investment efforts will be more effective and rewarding. If it unfortunately turns out that the entrepreneur was only interested in the funding and reveals his true uncooperative self after the investment, the VC still needs to maintain a close watch, to find ways to make changes or to make an early exit.

Of course, if the investment was made on the basis of capable management and great business plans and strategies, the company should progress well and management should best be left alone most of the time, with the VC advising and helping only when needed. Even in such a case, when called upon to help, the VC can respond better and faster, only if he has been in close touch with the company. The fact remains that for most, if not all, VC investments, there will inevitably be crises along the way. Therefore close monitoring is necessary so that the VC can at all times understand the situation well enough to choose the best course of action, from amongst options such as doing nothing and leaving it to the management, offering advice or assistance, exercising greater control of management, changing management, changing business strategies or directions, looking for M&A possibilities, or making a premature exit.

Post-investment monitoring is best done by the deal champion, since she has intimate knowledge of the company, having carried out extensive due diligence, and would have developed rapport with the founders and management, having interacted with them for some time. Some VCs prefer a separate monitoring team, since the skill sets of deal sourcing and deal making are different from those required for investment monitoring. Also, most investment staff prefer the excitement and glamour of deal making and accord lower priority and less time to monitoring. However, the handing over of a deal from the deal champion to a monitoring staff results in discontinuity. Some VCs prefer the deal champion to continue with monitoring, but have a monitoring team that audits investee companies on a periodic basis, and hence provides a check and balance against weak monitoring, biased reporting, or late reporting of problems by the deal champion.

After elaborating on the investment monitoring objectives, we shall discuss the monitoring of the investment portfolio, which is different from monitoring each investment, and present an example investment monitoring reporting format at the end of the chapter.

Keeping Current

It is obvious that close monitoring means keeping current with all developments in the investee company. There should be regular board meetings to review financial and management reports and to discuss major operational issues, policies, and strategies. Board meetings have to be supplemented by ad hoc meetings and phone calls. Such less formal contacts can be valuable to develop rapport, exchange views, and discuss details with the CEO and his executives. Regular visits to the operations would be necessary to get a good feel of the morale and to see progress made.

The VC has to pay attention to the current financial health of the company, especially matters affecting cash flow such as hiring of staff, overhead expenses, capital expenditures, inventory levels, and accounts receivable. The VC often has to deal direct with the finance manager of the company as the CEO usually concentrates on operational and marketing issues.

The VC has to avoid going overboard with loading the management with frequent demands for all sorts of reports and information. Usually the information that the VC needs would be exactly those that the CEO would in any case require to manage the company effectively.

Monitoring an investment is not only monitoring the investee company, but also monitoring external factors that may affect the company. The VC has to monitor the industry, competitors, the market, the economy and relevant laws and regulations to keep current of trends, changes, and emergence of new threats or opportunities. The VC would have to alert the board and the management to discuss developments that could have impact on the business.

Early Warning

The VC has to be alert to detect problems as they emerge so that they can be tackled more easily than when they become too serious. Sometimes management may not be aware or, if they know of the problem, may either be indifferent to or may conceal the matter.

The following are examples of detection of warning signs, which should trigger appropriate action by the VC:

o   Financial Warnings: Ratio analysis of monthly or quarterly financial statements may show alarming trends such as sales decline, margins deterioration, and swelling of inventories and accounts receivable. Analysis of cash flow projections may show cash flow tightening. Early action is required as cutting expenses significantly or raising funds takes time to effect.

o   Marketing Problems: Sales decline could be an indication of lack of, or loss of, market traction, unless it is temporary in nature. Decline in profit margins could also be due to loss of market traction or increased competition, requiring lowering of prices. The VC should investigate further, even though these problems may appear to be seasonal or temporary.

o   Swelling of Inventory: This could be due to too aggressive purchasing arising from overly optimistic anticipation of future sales, or errors in purchasing resulting in piling up of unusable or obsolete inventory. Investigation into the root cause is necessary to prevent further worsening, while taking action to dispose off excess inventory.

o   Ballooning of Accounts Receivable: Management may give the excuse that customers are being difficult and purposely delaying payments. Again the VC may have to investigate further to see whether the real reason for late payment is customers' dissatisfaction, which could have been due to poor product or service quality, or poor installation or customization work.

o   Sudden Spurt in Spending: After funding or after achievement of initial sales, management may get overly exuberant and launch heavy capital expenditures or rapid recruitment. The VC would have to ensure this does not get out of hand and may need to help management find ways to conserve cash by working with strategic partners, part-time staff or outsourcing.

o   Product Development Delays: Slippage in product development schedules or delays in product rollout may not necessarily be only due to technical difficulties. The entrepreneur may be attempting to repeatedly refine or redefine the product or to add too many extra features. The VC would have to help rework product strategies before market windows are missed.

o   Late or Lack of Notification to the Board: Major corporate actions taken by management without prior approval by the board, or with notification only after the fact, are signs of disregard towards proper corporate governance and disregard of shareholders' interests.

o   Delay in Response: Management becoming less open and responsive, with undue delays and inaccuracies in the information provided, are signs that management may be covering up some problems.

o   Late Financials: Late completion of financials is always a sign of problems, ranging from staffing problems in the Finance Department to as serious a problem as management manipulating the numbers.

o   Staff Resignations: This is a sign of possible management, remuneration, or morale problems at certain staff levels or groups. The CEO has to find out the reasons and take appropriate actions to contain or resolve the problem. The VC or another board member may have to interview the departing staff to ascertain the reasons.

o   Breakup of Founding Team: Many start-ups fail because of disagreement among the founders on the direction of the company, which often happens when the company faces a crisis. Founders have different solutions and pull the company in different directions. The VC may have to step in to find the best solution and to build consensus among the founders and management, before irreparable damage occurs. An adamant dissenting founder may have to be removed from having an executive position.

o   Evidence of Incompetence: Despite all the due diligence having shown otherwise, the CEO may turn out to be unsuitable for one reason or another. The VC would have to lead the board to make a change. Although difficult and disruptive, the earlier the change the better. Sometimes, one of the senior managers may show incompetence or inability to grow with the company, but the CEO may have blind faith or loyalty to a comrade and may refuse to remove the person. The VC would have to harness the board's support to force the CEO to take action.

o   Loss of Focus: If management makes all sorts of proposals to the board to diversify into unrelated businesses, to move into unfamiliar markets or to make acquisitions, on the basis of rather superficial justifications, the VC may conclude that the founders and management are losing focus or losing confidence in the original business. The board would have to review and perhaps redefine the business. If the future is bleak, the VC would have to plan an exit, recovering as much value as possible.

o   Lack of Performance: After the company has fallen behind schedules and targets a few times, the board would have to review the reasons and may have to make changes to the management or the business strategies. The VC cannot afford to wait passively for a recovery. Again, if there is no hope for recovery, the VC would have to work out a premature exit.

Besides the various possible actions described, the VC may respond to warning signs of emerging problems by taking a more active role in the management of the company. The board may authorize the formation of an Executive Committee, chaired by the VC, and with the CEO, COO, if any, CFO, and perhaps another board representative as members. The Executive Committee will discuss and make major management decisions, thus removing some of the executive powers of the CEO and enabling the VC to drive the company more directly.

When the board forms the Executive Committee, the management and in particular the CEO, will likely be disgruntled. Therefore it would be preferable if the formation of an Executive Committee had been agreed upon prior to the investment, if due diligence had shown a potential need to do so. Nevertheless, the Executive Committee is a powerful means for the VC to control the company, and may be disbanded when confidence of the management or the business is restored.

Adding Value

The VC firm adds value to an investee company by offering advice, effecting business introductions, and providing assistance, directly from the expertise of the VC partner sitting on the board or other partners in the firm who have relevant expertise, or indirectly through the firm's network of contacts. The advice and assistance extend beyond discussions at board meetings, into arranging meetings and visits to potential suppliers, customers and industry partners, as well as industry or market consultants and regulatory authorities, with the VC often accompanying and supporting the CEO. Sometimes the VC, as a director of the investee company, may represent the company and participate in marketing presentations, business negotiations, and recruitment interviews.

Some VCs charge a monthly "management fee" for such value-add services, but most do not, since the VCs benefit if the value-add services result in faster growth and enhancement of the value of investee companies. Examples of value-add services that a VC firm may provide to its investee companies include:

o   Strategic Business Advice: Giving advice on formulation of business plans, models and strategies, analyzing strengths and weakness, threats and opportunities facing the company, and helping to define goals and action plans.

o   Financial Expertise: Assisting the setting up of financial and costing systems and reports. Contributing to the board's review of financial statements and helping to point out financial weaknesses. Helping in the raising of debt financing, raising of a new equity round, or capital restructuring, when required.

o   Management Assistance: Mentoring the CEO, being a sounding board to thrash out business, operational or management issues with the CEO, and advising the CEO on best business practices, management principles, and concepts, and latest technology or industry developments, as well as helping to build the management team. Helping to formulate or review corporate policies and procedures, compensation, and stock option plans. Helping to recruit board members and senior management staff.

o   Business Networking: Introducing customers, suppliers, distributors, resellers, joint venture or strategic partners, sources of technology, and professional services and consultancy services providers. Helping to secure sales, supplier capacity, government approvals, and licenses.

o   International Expansion: Helping expansion into foreign markets by providing knowledge of market opportunities, business practices, and regulations as well as contacts with potential local partners and customers. Providing hand-holding support, if the VC has an office in the particular market.

o   Corporate Image: Helping to promote the investee's corporate image and credibility (through association with the VC) in corporate communications and marketing collateral.

o   Exit Process: Helping to look for and negotiate with strategic buyers, if necessary, or helping with the IPO process.

The VC has to be proactive in offering help, and of course, the type and extent of help that the VC provides also depends on the particular needs of the company and the receptiveness of the CEO and the management team to the VC's help.

Corporate Governance

Since the VC firm takes a minority stake for most of its investments, it is important that its shareholder interests are protected through good corporate governance and practices in the investee companies. Although the Investment and Shareholders Agreements contain clauses relating to management controls, minority protection, and shareholders' rights, it has to be ensured that the company's board and management are always aware of and adhere to the provisions. We discussed these provisions in Chapters 16 and 19.

It is now recognized that separating the roles of chairman of the board and CEO is important for good corporate governance. The VC may take on the role of non-executive chairman or perhaps appoint a semi-retired CEO, who was previously supported by the VC and who knows the investee company's business to some extent.

A strong board is a prerequisite for good corporate governance. The VC may have to help recruit suitable board members and to ensure that the board is active, independent, and committed. The board has to ensure that operational and financial policies and procedures are reviewed, implemented, and complied with. The board should set up a Compensation Committee and an Audit Committee, although these may not be required for a private company but would help prepare the management for eventual operation as a listed company. They would also serve to enhance corporate governance, ensure compensation plans are linked to performance and are adequate to motivate and retain good staff, and to assure compliance with financial policies and procedures.

Board members should also conscientiously take an active interest in the company's business and market and proactively try to add value in the areas as described in the previous section on Adding Value. For the board to be effective, board members should demand high standards from management in terms of openness, quality, and timeliness of management reports and promptness in follow-up actions required by the board.

A strong and active board will be of tremendous value in supplementing the VC's own efforts in monitoring and adding value to the investee company.

Ensuring Compliance

Another objective in monitoring is to ensure compliance with investment terms and conditions. The VC has to ensure that the company follows its proposed business plans and strategies and any deviations are justified and approved by the board. The investment funds are also to be used according to the plans, and major expenditures are to be approved by the board.

More specifically, there may be investment ratchets and milestones imposed at the time of the VC's investment and documented in the investment agreements. Depending on the deal structure, there may also be options for exercise of warrants, loan redemptions, conversions, or repayments that have expiry or maturity dates. The VC has to keep track of them so that timely and appropriate actions may be taken, instead of allowing expiry by default. Decisions on these actions depend on good knowledge of the current state and updated future potential of the company, which is derived from the close monitoring efforts.

Exploring Exit

It is inevitable that in many of the VC's investments, performance of the management or the company may disappoint and the VC sees no possibility of recovery within the next few years and no plausible action that can bring about recovery. The VC would have to find ways to divest and salvage as much as possible from the investment.

Even if the investee company is progressing well, the VC should constantly be on the lookout for divestment opportunities such as through a merger or a trade sale, which could bring better value than a later IPO. Also, engineering a merger or acquisition may accelerate the IPO and hence divestment process. It has been said that an investment gets into divestment mode as soon as the investment is funded.

In order to recognize suitable divestment opportunities in a timely fashion, the VC needs to keep close tabs on the progress of the investee company, and be plugged into the M&A network, by being in touch with investment bankers, advisors, brokers, and consultants.

Monitoring the Portfolio

It is necessary for the VC firm to designate a partner or the CFO to monitor a fund's portfolio of investments on an aggregate basis for a number of reasons. Firstly, during the investment phase of the fund, the mix of investments has to be monitored to ensure that certain fund allocation limits are not exceeded. These limits, imposed by Limited Partners and spelt out in the fund's charter, may be on the amounts of investments in companies categorized by stage of development, investment size, industry sector, or geographical territory, to ensure diversification of risks. Also, the fund's charter will specify an investment period, beyond which new investments may not be made unless with approval of the Advisory Committee. Some funds are focused on certain industry sectors, while some funds are barred from certain investments, such as those involving gambling. The partner in charge of monitoring the fund has to ensure that these and all other investment restrictions are complied with.

As a fund approaches its fully invested stage, the cash flow has to be managed carefully by the partner or CFO in charge of the fund. If the fund does not set aside a sufficient amount—usually 10 to 20 percent of the committed capital for follow-on investments—the VC will not be able to make a follow-on investment and will be badly diluted in an investee company showing strong performance. If there is a gap between being fully invested and receiving proceeds from divestments, the VC may not have funds to meet operational needs. This could easily happen to a young VC which is managing just one fund, and therefore cannot draw from other funds.

Besides managing cash flow carefully when the fund nears full investment, the timing and amount of distribution of divestment proceeds to Limited Partners will also have to be managed. A reserve for payment of management fees may need to be maintained. On the other hand, too big a reserve has to be avoided, or Limited Partners will receive smaller or later distributions, resulting in the Limited Partners experiencing a poorer IRR on the fund than would otherwise be the case.

The performance of the fund needs to be regularly analyzed, requiring the VC's investment managers to provide projections of the timing and value of divestments of companies remaining in the portfolio. The partner or CFO in charge of the fund may need to push investment managers to exert greater effort in seeking earlier divestments of poorer performing investments, so that the fund performance is not dragged down.

It is also necessary to monitor the group of investee companies that have become listed, to effect appropriate divestments without infringing SEC Rule 144 restrictions. Some VCs organize the management of portfolio companies such that when a company is listed, the monitoring responsibility passes to the partner or CFO in charge of the fund. Centralizing the divestment of listed companies enables more effective compliance with SEC restrictions, which may change from time to time, and working with stockbrokers and investment banks to sell or place out the shares.

Finally, the person in charge of the fund may have to manage the extension of the fund life, if necessary, and the winding up processes for the fund.

Monitoring Reports

An example format for a quarterly monitoring report is shown in Appendix 20A. These reports are stored in the deal database as described in Chapter 6. Supplementing these regular reports would be ad-hoc reports written by the monitoring staff as and when important issues arise and reports of visits to the company by a monitoring or audit team.

Chapter Recap

In this chapter we discussed the monitoring of investee companies to:

- o   Keep current of developments and progress
- o   Detect early warning signs of problems
- o   Add value and assist management
- o   Ensure good corporate governance
- o   Ensure compliance of investment terms
- o   Constantly explore exit opportunities

We also discussed monitoring of a fund's portfolio of investments to ensure compliance with the fund's investment charter and to manage cash flow, performance, divestments, possible extension of fund life, and winding up. We also saw an example format for the quarterly monitoring report.

APPENDIX 20A   QUARTERLY MONITORING REPORT

Date :

Name of Company	*Indicate Listed or Private*

Principal Business   :

Place of Business   :
CEO / CFO Name   :
Board Representative   :   *Name of VC's board representative*
Monitoring Officer   :   *Name of VC's monitoring staff*

I   INVESTMENT SUMMARY

Approved Investment Amount   :
Post-money Company Valuation   :
% Shareholding   :
Type of Security   :
Initial Investment Date   :
Total Amount Disbursed to date :

Current Company Valuation   :
Basis of Valuation   :

Capitalization Summary

Shareholder	Amount Invested	% Share

II   DIVESTMENT SUMMARY

Initial Divestment Date   :
Total Proceeds to date   :
Remaining % Shareholding   :

Realized Gain / (Loss)   :
Unrealized Gain / (Loss)   :
IRR to date   :

III   FINANCIAL PERFORMANCE

	yyyy	*yyyy*	*yyyy*	*yyyy*	*yyyy*
Projection Revenue EBITDA NPAT					
Actual Revenue EBITDA NPAT					

IV   STATUS & OUTLOOK

Brief description of status of the company and future outlook, including issues faced and management actions required.

V   VALUE ADDED

Record of VC's value adding contributions to the company (useful as examples for future fund-raising).

VI   INVESTMENT CONDITIONS

Investment terms and conditions that have been met or have to be met, with corresponding dates for compliance or expiry, as well as actions taken or to be taken.

VII   EXIT

Expected mode and timing of divestment and target company valuation at exit.

21

Realizing & Recovering Value

I n this chapter we discuss the last steps in the VC Process: realizing the value of the investment through divestment, or in the case of unsuccessful investments, recovering value from the failed investment. The aim is to find the best way and the best time to divest a given investment to achieve the highest possible return from that investment, whether the investment is successful or not. This requires the VC to be proactive, to plan the best exit strategy, to monitor the company's performance and market conditions closely, to modify the exit strategy if necessitated by changed conditions, and to work closely with other shareholders and the management to execute the exit plan.

In Chapter 8: Due Diligence Basics, we stated that part of the due diligence investigation is to check the feasibility of the proposed exit strategy and to examine alternative exit strategies if necessary. Therefore, at the time of the investment, there should already be a planned exit strategy. Also, certain conditions may be negotiated into the investment terms to facilitate and support the VC's exit, as described in Chapter 16, in the section on Exit Provisions, and perhaps even some of the business strategies may have to be geared towards being consistent with and supporting the planned exit strategy.

It is important to the VC that there is a clear and viable exit strategy. A VC fund has a limited life, at the end of which all its investments have to be divested. A forced premature exit is likely to result in an investment return that is inferior to a planned and well-executed exit.

The typical exit strategy for VC investments is through a public listing of the investee company. With this strategy, the VC and the company have to find the best timing for the IPO, given the company's current and future performance and the capital market conditions. Sometimes there may be a possibility to list in another stock market that can offer a higher valuation or better liquidity, and pursuing such a strategy also requires an action plan.

Another popular exit strategy is the sale of the VC's shares in the investee company, or perhaps all the shares, to a strategic or financial investor. The VC has to consider this choice as sometimes it may provide a higher return than an IPO, or sometimes the IPO route may not be viable. There are also other less common modes of exit such as buy-back or redemption.

If an investee company is not performing and is most unlikely to recover, the VC has to move quickly to divest, as the value of the company could further deteriorate with time. Having contingent recovery plans or exit strategies combined with close monitoring of the company will facilitate quick actions.

We shall now discuss in greater detail these and other issues that need to be taken into account by the VC when working towards realizing or recovering value from the investments. First we shall cover the exit options, such as IPO, trade sale, buy-back, and redemption. Then we shall discuss the need for the VC firm to have a distinct divestment function. Finally, we shall discuss salvaging value from a troubled investment.

IPO versus Trade Sale

The two principal modes of exit by a VC from an investment are through sales of its shares in the public market after the IPO of the investee company or through sales of its shares in a private transaction, called a trade sale. The trade sale may be a sale of the company or its assets for cash or for shares in the buying company, or for a combination of cash and shares. If the VC receives shares of the buyer, the eventual exit would be through sale of the shares in the public market if the buyer is already listed, or if not, after the buyer's IPO. In the latter case, the VC would require the buyer's commitment to IPO within an agreed period, and perhaps the VC would also have the option to sell its shares back to the buying company or to its shareholders, depending on the terms that have been agreed upon by the parties concerned.

Achieving a public listing is the preferred objective for shareholders, including the VC and the founders, as well as the management because the company will be fully valued by the market; will increase its capital base and hence enhance its ability to borrow; will raise its corporate standing and image and help to attract and retain staff, and give greater confidence to suppliers and customers; and will enhance ability to raise further capital in the future for expansion or acquisitions.

The VC would in most cases fully support an IPO. However, the VC should be aware that under some circumstances another mode of exit may be preferable and the VC may have to take proactive action to convince the other shareholders and the management, and to help plan and carry out the alternative process. In any case, even if an IPO appears to be the best alternative for an investee company in question, the VC should make it a rule to always keep an eye out for alternatives, as circumstances internal and external to the company may change, including changes in the capital markets.

Factors that may work against the preference for IPO as an exit for the VC relate to:

o   Listing requirements
o   Valuation
o   Liquidity
o   Timing
o   Cost

In some cases, the company may find it difficult to IPO because it may not be able to satisfy listing requirements or may not be attractive enough to generate sufficient IPO interest. For example, the company may have just a single product or a dominant or single customer. Or it may have unpredictable or widely variable earnings due to the nature of its business. The VCs would have to exit via a trade sale or engineer a merger or acquisition that will make the investee company qualify or be more attractive for an IPO.

Even if the company could qualify for IPO, the public market may not fully value the company if it is in an industry sector that is not well understood or has fallen out of fashion, or the technology is too specialized or technically too difficult to be explained clearly to the public. Lack of understanding or attractiveness in the public market would be accompanied by lack of liquidity. Hence the VC would also find difficulty in disposing the shares. A trade sale should then be explored, as an industrial buyer that understands the business and the technology and recognizes the synergies may be prepared to pay the right price or even a premium for the company. In an IPO, the offer of new shares to the public results in dilution to the VC. If the trade sale is at the same or higher valuation than what would have been achieved in an IPO, the VC would achieve a higher return because there is no dilution and perhaps also because of the earlier divestment and avoidance of market risks that may cause the share price to spiral down post-IPO.

Sometimes the desired objective may still be to IPO, but an option may have to be explored for the IPO to take place in a foreign capital market that may offer a much higher valuation of the company and perhaps other advantages such as better liquidity and opportunities for subsequent fund-raising. Companies in Asia, Australia, or Europe may wish to list in the U.S. A company in China may wish to list in Singapore. The VC should explore such opportunities as it is obviously to its benefit as well. Pursuing such alternatives may require the VC to assist the company in making an acquisition in the target market, so as to have a domestic presence to enable or enhance the listing.

In some countries that have a stock market with a main board and a second board for younger companies, it is usual that the main board has higher valuations and greater liquidity, but more stringent listing requirements. Therefore the VC may wish to influence the company to take longer for its IPO to aim for a main board listing.

Liquidity, or the lack of liquidity, may be a strong enough factor to swing preference towards a trade sale instead of an IPO. Lack of liquidity in the stock market may be due to lack of understanding or attractiveness of the business by the public, as pointed out, or may be due to the state of the capital market in the investee company's country arising from poor market sentiment or economic or political factors affecting market interest. If a favorable opportunity for a trade sale comes along, the VC may wish to grab the opportunity instead of facing the uncertainty of when and how strongly market sentiment may return. Market sentiment may affect an industry sector and may last longer than the overall market. Thus timing of exit is also an important factor for the VC to consider.

Sometimes the investee company may be progressing well along the road towards an IPO when an offer may be made by a large corporation to buy up the company or to buy out the VC's shares. If the valuation is attractive, the VC should seriously consider selling, and not face the risks that the IPO may not come about, whether through the company's internal problems or changes in external conditions. There have been cases of this happening, much to the VC's regret.

Timing of the IPO would be ideal if it coincides with the company reaching its peak performance and having a solid plan to jump to a higher level of performance with the funds raised from the listing; if the company has achieved a good track record and built up a proper management team; and if it coincides with an active IPO market, with strong public interest in the company's type of business. If any of these factors are unfavorable the timing for IPO may have to be delayed or a trade sale may have to be explored. A delay of IPO faces the risk of missing the IPO market window.

For the VC, timing may also be affected by the life of its fund that invested in the company. Considering that full divestment of the shares may take months after the IPO, due to lockup or Rule 144 restrictions, the VC may not have enough time for the whole process of IPO and divestment through the public market, before the life of the fund ends. Furthermore, if the VC owns a large block of shares, rapid selling by the VC and other financial investors after the lockup period would depress the share price, resulting in a lowering of the VC's investment return. However, the avenue is open for the VC to distribute shares of the listed company to the fund investors, called distribution in specie, which might save some time compared to disposing in the stock market and distributing cash. However, limited partners are not too happy to receive distributions in specie, as it entails extra effort on their part to dispose the shares.

The divestment effort may also be accelerated by a secondary offering or through block placement of shares to other investors. The viability of a secondary offering is subject to the company's post IPO performance and stock market conditions. A block placement would usually require a discounted price. The VC would have to consider all these factors when deciding between an IPO and a trade sale.

Another timing factor that affects the VC's exit from investee companies relates to its fund-raising efforts. Particularly for a young VC that is in the latter stage of its first fund, a good record is needed to raise the next fund. While a good investment record helps, it is divestments that provide real proof of performance. The young VC would then be tempted to rush the more ready investee companies to IPO, although it might have made more sense for them to wait longer. This practice is called *grandstanding* in the industry and is frowned upon by limited partners, as their investment return from the fund would not be as high as it could possibly be.

The IPO of a company entails not only high costs in terms of underwriting fees, legal and audit fees, and printing costs, but also in terms of diverting management attention and effort away from the business, and possibly even loss of some competitive edge due to the need for public disclosures. These may affect the company's performance and hence valuation. A trade sale, even if conducted through an investment bank, financial advisor, or broker, would be less costly.

All the above reasons make it appear that a trade sale may be better for the VC, and indeed this mode of exit is gaining in popularity. However, finding the right buyer is not easy. Without good business fit and synergy, the buyer may not pay an attractive enough price. On the other hand the management, fearing loss of independence, may not support the sale and in fact may even consciously or unwittingly hinder the transaction through lack of cooperation or enthusiasm when the buyer conducts due diligence of the company.

Sometimes the VC may seek an early exit because of breakdown in its relationships with the founders or management. There could be disagreement over business strategies or future directions for the company. The VC could be getting disenchanted with the company's future. The company may also prefer to secure a strategic partner that may provide needed support to take it to a higher level, provided the buyer assures the management of continued independence, an attractive stock option plan, and an IPO objective.

If the VC sees that the founders and management are running the company to the ground, it may have to quickly find a buyer for the company or the assets. A strategic buyer would have the resources to inject new management and may still be prepared to pay well for the business.

Just as an IPO requires a lot of preparation over an extended period of time, a trade sale also requires time and effort, not only to find the best matching buyer, but also making the company work towards enhancing those attributes that would be of most interest to strategic buyers, to increase its attractiveness and hence valuation. Similarly, negative attributes have to be reduced or removed. For example, restructuring of the company may be required to divest non-core assets or businesses, strengthening balance sheet items such as protecting intellectual property or reducing liabilities, or resolving contingencies such as contingent liabilities or pending litigations. Certain business strategies may need to be realigned to more closely fit those of the target buyers. All these require the cooperation of management, so they have to buy into the process. In some cases, the VC may have to work out an incentive scheme whereby key managers may be rewarded for a successful trade sale through a share of proceeds from the sale, and obviously also giving them some say in the choice of the buyer and allowing them to negotiate acceptable terms for the future working arrangements.

A trade sale buyer requirement may sometimes turn out to be a deal breaker. The buyer usually requires certain representations and warranties relating to the past conduct of the company from the company, its management, and shareholders. These are often too onerous for the VC to accept, especially since it had not been involved in the management of the company. However, if the buyer insists, and to avoid breaking the deal, the VC may negotiate a limited form of warranty, such as one limited by time and amount of indemnity, or limiting to acts or transactions involving fraud or misrepresentation. It may also be agreed that minor warranty breaches may be settled by sale price adjustments instead of resulting in voiding the deal, and a part of the transaction amount may be set aside in escrow during the warranty period.

It would be advisable for the VC to completely divest in a trade sale. Attempting to retain a stake for increased upside after the sale usually would not work. If the company does not IPO soon enough or does not IPO at all, it would be difficult to divest the retained small stake. Knowing that the VC has hardly any choice, the strategic owner would bargain a low price for the VC's remaining stake. Worse still, the strategic owner may let the acquisition languish while deriving all benefits in the parent company, or may even drive down the performance of the acquired company in order to force the VC to sell at a cheap price.

Buy Back or Redemption

A less common mode of exit would be through buy-back of the VC's shares by the founders or other shareholders. This would likely be a situation where the company's performance has fallen far short of expectations and hence an IPO or a trade sale would not have been feasible. If the VC had built in a put option (an option to sell the shares) into the investment terms, the shares could be sold back to the company or the founders at a predetermined price or on the basis of a pre-agreed formula, depending on how the terms were set. In some cases, the investment may have been structured in the form of a loan or redeemable shares, in which case the exit could be through maturity or calling of the loan, or redemption of the shares.

If the company or the founders are unable to fully pay for the put, the loan or the redemption, repayment by installments may have to be negotiated. In the case of a failed or failing investee company, the VC may face a voluntary or involuntary liquidation of the company, in which case little or none of the investment may be recovered.

Divestment Function

It is important for the VC firm to have a distinct divestment function within the organization, supported by clear divestment policies, procedures, and reports. Some VC firms leave this function to the individual investment staff who would handle the divestment of their respective investments according to their individual judgment. In such a case, the divestment function is relegated to a lower priority than the more glamorous and exciting job of chasing after and making deals. There is no divestment strategy or proactive action plan, and divestment is thought of only when the company goes IPO or goes down the drain. It may also happen that the investment staff in charge may still want to hang on to the investment, with the overly optimistic view that the listed company's share price will continue to rise or that the deteriorating company will recover. All too often this does not occur.

The divestment responsibility should be given to a senior partner, with supporting staff if necessary. All active investments will be constantly reviewed by this group, supplemented by visits to the investee companies to arrive at independent views on their status and future potential. This provides the check and balance against those investment staff who may fall in love with their investments. The divestment function and the monitoring function may logically be assigned to the same senior partner. The group would issue reports for discussion with the respective investment staff and jointly work out and constantly review divestment action plans.

The divestment group also keeps in close touch with investment bankers, financial advisors, and brokers, in order to spot opportunities and to explore possibilities for trade sales, mergers, and acquisitions. The group also works closely with selected stockbrokers and analysts to effect divestments of listed shares and to keep track of stock market conditions and sentiment.

The group should also issue divestment policies, procedures and guidelines, and monitor compliance. It is common that a fund's charter would spell out a requirement that listed shares of investee companies must be divested within a certain time from IPO, for example within eighteen months of IPO. Limited partners do not want the VC firm to engage in stock market speculations as this is not its forte. The divestment group will ensure that relevant fund charter requirements relating to divestments will be complied with. The group will also need to ensure that issues such as Rule 144 restrictions, stock registrations, stock placements, and secondary offerings are properly handled. This requires familiarity with stock market regulations and practices of the countries in which the investee companies are listed. Focusing the responsibility in a divestment group will foster efficiency, accuracy, and consistency in managing divestments.

On completion of divestment of an investee company, the group will issue a Divestment Report detailing the specific divestment strategies and actions and the cash flows for the investment. Outflows will be the investment disbursements for purchase of shares, perhaps in tranches, and exercise of warrants or options, if any. Inflows will be the net proceeds from sale of shares, and if any, interest payments, loan repayments, dividends, or redemptions. With the raw cash flow data showing amounts and dates, the IRR may be calculated on a monthly, quarterly, or yearly basis, as desired. The report will also show the return multiple on the investment.

This report, together with selected prior reports such as those spelling out the divestment action plans, would be filed into the deal database as described in Chapter 6. As indicated at the bottom of Appendix 6B of Chapter 6, links in the database record for the investee company will be provided to access the divestment reports. Thus complete case histories of all deals would be available, forming a useful knowledge repository for internal reference and training.

Recovering Value

Many of the VC's investments will inevitably get into trouble at one time or another. Many of them will recover and progress into successful companies. Some will not. Through the close monitoring of investee companies such situations should be detected early enough. In the previous chapter on Monitoring we reviewed a number of early warning signs of trouble. On detecting trouble, the VC needs to quickly assess whether:

- o   The problem is temporary and the company can recover on its own.
- o   Additional funding is required to overcome the problems.
- o   Strategic help or a work out is required.
- o   The company is beyond help.

If help is required, or if the company is assessed to be beyond help, the VC would have to weigh the costs and benefits or different responses, in consultation with other shareholders and the management if necessary, and then take appropriate action. We shall now discuss these various scenarios.

Down Round

Problems encountered by the company may require additional funding for the delays or increased expenses. If the management and the board consider that the company can recover with the buying of time or hiring of help, the company will quickly raise a new round of financing. The company valuation for this financing round will most likely be down from that of the previous round; hence it is called a down round. This is in contrast to a normal follow-on round of financing when a company is making good progress, as discussed in Chapter 2.

The consequence of a down round can be very severe on the founders, some existing shareholders, and the company. Ratchets and anti-dilution conditions of prior rounds may kick in resulting in significant dilution of founders' stakes as their shares are common shares, without anti-dilution rights. Investors at different prior rounds may have different degrees of anti-dilution protection, and hence some may suffer more than others. The company also suffers, as a down round is an indelible record of problems which will make it difficult to raise subsequent rounds.

Therefore a down round is proceeded with only if the survival of the company is at stake. If feasible, existing shareholders may instead carry out an internal round, contributed by all shareholders on a pro rata basis. In this case, the valuation of the company is irrelevant, since the shareholding structure does not change. For convenience, the valuation may be deemed to be that of the last round. However the VC, like the other investors would need to wary of putting in good money after bad. If an internal round is agreed upon, but if one or more of existing shareholders are unable or unwilling to participate in the round, the round may become a down round to punish the non-participants by diluting their stakes.

In a down round, the new investors have bargaining strength, given the desperation of the company. Frequently they will require senior rights over all existing shares, such as liquidation preference ahead of other securities and more board and voting rights. Often the new investors would require removal or waiver of many, if not all, of the preferred rights of prior rounds, such as requiring all current preferred shareholders to convert their preferred shares to common shares, thus losing all preferred rights. They may also require all outstanding shareholders' and directors' loans to be converted to equity. The severity of all these adjustments depends on how critical is the company's situation and the availability of alternative investors.

If the company is in a very desperate situation, the valuation of the down round may be so low that existing investors practically lose all their stakes, and the new investors own the whole company or almost all of the company. Such a round is called a *cram-down*. The new investors may subsequently set up a new stock option scheme for management, some of whom may be founders of the company.

Two points may be noted from a down-round situation. Firstly the VC should realize that investment terms may not be as ironclad as they may seem. Its preferred rights may have to be waived or removed in a down round. The VC may need to participate in the down round, to reduce the dilution effect and to enjoy the new preferred rights.

The second point is that after a down round, the investors in the last round will have the most rights and will benefit the most if the company recovers and becomes successful. This is the reverse of a normal situation of a company that progresses well, where the earlier round investors have the most rights and benefit the most, as they take higher risks. Down-round investors consider that past investments in the company have become worthless or nearly worthless, and are not sympathetic towards earlier investors.

Work Out

Sometimes the problems faced by a company may be strategic or structural and may require more than just additional financing. Change of strategic directions is not unusual in early stage companies as they struggle to find the best business strategies and the most rewarding growth markets.

Expenses may have to be incurred to hire consultants, to carry out new market studies, or to hire in new expertise. New strategic alliances, mergers or acquisitions may have to be forged to tap on the infrastructure, technology or other complementary resources. The VC has to play an active role to help brainstorm the necessary changes and to tap its own networks to assist.

If the problems are more deep-seated, management changes may be required, or a turn-around specialist may need to be recruited. A new CEO's business plan or a turnaround plan needs to be comprehensive and cohesive, tackling issues at the root causes, and requires full support of the board and shareholders. Unfortunately some boards take action too late or too superficially. The VC may have to put in extra effort to convince the board of the seriousness and the need for decisive actions.

Beyond Help

Finally, the VC may regretfully have to prepare for the worst, if recovery efforts do not work or may be too costly. If the company is beyond help, the VC may need to buy time with some quick measures to stop the bleeding and to preserve assets, and quickly find ways to sell the company or its assets such as the intellectual property. Such a distress sale is unlikely to recover much but is still better than nothing, which could be the case if the company has to be liquidated.

Post-mortem

For a failed investment, a divestment report should also be filed into the deal log database by the divestment team together with the investment staff in charge. Reasons for failure should be objectively captured, including not only mistakes made by the company, but also mistakes made in the assessment or due diligence by the VC. Again, such complete case histories of the deals enable the VC firm to be a learning organization and help it achieve high quality performance.

Chapter Recap

In this chapter we discussed how the VC firm realizes and recovers value from its investments. We compared the two common means of divestment or exit for the VC: an IPO and a trade sale. We discussed buy-back and redemption as other possible exits. We also discussed the advantages of having a distinct divestment function in the VC firm.

We discussed scenarios of an investee getting into trouble, requiring additional funding or strategic help, or may be beyond help, and elaborated on the severe implications of a down financing round.

We also stressed the advantages of having a divestment report to derive complete case histories of all deals.

PART VIII

ACHIEVING QUALITY PERFORMANCE

How does the VC firm know the quality of the performance of its investment funds year by year? How is the performance measured? What are the factors taken into consideration for such measurement? Besides the investment performance, what makes a VC firm a quality organization?

Chapter 22: FUND PERFORMANCE explains the methods used to measure performance of VC funds and the factors that affect such measurement. Chapter 23: QUALITIES OF A VC FIRM describes the desirable qualities of a VC firm from three perspectives—those desired by investors, those desired by entrepreneurs, and those best practices and systems that are desirable in a top class VC firm.

22

Fund Performance

Measuring the performance of a fund is important to the LPs of the fund and to the VC itself. LPs need the information to gauge their own performance and to compare the performance of the VCs that they have invested in, so that they can decide on future fund allocations. The VC needs the information to assess the results of the fund's investment policies, portfolio management quality, and exit strategies, so that these can be improved for future funds.

When the VC raises a new fund, potential investors require not only the performance data of each fund, but also the composite performance of all the funds combined that they have managed since day one. Some institutional LPs want detailed investment and returns data for each investment so that they can analyze performance by various industry, geographical or development stage categories. Another aggregation method would be to segment the winners and losers by investment amounts lost or gained. Another measure that the institutional investor may look at is the average holding period of investments.

Such an analysis will show the capabilities and risk profiles of the VC firm as well as the investment climate and liquidity of capital markets in their operating environments. For example, it could indicate that a VC firm has strength in certain industry sectors or geographical regions. The institutional LP will then want to see whether the focus of the new fund is consistent with the VC's strengths or whether steps were taken to correct the weaknesses.

The analysis could also show that one VC firm has a knack for hitting big winners among a slew of losers, while another VC firm has the ability to minimize losses and having only fairly good winners. Therefore one VC has a high risk strategy while the other takes lower risks. Both could perform just as well on an overall basis. The institutional LP would then consider its own risk appetite to decide on the allocation of funds to the two VCs.

Of course, just like any analysis using financial ratios, the measures should not be used in isolation and have to be related to each other, as well as be relevant to the operating environment, in order to arrive at a more accurate picture. When VCs raise new funds, they should therefore be prepared for thorough forensic examination of portfolios by some institutional LPs. In this chapter we shall look at the composite measures that LPs typically use to measure fund performance.

The usual composite performance measure is the IRR of the fund, but there are several ways of calculating this figure and there is not yet a universal industry accepted way. Therefore when the IRR of a fund is quoted, the basis used must be disclosed. The basis for IRR calculations could be the portfolio cash flows, on a gross, net, or average basis, or the cash flows experienced by the LP. In another calculation, all the investment time periods are shifted to a common starting point (time zero) and the IRR is calculated for the resulting cash flows. Another composite performance measure that is quick and easy to compute is the Return Multiple, which acts as a good companion measure to IRR. We shall discuss all these performance measures, as follows:

- o   Portfolio Gross IRR
- o   Portfolio Net IRR
- o   Portfolio Average IRR
- o   Limited Partner IRR
- o   Time Zero IRR
- o   Return Multiple

It should be noted that the performance measures calculated by the above methods are affected by the compounding period used, whether monthly or quarterly, and by how the annualized IRR is derived. For funds that are not yet fully divested, the method of valuation of the residual portfolio also affects the portfolio IRR. In the case of LP IRR, any time lag in the use of funds drawn down or in the distribution of proceeds to LPs will adversely affect the IRR derived by the LPs. We shall take these into account in our discussions.

Measurement Methods

Portfolio Gross IRR

The Portfolio Gross IRR, or simply the Gross IRR, is the composite IRR of the whole portfolio of the fund, with the cash outflows of investments and cash inflows of dividends, interest receipts, and proceeds of divestments laid out in monthly or quarterly periods, commencing from the date of disbursement of the first investment. A simplified example using yearly periods is in Figure 22.1.

FIGURE 22.1   PORTFOLIO GROSS IRR CALCULATION

($ million)

Year	1	2	3	4	5	6	IRR	
Investment								
#1	(10)	0	0	10			0%	
#2	(5)	5	20				156%	
#3		(5)	0	0	0	0	-	
#4		(10)	0	0	(2)	50	47%	
#5			(10)	0	5		-29%	
Total	(15)	(10)	10	10	3	50	34%	Gross IRR

(Figures in brackets are negative cash flows)

This example is a six-year $50 million fund. Investment #1 amounted to $10 million in Year 1 and returned $10 million in Year 4, resulting in an IRR of 0 percent for this deal. Investment #2 amounted to $5 million and was partially divested for $5 million in Year 2. The remaining shares were divested for $20 million in Year 3. Investment #3 was a total loss. Investment #4 amounted to $10 million made in Year 2 of the fund. It had a follow-on investment of $2 million in Year 5 and was divested in Year 6 with proceeds of $50 million. The 5th company returned only half the investment. A total of $42 million or 84 percent of the fund was invested.

Based on the total cash flow, as shown in the bottom line of the table, the Gross IRR of this portfolio of investments was 34 percent. The Gross IRR measures the overall performance of the portfolio. It allows comparability between portfolios of VCs, as it ignores the variability of fees, expenses, and carried interest from one fund to the next.

Portfolio Net IRR

The Portfolio Net IRR takes into account the fees, expenses, and carried interest charged to the fund. This measures the performance of the VC firm in managing a fund and net of costs. The chargeable costs include start-up expenses, placement fees, management fees, carried interest, investment costs that are allowed to be paid by the fund, and winding up costs. The net cash flow is used to calculate the Net IRR for the portfolio, as shown in Figure 22.2.

FIGURE 22.2   PORTFOLIO NET IRR CALCULATION

($ million)

Year	1	2	3	4	5	6	IRR	
Investment #1	(10)	0	0	10			0%	
#2	(5)	5	20				156%	
#3		(5)	0	0	0	0	-	
#4		(10)	0	0	(2)	50	47%	
#5			(10)	0	5		-29%	
Total	(15)	(10)	10	10	3	50	34%	Gross IRR
Fees (2%) & Expenses	(2.1)	(1.1)	(1.1)	(1.1)	(1.1)	(1.3)		
Carried			(4.0)	0	1.0	(6.6)		
Total	(17.1)	(11.1)	4.9	8.9	2.9	42.1	21%	Net IRR

The portfolio for Figure 22.2 is identical to that of Figure 22.1, but now includes the cash flows for fees, expenses, and carried interest. For simplicity, it is assumed that the management fee was fixed at 2 percent of the committed capital of $50 million, which amounted to one million a year. Chargeable expenses amounted to $0.1 million a year. Start-up cost was one million and the winding up cost was $0.2 million. Carried interest paid by the fund to the GP was based on 20 percent of the profit on a deal by deal basis. The carried interest of $4 million in Year 3 was for Investment #2. There was no carried interest in Year 4 as no profit was made. In Year 5, there was a claw back of one million paid by the GP back to the fund, for 20 percent of the $5 million lost in Investment #5. The $6.6 million carried interest in Year 6 was for the total profit of $33 million for Investments #3 and #4 taken together.

The net cash flow after deducting the fees, expenses, and carried interest, as shown in the bottom line of the table, generated Net IRR of 21 percent. It can be seen that the management fees, chargeable expenses, and carried interest can add up to a significant reduction of the Gross IRR.

If the carried interest is paid only after all drawn down capital is returned to LPs, and not on a deal by deal basis, the fund cash flow will be as shown in Figure 22.3.

FIGURE 22.3   PORTFOLIO NET IRR – CARRIED AFTER RETURN OF CAPITAL

($ million)

Year	1	2	3	4	5	6		
Investments	(15)	(15)	(10)		(2)			
Proceeds		5	20	10	5	50		
Fees (2%) & Expenses	(2.1)	(1.1)	(1.1)	(1.1)	(1.1)	(1.3)		
Carried						(9.6)		
Total	(17.1)	(11.1)	8.9	8.9	1.9	39.1	**22%**	**Net IRR**

The Net IRR has improved to 22 percent due to the later payment of carried interest.

Portfolio Average IRR

Another method for measuring performance of a portfolio is to take the average of the IRR of each investment. One could take the simple average or the weighted average, weighted by size of investment.

A problem occurs if an investment ends up in a loss of part or all of the capital. The IRR for that investment will be negative. This is likely to happen to several of the investments in a VC portfolio. The simple or weighted average could still be mathematically calculated, but the result is not very meaningful. An alternative would be to segregate out the unprofitable investments and take the average for the profitable ones, but this is also unsatisfactory as it does not reflect the performance of the whole portfolio. This method is therefore not commonly used.

Limited Partner IRR

Ideally the timing of cash flows of drawdowns from, and distributions to, the LPs almost coincide with the cash flows for investment disbursements and receipts of dividends, interest, and divestment proceeds. If this is the case, the IRR to the LP is the Portfolio Net IRR.

In practice, there could be some lead or lag time between the two cash flows. There may be a need to have a higher initial drawdown if the VC does not have fees from other funds to cover initial expenses. There could be unexpected delays in closing a deal, such as delay in the legal documentation or some last minute negotiations. This results in a delay in disbursing the funds after drawing down from the LPs. Distributions to LPs are not made in dribs and drabs so as not to cause administrative inconvenience to all parties. If the GP is slack in managing the cash flow, the IRR to the LP can be significantly affected. Let us look at the examples in Figures 22.4 and 22.5.

FIGURE 22.4 LP IRR CALCULATION – TIGHT CASH FLOW

FUND CASH FLOW   ($ million)

Year	1	2	3	4	5	6
Drawdowns	17.5	15	10			
Investments	(15)	(15)	(10)		(2)	
Proceeds		5	20	10	5	50
Fees (2%) & Expenses	(2.1)	(1.1)	(1.1)	(1.1)	(1.1)	(1.3)
Carried						(9.6)
Distributions		(4)	(19)	(9)	(1.5)	(39.6)
Cash Balance	0.4	(0.1)	(0.1)	(0.1)	0.4	(0.5)
Cumulative Cash Balance	0.4	0.3	0.2	0.1	0.5	0.0

LP CASH FLOW

Drawdowns	(17.5)	(15)	(10)					
Distributions		4	19	9	1.5	39.6		
LP Cash Flow	(17.5)	(11)	9	9	1.5	39.6	22%	LP IRR

Figure 22.4 shows a case of tight management of cash flows by the GP. A cumulative balance of $0.5 million or less was maintained in the fund. Drawdowns were minimized and distributions were prompt. The LP IRR was 22 percent, similar to that in Figure 22.3.

Figure 22.5 shows a case of slack cash flow management. The initial drawdown was too large and the first distribution was made a year later. The GP maintained a high cumulative cash balance of more than $4.5 million in the fund. The LP IRR was reduced to 18 percent.

FIGURE 22.5 LP IRR CALCULATION – SLACK CASH FLOW

FUND CASH FLOW   ($ million)

Year	1	2	3	4	5	6
Drawdowns	22	15	10			
Investments	(15)	(15)	(10)		(2)	
Proceeds		5	20	10	5	50
Fees (2%) & Expenses	(2.1)	(1.1)	(1.1)	(1.1)	(1.1)	(1.3)
Carried						(9.6)
Distributions			(20)	(10)	(4)	(43.6)
Cash Balance	4.9	3.9	(1.1)	(1.1)	(2.1)	(4.5)
Cumulative Cash Balance	4.9	8.8	7.7	6.6	4.5	0.0

LP CASH FLOW

Drawdowns	(22)	(15)	(10)					
Distributions			20	10	4	43.6		
LP Cash Flow	(22)	(15)	10	10	4	43.6	18%	LP IRR

Time Zero IRR

The VC industry has devised another way of analyzing the portfolio of investments. All investments in the portfolio are shifted in time to the same initial investment date and the resultant cash flow is used to calculate the gross IRR. This value is called the Time Zero IRR or Indexed To Zero IRR. Using the same portfolio as in previous examples, Figure 22.6 shows how the investment cash flows would be laid out.

FIGURE 22.6   TIME ZERO IRR CALCULATION

($ million)

Year	1	2	3	4	5	6	IRR	
Investment								
#1	(10)	0	0	10			0%	
#2	(5)	5	20				156%	
#3	(5)	0	0	0	0		-	
#4	(10)	0	0	(2)	50		47%	
#5	(10)	0	5				-29%	
Total	(40)	5	25	8	50	0	30%	Time Zero IRR

The Time Zero method would tend to increase the gross IRR value if the fund has bigger winners later in the fund life. Pulling forward such investments increases their time value, hence increasing the overall IRR. If the fund has substantial early winners, then the gross IRR value would be diluted. In the example above, the Gross IRR is reduced from 34 percent to 30 percent because the pulling forward of Investments #3, 4 and 5 diluted the impact of Investment #2, which was the big winner with IRR of 156 percent.

Periods of investment inactivity and different investment rates would affect the IRR of the portfolio. Indexing all investments to time zero will remove this distortion and allow comparability between portfolios.

Return Multiple

The Return Multiple measured at the portfolio level is simply the ratio of the total divestments proceeds to the total investment amount for the portfolio. This measure can also be made at the LP level, which would then be the total distribution received from the fund divided by the capital disbursed to the fund. These measures do not take into account the time value of money. They measure the absolute profits made by the fund.

Referring to Figure 22.3, the total investment in the portfolio was $42 million and total amount of proceeds received was $90 million. Hence the gross return multiple for the portfolio was $90/42 = 2.14$. Referring to Figure 22.4, the total capital drawn down was $42.5 million and the total amount of distributions to LPs was $73.1. Hence the return multiple to LPs was $73.1/42.5 = 1.72$.

The return multiple measure complements the IRR measure. Since IRR takes into account the time value of money, a high IRR may not necessarily mean a high return in absolute dollars. For example, an investment of one million generating a return of $3 million after one year gives an IRR of 200 percent. If the one million returns $20 million after five years, which is the typical *holding period* for VC investments, the IRR is 82 percent. If only IRR is used as a measure, the second investment appears to be inferior. In practice, the VC will desire a high return over a reasonable holding period, say four to six years, more than a quick flip that gives high IRR but a low absolute return. Using IRR and return multiple together gives a better picture of the investment performance.

Instead of return multiple, the average investment holding period may be used with the IRR figure. Calculating the average holding period of all investments in a fund is a good indicator of the gestation period for investments in a particular industry sector or geographical area. Obviously a fund focused on very early stage investments will have a longer average holding period.

Appropriate Measures

The VC industry has not settled on a standard measure or a standard set of measures. It would be appropriate to use the Portfolio Gross IRR, the Limited Partner IRR, and the respective Return Multiples as a set of measures for a fund. The Portfolio Gross IRR together with the Portfolio Return Multiple measure the performance of the portfolio of investments, while the Limited Partner IRR and Limited Partner Return Multiple take into account the GP's costs and reflect the actual return obtained by the LP.

Factors Affecting Measurement

We have discussed the impact of time lags in cash flows on the measurement of IRR to LPs. We shall now discuss the impact of the compounding period and the valuation of the portfolio.

Compounding Period

If monthly or quarterly periods are used for the cash flows, there are two ways to calculate the annualized IRR which give different results. One way is to multiply by the number of months or number of quarters in a year. The other way is to compound the monthly or quarterly periods. For example, the monthly IRR may be worked out to be 3 percent. Simply multiplying 3 percent by twelve derives 36 percent as the annualized IRR. Compounding over twelve periods using the formula:

$$IRR_{(annualized)} = (1 + r)^n - 1$$

where r = 3 percent and n = 12, results in $IRR_{(annualized)} = (1 + 0.03)^{12} - 1 = 42.6\%$, different from the 36 percent derived from the simple annualization.

If quarterly periods are used, n would equal 4. It is a widely accepted practice to compound to derive the annualized IRR.

Valuation Policy

For funds that are not yet fully divested, the performance to date can be measured by applying a value to the remnant portfolio. The valuation of this remnant portfolio, known as the *residual portfolio value*, affects the IRR value. The residual portfolio value consists of the cost of the remaining investments plus unrealized gains or losses of each of them. Again, there is not yet an industry-accepted practice on how the unrealized gains or losses are to be determined, although VC associations, particularly in the U.S. and Europe, publish guidelines. Therefore when VCs quote their interim IRRs for incompletely divested portfolios, the portfolio valuation policy should also be disclosed.

An example of an acceptable valuation policy for a residual portfolio would be:

(a) For listed companies in the portfolio:

    (i)   If the shares are freely tradable, they will be valued at the last transacted price on the valuation date.

    (ii) If the shares are illiquid, for example if they are under lockup, or the trading volume for the stock is very low compared to the amount of stock held, the shares will be valued at a discount from the market value. Such a discount will range between 10 percent and 25 percent depending on the length of the lockup or the severity of the lack of liquidity or other trading restrictions.

(b) For unlisted companies in the portfolio:

    (i)   If the company's performance has been consistently below expectations, and is unlikely to recover in the short term, the value of the company will be written down by 25 percent, 50 percent, or 75 percent from cost, depending on the severity of the poor performance and inability to recover.

    (ii) If there has been a material arm's length investment into the company, the company will be valued by that transaction, whether higher or lower as the case may be.

    (iii) If there has been a material partial divestment, then the remaining shareholding will be valued at the divestment valuation.

    (iv) All other unlisted shares will be valued at cost.

(c) Other securities, such as loans (both convertible and non-convertible) and warrants, will be valued at cost. Free warrants will be valued at zero cost.

Many VCs take a conservative approach and do not mark up the valuation even if the company's performance justifies it. The view is that performance can go up or down from year to year. It is only if there is independent market valuation, for example an IPO or a major third party investment, would the valuation be marked up. However the VC should be more ready to mark down valuations, if such independent valuation is lower than the current valuation or if the company's performance drops significantly.

There are VCs that mark their investees to market values or current "fair values" each time they carry out a portfolio valuation exercise. "Fair value" is defined by U.S. GAAP as "the amount at which an investment could be exchanged in a current transaction between willing parties, other than in a forced liquidation sale." Such VCs may engage valuers such as accounting firms to carry out independent valuations; benchmark against comparable companies that had recent financing rounds; or adopt industry recommended guidelines using appropriate performance or earnings multiples applied to sustainable earnings and incorporating appropriate market discounts.

While many VCs have started to adopt "fair value" guidelines, most have decided to wait and see, maintaining the more conservative approach as described above. They argue that the guidelines and the definitions of "appropriate" multiples or discounts and "sustainable" earnings leave a lot of room to interpretation. They are also not comfortable with writing up the value of an investment in the absence of an outside financing round or a liquidity event. LPs and accounting firms are also mixed on these issues. While some accounting firms feel that adopting fair values will result in more GAAP-compliant financial statements, others accept the conservative approach, so long as the policies are clearly spelt out and consistently applied.

In any case, it is important for a VC to have clearly written valuation policies and guidelines, which are comprehensive enough to cover various *valuation events*. As the name implies, a valuation event occurs when an investee company experiences an event that affects its valuation, such as an IPO, a material investment into the company, or a significant drop in performance. The VC usually has a valuation committee consisting of senior partners to determine the valuations based on the assessments made by the investment managers. The decisions of the valuation committee are usually ratified by the Advisory Committee. A typical Valuation Report format is given in Appendix 22A at the end of this chapter for reference.

Factors Affecting Performance

The obvious factors that affect the performance of a VC fund are the capability and experience of the fund management team, the adoption of right investment strategies, instituting best practices in the entire VC Process, and providing a rewarding and motivating environment for the investment and support staff. External factors also have impact, such as the investment climate of the country, the political stability, government regulations, economic growth, and currency stability.

Another important factor is the skew effect discussed in Chapter 2, where the staging of investments allows the VC to pour more money into the more successful companies and hence skew the overall performance of the portfolio towards a higher return. Less obvious is the impact of cash flow management which we have discussed earlier in this chapter.

There are two other factors that are worth a little discussion. Firstly, the timing for the establishment of a fund can play an important part. Secondly, a star investment that gives a stellar return can also skew the portfolio performance significantly higher.

Vintage Year

If a fund is set up when stock market sentiment is down and fewer venture funds are chasing after and bidding for deals, company valuations will be low and the VC can cherry-pick the quality deals. If it also happens that four or five years later, when the fund's investments mature, the IPO market is booming, the fund will be able to exit from the investments at high valuations. It is also likely that the portfolio companies would be growing well along with the economic recovery. The fund's returns will therefore be superior if not spectacular.

The converse is also true. If a fund is established during boom times and experiences an economic downturn about five years later, it is likely to perform poorly. Such funds have to invest at high valuations and will find difficulty or delays in getting exits, and if they do, the divestments will be at low valuations, resulting in a poorly performing fund.

Striking examples would be funds active during the dot-com era. Those VCs which invested early paid reasonable valuations and several years later, the dot-com IPO madness resulted in astronomical valuations, which generated returns to VCs in the hundreds of multiples, if not more. Those funds that were started a year or two later invested at high valuations (of course with the hope that they would go up even higher), but were caught by the crash, and obviously they performed abysmally. Less extreme, but still having significant impact, would be the cycles of industries such as the semiconductor or computer industry, and economic cycles of a country or region.

If the year a fund is started, called its *vintage year*, coincides roughly with the start of a cycle of industry or economic growth, the efforts put in by the GP will be enhanced. Unfortunately, the VC business cannot be operated in a start-stop manner. The GP needs to raise a new fund when the existing fund is close to being fully invested, and cannot afford to wait a few years for the right timing. However, there is some leeway for the GP to bring forward or push back raising a new fund by a year or so.

Star Investments

Let us look again at the example portfolio in this chapter, given in Figure 22.1. Let us replace the star performer, Investment #2, with a lackluster investment, resulting in Figure 22.7.

FIGURE 22.7 ABSENCE OF A STAR INVESTMENT

($ million)

Year	1	2	3	4	5	6	IRR	
Investment								
#1	(10)	0	0	10			0%	
#2	(5)	0	5				0%	
#3		(5)	0	0	0	0	-	
#4		(10)	0	0	(2)	50	47%	
#5			(10)	0	5		-29%	
Total	(15)	(15)	(5)	10	3	50	**16%**	**Gross IRR**

The Portfolio Gross IRR is reduced from the 34 percent in Figure 22.1 to 16 percent as shown in Figure 22.7. Since LPs expect at least 20 percent

IRR, the fund performance has dropped from stellar to poor, just by the absence of a star investment. You can imagine how well a fund will perform if it has two or more star investments that give more than ten times return multiples.

Limited partners would usually look deeper when they assess a VC's set of portfolios to see whether there is a masking effect of star investments on the other investments. A portfolio may have a star investment but if all the other investments are mediocre, the LP would need to assess whether the star investment was merely a lucky shot.

Performance Benchmarks

There are organizations such as Venture Economics, a division of Thomson Financial, Private Equity Intelligence Ltd., and InsiderVC.com that provide performance data of VC funds, besides information such as partnership terms, fund strategies, and focus, as well as information on portfolio companies. The information is useful to LPs to help assess GPs and determine fund allocations. The information is also useful to GPs to benchmark themselves with other funds or with industry aggregated data.

However, the data is mainly on U.S. funds with increasing information on European funds. There is a lack of data on the performance of Asian based VC funds.

Disclosure

We discussed the issue of disclosure in Chapter 5, in relation to the terms and conditions of the Limited Partnership Agreement. Most VCs abhor revealing fund performance data and would oblige if only industry aggregated information is revealed.

Even if only returns achieved by funds are revealed, VCs are concerned about comparability due to differences in measurement and portfolio valuation, as discussed in this chapter. For fully divested funds, the IRR that is quoted would be different if it is a portfolio gross return, net return, time zero return, or return to LPs. For partially divested funds, the return depends on how the residual portfolio is valued.

VCs are also concerned that for a partially divested fund, the ultimate return when the fund is fully divested could be vastly higher, if there are gems in the residual portfolio. For a fund at its early years, it is typical that the performance could be poor or even under water, which is the well-known *hockey stick* growth curve. The interim IRR figure could then be misleading.

Besides these concerns about interpretation and comparability of data, there is of course the concern about confidentiality, particularly information that could reveal the performance of investee companies. A precautionary write-down of an investee could prove to be self-fulfilling if word spreads out to its customers, suppliers, and staff. The VC could also be in breach of a confidentiality agreement if sensitive information of an investee company is revealed.

VC funds that are listed face the same problem as those that have state pension funds as limited partners. A state pension fund may be forced to reveal confidential information relating to its investments in VC funds by the Open Records Act, as discussed in the section on Disclosure in Chapter 5. A listed VC fund has to disclose information on its larger investments that have material impact on the performance and prospects of the fund. The GP has to balance between complying with disclosure requirements and protecting the confidentiality of investee companies.

As stated in Chapter 5, a compromise is likely to be reached where overall return data for a fund may be revealed, but valuation and performance of individual investments will likely remain confidential.

Chapter Recap

In this chapter, we explored the following:

- o   The importance of fund performance measures
- o   Common fund performance measures:
    - o   Portfolio gross IRR
    - o   Portfolio net IRR
    - o   Limited partner IRR
    - o   Time zero IRR
    - o   Return multiple
- o   Factors that affect the measurements:
    - o   Time lags in cash flow to LPs
    - o   Compounding period
    - o   Portfolio valuation policy
- o   Less obvious factors that affect fund performance:
    - o   Vintage year
    - o   Star investment
- o   Performance benchmarks
- o   Disclosure issues

APPENDIX 22A   VALUATION REPORT

SINGULAR VENTURES INC
VALUATION REPORT
Date

Company Name   :
Company Location   :
Principal Activities   :
Status Code   :
Key Management   :
Singular Ventures Rep :
Currency Used   :

INVESTMENT HISTORY

Investment Date	Amount Invested	Financial Instrument	Price per Share	Post-money Valuation	Cumulative Shareholding (%)

PROCEEDS FROM DIVESTMENT

Date of Receipt	Nature of Proceeds*	Amount Received	Cumulative Amount Received

(*Interest, dividend, redemption, or sale of shares, etc)

OPERATING HIGHLIGHTS

FINANCIAL HIGHLIGHTS

Year Ended	Revenue	Gross Margin (%)	Profit Before Interest and Tax	Net Profit After Tax	Net Tangible Assets

CONSOLIDATED BALANCE SHEET SUMMARY
as at financial year ended _____

Current Assets	Current Liabilities
Fixed Assets	Long Term Debt
Other Assets	Convertible Bonds
	Minority Interest
	Share Capital
	Retained Earnings
	Other Reserves

CURRENT ISSUES

Issue	Corrective Action	Responsible Person	Date of Completion

VALUATION

Previous Valuation	
Current Valuation	

BASIS FOR VALUATION

23

Qualities of a VC Firm

Throughout this book we have discussed many best practices that a VC firm could adopt in its work processes. We conclude the book with suggestions on the qualities and high standards that a VC firm should aspire to achieve. The qualities of a VC firm arise from expectations of its three groups of stakeholders:

o   Limited Partners of the VC's funds
o   Entrepreneurs and investee companies
o   Staff of the firm

Each group has a different perspective of the VC firm and hence a different set of expectations of quality and value. We shall describe each of these perspectives in turn. Many of these qualities have been described in greater detail elsewhere in this book as they are built into the suggested best practices. However, at the risk of some repetition and paraphrasing, it would be valuable to see these qualities and best practices all together and contrasted in the light of the different expectations of stakeholders.

Limited Partner Perspective

Limited Partners (LPs) invest in the VC's funds to derive satisfactorily high returns for the risks involved. Their expectation is that a quality VC firm would have strong capability to achieve or exceed the target returns. They expect the firm to have quality staff with relevant qualifications and experience, and proper internal control systems and best practices. They also expect to be kept informed of investment activities and the status of investments in a prompt and open manner.

LPs will therefore focus on the quality of the following aspects of the VC firm:

- o Investment staff:
    - o Qualifications, experience, local knowledge, and networking strengths
    - o Investment ability: Sourcing and making good investments, managing risks, and exiting profitably
    - o Portfolio management capability: Adding value, monitoring, and working out portfolio companies
    - o Team spirit

- o Investment strategies:
    - o Winning strategies to source and pick out good investment opportunities
    - o Consistency of strategies with skill sets of staff as well as with constraints and opportunities in the investment territory

- o Internal systems:
    - o Documented systems and procedures
    - o Proper controls and compliance procedures
    - o System of incentives and accountability

- o Reporting systems:
    - o Prompt, open, and full disclosures of investment activities and status of investments

We have discussed qualities of investment staff and investment strategies of VC firms elsewhere in this book. Internal systems will be discussed later in this chapter in the section on the internal qualities of the VC firm. Here we shall focus on the quality of reports and other communications from the VC to its LPs.

The Limited Partnership Agreement (LPA) between the LPs and the VC provides for regular reporting of investment activities and the status of the investment portfolio, such as quarterly and annual reports. LPs expect the reports to be submitted on schedule and provide transparent details and balanced assessments of the performance of the investee companies. LPs also expect the VC to go beyond the bare provisions of the LPA, by alerting them promptly of significant changes in between reports. Such changes include not only significant new investments, divestments or swings in investee company performance, but also staff movements and changes in the investment climate or regulatory environment. Qualities such as promptness, openness, and transparency will build the trust and confidence of LPs which will also help in future fund-raising.

Besides regular and ad-hoc reports, the VC communicates with its LPs through an annual meeting and regular meetings of its Advisory Committee which has the major LPs as members, as well as ad-hoc visits by LPs to the VC for portfolio briefings, to meet new staff, or to be accompanied on visits to investee companies.

Reports

Some LPs require quarterly reports, while others may require semi-annual reports. The Annual Report will be a full-fledged report, like any corporate annual report, while the quarterly or semi-annual reports will be less detailed, and sometimes limited to just reports of new investments and divestments.

A typical format of an Annual Report is shown in Figure 23.1. The general partner's letter, like a corporate chairman's letter to shareholders, gives the highlights of the status of the fund, in terms of the amount of committed capital drawn down and invested; the recent new and follow-on investments, divestments, liquidity events such as trade sales or IPOs, valuation events such as write-ups, write-downs or write-offs, valuation and performance of the portfolio to date, distributions made to LPs; updates on the investment climate, capital markets, regulatory environment and staff movements; and a brief prognosis of the outlook for the fund. An example of a GP's letter is given in Appendix 23A on page 461.

FIGURE 23.1   ANNUAL REPORT FORMAT

GP's Letter	Highlights of fund status, investment activities, staffing and outlook
Financial Statements	Partnership financial statements Limited Partners' capital accounts
Fund Performance	Fund performance to date
Portfolio Summary	Summary listing of the portfolio
Company Write-Ups	Status of each investee company

The second section of the annual report would contain the financial statements for the fund and a statement of changes in LPs' capital accounts. The latter statement is a tabulation of the change in each LP's capital account over the period. The change is derived as illustrated in Figure 23.2.

FIGURE 23.2   LP's CAPITAL ACCOUNT STATEMENT

SINGULAR VENTURES FUND I
PARTNER'S CAPITAL ACCOUNT
As at December 31, 2002

($'000)

Contributed Capital		1,000
Cumulative Operating Income	(100)	
Realized Gains	900	
Unrealized Gains	1,200	
Cumulative Net Income		2,000
Distributions		(1,400)
Remaining Capital		1,600

The third section is a listing showing the performance of each investment to date, with the column headings as shown in Figure 23.3.

FIGURE 23.3   FUND PERFORMANCE DATA

Column Heading	Explanation
Portfolio Company	Name of portfolio company
Investment Date	Date of initial investment
Divestment Date	Date of full divestment
Amount Invested	Total investment amount
Realized Proceeds	Total proceeds of divestment
Unrealized Value	Valuation of remaining investment
Total Value	Total of realized and unrealized amounts
Return Multiple	Multiple of total value against cost
IRR	Internal rate of return on the investment

The bottom of this tabulation will show the overall totals as well as the return multiple and IRR for the fund to date.

The fourth section of the annual report would be a listing of all the portfolio companies, providing details of Company Name, Location, Type of Business, Type of Securities Held, Date of Purchase, Cost, Valuation, Basis for Valuation, and Percent of Company Owned on a fully diluted basis.

The fifth and final section will be write-ups of each active portfolio company (i.e., excluding those that are fully divested), giving a summary of the latest financials and a brief on the progress of each company.

Annual Meetings

Being a partnership and not an incorporated company, there is no requirement for an annual general meeting. However, the VC will still hold an annual meeting, usually called a partners' meeting. The meeting may be held in a resort and is an occasion for the GP to foster closer relationships with LPs. In the formal part of the meeting, the GP will present details of portfolio performance and highlight interesting investments, perhaps supplemented with presentations by the companies themselves. The GP will also take the opportunity to introduce new staff, and advise latest economic and political developments of the investment territories, highlighting new investment opportunities and strategies.

Sometimes the meeting may be held in a country or region within the VC's investment area of interest, and the opportunity will be taken to be briefed by local government officials and financial authorities, as well as to visit existing or potential investee companies in that locale. There would also be an informal part of the meeting for LPs and spouses to socially interact with staff.

Advisory Committee Meetings

The VC's Advisory Committee, which consists of representatives from the major LPs, will usually meet twice a year, once at mid-year and once after the year end, perhaps just after the annual partners' meeting. At the mid-year meeting, the Advisory Committee would review the Valuation Report, which is a report providing the GP's valuation of each of the remaining investments in the portfolio and explaining the rationale for the basis used, supported by the semi-annual status reports of the status of the companies. VCs would apply valuation policies similar to those described in Chapter 22.

The Advisory Committee's review of the Valuation Report is to assure itself that the valuations are fair and reasonable, since there can be subjectivity in some cases. There could also be conflict of interest on the part of the GP, if management fees are tied to the portfolio valuation. For example, if the management fee is partly based on the outstanding total amount invested at cost, the GP needs to be ready to write off investments that have clearly become unrecoverable, instead of keeping them in the books and inflating the fees.

Another matter in the Advisory Committee meeting agenda may be a review of the consistency and compliance with fund objectives and strategies, and consideration of requests by the GP, if any, to waive certain fund charter restrictions, such as exceeding the investment limit for an exceptionally promising investment. The Committee may also need to resolve conflict of interest issues such as making an investment into the portfolio company of the VC's prior fund. The GP will also report significant changes affecting its portfolio, operation, or investment environment.

Entrepreneur Perspective

Some entrepreneurs do not pay attention to the qualities of the VC; caring only about getting the funding and getting it at as high a valuation as possible. After the funding they hope they will be left alone and neither would they want to bother with the VC. This would be a totally mistaken view.

They should realize that the VC will be monitoring its investments closely, will want to ensure that the proposed plans are well executed, and milestones are met if not exceeded. If the company stumbles badly, the VC will unhesitatingly move in and make changes, including changing the management. Given such an investor and a partnership that will last several years, the entrepreneur should appreciate the importance of finding the best quality partner.

Just as a VC would carry out due diligence, the entrepreneur should conduct due diligence checks on the VCs under consideration, by talking to their investee companies (both successful and unsuccessful ones), checking with bankers, lawyers, accountants and investment advisers, questioning the GPs and examining their backgrounds and track records.

The qualities that the entrepreneur should look out for in a VC firm and in the VC staff in charge of the investment should be:

- o Value add services:
    - o Strong depth and range of value added services as described in Chapter 20

- o Personal rapport (with the investment staff in charge):
    - o Personal chemistry and shared vision for the business
    - o Understanding of business and relevant operating experience

- o Track record:
    - o Successful investments in related fields

- o　Record of active assistance and advice to investee companies
- o　Record of fair treatment of investee companies

- o　Funding support:
  - o　Large fund size without investment size limitations
  - o　Syndication ability
  - o　Investing fund is not near end of life, and hence has follow-on funding flexibility

- o　Reputation:
  - o　Highly reputed in the financial community with well-known sponsors and limited partners

From the VC's perspective, knowing that the above qualities and attributes are what entrepreneurs seek, it should pay attention to developing and enhancing these qualities. For example, the VC should devote time and effort to expand its network and to actively find ways to add value to its investee companies. Such efforts not only increase value of the investments, but also boost the reputation of the VC, which in turn help to attract good deals.

Internal Perspective

It is obvious that the VC firm should aim to build a top quality organization. It is beyond the scope of this book to go into all the attributes that make up a top quality organization. The best practices and qualities of the various VC investment processes are described in this book. Examples of process documentation and data capture are given and these provide audit trails and serve as learning materials. We have also discussed the organization structure, the necessary skill sets and qualities required of investment staff and incentive schemes for investment staff. In the above sections we have described the qualities that LPs and entrepreneurs look for in VCs, and these are also qualities that need to be internalized to build a quality VC firm.

In this section, we shall round off by highlighting two internal systems that could further enhance the quality of the organization: the Internal Control Procedures and the VC Management System Software.

Internal Control Procedures

It is important that the VC should have comprehensive documented Internal Control Procedures (ICP) in view of the fiduciary responsibilities involved, and the need for audit trails and compliance with regulatory or licensing authorities. A system must also be put in place to ensure compliance with the procedures.

The VC's ICP manual should have statements of investment policies, strategies, financial and administrative procedures and authority limits, code of conduct, and management of conflict of interest situations. It is important to properly document the entire investment process, specifying the necessary documentation, due diligence methodologies and checklists and the sequence of internal approvals that must be secured at each step of the process, as well as the committees or designated persons that are authorized to give such approvals. Adequate quality control checkpoints, check and balance measures, as well as compliance standards must be built into the manual.

VC Management System Software

If the VC firm does not have one already, it should quickly evaluate and implement a management system software package that not only allows automation of processes but also ready retrieval of deal and investment data, processing of analytics and reports, portfolio and contact management, investor relations management, and knowledge management. Additional features of such software available in the market also enable management of the fund-raising process, management of LP capital accounts, integration with the general ledger, Web-based interface, and integration with e-mail and other office applications. Early implementation of a computerized system incurs less transition pain and greater benefits of an efficient organization. In this book we have made recommendations for database capture documents and reports, and a deal log database system that integrates all the deal data and forms the basis for the VC's knowledge management system. Adoption of all these recommendations and best practices will go a long way towards building a world-class VC firm.

Chapter Recap

In this chapter we discussed the qualities of a VC firm as expected by three groups of stakeholders:

- o Limited Partners
- o Entrepreneurs
- o Staff

In discussing the expectations of Limited Partners with regard to communications and reports, we detailed the Annual Report that is submitted and the meetings with Limited Partners that are held by the VC. In discussing the internal qualities that a VC should develop, we highlighted the Internal Control Procedures and Management System Software that a VC should implement.

APPENDIX 23A   GP's LETTER TO SHAREHOLDERS

SINGULAR VENTURES

6 February 2003

To Our Partners

Singular Ventures Fund I has completed its fifth year, since the final closing in January 1998 with a committed capital of $200 million. Eighty-eight percent of the committed capital (i.e., $176 million) has been invested in a portfolio of 40 companies, of which 26 were in USA and 14 in Asia. As at end of 2002 we had realized $138 million in proceeds from divestments, with 28 companies valued at $231 million remaining in the portfolio being actively monitored. The total portfolio valuation of $369 million was about 110% above cost (i.e., the fund achieved a total realized and unrealized gain of $193 million over the $176 million invested.

Two distributions were made in 2002 totaling 15% of committed capital to reach cumulative distribution of 85%. As the fund has completed its investment period, there will be no more new investments and only follow-on investments will continue to be made for the remainder of the fund life.

Several of our portfolio companies are delaying their public listing plans in view of the weak public markets. We are encouraged by signs of economic recovery and expect to realize further gains from divestments late this year or early next year. In the meantime, we continue to work closely with our portfolio companies, several of which have been affected by the global slowdown in IT spending and the downturn in PC markets, and may require follow-on funding.

There were no staff movements in 2002. Our professional staff strength remains at 8, in our offices in San Francisco, Hong Kong, and Singapore. After some delay, Singular Ventures Fund II shall be closed shortly, and we take this opportunity to thank our Partners who continue to support us.

The following are the highlights of our investment activities and performance in calendar year 2002 and previous years.

New & Follow-on Investments

In 2002 we made two new investments and one follow-on investment. We invested $10 million in NetEagle Inc, headquartered in San Francisco, to complete its development of network application monitoring software. Although there are established players in this field, NetEagle believes it can capture market share through its cost competitiveness arising from its software development operation in India and its user-friendly graphical interface. The two founders have extensive experience in the R&D and marketing of such software in the leading companies.

The other new investment was a $5 million funding of FoneApp based in Hong Kong, a developer of Chinese mobile phone online games and other applications. The market is expected to be huge and the business model is based on revenue sharing with mobile phone operators. The company is carrying out beta-site testing and the response of mobile phone operators is enthusiastic.

A follow-on investment of $3 million was made in Airwaves, which required increased working capital to ramp up production of its wireless digital audio module, which is being shipped to two Japanese producers of consumer audio equipment.

The cumulative total number of companies in the portfolio was 40 as at the end of the year as shown in Chart 1, and the cumulative amount invested was $176 million, at cost, as shown in Chart 2.

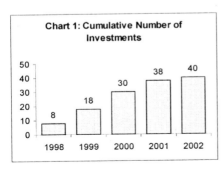

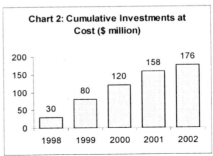

Portfolio Performance

The valuation of our portfolio increased from $312 million at the end of 2001 to $369 million at the end of 2002. This was mainly due to the increase in valuation of BroadGain, which produces advanced ADSL equipment, arising from its successful IPO on NASDAQ in August last year. The valuation of $369 million was 2.10 times the portfolio cost of $176 million.

The performance of our portfolio in 2002 compared to 2001 is summarized as follows:

($ million)	2002	2001
Portfolio Valuation	369	312
Investment at Cost	176	158
Total Gain	193	154
Realized Gains	102	89
Unrealized Gains	91	65
Total Gain	193	154

Chart 3 shows the portfolio valuation against cost of investments as at the end of each year.

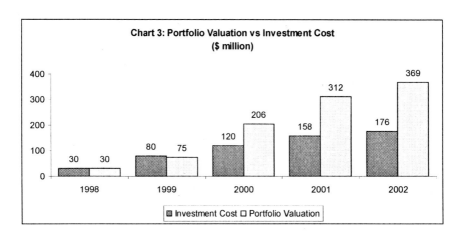

Chart 3: Portfolio Valuation vs Investment Cost ($ million)

Divestments

In 2002 we completed divestment of three listed companies, Clinicast, Onco, and Yentech which were cumulatively divested profitably at 2.9 times, 11.1 times, and 3.4 times the cost of investment respectively, realizing total proceeds of $77 million on a total cost of $12 million. We continued to divest the shares of listed companies such as Genex, and NetFind, but progress was slow because of their depressed share prices. We wrote down Silverex to 50% of cost due to its poor performance from which it is unlikely to recover.

We have now fully divested out of 12 companies, leaving 28 companies in our portfolio being actively monitored. The cumulative number of companies fully divested over the years is shown in Chart 4.

The rate of divestments in dollar terms is shown in Chart 5. The cumulative divestment of $36 million represents 20.5% of the portfolio at cost.

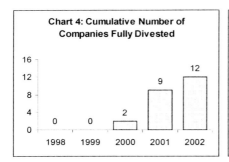

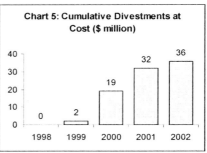

Divestments made in 2002 amounted to $4 million at cost, and netted $13 million in proceeds to realize a gain of $9 million. This resulted in cumulative realized gain of $102 million as at end of 2002. Chart 6 on the next page shows the cumulative realized gains over the years.

With the IPO of BroadGain, the total number of listed companies is currently 11, out of the portfolio of 40 companies. The rate of increase in the number of listed companies in the portfolio is shown in Chart 7.

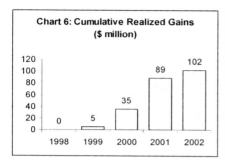

Chart 6: Cumulative Realized Gains ($ million)

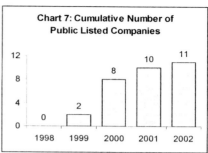

Chart 7: Cumulative Number of Public Listed Companies

Distributions

We made a 15% distribution in July 2002 followed by 10% in September 2002, which together with distributions of 12.5% in 2000 and 20% in 2001, resulted in cumulative distribution of 57.5% of committed capital, or $115 million in total. In comparison with published benchmarks of U.S.-based venture funds of the same vintage year, Singular Ventures Fund I ranks in the upper quartile range.

Outlook

We were holding investments in 28 companies at a total valuation of $231 million as at the end of last year. We are seeing signs of recovery in technology stocks and several of our portfolio companies should be able to proceed with their IPO plans later this year. The expected recovery in IT spending augurs well for many of our portfolio companies. We believe our good performance with this fund has given most of you the confidence to continue support with our Fund II, for which we express our sincere gratitude. We look forward to meeting you at the Annual Meeting on Friday, March 21.

Sincerely
Singular Ventures Fund I

List of Abbreviations

CEO	Chief Executive Officer
CFO	Chief Financial Officer
COO	Chief Operating Officer
CPS	Convertible Preferred Shares
CTO	Chief Technical Officer or Chief Technology Officer
CV	Curriculum Vitae
EBITDA	Earnings Before Interest, Tax, Depreciation and Amortization
ERISA	Employee Retirement Income Security Act
ESOP	Employee Stock Options Plan
ESOS	Employee Stock Options Scheme
fab	fabrication (as in wafer fab)
GAAP	Generally Accepted Accounting Principles
GP	General Partner or General Partnership
HR	Human Resources
IPO	Initial Public Offering
IQC	Incoming Quality Control
IRR	Internal Rate of Return
IT	Information Technology
LLC	Limited Liability Company
LLP	Limited Liability Partnership
LP	Limited Partner
LPA	Limited Partnership Agreement
M&A	Mergers & Acquisitions
MBA	Master of Business Administration
MRP	Manufacturing Resources Planning or Materials Requirement Planning
NDA	Non-Disclosure Agreement
NTA	Net Tangible Assets
PDCA	Plan-Do-Check-Act (as in PDCA Cycle, a quality management concept)
P-E	Price-Earnings (as in Price-Earnings Ratio)
PER	Price-Earnings Ratio
QA	Quality Assurance
R&D	Research & Development

RCPS	Redeemable Convertible Preferred Shares
RPS	Redeemable Preferred Shares
SEC	Securities and Exchange Commission
UBTI	Unrelated Business Taxable Income
VC	Venture Capital, Venture Capitalist (individual) or Venture Capital firm, according to the context

(Abbreviations that are explained in the text and used only in proximity of the explanation are excluded.)

Index

(Note: where multiple pages are referenced, the page containing the definition or explanation, or the most relevant pages, if any, are in **bold**)

A

accredited investor, 86
acquisition
    affecting ESOP, 335
    as liquidity event, 276, 305
    for exit, 113, 410, 417-418, 423
    for expansion, 27, 32, 113, 208, 406
    funding, 32, 208, 297, 298, 308, 311, 417
    management covenant, 331, 391
    of later stage company, 317-320
Act stage, 144, **151**, 153, 160, 171
adaptability, 159, 160, **163**
adding value, 16, 19, 21, 41, 54, 59, 76, 94, 99, 109, 113, 114, 130, 269, 308, 309, 328, 401, **407-408,** 409, 452, 458
    business networking, 408
    corporate image, 408
    exit process, 408
    financial expertise, 407
    international expansion, 408
    management assistance, 408
    strategic business advice, 407
    strong board, 409
Advisory Committee, 80, 81, 90
    conflicts of interest, 53, 97, **101-102**
    corporate governance, 95, 98, 100, 101, 411, 443
    meetings, 453, **456-457**
affirmative covenants, 390, 391
ancillary document, 386
angel, 15, 30, 32, 42-44, **45**, 71, 115, 116, 137, 157, 269, 270, 278-280, 288, 289, 327
annual meeting, 50, 77, 453, **455**, 465
Annual Report, 453-455
    GP's Letter, **453**, 454, **461-465**
annualization, 441
Anthony, Scott, 108
anti-dilution, 243, 268, 274, **285-293**, 306, 311, 325, 329, 346, 387, 425
    broad-based, 274, **289**, 291, 306
    full ratchet, 274, **286**, 289, 291, 306, 329
    impact on returns, 299
    in employee stock plans, 288-289, 291, 334, **335**, 392
    narrow-based, 274, 289, **290-291**, 306
    pay-or-play, 274, **291-292**, 310
    pay-to-play, 292
    preemptive, **292-293**, 392
    right of first refusal, 293
    weighted average, 289
ARD, 11, 12
automatic conversion, 325, **339-340**
average entry valuation, **224-226**, 234

B

benchmarks
    for the fund, 95, **446**, 465
    for the investee, 193, 226, 248, 249, 443
beta site, 31
Blue Ocean, 112, 131

board representation, 325, **330-331**
board representative, 309, 330, 392, 406, 413
board seat, 87, 101, 297, 330
bond, **272-273**, 450
bootstrap, **29-30**, 32
breakup value, 226, **246**
burn rate, 29, 128, **133**, 204, 206, 210, 302, 326, 375
business angel, *see* angel
business model, 108, 109, 112, 116, 128, 131, 173, 174, 181, 252, 462
buy-back, 325, 335, **340**, 362, 385, 416, 422
Buy-Back Agreement, 385
Bygrave, William, 11

C
call option, 318, 340
capital account, 49, 58, **454**, 459
capital call, 49, 58, **92**, 93, 101
capital commitment
    of the fund (committed capital), 47, 53, 55, 60, 74, 75, 80, **91-93**, 94, 95, 96, 97-99, 103, 411, 435, 453, 461, 465
    of the GP or VC, 47, 49, 60, 80, **100**
    of the investee, 350
    of the LP (committed capital), 48, 85, 86, 89, **91-93**, 95
capitalization table, **42-44**, 205, 315, 325, **327-328**, 374, 388
carried interest
    to investment staff, 56, 57, **60**, 79, 101
    to the GP, **48**, 49-54, **55-56**, 74, 76, 77, 80, 81, 84, 91, 93, 94, **95-96**, 98, 99, 103, 434-436
    to the LP, 49, **55**, 84, 85, 93, 95
    to the placement agent, 70

case studies
    Brightek Inc, 135-136
    Stamptek Pte Ltd, 314-315
    Transpac Capital Pte Ltd, 83-84
    VC Method cases, 230-239
CEO
    as business angel, 14, 45
    as Entrepreneur-In-Residence, 116
    for networking, 112, 115, 116
    in deal screening, 128, **133**
    in management due diligence, 157, 158-159, **160-161**, 162-166, 171
    in monitoring, 403, 405-407, 409
    in recovering value, 427
    in value adding, 408, 409
    of the investee, 314-315, 335, 397
Check stage, 144, **151**, 153, 160
Christensen, Clayton, 108, 112, 178
claw back, **96**, 435
closing
    of a fund, 60, 80, 91, **92**, 461
    of an investment, 21, 241, 330, 351, 388, 390, 401, 436
commitment of capital, *see* capital commitment
committed capital, *see* capital commitment
common shares
    as an investment security, 268, **269**, 270, 272, 275, 276, 278, 281, 282-284, 288, 293-294, 385, 426
    in deal structuring, 304-306, 311
    in the term sheet, 327, 332, 335, 339, 340, 345, 347, 349, 353
    of a fund, 51
    of an investee, 43, 222, 268, **269**, 379, 425

Compensation Committee, 334-
336, 351, 409
compensation/incentivization
of investment staff, 56, **60**, 79,
100, 458
of management, 158, 159, 160,
166-167, 207, 214, 247, 301,
307, 325, **332-336**, 337, 361,
363, 397, 408, 409, 421, 452
of marketing staff, 177, **179-180**
of the GP, *see* fund
compensation
completion, *see* legal completion
completion date, **372**, 376, 380,
397-398
compliance
of the GP, 58, 90, 423, 452,
456, 459
of the investee, 190, 193, 198-
201, 203, 216, 379, 381, 391,
398, **409-410**, 414
of the transaction, 316, 320,
352, 386, 412
compounding period, 432, **441**
conditions precedent, 19, 21, 325,
329, **343-344**, 345, 354, **371-
381**, 387, 398
actions by both parties, 371-
372, 381
actions by investee, 329-330,
371, **379-381**
actions by investor, 329, 371,
372-379
ceasing fund-raising effort, 379
complying with representations
and warranties, 381
corporate restructuring, 379
effecting employment contracts,
380
ensuring no adverse change,
380
establishing an ESOP, 380

final due diligence, 377-379
investment agreements, 381
investment approval, 372-376
lawyers, 381
passing corporate resolutions,
380
special audit, 377-379
syndication, 376
Confidentiality Agreement, *see*
Non-Disclosure Agreement
conflict of interest
of the GP or fund, *see* fund
conflicts of interest
of the investee, 215, 317, 353,
388
of the LP, 45, 49
of the placement agent, 69
consolidation (of industry), 116,
302, 312, **319-320**, 365
controlled investment, 309
controls, *see* covenants
conversion, 205, 221, 222, 274,
379, 387, 410
as a performance ratchet, 274,
282-284, 306
as an anti-dilution adjustment,
286-291, 347
automatic, 325, **339-340**
in the term sheet, 325, 329, 333,
343
rights, 281-282, 345-346
convertible loan, 268, **271-272**,
273, 284, 290, 304, 306, 309
convertible preferred shares, *see*
preferred shares
corporate governance
of the GP, 89, 90, 91, **97-101**
see also Advisory Committee
of the investee, 21, 401, 405,
408-409
corporate restructuring, 309, 310,
371, **379**

Co-Sale Agreement, 385
cost to create, 226, **250**
covenants
    of the GP or fund, *see* fund
        covenants and controls
    of the investee, 15, 214, 220,
        351, 374, 378, **390-392**, 396
cram-down, 310, 426

D

deadlock, 330, 395, **397**
deal alert, 118, 122, 123, 125, **126-
    127, 139-140**
deal database, 108, 112, **117-118**,
    412, 424, 427, 459
    see also deal log
deal flow, 79, **107**, 115, 117, 118
deal log, **117-118**, **121-123**, 127, 139,
    427, 459
deal meeting, 57, 117, 125, **126**,
    127, 137, 146, 372
deal negotiation, 19, 20, 21, 126,
    155, 167, 307, **359-368**
    approach, 366-367
    deal issues, 366
    entrepreneur's objectives and
        concerns, 363-364
    factors, 359-366
    techniques, 367-368
    VC market, 364-366
    VC's objectives and concerns,
        360-363
deal proposal, 19, 114, 117
deal screening, 19, 20, 94, 113, **125-
    138**, 143, 144
    see also showstoppers
deal sourcing, 18, 19, 42, 57, 78,
    82, **107-118**, 402, 452
    best team, 112-113
    creating deals, 116
    growth sectors, 111
    high returns, 113

how to look, 114-116
    opportunistic approach, 114-
        115
    systematic approach, 115-116
    uniqueness and value creation,
        111-112
    what to look for, 108-110
    where to look, 110-113
deal structure, 20, 110, 140, 152,
    212, 272, 275, 283, **301-320**,
    323, 325, **326-328**, 374, 410,
    422
    amount of investment, 326
    capitalization table, 327-328
    company valuation, 327
    type of security, 327
    use of funds, 328
deal structuring, 19, 20, 126, **301-
    320**, 379
    amount of investment, 302-303
    balancing factors, 306-307
    case study: Stamptek Pte Ltd,
        314-315
    elements, 302-307
    industry consolidation, 319-320
    later stage deals, 311-312
    leveraged buyout, 316-318
    management buy-in, 319
    management buyout, 316-318
    of later stage deals, 311-320
    preferential rights, 305-306
    privatization, 316
    recapitalization, 312-313
    related issues, *see* deal
        structuring related issues
    turnaround, 320
    type of security, 304-305
    valuation, 303-304
deal structuring related issues, 307-
    311
    controlled investments, 309
    corporate structure, 309-310

existing investors, 310-311
investment tranches, 307-308
keeping it simple, 311
syndication, 308-309
use of funds, 308
debt
senior, 273, 317
subordinated, 271, 273, 317
default, *see*:
fund covenants and controls
Investment Agreement
redemption
representations and
warranties
Shareholders Agreement
demand registration, 274, 293, **295-296**, 297, 298
Deming, Edwards, 144
development stage, *see* product
development
dilution %, 229, 232, 234, 236, 238,
254, **255**, 256-258, 260-262,
263
dilution formula, 231, 234, 236,
254-258, 260-262
disclosure of fund information, 73,
91, **103, 446-447**
discount rate, 230, 231, 233, 234,
236, **239-240, 242**
discounted free cash flow, 226,
247-248
discounting formula, 230, **254**, 262
disruptive innovation, **108**, 131
distribution, *see* fund distribution
distribution strategy, 170, 177, **179**
divestment
function, 57, 412, 416, **422-424**,
427
in fund performance, 433, 436,
439, 442, 444
in the VC Method, 228, 231,
234, 235, 237

opportunities, 21, 54, 410
policies, 53, 76, 80, 93-95, 98-100, 102, 422, 423
proceeds, 40, 41, 55, 72, 76, 91,
93, 95, 98, 411, 424, 455, 461
process, 55, 56, 57, 75, 99, 110,
126, 306, 339, 410, 411, 412,
415, 418-420, 422-424
report, 123, **413**, 422, **424, 427**,
453, 455, 461, **464**
see also:
exit difficulty
exit opportunity
exit options/strategies
exit process
exit provisions
exit valuation
dividend
accrued, 275, 285, 346, 348
cumulative, 274, **275**, 305
from the fund, 48, 49, 51, 72
from the investee, 76, 205, 247,
312, 314, 331, 350, 396, 424,
433, 436
guaranteed cumulative, 274, **275**
non-cumulative preferred, **275**,
305
of stock, 291, 346
participation, 268, 269
preferred, 274, **275**, 294, **305**,
325, 329, 349, 387
Do stage, 144, 145, 148, **149-151**,
152, 159, 160, 186, 189, 203,
204
domain expertise, 159, **164-165**
Doriot, Georges, 12
dot-com crash, 32, 35, 73, 276, 284
double dip, **277**, 279
down round, **29**, 32, 223, 276, 285,
286, 288, 291, 292, 310, 340,
425-426
drag along, 274, 325, **337, 353**, 396

drawdown, 48, 91, 92, 103, 436, 437, 438

due diligence basics, 143-155

due diligence conclusion, 153-155

due diligence expenses, 77, 341, 351, 394

due diligence (final), *see* final due diligence

due diligence framework, 20, **146-148**, 149, 152, 153, 158, 159, 161, 170, 171, 185, 186-188, 190, 192, 204-205

due diligence in screening deals, 125-127, 130, 137, 138

due diligence interview, 59, **150**, 160, 162, 163, 165, 171, 186, 188, 190, 193, 203, 215, 375

due diligence of early stage companies, 133, 157, 161, 164-166, 185, 196, 197, 206, 214, 379

due diligence of environmental factors, 146

due diligence of exit options, 147, 148, 415

due diligence of expected return, 147, 148, **210-212**, 362

due diligence of financial aspects, *see* financial due diligence

due diligence of intellectual property, 214, 215, 388

due diligence of later stage deals, 312-313, 316-320

due diligence of legal aspects, *see* legal due diligence

due diligence of management, *see* management due diligence

due diligence of manufacturing, *see* manufacturing due diligence

due diligence of marketing, *see* marketing due diligence

due diligence of technology, 143, **146-148**, 149, 150, 154, 155, 163, 164, 172, 173, 175, 177, 179, 182, 188, **196-198**, 204, 214

due diligence of the market, *see* marketing due diligence

due diligence of the VC firm, 65, 83, 457

due diligence of valuation, 148, **219-252**

due diligence reports, 352, 374, 375

due diligence sources, 146-148, **149-150**, 159, 160, 170, 171, 187, 205

E

early stage companies, 13, 109, 311, 426

financing of, 27-36, 303

fund focused on, 30, 45, 54, 74, 440

investment terms in, 280, 281, 305, 309, 391

stock options plan in, 333

see also:

due diligence of early stage companies

valuation of early stage companies

early warning, 21, **403-407**, 424

ballooning of accounts receivables, 404

breakup of founding team, 405

delay in response, 405

evidence of incompetence, 406

financial warnings, 404

lack of performance, 406

late financials, 405

late or lack of notification to the Board, 405

loss of focus, 406

marketing problems, 404

product development delays, 405
staff resignations, 405
sudden spurt in spending, 404
swelling of inventory, 404
EBITDA multiple, 226, **244**
economies of scale
    for the GP, 58, 67
    for the investee, 109, 113, 128, 129, 181, 207, 319
employee stock options
    affecting anti-dilution, 288, 289, 291, 334, 335, 392
    affecting dilution/valuation, 43, 137, 222, 229, 235, 261, 264, 270, 303, 310, 332, 380
    exercising, 221, 298, 333, 335
    incentivizing management, 137, 222, 270, 276, 303, 310, 313, 315, 317, 325, 332, 333, 337, 353, 363
Employee Stock Options Plan, 332-336
    administration, 332, 334-336
    anti-dilution, 334, 335
    basis for award, 333, 334
    eligibility, 333, 334
    exercise price, 333, 334
    option terms, 333-335
    size, 333-335
    vesting, 333-335
    voting rights, 335
Employee Stock Ownership Scheme, 387, **392**
employment agreement/contract, 160, 166, 212, 214, 215, 344, **353**, 371, **380**, 385, 388, **397**
Entrepreneur-In-Residence, 116
entrepreneurship, 14, 45, 74, 159, 160, **162**
entry barriers, 108, 109, 131, 132, 175, 214

entry valuation, 17, 110, 113, 148, **224-226**, 229-238, 243, 264-266, 282, 303
equity account, 272
ERISA, **86-87**, 101
escrow, 96, 282, 422
example documents
    Deal Alert, 139-140
    Deal Log, 121-123
    GP's Letter, 461-465
    Monitoring Report, 413-414
    Non-Disclosure Agreement, 119-120
    Term Sheet, 343-355
    Valuation Report, 449-450
exclusivity period, 325, **341-342**, **354**
Executive Committee, 362, **406-407**
exempt transfer of shares, **337**, 396
exercise price of stock option, **333**, 334
exercise price of warrant, 273
exit details, 78, 414
exit difficulty, 108, 110, 128, **130**, 251, 284, 309, 313, 361, 444
exit opportunity, 41, 57, 60, 220, 401, **410**
exit options/strategies, 140, 147, 148, 213, 284, 307, 309, 316, 374, 385, 401, 402, 406, 410, **415-422**, 431
exit process, 16, 408, 452
exit provisions, 293, 301, 325, **338-340**, 361, 362
    automatic conversion, 339-340
    buy-back rights, 340
    IPO conditions, 339
Exit Rights Agreement, 385
exit valuation, 16, 17, 110, 113, 223, **224-226**, **229-237**, **240-241**, 251, 264-266, 414, 444

expansion stage, 27, 28

F

final due diligence, 342, 343, 354, 371, **377-379**
finance department
  of the GP, 58
  of the investee, **198**, 203, 206, 405
finance manager, 203, 403
finance staff, 190, 191
financial due diligence, 20, 146-147, **203-212**
  future performance, 206-209
  past performance, 205-206
  present performance, 206
  returns, 210-212
  risks, 209-210
financing round
  1st, 2nd, 3rd round, 30-31
  bootstrap, 29-30
  characteristics, 32
  examples, 33-36
  Initial Public Offering, 32
  other rounds, 32
  Rolodex, 30
  seed, 30
  Series A, B, C rounds, 30-31
  see also:
    cram-down
    down round
    follow-on
    mezzanine
financing rounds and corporate development, 27-29
financing rounds and dilution, **256**, 270-271, 313, 425-426
financing rounds and milestones, 16
financing rounds and returns, 18, 25-26, 37, **210-211**, 264
financing rounds and valuation, 42-43, 223-226, 229-242, **248**, 303
finder's fee, 77, **115**, 341
finding deals, see deal sourcing
first closing, 80, 91, 92
  see also closing
follow-on, **36-38**, **40-41**, 53, 55, 58, 75, 92, 98, 102, 232-235, 309, 411, 425, 433, 453, 458, 461, 462
for-cause provisions, 103
fully diluted, 221, 222, 290, 291, 455
fund charter, 53, 55, 102, 411, 423, 456
Fund Company, **46**, 47, 50-52, 79, 81, 91
  see also Limited Liability Partnership
fund company structure, 46-52
  corporation, 50-52
  limited liability partnership, 46-50
fund compensation, **53-56**, 79-81, 90, 91, **93-96**
  carried interest, see carried interest
  management fee, see management fee
  other income & expenses, 96
fund conflicts of interest, 80, 81, 90, 91, 97, **101-102**, 130
  GP's internal controls, 459
  GP's management fee, 456
  GP's other business activities, 102
  GP's personal investments, 102
  investment into portfolio of old fund, 102, 456
  investment by parallel funds, 53, 102
fund covenants and controls, 76, 90, 91, **97-101**

appointment, 97
contingent liabilities, 99
debt, 99
default of limited partners, 101
divestment decisions, 99
extension of fund life, 100
fund size, 97
GP's co-investment, 100
GP's contribution, 100
investment decisions, 97
investment into other funds,
    98-99
investment into public
    securities, 99
investment limits, 97-98
investment period, 98
involvement of limited partners,
    100
liability and indemnification,
    101
portfolio valuation policy, 99
raising new funds, 100
regulatory requirements, 101
reinvestment of proceeds, 98
services, 97
staffing and compensation
    changes, 100-101
fund distribution, 48, 49, 51, 58,
    60, 453, 454, 461, 465
in relation to fund performance,
    411, 433, **436-440**
in relation to fund-raising, **76**,
    80, 87, 91, **93**, 95
in specie, 49-50, **93**, **419**
fund focus, 30, 69, **73-74**, 78, 85,
    97, 98, 100, 116, 128, **129-
    130**, 312, 411, 431, 440, 446
fund life, 46, 50, 52, 55, 56, 72, **74-
    75**, 80, 91, 94-96, 98, 99,
    240, 285, 313, 362, 415, 419,
    439, 458, 461
extension, 55, **100**, 412

fund management, 53, 81, 83, 99,
    443
fund management company, 56,
    85, 91
    see also General Partner
fund manager, **46**, 54, 73, 99
    see also General Partner
fund objectives, 13, 15, 17, 38, 45,
    46, 71, 73, **75**, 80, 82, 91,
    313, **360-363**, 366, 456
fund-of-funds, 70, **71**
fund performance, 99, 411, **431-
    447**, 454, 455
appropriate measures, 440
benchmarks, 446
compounding period, 441
disclosure, 446-447
factors affecting measurement,
    441-443
factors affecting performance,
    443-446
limited partner IRR, 436-438
measurement methods, 432-440
performance benchmarks, 446
portfolio average IRR, 436
portfolio gross IRR, 433-434
portfolio net IRR, 434-436
return multiple, 439-440
star investments, 445-446
time zero IRR, 438-439
valuation policy, 441-443
vintage year, 444-445
fund policies and strategies, 46, 53,
    69, **73-77**, 79, 80, 81, 82, 89,
    90, 96, 128, 129, 431, 459
distribution of proceeds, 76
divestment, 75
focus, 73-74
investment expenses, 77
investment limits, 75-76
investment objective, 75
investment policies, 75-76

investment strategies, 75
life, 74-75
monitoring, 75
other income, 76-77
size, 74-75
valuation policy, 76
see also:
    divestment
    fund distribution
    fund focus
    fund objectives
    valuation of portfolio
fund-raising by a company, 30-36,
    43-44, 208, 250, 284, 303,
    314, 371, 379, 407, 418
fund-raising by a VC firm, 18, **65-
    87**, 91, 93, 100, 117, 414,
    420, 445, 453, 459
    fund policies and strategies, 73-
      77
    investor criteria, 77-79
    limited partners, 70-73
    new VCs, 54, 83-86
    offering document, 79-81
    placement agent, 68-70
    regulatory requirements, 86-87
    road show, 82-83
    VC market cycles, 29, 66-68,
      365
fund size, 54, 60, 68, **74-75**, 78, 91,
    92, **97**, 100, 102, 458

G
gatekeeper, **71**, 93
General Meeting, 50, 89, 395, 396,
    455
General Partner, **46**, 73, 77, 79, 89,
    91, 116, 375
    see also Management Company
going-concern, 246
Gompers, Paul, 66, 84
goodwill, 245, 246, 349

GP's Letter, **453**, 454, **461-465**
grandstanding, 420

H
Human Resource, 56, 58, 188, **198**
hurdle rate, 96

I
incentive options, 288
incentive shares, 325, **332**
Incoming Quality Control, 188,
    189, **194-195**, 200
incubators, 15, 45, 115, 116
information rights, 325, **338**, 391
initial closing, *see* first closing
initial concept stage, 27, 29
Initial Public Offering
    dilution, 230-232, 235-239, 258,
      418
    S-1 form, 294
    versus trade sale, 416-422
innovation, 14
    disruptive, 108, 131
    sustaining, 108
    value, 112, 131
InsiderVC.com, 446
integrity, 133, 159, 160, **161-162**
intellectual property
    definition, 196
    infringement, 134, 393, 394
    problems, 128, **134**, 215
    protection, 30, 214, 309, 310,
      391-393, 421
    rights agreement, 344, 385, 387,
      393, 397
    transaction, 331, 350, 427
    transfer, 214, 310, 329, 353,
      380, 393
    valuation, 220, 245
    see also due diligence of
      intellectual property
internal control procedures, 459

internal documents, *see*:
  example documents
  internal control procedures
  investment proposal
interview
  of management, 160, 162, 163,
    165, 171, 186, 188, 190, 193,
    203, 215
  of the GP, 65
  skills, 59
  techniques, 150, 160, 162, 165
  see also due diligence interview
Investment Agreement, 208, 215,
    329, 344, 347, 351, 372, 376,
    380, 381, 384, 385, **386-394**,
    395-398, 410
  affirmative covenants, 390-391
  capitalization, 388
  company operations, 390
  completion terms, 388
  conditions precedent, 387
  confidentiality, 392-393
  default, 393-394
  definitions, 387
  employee stock options
    scheme, 392
  employee stock ownership
    scheme, 392
  expenses, 394
  governing law, 394
  indemnification, 394
  information rights, 391
  intellectual property rights, 393
  minority protection rights, 391
  negative covenants, 391-392
  non-competition, 393
  preamble, 387
  representations and warranties,
    388-390
  Securities Purchase Agreement,
    385
  Stock Purchase Agreement, 385

  terms for the purchase, 387
  type of security, 387
  use of proceeds, 390
investment amount, 53, 94, 102,
    115, 122, 220, 229, 237, 238,
    241, 259, 263, 264, 276-280,
    326, 328, 376, 413, 431, 439,
    455
investment by parallel funds, *see*
  fund conflicts of interest
Investment Committee, 56, 57, 85,
    97, 343, 368, 372, 374, **375-
    376**, 377
investment decisions, *see* fund
  covenants and controls
investment division, 56-58
investment documentation, 19, 21,
    212, **383-398**
  see also:
    employment agreement
    Investment Agreement
    legal completion
    Shareholders Agreement
investment expenses, *see* fund
  policies and strategies
investment focus, *see* fund focus
investment into other funds, *see*
  fund covenants and controls
investment into portfolio of old
  fund, *see* fund conflicts of
  interest
investment into public securities,
  see fund covenants and controls
investment limits, 75-76, 97-98
investment objectives, *see* fund
  objectives
investment of proceeds, *see*
  reinvestment of proceeds
investment period, *see* fund
  covenants and controls
investment personal to GP, *see*
  fund conflicts of interest

investment policies, *see* fund policies and strategies

investment process, *see* VC Process

investment proposal (of GP), 57, 122, 123, 127, **372-375**

investment securities, 19-20, 25, **267-299**, 304, 310, 323

see also:
   bond
   common shares
   convertible loan
   debt
   options
   preferred shares
   warrant

investment size, 75, 129, 241, 411, 458

investment staff, 18, 54, 56, 57, **58-60**, 107, 114, 117, 122, 126, 375, 402, 422, 423, 427, **452**, 457, 458

   incentivization, 60
   profiles, 59-60

investment staging, *see* staging

investment strategies, *see* fund policies and strategies

investment tranche, 155, **307-308**, 326, 345, 347, 424

investor criteria, 65, **77-79**

investor objectives, 11, 68

investor relations, 50, 56, 69, 455, 459

investor rights, 93

IPO, *see* Initial Public Offering

IT, 56, 58, 73, 461, 465

K

key performance indicators, 145

key person insurance, 325, **332**

Kim, W. Chan, 112, 131

know-how, 111, 196, 293, 310, 392

knowledge management system, 112, 118, 123, 127, 459

L

Lake, Rick, 11

Lake, Ronald, 11

later stage companies, 27, 73, 109, 196, 197, 208, 227, 249, 250, 302, 308, **311-320**

lawyers, 79, 212, 214, 324, 331, 340, 371, 372, 377, **381**, 384, 386, 390, 397, 457

legal completion, 329, 371, 372, 377, 380, 381, **397-398**

legal documentation, 58, 324, 341, 342, 354, 381, 436

   see also investment documentation

legal due diligence, 20, 146-147, **212-216**, 343

   commercial agreements, 213-214
   corporate documents, 213
   intellectual property, 214
   issue of stock, 215
   legal actions, 215
   regulatory requirements, 215-216
   staff, 214-215

Lerner, Josh, 66, 84

leveraged buyout, 312, **316-318**

Limited Liability Company (LLC), 47

Limited Liability Partnership (LLP), 12, **46-50**, 51, 89, 213

   advantages, 48-50
   structure, 46-48
   see also Fund Company

Limited Partner, *see* LP

limited partnership, *see* Limited Liability Partnership

Limited Partnership Agreement, 18, 46, 50, 55, 76, 77, 81, **89-**

104, 446, 452, 453
capital calls, 92
capital commitments, 91-93
carried interest, 95-96
closings, 92
compensation, 93-96
conflicts of interest, 101-102
covenants and controls, 97-101
disclosure, 103
distributions, 93
investor rights, 93
management fee, 94-95
organization, 90-91
other income & expenses, 96
partnership information, 91
termination, 103-104
liquidation preference, **269**, 270,
 274, **276-281, 305-306**, 325,
 329, **346**, 365, 387, 426
 multiple, 274, **277**, 279-281,
 305, 365
 participating, 274, **277**, 279,
 281, 305, 365
 participating multiple, 274, **277**,
 279-281, 305, 346
 simple, **270**, 274, 276-279, 281,
 305
 with yield, **276**, 279, 281, 305
liquidation value, 246
liquidity event, 443, 453
living dead, **39**, 284
lockup, **295**, 315, 419, 442
loss carry forward, 96
LP as sponsor, 49, 55, 80, 81, 84,
 85, 93, 121, 150, 458
LP as stakeholder, 451-457
LP criteria, *see* investor criteria
LP default, *see* fund covenants and
 controls
LP IRR, 432, 433, **436-438**, 440
LP objectives, *see* investor
 objectives

LP relations, *see* investor relations
LP rights, *see* investor rights
LP types, 70-71
LP's capital account, *see* capital
 account
LP's capital call, *see* capital call
LP's committed capital, *see* capital
 commitment
LP's disclosure of fund
 information, *see* disclosure of
 fund information
LP's involvement in fund, *see* fund
 covenants and controls
LP's regulatory requirements, **86-
 87**, 101
 accredited investors, 86
 ERISA, 86-87
 UBTI, 87
LP's return, 54, 56, 240, 281

M

management buy-in, 302, 312, **319**,
 320
management buyout, 13, 32, 122,
 208, 312, 316-318
Management Company
 investment division, 56-58
 investment staff, 56-61
 finance department, 58
 organization, 56-58
 see also: General Partner
management controls, 325, **330-
 332**, 374, 409
 board representation, 330-331
 key person insurance, 332
 minority protection, 331
 operational controls, 331
 voting rights, 330
management due diligence, 20,
 146-147, **157-167**, 204, 209,
 210
 adaptability, 163-164

commitment, 163
compensation, 166-167
domain expertise, 164-165
entrepreneurship, 162
integrity, 161-162
relationship with the VC, 166
team dynamics, 165
the CEO, 160-161
management fee, 48, 49, **53-55**, 56, 74, 80, 81, 85, 281, 411, 456
charged to investee, 76, 407
for extended fund life, 55, 75
in fund performance, 434, 435
in the limited partnership agreement, 89, 91-93, **94-95**, 97-100
structure, 46, **94-95**
management incentives, 301, 325, **332-336**
incentive shares, 325, **332**
see also:
employee stock options
Employee Stock Options Plan
Employee Stock Ownership Scheme
management system software, 458, **459**
manufacturing due diligence, 20, 146-147, **185-201**, 204, 209, 210
finance, 198
human resource, 198
incoming quality control, 194-195
manufacturing engineering, 193-194
manufacturing objectives, 186
materials, 188-191
plant tour, 199-201
production, 192-193
quality assurance, 195-196

research and development, 196-198
Manufacturing Engineering, 188, **193-194**, 196, 201
market development, 27, 178, 311
market launch, 27, 43, 135
marketing due diligence, 20, 146-147, **169-183**, 204, 209, 210
market characteristics, 175-176
market need, 172-174
market potential, 174-175
market risks, 180-183
market shifts, 182-183
market traction, 181-182
marketing staff incentivization, 179-180
see also marketing strategies
marketing strategies, 176-180
distribution, 179
objectives, 177
pricing, 178
product strategy, 177-178
promotion, 178-179
staffing and incentives, 179-180
Materials, **188-191**, 201
Mauborgne, Renee, 112, 131
merger, 32, 113, 130, 276, 277, 305, 335, 346, 349, 352, 385, 391, 401, 410, 417, 423, 427
mergers and acquisitions, 45, 57, 110, 116, 305, 402, 410, 423
see also:
acquisition
merger
mezzanine
funds, 31, 32, 122, 273, 316, 317
round, **31**, 32
stage, 13, **27**, 240
milestone, 16, 25, **28-31**, 38, 155, 208, 222, 241, 243, 284, 302, 303, 307, 308, 326, 332, **345**, 366, 392, 410, 457

minority protection, 325, **331, 349-351, 391,** 409
monitoring, 16, 19, 21, 41, 54, 57-59, 76, 80, 94, 126, 155, 307, 308, **401-414,** 416, 423, 424, 452, 457
  adding value, 407-408
  corporate governance, 408-409
  early warning, 403-407
  ensuring compliance, 409-410
  exploring exit, 410
  function, 423, 452
  keeping current, 403
  objectives, 401
  portfolio, 410-412
  report, 412, **413-414**
monitoring fee, 94
monitoring group, 57
multiple funds, 46, **52-53,** 102

N
negative covenants, 15, 390, **391-392,** 396
negotiation of deal, *see* deal negotiation
negotiation of legal documents, 371, 379, 384, 386, 389, 392, 394
negotiation of preferential terms, 271, 276, 291, 292
negotiation of term sheet, 323, 326, 327, 341, 386
negotiation of valuation, 110, 130, 220, 226, 243, 245, 303, 317, 327, 379, 389
negotiation skills, 21, 57, 220
negotiation with LPs, 53, 97
net tangible assets, 139, 226, 245
net tangible assets multiple, 245
net worth, 71, 86, 226, **245,** 340
networking, 57, **60,** 114, 364, **408,** 452

no-fault provisions, 103
Non-Competition Agreement, 214, 215, 385
Non-Disclosure Agreement, 108, **117, 119-120**

O
offering document, 65, 73, **79-81,** 82
Open Records Act, 103, 447
operational controls, 325, **331**
opportunistic approach, 74, 78, 113, **114-115,** 116
options
  dilution effect, 137, 221-224, 229, **235,** 264, 288-291, 310, 332, 334, 335, 347, 380, 426
  for board members, 76, 328, 333, 336
  see also warrant

P
parallel fund, 52, 53, 69, 100, 102
partners' meeting, 455, 456
patent, 26, 30, 111, 196, 212, 214, 245, 246, 310, 377, 386
pay-or-play, *see* anti-dilution
pay-to-play, *see* anti-dilution
PDCA approach, **153,** 158, 169, 171, 185, 186
PDCA cycle, **144-145,** 149, 186
  see also:
    Act stage
    Check stage
    Do stage
    Plan stage
piggyback, 274, 293, **298**
placement agent, 66, **68-70,** 77, 82, 84
Plan stage, 144, **145,** 149, 152, 153, 158, 169, 186, 203
plant tour, 188, 193, **199-201**
portfolio IRR, 17, 40, 41, 433

see also fund performance

portfolio performance, 40, 41, 444, 455, 463

see also fund performance

portfolio valuation, *see* valuation of portfolio

post-dilution shareholding, 229, 231, 232, 234, 236-238, **255-258**, 260-263, 265-266

post-money, 30-36, 38, 210, **221-223**, 224, 225, 230-232, 236-239, 248, 257, 259, 263, 285, 286, 413

post-mortem, 375, **427**

pre-dilution shareholding, 229, 231, 232, 234, 236-238, **255-258**, 260-263, 265-266

preemptive right, *see* anti-dilution

preferential rights, 15, 205, 268, 269, 270, **273-299**, 301, 302, 304, **305-306**, 325, 328-329, 336, 340

see also:
anti-dilution
conversion rights
liquidation preference
preferred dividend
redemption
registration rights

preferred dividend, *see* dividend

preferred (preference) shares, 30, 268, **269-271**, 272, 274-278, 293, 294, 304, 305, 327, 328, 336, 339, 340, 379, 385, 426

convertible, **281-284**, 285, 343

redeemable, 51, **284-285**, 306, 343

same/different series, 274, 292, 296, 305

Series A, B, C, 30, 42, 43, 271, 328

pre-money, 33-36, 38, 122, **221-223**, 224, 225, 230, 238, 239, 248, 285, 286, 327

price per share, **221**, 227, 254, **259**, **263**, 264, 270, 282, 286-288, 290, 328, 339

price-earnings ratio, 220, 226, **227-228**, 229-231, 240-242, 244, 245, 249, 251

pricing strategy, 170, 176, **178**

private equity, **13**, 14, 54, 72, 75, 85, 312, 316

Private Equity Intelligence Ltd, 446

privatization, 302, 312, **316**

probability
and IRR, **212**, 361
and risk, 143, **154-155**
and valuation, 251-252

product development, 26, 27, 43, 164, 250, 405

product strategy, 170, 176, **177-178**

Production, 149, 187, 188, **192-193**

profit guarantee, 303, 368

profitable stage, 27

profits before tax, 227

promotion strategy, 170, 177, **178-179**

proof of concept, **26**, 27, 30, 197

Put Agreement, 385

put option, 274, 340, **422**

Q

qualities of a VC firm, *see* VC firm qualities

Quality Assurance, 187, 188, **195-196**

R

R&D, 132, 164, 185, 188, **196-198**, 201, 207, 462

raising funds, *see*:
fund-raising by a company
fund-raising by a VC firm

ratchet, 205, 220, 243, 274, **282,** 283, 284, 299, 303, 304, 306, 311, 312, 366, 368, 410, 425
  broad-based, 274, **289,** 291, 306
  ceiling, 283
  floor, 283
  full, 274, **286,** 291, 306, 329
  narrow-based, 274, 289, **290,** 291, 306
Raynor, Michael, 108, 178
realizing value, 19, 21, 93, **415-424**
  buy-back, 422
  divestment function, 422-424
  IPO versus trade sale, 416-422
  redemption, 422
recapitalization, 291, 302, 308, **312-315,** 316
recovering value, 21, 93, 415, 416, **424-427**
  beyond help, 427
  down round, 425-426
  post-mortem, 427
  work out, 426-427
Red Ocean, 112, 131
redeemable preferred shares, *see* preferred shares
redemption, 51, 268, 274, **284-285,** 306, 312, 325, 329, 338, 340, **347-348,** 393, 410, 416, **422,** 424
  default, 338, 344, **347-348**
  premium, 274, **285**
  see also:
    buy-back
    put option
referral fee, 115
  see also finder's fee
registration rights, 268, **293-299,** 329, 387, 388
  Agreement, 296, **385**
  demand, 274, 293, **295,** 296-298
  piggyback, 274, 293, **298**

S-3, 274, 293, **297-298**
shelf, 297
registration statement, 294-296
regulatory issues
  of limited partners, *see* LP's regulatory requirements
  of the GP, 58, 101, 110, 453, **459**
  of the investee, 143, 175, 182, 198, 215, **215-216,** 220, 377, 378, 407
reinvestment of proceeds, 72, **98**
relationship of GP and investee, 107, 158, 159, **166,** 366, 367, 420
representations and warranties, 212, 215, 312, 325, **340,** 351, 353, 354, 387, **388-390**
  default/breach/compliance, 312, 344, 347, 371, **381,** 390, 394, 398, 421
  indemnification, 312, 389, 390, **394,** 421
reputation
  of the entrepreneur, 364
  of the GP, 67, 114, 361, 363, **458**
research institute, 115, 116, 292
residual portfolio value, 432, **441,** 446, 447
restricted shares, 296-297
retention %, 229, 254, **260,** 261, 262, **263**
return multiple
  of investment, 37, 40, 210, **211,** **225,** 226, 234, 240, 315, 424, 446, 455
  of portfolio, 432, **439-440,** 455
revenue model, 145, **173**
revenue multiple, 226, **249**
revenue stage, 27
right of first offer, 352

right of first refusal, 274, **293**, 325, **336-337**, 352, 353, 396
road show, 65, 70, **82-83**
Rolodex, **30**, 32, 34
Roth, Erik, 108
rounds of financing, *see* financing rounds
Rule 144, **293-297**, 412, 419, 423
runway, 302, **303**, 326

S

S-1 registration, **294**, 297
S-3 registration, 274, 293, **297-298**
Sahlman, William, 219
scale, *see* economies of scale
scenarios, 21, **209-212**, **251-252**, 264, 299, 375, 425
screening, *see* deal screening
SEC, 294, 295, 297, 298, 412
Securities Act, 86, **294**, 296
Securities Purchase Agreement, 385
seed round, 26, **30**, 32-38, 42-43, 225
seed stage, **27**, 30, 73, 121, 211, 239, 248, 311, 332
senior debt, 273, 317
Series A, B and C rounds, 25, **30-31**, 43, 303
Series A, B, C shares, *see* preferred shares
share issue formula, 238, 254, **258-259**, **263**
Share Subscription Agreement, *see* Investment Agreement
share transfer
    exempt, 325, **337**, 396
    limited partner, 101
    management/founders, 325, **338**, 347, 352, 353, 396
    shareholders, 293, 337, 352, 385, 395, 396

staff of the GP, 60
shareholder rights, 301, 325, **336-338**
    drag along rights, 337
    exempt transfer of shares, 337
    information rights, 338
    management share transfers, 338
    right of first refusal, 336-337
    tag along rights, 337
Shareholders Agreement, 344, **384**, 385, 390, **394-397**, 409
    board meetings, 395-396
    deadlock, 397
    default, 396-397
    definitions, 395
    employee stock options, 396
    expenses, 397
    general meetings, 396
    governing law, 397
    preamble, 395
    sale and transfer of shares, 396
shelf registration, 297
Shewhart, Walter, 144
shopped deal, 128, **130**
showstoppers, 126, **127-137**, 164
    cannot scale up, 129
    commercialization difficulties, 134-136
    competitor of portfolio company, 130
    execution weakness, 134
    high burn rate, 133
    intellectual property problems, 134
    intense competition, 131
    lack of focus, 128
    low margins, 132
    management change, 133
    market acceptance problems, 132
    no CEO, 133

no exit, 130-131
outside fund focus, 129-130
price control, 131
shareholder conflicts, 136-137
shareholder dilution, 137
shopped deal, 130
slow growth, 129
valuation too high, 130
skew, **25**, 26, **38-41**, 444
sourcing deals, *see* deal sourcing
special audit, 206, 371, **377-379**
sponsor, **49**, 55, 80, 81, 84, 85, 93,
    121, 150, 458
stages of corporate development,
    26-27
    see also:
        development stage
        early stage companies
        expansion stage
        initial concept stage
        later stage companies
        market development
        market launch
        mezzanine stage
        product development
        proof of concept
        revenue stage
        seed stage
        start-up stage
staging, 16, **25-26**, **36-41**, 224, 302,
    303, 307, 444
star investment, 444, **445-446**
start-up
    costs, 133, 208, 245, 434, 435
    funding, 14, 45, 73, 133, 137,
        157, 196, 269, 270, 280, 281,
        303, 308
    risks/problems, 13, 83, 163,
        165, 181, 207, 237, 326, 331,
        332, 405
    stage, **27**, 28, 121, 163, 211, 240,
        281, 311

    see also:
        due diligence of early stage
          companies
        valuation of start-ups
step-down (in valuation), 223
step-up (in valuation), 29, 34, 36,
    223, 242
stock options, *see* options
Stock Options Plan, *see* Employee
    Stock Options Plan
Stock Ownership Scheme, *see*
    Employee Stock Ownership
    Scheme
Stock Purchase Agreement, 385
subordinated debt, 271, 273, 317
subscribers multiple, 226, **249-250**
Sun Tzu, 359
super-majority, 89, 102, 103, **396**
sustaining innovation, 108
syndication, 115, **308-309**, 371,
    376, 458
systematic deal sourcing, 114-116

T
tag along rights, 274, 312, 325, **337**,
    353, 396
team dynamics, 159, **165**
technology, 12-14, 29, 32, 34, 36,
    59, 67, 73, 111, 116, 292-
    293, 306, 310, 319, 332, 373,
    393, 408, 418, 427, 465
    screening, 128, 131, 132, 134-
        136
    valuation, 220, 228, 249
    see also due diligence of
        technology
term sheet, 19, 21, 82, 122, 123,
    274, 289, **323-355**, 365-367,
    371, 372, 374-377, 379, 381,
    383, 384, 386-388, 392, 396
    conditions precedent, 329-330
    confidentiality, 341

deal structure, 326-328
exclusivity, 341-342
exit provisions, 338-340
expenses, 341
governing law, 341
management controls, 330-332
management incentives, 332-336
organization, 324, 325
preamble, 324
preferential rights, 328-329
representations and warranties, 340
shareholder rights, 336-338
VC internal approval, 341
terminal year, **229**, 230-232, 234, 236, 237, **240-242**, 252
Thomson Financial, 446
Timmons, Jeffry, 11
Total Quality Management, 144, 192
trade sale, 16, 34, 113, 131, 152, 213, 225, 226, 229, 232-234, 241, 277, 281, 316, 362, 385, 410, 416, 422, 423, 453
versus IPO, 416-422
Transpac, 83-85
Transtech, 83-84
turnaround, 246, 302, 312, **320**, 427

U
UBTI, **87**, 101
unique selling proposition, 146

V
valuation committee, 443
valuation concepts, 148, **221-226**
entry valuation, 224-226
exit valuation, 224-226
post-money valuation, 221-223
pre-money valuation, 221-223
step-down in valuation, 223
step-up in valuation, 223
valuation event, **443**, 453
valuation factors, **219-220**, 242
valuation for financing rounds, 32, 223, 239, **241-242**, 248, 443
valuation for stages of development, 32, 248
valuation from VC perspective, 242-243
valuation methods, 130, **226-242**, **244-251**
breakup value, 246
cost to create, 250
discounted free cash flow, 247-248
EBITDA multiple, 244
effect of cash or debt, 250-251
liquidation value, 246
net tangible assets multiple, 245
net worth, 245
price-earnings ratio, 227-228
revenue multiple, 249
subscribers multiple, 249-250
using scenarios, 251-252
VC industry averages, 248
VC Method, *see* VC Method
valuation of early stage companies, 219, 250, 309
see also valuation of start-ups
valuation of intellectual property and technology, 220, 228, 245, 249
valuation of portfolio, 79, 82, 99, **441-443**, 446, 456, 461, 463
valuation of start-ups, 227, 237, 240, 248, 250, 332
valuation of technology, *see* valuation of intellectual property and technology
valuation report, 443, **449-450**, 456
value innovation, 112, 131
Varitronix, 113, 175

VC as a funding source, 14-15
VC definition, 13-14
VC financing, 15, 18, **25-44**, 288,
    302, 388
    capitalization table, 42-44
    rounds of financing, 27-36
    skew effect, 38-41
    stages of corporate
        development, 26-27
    staging of investments, 36-38
VC firm, *see* General Partner
VC firm qualities, 21, **451-459**
    entrepreneur perspective, 457-
        458
    internal perspective, 458-459
    limited partner perspective,
        451-457
VC fund, *see* Fund Company
VC fund-raising, *see* fund-raising
VC industry averages, 226, 243,
    248
VC investment characteristics, 15-
    16
VC listed fund, **72-73**, 86
VC market cycles, 66-68
VC Method, **228-242**, 251-252,
    254-262, 262-266
    calculation examples, 230-239
    conclusion, 242
    derivation of formulas, 254-262
    discount rate, 239-240
    financing rounds, 241-242
    spreadsheet model, 264-266
    summary of formulas, 262-263

terminal value, 240-241
terminal year, 240-241
using scenarios, 251-252
VC organization, 45-60
    compensation structure, 53-56
    fund company structure, 46-52
    investment staff, 58-60
    management company
        organization, 56-58
    multiple funds, 52-53
VC perspectives on valuation, 242-
    243
VC Process, **16-21**, 41, 107, 126,
    415, 444
VC role, 14
Venture Economics, 248, 446
VentureOne, 248
vesting period, 60, **333-334**
veto right, 311, 330, **349**
vintage year, **444-445**, 465
voting right, 269, 325, **330**, 334,
    335, 346, **349**, 352, 353, 387,
    426

W
warrant, 205, 221, 224, 267, **268**,
    272-273, 290, 291, 304, 312,
    327, 347, 385, 388, 410, 424,
    442
Warrant Purchase Agreement, 385
warranties, *see* representations and
    warranties
work out, 424, **426-42**

About the Author

Lin Hong Wong is presently Managing Director of Wingz Capital Pte Ltd, a company in Singapore that he set up to offer management and financial advisory services.

Lin Hong has ten years experience as a senior partner in a leading Asian venture capital firm, two and a half years in the mentoring and incubation of start-ups, nine years as a CEO in high-tech manufacturing firms and eleven years in the Singapore Economic Development Board, promoting the development of the electronics industry. He was previously the Managing Director for Business Development in Temasek Capital (Pte) Ltd from October 2000 to March 2003. (Temasek Capital was the private equity arm of Temasek Holdings, a Singapore government-owned investment firm with a global portfolio of more than US$50 billion.) His responsibility was to set up Temasek's incubation program, which provided funding, support and mentoring services to start-ups and early stage companies. The program was successfully established in Singapore, Chennai and Shenzhen and several investments into start-ups were made in these cities.

Prior to joining Temasek, Lin Hong was the EVP of Transpac Capital Pte Ltd, from 1990 to 2000. Transpac was established in 1986 (then known as Transtech) and grew to become one of the largest venture capital firms in South-East Asia, managing more than US$820 million of funds in 2000, which were invested in a broad range of companies in Asia and USA. Prior to Transpac, Lin Hong was the CEO of U.S. subsidiaries manufacturing disk drives in Singapore, from 1981 to 1990. This included starting up from scratch, Computer Memories Far East Ltd in 1983, which was sold to Micropolis Ltd for about US$30 million in 1986, resulting in a significant capital gain for the owners of Computer Memories.

Lin Hong and his management team restarted under Micropolis in 1986 and grew the Singapore operations to achieve a revenue run rate of US$400 million at the time of his departure in 1990. Lin Hong started work in 1970 in the Singapore Economic Development Board, heading the electronics group, where he spent eleven years promoting the development of the electronics industry in Singapore, which is now the largest industrial sector in the economy.

Lin Hong has a bachelor degree in electrical engineering and a diploma in business administration. He has served on the boards of listed companies (in USA and Singapore), boards of private companies, boards of governors of educational institutes and various government committees. He was awarded a Singapore Public Service Medal in 1992.